Here, There and Everywhere

Here, There and Everywhere

My Life Recording the Music of THE BEATLES

Geoff Emerick
and Howard Massey

GOTHAM BOOKS

GOTHAM BOOKS
Published by Penguin Group (USA) Inc.
375 Hudson Street, New York, New York 10014, U.S.A.
Penguin Group (Canada), 90 Eglinton Avenue East, Suite 700, Toronto, Ontario M4P 2Y3, Canada
(a division of Pearson Penguin Canada Inc.); Penguin Books Ltd, 80 Strand, London WC2R 0RL,
England; Penguin Ireland, 25 St Stephen's Green, Dublin 2, Ireland (a division of Penguin Books Ltd);
Penguin Group (Australia), 250 Camberwell Road, Camberwell, Victoria 3124, Australia
(a division of Pearson Australia Group Pty Ltd); Penguin Books India Pvt Ltd, 11 Community Centre,
Panchsheel Park, New Delhi - 110 017, India; Penguin Group (NZ), cnr Airborne and Rosedale Roads,
Albany, Auckland 1310, New Zealand (a division of Pearson New Zealand Ltd); Penguin Books
(South Africa) (Pty) Ltd, 24 Sturdee Avenue, Rosebank, Johannesburg 2196, South Africa

Penguin Books Ltd, Registered Offices: 80 Strand, London WC2R 0RL, England

Published by Gotham Books, a division of Penguin Group (USA) Inc.

First printing, March 2006
1   3   5   7   9   10   8   6   4   2

Copyright © 2006 by Emerick Softpaw Productions, Inc. and Howard Massey
All rights reserved

Gotham Books and the skyscraper logo are trademarks of Penguin Group (USA) Inc.

LIBRARY OF CONGRESS CATALOGING-IN-PUBLICATION DATA
has been applied for.

ISBN 1-592-40179-1

Printed in the United States of America
Set in Minion
Designed by Alice Sorensen

To the memories
of my mother and father,
Mabel and George,
and my dear wife,
Nicole

· Contents ·

· Foreword ·

by Elvis Costello

It has been ten years since Geoff Emerick and I last worked together. One of my favorite memories of that last occasion is Geoff politely cursing the recording desk when it proved impossible to make it distort in an attractive and interesting fashion.

So many of the sounds in today's recording studios come out of little boxes that merely imitate the sonic innovations of the past. The range of choices is vast but, in unimaginative hands, it seems to create fewer surprises.

Despite all the endless theorizing about pop music of the 1960s, the contribution of a small handful of engineers is still not fully appreciated. Inspired by particular musicians, these innovations brought about a change in the very nature of the recording studio, from a place where musical performances were simply captured in the best available fidelity to an experimental workshop in which the transformation and even the distortion of the very sound of an instrument or voice became an element in the composition. Not that you would ever hear any of this grand talk from Geoff Emerick. You could not meet a more modest and self-effacing man.

When we first worked together in 1981, I had decided to take a very different approach to the recording of what would become the album *Imperial Bedroom*. My first album had been recorded in a total of twenty-four hours of studio time; the second took eleven days. Now the Attractions and I had booked AIR Studios for twelve weeks and granted ourselves the license to work on the *sound* of the record until it reflected the mood of the songs. We would hire anything that seemed to help: a harpsichord, a trio of French horns, or even a small orchestra. If we were not to be railroaded to that deadly place called "Geniusville," where every passing notion in the mind of the musical submariner is mistaken for sunken treasure (believe me, the recording studio can have more than a passing resemblance to the depths of the ocean), we would need someone to retain perspective, to bring some kind of order, and to occasionally act as a referee.

This is how I met Geoff Emerick, a tall, gentle man with a resonant voice and, at that time, an occasionally jittery pattern of speech that I put down to his almost constant intake of vending-machine coffee that blended nicely with the taste and aroma of melted plastic. Over our weeks in the studio, an instrumental tone or sonic effect that seemed fleetingly familiar would suddenly appear, but we never got the impression that Geoff was shaping the sound from a clichéd "box of tricks." The songs and the moods of the performance always took precedence over the way they might be filtered, altered, or changed on their way to tape. By the end of our time together, we found that Geoff had helped us produce the richest and most varied-sounding record of our career to date.

I had made the band promise that they would not pester Geoff for Beatles stories, but as we got deeper into the process of recording and mixing, the occasional anecdote would emerge. These tales never sounded worn out or rehearsed. There was never a hint of self-aggrandizement or boastfulness about them. They were usually used as examples of how a problem might be solved. The fact that the "problem" might have generated the sound of "Being For The Benefit Of Mr. Kite" seemed merely incidental.

Well, now we can all enjoy Geoff's reminiscences about his most famous work. Without meaning any disrespect to George Martin, I think I could find many contemporary musicians and record makers who might agree with me that Geoff Emerick would be regarded as the coproducer of *Sgt. Pepper's Lonely Hearts Club Band* by modern definitions. What makes this memoir so entertaining to read is that these fabulous inventions and innovations always seemed to be made out of elastic bands, sticky tape, and empty cotton reels. It was the stuff of the hobby shop or do-it-yourself enthusiast rather than the computer-assisted boffin, and always in service of a brilliant musical idea rather than in place of it. None of this is told with any sense of pomp or portentousness, although there is certainly plenty of youthful enthusiasm, described in the accounts of Geoff's work as a teenage assistant engineer on the very first Beatles' sessions.

The fact that four young musicians from Liverpool were assigned to the EMI *comedy* imprint, Parlophone, and staff producer responsible for the comedy output, gives us a glimpse of a number of casual regional assumptions and the hierarchies of early '60s England. American readers may only be able to equate the class-bound stiffness of Abbey Road to something out of *Monty Python*. I remember Geoff telling me about the staff engineer's Rebellion of the White Coats, in which they donned ludicrously mismatched sizes in response to a management directive that they once again wear these garments—last seen in the days when they had to handle the more volatile wax medium of recording—just as hair started to creep over collars that were now sporting floral ties.

The book captures the mood of claustrophobic England that was suddenly illuminated by such imaginative music. It was still postwar England, in which the buses stopped running very shortly after the pubs shut. If I had to give a précis of the contents, it would be in the sentence, "We recorded 'Tomorrow Never Knows' and then I went home and had some nice biscuits."

Geoff would be the first to say that none of the sonic flights of fancy that he helped shape in the music of the Beatles would have been possible without the incredible apprenticeship and experience offered by working at Abbey Road in the early to mid-sixties. How else could anyone find themselves working with Otto Klemperer and a symphony orchestra in the morning and Judy Garland in the afternoon, with chances of a late session with The Massed Alberts? Needless to say, it will always be the sessions with the Beatles that arouse the greatest curiosity. For once, you are not hearing an account of the events from someone with a vested interest in your agreeing with their mad theory. This is the view of a contributing participant, one who offers unique anecdotes and some surprisingly critical opinions.

I've had the experience of arriving early for a session and overhearing Geoff lost in playing the piano for his own amusement. He plays very well, in an elaborate, romantic style. However, it takes a very unique temperament to sit behind his other instrument, the mixing desk. It seems best if you have enormous patience, good judgment, generosity, and a self-deprecating sense of humor. You will find all of these qualities in the pages of this book. I am very glad that Geoff has gotten to tell his tale.

October 2005

· Prologue ·

1966

Silence. Shadows in the dark, curtains rustling in the cool April breeze. I rolled over in bed and cast a weary eye at the clock. Damn! Still middle of the night, exactly four minutes later than the last time I looked.

I'd been tossing and turning for hours. What had I let myself in for? Why on earth did I ever take George Martin up on his offer? I was only nineteen, after all. I shouldn't have a care in the world. I should be out with my mates, meeting girls, having a laugh.

Instead, I'd made a commitment to spend the next months of my life cloistered in a recording studio day and night, shouldering the responsibility of making the most popular group of musicians in the world sound even better than they ever had before. And it would all be starting in just a few hours' time.

I needed to get some sleep, but I couldn't turn off my brain, couldn't ease myself into slumber. No matter how hard I tried to fight them off, bleak thoughts consumed me. That Lennon, with that sharp tongue of his, he'll have my guts for garters, I just know it. And what about Harrison? He always seemed so dour, so suspicious of everyone—you never knew quite where you stood with him. I pictured the four of them—even friendly, charming Paul—ganging up on me, reducing me to tears, banishing me from the studio in disgrace and shame.

Dinner began repeating on me. I knew I was working myself up into a state, but I was powerless to stop either the stomach churning or the mental agitation. Just hours before, in the bright sunshine of daylight, I'd been confident, even brash, certain that I could handle anything the Beatles might throw at me. But now, in the darkness of night, sleep-deprived, alone in my bed, I could only feel fear, anxiety, worry.

I was terrified.

How had it all come to this? I began reflecting on the events that had led up to this point, like a tape rewound and played back over and over again. As the sweet arms of Morpheus began to embrace me, I was carried back to a rainy morning just two weeks previous.

"Give us a ciggie, will you, mate?"

Phil McDonald was bumming a smoke from me as we sat in the cramped, brightly lit control room, waiting for yet another recording session to begin. Forced to adhere to a strict dress code, we were both dressed conservatively in shirt and tie, despite the fact that most of the rest of our generation were parading around Swinging London garbed in brightly colored Carnaby Street "mod" gear. Just a year younger than me, Phil had been at EMI Studios for only a few months (it wouldn't be called "Abbey Road," after the Beatles' album of the same name, until 1970) and so was still serving his apprenticeship as an assistant engineer. We'd developed a good camaraderie, though once the tape started rolling, I became his boss. In the lull between the time we'd set up the microphones and the moment the doors would burst open with the loud bustle of musicians arriving, we'd quietly share a cigarette, making our personal contribution to the stale, smoky air that permeated the EMI complex.

The phone beside the mixing console rang loudly, shattering the peaceful atmosphere.

"Studio," Phil answered crisply. "Yes, he's right here. Do you want to speak with him?"

I began to walk toward the phone, but Phil waved me off. "Okay, I'll tell him." Turning to me, he reported with the slightest twinkle in his eye, "They want to see you in the manager's office, sharpish. I reckon you're in deep shit for something. Don't worry, I'll do a good job replacing you as EMI's latest boy wonder."

"Yeah, right—once you figure out which end of the microphone to stick up your arse, you'll make a fine engineer," I retorted. But as I headed down the corridor, I had a growing sense of unease. Had someone reported me for messing about with the wiring or for using a nonstandard microphone positioning? Was I in some kind of trouble? I'd been breaking so many rules lately, it was hard to think of which transgression was getting me called on the carpet.

The door to the studio manager's office was ajar. "Come in, Geoffrey," said the imperious Mr. E. H. Fowler. Fowler, who was in charge of day-to-day operations for the entire facility, had originally been a classical music recording engineer and was generally an innocuous figure, though he had a few quirks. At lunchtime he used to wander around the studios and turn all the lights off to save electricity; at 1:55 he'd come back and turn the lights back on. There was something in the tone of his voice that told me I wasn't in trouble after all.

I stepped inside. Seated beside Fowler's desk was George Martin, the lanky, aristocratic record producer I had worked with for the past three and a half years on sessions with the Beatles as well as with Cilla Black, Billy J. Kramer, and other artists in the Brian Epstein fold. George was well known for getting to the point, and he didn't beat around the bush that morning. Without waiting for Fowler to say a word, he turned toward me and dropped a bombshell.

"Geoff, we'd like you to take over Norman's job. What do you say?"

Norman Smith had been the Beatles' regular engineer since their very first artist test, back in June of 1962. He had manned the mixing console for every one of their records since then, including the hit singles that had launched them to international stardom. Norman was an older man—probably George Martin's age, though none of us ever knew exactly how old Norman was, since it was common practice to lie about your age on job applications in those days—and quite authoritarian. He certainly knew his stuff. I had learned a great deal assisting for him, and there was no question that he was an integral part of the Beatles' early success. In all my dealings with the band, I had gotten the sense that they were quite happy with the work he did for them.

Norman was ambitious, though. He was an amateur songwriter and he had dreams of being a recording artist in his own right. But most of all he wanted to become a producer; there was gossip that he even had aspirations of eventually taking over George Martin's role. We had heard rumors through the studio grapevine that Norman had been lobbying top management for a promotion throughout the *Rubber Soul* sessions in the fall of 1965, but with a catch: he wanted to be a staff producer for EMI *and* continue engineering for the Beatles at the same time.

George Martin, who was also head of the Parlophone label, put his foot down: that was not going to happen. Either Norman could continue to be the Beatles' engineer or he could be a staff producer, but not both. With one eye on a promising young band he had spotted in a London club and hoped to sign to the label—they went by the name of Pink Floyd—Norman decided to leave the engineer's chair for good, even though it meant parting ways with the biggest act in the world.

Once Norman became a producer, the studio needed an engineer to replace him, and for reasons I still didn't quite understand, I had gotten the promotion, despite the fact that I was only eighteen years old at the time. Perhaps I was given the position simply because I was more popular than some of the older, more experienced assistant engineers; so much of the job had to do with diplomacy and studio etiquette. Certainly George Martin and I had gotten along well during the times I had assisted him. Frequently, we had found ourselves thinking the same thought at the same time; we could almost communicate without speaking.

But this time around I found it impossible to read his mind. What he was saying to me was simply unfathomable: even though I had less than six months of experience in the job, he was asking me to become the *Beatles'* engineer.

"You're joking, right?" was all I could stammer in response. Blushing furiously, I immediately realized that it was a pathetic reply.

"No, I'm not bloody joking." George laughed. Sensing my discomfort, he continued in a rather softer voice. "Look, the boys are scheduled to begin work on their new album in two weeks' time. I'm offering you the opportunity to engineer it for me. Even though you're young, I think you're ready. But I need your answer now, today."

I looked to Fowler for guidance, but he was preoccupied, absentmindedly cleaning his glasses with a tattered handkerchief. *Easy for him*, I thought. *He's not the one being put on the spot.* My breathing began to shallow; panic set in. Sure, there were times when I'd daydreamed about recording the Beatles—they were, after all, not only EMI's biggest act, they were the most famous band in the world. I knew that the offer George was making was potentially the fastest way to advance my career. But could I really handle that kind of responsibility? As George Martin studied me impatiently, I began playing an "eenie, meenie, minie, moe" game in my head. Incongruously, I thought, *If it lands on "moe," I'll say yes.* To my dismay—or was it to my delight?—it did. Or perhaps I just rigged the game that way.

Feeling strangely removed, as if I were observing this awkward, gangly teenager instead of actually inhabiting his body, I somehow managed to get out four words.

"Yes, I'll do it."

But all I could think was *I hope I don't screw this up.*

The first session for what would ultimately become the album known as *Revolver* was due to start at 8 P.M. on Wednesday, April 6, 1966. At around six, the two longtime Beatles roadies—Neil Aspinall and Mal Evans—rolled up in their beat-up white van and began hauling the group's equipment into EMI's Studio Three.

Earlier that day, I had been pleased to learn that Phil had landed the job of assisting me on the project. Now he and I busied ourselves in the studio, directing the maintenance engineers to set up the microphones in the same standard positions that Norman Smith had always used. As each mic was plugged in, Phil walked around and uttered the time-honored phrase, "Testing, one, two, three," while I sat in the control room making sure the signal was arriving at the mixing desk without noise or distortion.

Shortly before eight o'clock, George Martin arrived and stuck his head in. "All right, Geoff?" he asked casually.

"Fine, George," I replied, trying to sound just as casual—but probably failing miserably.

"Right, then," he said as he headed out to the canteen for a quick cup of tea. Moments after he disappeared, the studio door swung open and the four Beatles walked in, laughing and joking as usual. Their hair was a bit longer, and they were dressed casually instead of wearing their usual tailored suits and skinny ties, but other than that they seemed unchanged by the phenomenal success they'd enjoyed since I'd last seen them. Mal ran off to fetch George Martin, and I got on the intercom to alert Phil—who was in the machine room, ready to operate the tape recorder—that the session was about to start.

Battling the butterflies in my stomach, I lit what must have been my fiftieth cigarette of the day and leaned back in my chair, savoring the stillness. It was a moment that had become ritual to me, but this time it really felt like the calm before the storm. *My entire life is about to change*, I thought. The only thing was, I didn't know if it was about to change for the better or the worse. If all went smoothly, my career would probably take off like a shot. If it didn't . . . well, I preferred not to think about that.

I assumed, naturally enough, that the four Beatles knew that Norman Smith was out and that I was to be their new engineer, and I wondered how they felt about the switch. Lennon and Harrison were the two that I feared the most; John because he could be caustic, even downright nasty, and George because of his sarcastic tongue and furtive nature. Ringo was generally bland, just one of the lads, really, though he had a strange sense of humor and was actually the most cynical of the four. Paul, on the other hand, was usually friendly and amiable, though assertive when he needed to be. He and I had established the closest relationship since I'd first started working with the band back in 1962.

My quiet contemplation was interrupted by George Martin opening the control room door, cup of tea in hand. "Everything ready to go?" he asked me.

"Yes, Phil is standing by and all the mics are up and working," I answered dutifully.

His response floored me. "Well, I suppose I better go out there and tell them the news." George carefully placed his cup of tea on the small producer's table beside the mixing console and walked out.

Tell them the news?? My jaw dropped. They didn't know after all! My God, why had I ever agreed to do this? I looked out through the glass window that separated the control room from the studio. Lennon and Harrison were tuning their guitars, while Paul and Ringo were clowning around at the piano. Through the open microphones, I could hear the conversation as George Martin entered the room.

"Afternoon, 'enry," said Lennon in his flat, nasal voice. Because there were two Georges involved in the recording sessions—Harrison and Martin—George Martin was usually referred to as "George H," since his middle name was Henry. It was an arrangement I always found a little odd, since George Harrison was also a George H. John was the only one of the four who was actually cheeky enough to call the schoolmasterly Martin solely by his middle name, which he tended to do when he was especially exuberant . . . or especially irritated. Paul and Ringo greeted their producer with a much more respectful "Hello, George H, how have you been?" As the pleasantries were exchanged, I started to feel a sense of relief—at least everyone seemed to be in a good mood.

Everyone, that is, except George Harrison. Peering sullenly over his guitar, he dispensed with the niceties and spat out two words that shot like an arrow through my heart.

"Where's Norman?" he demanded.

All four pairs of eyes turned to George Martin. The brief pause that followed seemed like an eternity to me. Perched on the edge of my chair in the control room, I stopped breathing.

"Well, boys, I have a bit of news," Martin replied after a beat or two. "Norman's out, and Geoff's going to be carrying on in his place."

That was it. No further explanation, no words of encouragement, no praise for my abilities. Just the facts, plain and unadorned. I thought I could see George Harrison scowling. John and Ringo appeared clearly apprehensive.

But Paul didn't seem fazed at all. "Oh, well then," he said with a grin. "We'll be all right with Geoff; he's a good lad."

Another pause, this one a bit longer. I allowed myself to breathe again, but I could hear my heart pounding.

Then, just as abruptly, it was over. John shrugged his shoulders, turned his back on the others and continued tuning his guitar; Ringo returned his attention to the piano. With an ominous glare, George Harrison muttered something I couldn't quite make out but then joined Lennon at the guitar amplifiers. Paul got up and began walking toward the drum kit, looking quite pleased with himself. In fact, with the passage of time I've almost convinced myself that he and George Martin exchanged winks.

Looking back all these years later, it seems to me that the change in engineering seats was probably done with Paul's advance knowledge and tacit approval. Perhaps it was even done at his instigation. It's hard to imagine that George Martin would have made that kind of momentous decision without discussing it with any of the group, and he seemed to have the closest relationship with Paul, who was always the most concerned about getting the sound right in the studio. And while I'd like to believe that Paul had fostered a friendship with me since our earliest years of working together because he liked me, it's also possible that he had an ulterior motive, that he was scouting me out as a possible replacement for Norman.

There were certainly other engineers at EMI more experienced and qualified than I was, but they were almost Norman Smith's age. Perhaps Paul simply wanted someone a bit younger, someone closer in both age and outlook, especially since the band was growing by leaps and bounds musically and starting to experiment more. John, Ringo, and George Harrison didn't care about details like that the way that Paul did, so I could see how George Martin opted to avoid controversy by keeping it secret from them for as long as possible.

But sitting in that control room, waiting to see how I would be received, I wasn't thinking about that. I was simply a jumble of emotions: filled with nervous excitement, worried that I would screw up, horrified that George Martin was springing this on them at the last moment . . . and fearful that the group would reject me out of hand.

With the issue resolved, the Beatles soon settled down to business. Wiping the sweat from my brow, I decided to venture into the studio to find out what it was we were going to be working on that evening.

"Hello, Geoff," Paul said brightly as I walked in the room. The other three basically ignored me. John was deep in discussion with George Martin;

clearly the first song we were going to be working on was one of his. He had no title for it at the time, so the tape box was simply labeled "Mark I." The eventual title—"Tomorrow Never Knows"—was actually one of Ringo's many malapropisms. It belied the deep nature of the lyric, which was partially adapted from *The Tibetan Book of the Dead*.

There's a misconception in the public's mind that John and Paul always wrote songs together. Perhaps they did in the early days—which is why they had agreed to credit all their songs to "Lennon/McCartney" and split the royalties equally—but by the time the *Revolver* sessions began, they were more usually writing separately. Each would critique the other's work and offer suggestions; sometimes one would contribute a middle section to the other's song, or rewrite a verse or chorus. But pretty much every song they recorded was written individually. Almost without exception, the main writer of the song took the lead vocal.

"This one's completely different than anything we've ever done before," John was saying to George Martin. "It's only got the one chord, and the whole thing is meant to be like a drone." Monotonic songs were becoming increasingly popular in those early, heady days of psychedelia; I suppose they were meant to be listened to while you were stoned, or tripping. To my mind, that was really the only way they could be appreciated. But my musical tastes didn't matter here: my job was to give the artist and producer the kinds of sounds they wanted. So my ears perked up when I heard John's final direction to George: ". . . and I want my voice to sound like the Dalai Lama chanting from a mountaintop, miles away."

That was typical John Lennon. Despite the fact that he was one of the greatest rock 'n' roll singers of all time, he hated the sound of his own voice and was constantly imploring us to make him sound different. "Can you squeeze that up there?" he would say, or "Can you make it sound nasally? No, I'll sing it nasally—that's it." Anything to disguise his voice.

John always had plenty of ideas about how he wanted his songs to sound; he knew in his mind what he wanted to hear. The problem was that, unlike Paul, he had great difficulty expressing those thoughts in anything but the most abstract terms. Whereas Paul might say, "This song needs brass and timpani," John's direction might be more like "Give me the feel of James Dean gunning his motorcycle down a highway."

Or, "Make me sound like the Dalai Lama chanting from a mountaintop."

George Martin looked over at me with a nod as he reassured John. "Got it. I'm sure Geoff and I will come up with something." Which meant, of course, that he was sure *Geoff* would come up with something. I looked around the room in a panic. I thought I had a vague idea of what John wanted, but I had no clear sense of how to achieve it. Fortunately, I had a little time to think about it, because John decided to start the recording process by having me make a loop of him playing a simple guitar figure, with Ringo accompanying him on drums. (A loop is created by splicing the end of a section of music to the beginning so that it plays continuously.) Because John wanted a thunderous sound, the decision was made to play the part at a fast tempo and then slow the tape down on playback: this would serve not only to return the tempo to the desired speed but also to make the guitar and drums—and the reverb they were drenched in—sound otherworldly.

The whole time, I kept thinking about what the Dalai Lama might sound like if he were standing on Highgate Hill, a few miles away from the studio. I began doing a mental inventory of the equipment we had on hand. Clearly, none of the standard studio tricks available at the mixing console would do the job alone. We also had an echo chamber, and lots of amplifiers in the studio, but I couldn't see how they could help, either.

But perhaps there *was* one amplifier that might work, even though nobody had ever put a vocal through it. The studio's Hammond organ was hooked up to a system called a Leslie—a large wooden box that contained an amp and two sets of revolving speakers, one that carried low bass frequencies and the other that carried high treble frequencies; it was the effect of those spinning speakers that was largely responsible for the characteristic Hammond organ sound. In my mind, I could almost hear what John's voice might sound like if it were coming from a Leslie. It would take a little time to set up, but I thought it might just give him what he was after.

"I think I have an idea about what to do for John's voice," I announced to George in the control room as we finished editing the loop. Excitedly, I explained my concept to him. Though his brows furrowed for a moment, he nodded his assent. Then he went out into the studio and told the four Beatles, who were standing around impatiently waiting for the loop to be constructed, to take a tea break while "Geoff sorts out something for the vocal."

Less than half an hour later, Ken Townsend, our maintenance engineer, had the required wiring completed. Phil and I tested the apparatus, carefully placing two microphones near the Leslie speakers. It certainly sounded different enough; I could only hope that it would satisfy Lennon. I took a deep breath and informed George Martin that we were ready to go.

Setting down their cups of tea, John settled behind the mic and Ringo behind his kit, ready to overdub vocals and drums on top of the recorded loop; Paul and George Harrison headed up to the control room. Once everyone was in place and ready to go, George Martin got on the talkback mic: "Stand by . . . here it comes." Then Phil started the loop playing back. Ringo began playing along, hitting the drums with a fury, and John began singing, eyes closed, head back.

"Turn off your mind, relax and float downstream . . ." Lennon's voice sounded like it never had before, eerily disconnected, distant yet compelling. The effect seemed to perfectly complement the esoteric lyrics he was chanting. Everyone in the control room—including George Harrison—looked stunned.

Through the glass we could see John begin smiling. At the end of the first verse, he gave an exuberant thumbs-up and McCartney and Harrison began slapping each other on the back.

"It's the Dalai Lennon!" Paul shouted.

George Martin shot me a wry grin. "Nice one, Geoff," he said. For someone not prone to paying compliments, that was high praise indeed. For the first time that day, the butterflies in my midsection stopped fluttering.

Moments later, the first take was complete and John and Ringo had joined us in the control room to listen to it. Lennon was clearly bowled over by what he was hearing. "That is bloody marvelous," he kept saying over and over again. Then he addressed me directly for the first time that evening, adopting his finest snooty upper-class accent. "I say, dear boy," he joked, "tell us all precisely how you accomplished that little miracle."

I did my best to explain what I had done and how a Leslie worked, but most of it seemed to go over John's head; all he really got out of it was the concept of a rotating speaker. In my experience, there are few musicians who are technically savvy—their focus is on the musical content and nothing else, which is as it should be—but Lennon was more technically challenged than most.

"Couldn't we get the same effect by dangling me from a rope and swinging me around the microphone instead?" he asked innocently, throwing the others into paroxysms of laughter.

"Yer daft, John, you are," McCartney teased affectionately, but Lennon persisted. In the background, I could see George Martin shaking his head bemusedly, like a schoolteacher enjoying the naivete of one of his young charges.

Lennon was not to be dissuaded quite so easily, though. The following year, when we were doing the *Sgt. Pepper* album, Beatles roadie Mal Evans was actually dispatched to go out and buy a rope strong enough to support John from the rafters of the studio ceiling so that he could be swung like a bell. Fortunately for us all, Mal would be unsuccessful in his quest—or per-haps, cognizant of the danger (and foolishness) of the notion, he deliberately avoided carrying out his employer's wishes. In any event, the idea was qui-etly dropped, although Lennon continued to search for new ways to disguise his voice, often referring to the way "our Geoffrey" had levitated him up to the mountaintop for the recording of "Tomorrow Never Knows."

Later that first evening, John gave me a friendly grin and began a casual conversation—his way of showing that I was accepted and had passed his personal muster. "Have you heard that new Tiny Tim record?" he asked.

I hadn't, but I was determined to present myself as being both knowl-edgeable and hip. "Yeah, they're great," I bluffed.

Lennon burst out in derisive laughter: "*They're* great? It's just one bloke, don't you know even that? Nobody's really sure if it's actually a guy or some drag queen."

I turned beet red and slunk out of the studio, tail between my legs. I had learned one important lesson: you couldn't pull the wool over John Lennon's eyes.

While they were listening to the first playback of "Tomorrow Never Knows," John and George Harrison had been excitedly discussing ideas for guitar parts. Harrison eagerly suggested that a tamboura—one of his new collection of Indian instruments—be added. "It's perfect for this track, John," he was explaining in his deadpan monotone. "It's just kind of a dron-ing sound and I think it will make the whole thing quite Eastern."

Lennon was nodding his head; you could tell he liked the idea, but he wasn't about to say so. Most of the time he treated his younger bandmate more like a kid brother or even as a subordinate. It was rare when John gave George the respect he deserved.

But my attention was drawn to Paul and Ringo, who were huddled to-gether talking about the drumming. Paul was a musician's musician—he could play many different instruments, including drums, so he was the one who most often worked with Ringo on developing the drum part. Paul was suggesting that "Ring" (as we usually called him) add a little skip to the basic beat he was playing. The pattern he was tapping out on the mixing console was somewhat reminiscent of the one Ringo had played on their recent hit single "Ticket To Ride." Ringo said little, but listened intently. As the last of the four Beatles to join, he was used to taking direction from the others, es-pecially Paul. Ringo made an important contribution to the band's sound—

there's no question about that—but unless he felt strongly about something, he rarely spoke up in the studio.

While Paul was focusing on the drum pattern, I was concentrating on the actual sound of the drums. Norman's standard mic positioning might have been fine for just any Beatles song, but somehow it seemed too ordinary for the unique nature of this particular track. With Lennon's words rolling around my brain ("This one's completely different than anything we've ever done before"), I began hearing a drum sound in my head, and I thought I knew how to achieve it. The problem was that my idea was in direct contravention of EMI's strict recording rules.

Concerned about wear and tear on their expensive collection of microphones, the top studio brass had warned us never to place mics any closer than two feet to drums, especially the bass drum, which put out such a wallop of low frequencies. It seemed to me, though, that if I moved all the drum mics in closer—say, just a few inches away—we would hear a distinctly different tonal quality, one which I thought would suit the song. I knew I might get a bollocking from the studio manager for doing so, but my curiosity was piqued: I really wanted to hear what it would sound like. After a moment's thought, I decided, what the hell. This was the Beatles we were talking about. If I couldn't try things out at their sessions, I probably would never get the opportunity on anybody else's session.

Without saying a word, I quietly slipped out to the studio and moved both the snare drum mic and the single overhead mic in close. But before I also moved the microphone that was aimed at Ringo's bass drum, there was something else I wanted to try, because I felt that the bass drum was ringing too much—in studio parlance, it was too "live." Ringo, who was a heavier chain smoker than the other three, had a habit of keeping his packet of cigarettes close at hand, right on the snare drum, even while he was playing. In some ways, I think that might have even contributed to his unique drum sound, because it served to slightly muffle the drumskin.

Applying the same principle, I decided to do something to dampen the bass drum. Sitting atop one of the instrument cases was an old woolen sweater—one which had been specially knitted with eight arms to promote the group's recent film, which was originally called *Eight Arms to Hold You* before it was renamed *Help!* I suppose it had since been appropriated by Mal as packing material, but I had a better use for it. As quickly as I could, I removed the bass drum's front skin—the one with the famous "dropped-T" Beatles logo on it—and stuffed the sweater inside so that it was flush against the rear beater skin. Then I replaced the front skin and positioned the bass drum mic directly in front of it, angled down slightly but so close that it was almost touching.

I returned to the control room, where the four Beatles were gulping down cups of tea, and unobtrusively turned the mixer's inputs down so that they wouldn't overload when Ringo resumed playing. Then it was time for me to put into action the final stage of my plan to improve the drum sound. I connected the studio's Fairchild limiter (a device that reduces peaks in the signal) so that it affected the drum channels alone, and then turned its input up. My idea was to purposely overload its circuitry, again in direct violation of the EMI recording rules. The resulting "pumping" would, I thought, add an extra degree of excitement to the sound of the drums. At the same time, I was saying a silent prayer that the mics wouldn't be damaged—if they were, my job would probably be on the line. I have to admit to having felt a little bit invulnerable, though: in the back of my mind, I assumed that John Lennon—ecstatic over his new vocal sound and still raving about it to anyone who would listen—would probably rise to my defense if management did threaten to fire me.

As the band reassembled in the studio to make a second attempt at recording the backing track to "Mark I," I asked Ringo to pound on each of his drums and cymbals. Happily, none of the mics were distorting. In fact, the drums already sounded great to my ears, a combination of the close miking and the Fairchild working away. There was no comment from George Martin, whose attention was diverted elsewhere; he was no doubt thinking about arrangement ideas. My fingers tightened over the controls of the mixing desk; I was tingling with anticipation. So far, so good—but the proof would come when the whole band began playing.

"Ready, John?" asked Martin. A nod from Lennon signaled that he was about to begin his count-in, so I instructed Phil McDonald to roll tape. ". . . two, three, four," intoned John, and then Ringo entered with a furious cymbal crash and bass drum hit. It sounded magnificent! Thirty seconds in, someone in the band made a mistake, though, and they all stopped playing. I knew from my assisting days that Lennon would want to start another take immediately—he was always impatient, ready to go—so I quickly announced "take three" on the talkback microphone and the group began playing the song again, perfectly this time around.

"I think we've got it," John announced excitedly after the last note died away. George Martin waved everyone into the control room to hear the playback. This time around, I was far less nervous—I felt I had come up with exactly the drum sound that worked best for the song. Ten seconds after starting the tape playing for the four Beatles, I knew my instincts were correct.

"What on earth did you do to my drums?" Ringo was asking me. "They sound fantastic!"

Paul and John began whooping it up, and even the normally dour George Harrison was smiling broadly. "That's the one, boys," George Martin agreed, nodding in my direction. "Good work; now let's knock it on the head for the night."

It was after 2 A.M., and though, to my great relief, the evening had ended in triumph, my primary feeling was exhaustion. Everyone else was in high spirits; I was just plain knackered.

In the now-empty control room, Phil McDonald and I took a few moments to have a smoke and reflect quietly on all that had transpired. "You did it, Geoff," he said softly. "You completely won them over."

And indeed I had; even George Harrison had given me an uncharacteristically friendly "Take care, be safe" on his way out. Stubbing out my cigarette in the beat-up old ashtray on top of the mixing desk, I slowly made my way down the hallway and climbed into the car that was waiting to take me to my parents' North London home, the faint glow of dawn beginning to appear on the horizon.

· 1 ·

Hidden Treasure

In the depths of my grandmother's damp, musty basement awaited hidden treasure, the box that was to literally change my life.

Not that I had any idea what was inside—after all, I was only six years old. As an only child, I had grown accustomed to spending long hours on my own. My father worked from dawn to dusk in his butcher shop, and my mum, who was a full-time housewife despite having been trained as a court dressmaker (as a young woman, in the prewar years, she had made clothes for the Royal Family), seemed to always be busy puttering around the house doing one thing or another. On this particular chilly afternoon in the spring of 1953, I had decided to while away the hours indoors, poking around in the nether regions of my grandmother's house, where my parents and I lived. To anyone else's eyes it was a gloomy, airless basement filled with spiders and cobwebs, dust and junk. But to my young eyes, it was a secret inner sanctum that contained untold mysteries, exotic relics of a prewar era I had never known.

The war was something that everyone in Britain still talked about in hushed tones. There was evidence of it everywhere, from the battle-scarred veterans you saw on the streets, to the bomb sites that still remained as mute testimony to the horrific pounding London had taken. In fact, there was a bomb site just up the road from where I lived; in our innocence, all the neighborhood kids used it as a makeshift playground, a mysterious place where we formed secret societies. But though the war was unreal to me, I knew at an early age that it had affected my life. For one thing, it was the reason why my dad had to spend Sundays hunched over the kitchen table sorting through the ration coupons he had received during the week, quietly filling out all the proper government forms. It was also the reason why we lived where we did. The neighborhood where my parents grew up and met— Clerkenwell, in central London—was being bombed so heavily during the war years that they had been forced to flee and move to my grandmother's home in the relatively unscathed North London suburb of Crouch End.

I was raised in that house, a small Edwardian terrace on a hilly street. The view was dominated by the past and the future: the bygone splendor of Alexandra Palace, atop which sat a huge and ugly BBC television transmission tower—the first in all of Britain. Our house was plainly decorated yet bright and cheerful, and it still sported gaslight fittings, though we had electricity by the time I was born. The kitchen range was the old-fashioned black galvanized iron type that had probably been there since the house was first constructed; my mother would spend long hours standing over that stove preparing meals for us, humming softly along with the sounds of light orchestral music emanating from the radio in the front room. The radio was almost always on in our house, a cheerful, comforting presence. My dad enjoyed the sound of big bands—he was a Gene Krupa fan, and he used to drum along on the tabletop with a couple of spoons whenever "Drum Boogie" would come on the air.

It was a happy enough middle-class existence, marked by eccentric neighbors (the aptly named Mrs. House, who lived next door, was so obsessed with keeping her garden tidy that she sometimes swept the lawn with a broom) and childhood pranks. All in all, I suppose I led what most might call a normal childhood, though I was soon to develop a number of interests that would lead me to pursue a career that was far from ordinary.

For one thing, I always was attracted to music, even though none of the members of my family had any particular musical talents. My great-uncle George had an old piano in his front room—it was built in Paris in the 1850s, before there was electricity, so it had a pair of built-in brass candlesticks that stuck out in front. His house was dark and forbidding, with heavy curtains to keep the draft out, but I was always happy to visit, because it gave me an opportunity to tinker on that piano. Much to my parents' amazement, I found myself able to pick out simple tunes I had heard on the radio, playing solely by ear. I have no explanation for how I was able to do it; for some reason I just knew where the notes fell, and it was only a matter of going from one note to another to make up the tune.

That must have gotten my parents thinking, because one year their Christmas gift to me was a bright red toy record player (known in those days as a "gramophone"). My eyes were big as saucers as I pulled it out of its wrapping, and within moments, I was playing the two tiny records it came with, singing and clapping along to the children's songs that magically floated from thin air. In the weeks to come, I would spin those two records over and over again, until their grooves were nearly worn out.

Then came that fateful afternoon in my grandmother's basement. Pushing aside the pile of gas masks that sat atop the mysterious box, I excitedly tore the lid open, hoping that within I would find a pot of gold . . . or at least a pile of comic books.

"Mum! Come look at this!" No answer. I raised my shrill voice up a notch: "Mum!!"

Above my head I heard chairs creaking and the unmistakable footsteps of my mother approaching the basement stairs.

"Whatever is it, Geoffrey? What's got you so excited?"

I was literally jumping up and down, unable to contain myself as I begged her to ask Nan if I could have what I had found.

Inside the box were dozens of old gramophone records. I had never imagined that so many records even existed . . . and I couldn't wait to hear what they sounded like.

My grandmother must have wondered what on earth a six-year-old would want with a collection of old classical and operatic records, but she quickly gave her assent. My dad was enlisted to haul the heavy box upstairs, where, to my delight, I discovered that my toy player could accommodate grown-up records, too. Probably with a sense of relief that he would never again have to listen to another chorus of "Pop Goes the Weasel," my father carefully blew the dust off the record on top of the pile and gently placed it on the green felt mat of the turntable. As the needle dropped down, the scratchy sounds of "*Un bel di*," the famous aria from *Madame Butterfly*, filled the room.

Instantly, rapturously, I was in love.

I spent the next several months playing those records endlessly— *Pagliacci*, "The Volga Boat Song," *Rhapsody in Blue*, even the *Brandenburg* Concerto no. 2 (a composition that would serve to inspire Paul McCartney years later when he was recording "Penny Lane"). And the more I played them, the more I got out of them. The music would not only evoke emotions in me—joy, sadness, longing, excitement—but also conjure up images in my mind.

At the time, I was attending Rokesley Infant School (the equivalent to an American kindergarten) and my ears perked up when our teacher announced that a professional musician named Leon Goossens—a famous oboist—would soon be making a visit. The talk he gave made quite an impression on me. After describing the hard work and determination it took to follow his dream, Goossens showed a short film of the BBC Symphony Orchestra in concert. As I watched the film, I found my attention focusing on the conductor. It began to dawn on me that it was he who was responsible for how fast or slow they were playing, and as I followed the arc of his baton I realized that he was coaxing various sections to play louder or softer, too.

At home, I began listening to my beloved records differently. Using a pencil as a baton, I began imitating the movements of the conductor, urging the imaginary musicians in my room on to new heights of performance. *If only they could play faster here,* I would think. *If only the violins could be louder, the flutes softer, the trumpets less harsh.* In my childish naivete, I found myself increasingly frustrated that the orchestra on the recording refused to respond to my urgent summonings. I began wishing there was some way I could affect the sound I was hearing.

At the time, I had no idea what role a producer or recording engineer played; I didn't even know that such jobs existed, much less what a recording studio was. But I am convinced that those long hours up in my room, waving a pencil at phantom musicians playing through a tiny speaker in a toy gramophone, served as the catalyst that eventually propelled me toward a lifetime of making records.

In addition to my growing appreciation for the aesthetics of music, I was beginning to develop an interest in the technical aspects as well. I would stare at each record as it spun around, totally absorbed, observing how the needle was bouncing along. I didn't quite understand how it all worked, but I instinctively realized that there had to be some connection between the way the needle was moving and the sound I was hearing.

Encouraging my keen interest in all things musical, my father came home from work one day and presented me with a radio of my own: a crystal set called a Cat's Whisker. It was tiny, consisting of a delicate tuning device and a small set of earphones for listening. I kept it in my bedroom, and I'd play it late at night when I was supposed to be sleeping.

That little radio, primitive though it was, made a big difference in my life. The only commercial station in those days was the rather exotic Radio Luxembourg, broadcast from the European mainland. Their disk jockeys played exciting skiffle and rock 'n' roll records instead of the bland music of my parents' generation, and, like so many other British youths of my generation, that was how I discovered pop music. Each Sunday night at 11 P.M. I would silently rise from my bed and carefully tuck the Cat's Whisker under my pillow, then, checking to make sure there was no one at my door, don the earphones. With bated breath and a trembling hand, I would methodically search the crystal for just the right spot that would allow me to hear that week's Top Twenty.

Those records sounded raucous to my classically tuned ears, but there was something exhilarating about them, too. They were like a breath of fresh air, and I found myself drawn more and more to pop records, though I still retained my appreciation for classical and operatic pieces. Somehow my musical tastes were broadening, not just shifting.

The big breakthrough for me, as well as for millions of other young people in England and America, came when Bill Haley and the Comets exploded onto the scene. Their rough, driving sound made an impact on me that was almost indescribable. When "Rock Around The Clock" would come on, I could feel my pulse quicken, and my feet would start to move to the beat, as if they had a mind of their own. It was a visceral, emotional response—one that was different from what I felt when I listened to more "serious" music, but no less compelling.

By this time, I had successfully lobbied my parents into buying me a more grown-up gramophone. It was still a windup model, but it was made by HMV, the big music chain in England. It had a more austere, respectable look to it than my first one: black instead of childish bright red, it sported a nifty dog-and-trumpet logo, and it had a greatly improved sound, too.

I was also starting to explore my own musical ability. In junior school, we were encouraged to take up a musical instrument. With memories of Leon Goossens's visit still lingering, I decided to learn to play the recorder. I eagerly looked forward to the lessons each week, and I also discovered to my delight that, just as on the piano, I was able to play the recorder by ear, picking out familiar melodies with ease. I even fancied myself as a bit of a composer; at one point, I wrote down a random series of notes and presented it to our teacher, Miss Weeds, as a finished composition, requesting that she play it. She took one look at my chicken scratch and declared it totally unplayable.

Undeterred, my musical progress continued, not least thanks to the generosity of my uncle George, who had decided to give us his old piano in order to encourage my playing. On the day it was due to arrive, I stood on the street corner, anxiously eyeing every lorry that drove up the street. When the big truck finally pulled up in front of my house, I ran over to the deliverymen, supervising their every move as they carefully carried the piano into our front room.

"Play us a tune then, lad," demanded the burly foreman as he set it down in the designated spot, wiping the sweat from his brow.

Obligingly, I plunked out the familiar first few notes of Beethoven's Ninth. He rudely interrupted me.

"Nah, what's that lot? Play us some real music!"

Unabashed, I pounded out a furious version of Chopsticks, then crossed my arms and gave him what I thought was a look to kill . . . which only had the effect of sending him into a fit of laughter.

Clearly, he was no aficionado of the finer things in life.

Something else of significance happened to me when I was a child: I saw a spaceship. It only happened once, and, no, there were no little green men, and, no, I wasn't abducted and flown off to Mars. It sounds crazy, but I know what I saw, and the memory is indelibly etched in my consciousness.

It was about nine o'clock in the evening on a cold winter night; the moonless sky was pitch-black and clear. I was alone in my bedroom, standing near the window, when this huge thing suddenly appeared out of nowhere, hovering directly overhead. Irregular in shape and full of craterlike indents, it was pulsating and glowing a fiery red. There was no sound associated with it, which made the whole experience all the more surreal. After a moment or two, it shot off at a high rate of speed and off in the distance I could see it making rapid, sharp maneuvers, moving in ninety-degree directions. Obviously, someone or something was steering it.

Torn between fear and an intense desire to see what it did next, I stood rooted to my spot for a good minute or two before I decided I needed to alert my parents. Running downstairs at full speed, shouting at the top of my lungs, I burst into the kitchen, where they were doing the washing-up. Dismissive yet curious, they followed me back up to my bedroom, but of course by this time all traces of the spaceship—or whatever it was—had disappeared.

My parents arrived at the only sensible conclusion: that I had been having a nightmare and had imagined the whole thing. But I am certain that I was fully awake the entire time. When they were unable to convince me otherwise, the matter was quietly dropped in the Emerick household . . . until a week later, when the local newspaper came out. In the letters to the editor section, there was a query from a man who lived just down the road from us—he was not a neighbor we knew well, but it was an address I recognized. On the night in question, he wrote, he had seen something odd outside his window and was inquiring as to whether anyone else had also seen it. His description of the alien craft and its bizarre movements fitted mine perfectly. For a few days, I contemplated knocking on the fellow's door to assure him that he wasn't going mad, but in the end I decided against it. As grown-up as I may have felt, deep down I realized that I was still only a child, and I thought he might not take me seriously.

Seeing that UFO had no great effect on my life—it was just something that happened, something for which I have no explanation. Years later, when I was in the studio working with the Beatles, I had the opportunity during a late-night break to relate the story to Paul and John. John, as was his wont, was immediately dismissive, even derisive, but Paul was sympathetic; he believed me then, and I think he believes me to this day. We had a long conversation that evening, at the end of which Paul and I concluded solemnly that there simply are some things in this world that are beyond our ability to comprehend. "Bollocks," snorted John as he headed off for a cup of tea.

I have often wondered if John Lennon felt any different after he himself spotted a flying saucer hovering over the East River while living in New York City in the mid-1970s. Sadly, I never got the chance to ask him.

By my preteen years, my interests had expanded significantly beyond playing records and listening avidly to the radio. I was beginning to become more visually oriented, spending long hours tinkering with my camera, experimenting with various lenses. Unlike most of the other kids my age, I was never too keen on sports, though. At one point, I was asked to play on the school rugby team simply because I was tall, but it didn't last for long because my limited skills were costing the team too many points.

As I grew older, I also began developing a growing appreciation for the cinema. After I saw the movie *The Eddy Duchin Story*, I briefly began fantasizing about becoming a classical concert pianist. But I soon realized that I had neither the native ability nor the willingness to put in all the hours of training and practice that were required, and the idea faded. It was an inspiring film, though, and it did spark me into starting to think about my future, about what I wanted to make of my life. My dad made no secret of his desire for me to follow in his footsteps. His father had been a butcher, and so had his father's father. But there was no way I could face a lifetime of chopping up raw meat. The very thought—and smell—of the blood and guts made me feel physically ill. To his credit, my dad never pushed me into it.

Once he saw that I intended to take my life in a different direction, he provided me with quiet encouragement to do whatever it was I wanted to do.

The problem was, having decided that I was going to be neither a concert pianist nor a butcher, I had no idea what I *did* want—and there seemed to be an impossibly wide range of choices between the two. It really wasn't too early for me to begin thinking about my future, either. In the English system, you completed school when you were fifteen or so, and either left to pursue a trade or—if you had good grades, money, and/or connections—went on to university, something that wasn't an option for me.

Then one hot summer afternoon, in the middle of the school holidays, I discovered my calling. For some time, I had been intrigued by the tiny television in our front room, even though the BBC was the only channel on the air. I was especially fascinated by the experimental stereo broadcasts their technicians ran on Saturday mornings, when presumably they thought few people would be watching. Viewers were instructed to position their radio left of the TV in order to hear the stereo effect, with the radio speaker playing the left channel of the accompanying music and the television speaker playing the right channel. It was a clever, though primitive, idea, and I was captivated by the full, rich sound that resulted.

That's why my eye was drawn to an advert in the local newspaper announcing the dates and times of the upcoming annual Television and Radio Show, held in the cavernous Earl's Court in southwest London. This was a trade show, open to the public, in which the various manufacturers showed their wares—the newest models of televisions, radios, and record players on the market. Bored and looking for something to do, I decided to attend, even though none of my mates were interested in accompanying me, preferring to spend their summer afternoons chasing a football in the park. I didn't really know what to expect; I thought I might catch a glimpse of a real-life TV camera and perhaps gain a little insight into some of the hobbies I was interested in. But what I discovered that day was to have a profound impact on the rest of my life.

The BBC, naturally enough, had the largest display area at the show; in fact, they were doing a live orchestral radio broadcast on the day I attended. I jostled my way to the front of the queue and watched, wide-eyed, as a dapper, mustachioed announcer dressed in a formal tuxedo stepped before a microphone.

As he introduced the programme, he pointed out the numerous microphones situated in and around the orchestra, explaining that their purpose was to capture the sound. The signal from those microphones, he said, traveled down electrical wires into something he called a "mixing console."

My attention shifted to the huge electrical apparatus he was indicating, behind which stood a stocky fellow in a white coat, wearing clunky earphones as he fiddled with various mysterious-looking knobs and dials. On the wall behind him were two illuminated signs, one of which read "On Air," and the other which read "Control Room." *Control* room. Of course! This was where the magic all happened, and it was all under the control not of the conductor, but of the mysterious fellow in the white lab coat. What was it the announcer called him again?

Oh, yes. The *sound engineer.*

For the next hour I stood rooted to that spot, mouth agape, as the broadcast commenced and the BBC Light Orchestra—two dozen or so bored-looking musicians also incongruously clad in tuxedos despite the sweltering heat—played their way through a medley of show tunes. But I paid them almost no mind, so transfixed was I with what the sound engineer was doing. With his every gesture and turn of a knob I strained to hear the difference he was making in the thunderous sound emanating from the huge speakers mounted overhead—far clearer and far more overwhelming than anything I had ever heard coming from my radio or television at home.

When the broadcast concluded, I was filled with an excitement I hadn't known since I had first discovered that cache of gramophone records in my grandmother's basement. But there was to be yet another important discovery that day. As I slowly worked my way past the crowds in the aisles, I began noticing that some of the booths had mysterious boxes that weren't television sets and weren't radios or even gramophone players. Pushing my way up front for a closer look, I noticed that these boxes had two things spinning on them, but they weren't record platters.

"What's the matter, sonny, haven't you ever seen a tape recorder before?" One of the demonstrators at the booth was addressing me, studying me with wry amusement.

"Er, no, sir," I stammered. "What's it for?"

"You use it to record the sound of your own voice, or that of your mates," he replied. "You can even use it to record music right off your radio."

Record music off the radio? I was flabbergasted. For the next fifteen minutes I watched excitedly as the technology—primitive by today's standards, but positively mind-boggling at the time—was explained and demonstrated. It seemed so incredible yet somehow I seemed to grasp the concept almost right away. It was amazing, sheer serendipity. In one afternoon I had not only discovered what a sound engineer was, but I also learned how recording worked. In the closeted little world I lived in at the time, that was quite a revelation.

Over the next few years, I made a point of attending the TV and Radio Show every summer, sometimes going two or three days in a row, always by myself. I'd take my time going from booth to booth, watching demonstrations, chatting with the salespeople, trying things out. I'd return home with a pile of glossy product brochures, which I would read and reread before organizing and filing them carefully away. All these technical innovations seemed to dovetail nicely with my keen interest in music of all genres, and slowly but surely I began thinking that what I wanted to do with my life was to somehow be involved in the creation of recorded music. Somehow, I wanted to be in the place where the magic happened.

When I was twelve I began attending the all-boys Crouch End Secondary Modern School. I was a generally indifferent student, though I did fairly well in math and history, and I developed an affinity for art, technical drawing, and chemistry. My love for music continued unabated: though I was resistant to the idea of formal music training, I enjoyed singing in the boy's choir because it gave me an increased appreciation for harmony. The local lending library also gave me new opportunities to expand my horizons in listening. They didn't have any pop records—that would have been way too progressive for the era—but I was able to take home quite a few classical and operatic pieces that I'd never heard before. For some reason, I leaned toward the more obscure recordings; somehow, the less popular the piece, the more interested I was in hearing it.

With my increased maturity came increased responsibility. My parents were giving me a modest weekly allowance, but my dad wanted me to learn the importance of self-reliance and so he had a word with the local greengrocer. Before I knew it, I had an after-school job stocking shelves and packing orders for customers. I didn't mind the work, actually—it provided me with extra pocket money, some of which I spent on chemistry and film developing supplies, but most of which went toward buying records.

There was "Rock Around The Clock," of course—I had to have that. And the latest singles from American artists such as Elvis Presley, Little Richard, Chuck Berry, the Platters, the Everly Brothers, Buddy Holly, and Jerry Lee Lewis, as well as English favorites like Cliff Richard and the Shadows. For some reason, I never used to listen to lyrics all that closely. Perhaps it was because of my taste for opera and classical music that the vocal always seemed like just another instrument to me. I was attracted to it solely for the way it fit in with the backing, not for the words that were being sung. Lyrics simply never sold me on a particular song—it was the overall sound that did.

There was a secondhand shop in our neighborhood that became one of my favorite places to visit because I never knew what I'd find there. One day when I was about thirteen I wandered in and saw that they had an old cream-colored drum kit on display. It was fairly tatty, although when it was new, it probably would have been a great piece of gear. But the price was right—three pounds, complete with cymbals—so I bought it on the spot. Fortunately for my parents, I didn't have room for the drums at home, so I brought them round to my mate Tony Cook's house, where I banged away on them for a few weeks before losing interest. Years later, when I was working with the Beatles and other bands in the recording studio, I'd sometimes reflect on that experience and think that even if I couldn't play drums, at least I knew how to make them sound great.

At some point I bought an old Hofner guitar from that shop, too, and I tried to learn to play it, but with no better results. One problem was that its electronics didn't work. I ended up trying to rebuild it; I veneered it in mahogany and spent a great deal of time trying to smarten it up.

Funnily enough, although I loved the sound of bass, I had no interest in learning to play that instrument, mainly because you couldn't really hear it clearly in those days. There wasn't the necessary equipment to get it on vinyl properly in England at that time, so it didn't seem to have that much importance, and if you heard it on TV or on radio, it was coming through a tiny speaker and so was nearly inaudible. Quite ironic, considering that so much of my later reputation as a recording engineer came from the bass sounds I devised with Paul McCartney.

Eventually I realized that what I really wanted, more than any musical instrument, was a tape recorder. The modest salary from my after-school job wasn't nearly enough to cover the cost, so I made the difficult decision to sell the train set my parents had bought me the previous Christmas and soon became the proud owner of a shiny new Brenell two-track model, complete with a microphone and an instruction book that explained the procedure for using a razor blade to cut and splice sections of tape together. After a little bit of practice, I became fairly proficient at splicing and was soon eagerly taping songs off the radio, cutting out the announcer's intruding voice, and piecing them together in the order I wanted to hear them—much like the process of sequencing an album. The Brenell also came with a Superimposition button, which disabled the erase head so you could add new parts on top of preexisting recordings. Just for a laugh, I'd tape myself playing some chords on the piano and then add a melody and a bass part. To my young ears, it sounded almost like a record!

My enthusiasm rubbed off on my friends, too; within a short time they all got tape recorders of their own. We'd swap tapes and talk enthusiastically about which songs we were planning on purloining from which radio programs. Interestingly, that was almost a precursor to today's downloading.

Despite my aversion to taking formal lessons, during my last year in school, I actually began participating in music classes. I had gotten into the habit of sneaking into the piano practice room after school hours to play *Rhapsody in Blue* and other favorite tunes, just to amuse myself. Unbenownst to me, the school's music instructor, Mr. Salter, decided to stay late one afternoon, and stuck his head in to see who was making all the racket. Lost in my own private rhapsody, I failed to notice him for several minutes. My self-absorbed performance must have made a favorable impression on him, because instead of giving me detention, he proposed that I begin accompanying the class on piano as they sang. It soon became apparent to me that his offer wasn't altogether altruistic: as I sat behind the piano at the front of the classroom doing all the work, he would use the time to sit in the back of the room and grade exam papers, saving himself the bother of bringing them home. It was all good fun, though, and I soon got my mate Howard Packham to play duets with me. We'd start with songs from the school repertoire but, to the class's delight, would inevitably end up performing bawdy songs. After a few weeks of perfecting our routine, we figured we might as well get something for our trouble, so, even though we were underage, we took our double act to the local pub, where we'd play on their beat-up old piano for pints of lager on a Saturday night.

Mr. Salter would also bring records to school and play us things like Ravel's *Bolero*, which I loved, and Holst's *The Planets*. More significantly, he'd play recordings of different orchestras playing the same piece, one after another, making me aware of slight variations in both musical approach and recording technique and thus further honing my burgeoning critical listening skills.

Another instructor who had a big influence on me in secondary school was Mr. Stonely. He was a physical education teacher who taught history as well. He also had an interest in opera, and so he arranged a school trip one evening to see *Pagliacci* at the famed Covent Garden Opera House. It was an optional trip, but I eagerly volunteered, anxious to see my first live opera. Only about fifteen of us went on the bus, making it rather a solemn occasion, with few schoolboy hijinks. Of course, we did all get one fit of the giggles during a quiet passage, invoking the disdain of the audience members around us who attempted to shush us—making us laugh all the harder! But the entire event completely awed me, from the moment we entered the imposing theater to the very last curtain call. It was the first time I heard a full symphony orchestra playing in person, and I was stunned by the sound of it.

Unfortunately, instructors like Mr. Salter and Mr. Stonely were the exception, not the rule, and before long I realized I had better begin making preparations for finding some kind of gainful employment in the real world. I had no intention of continuing on in university; there was simply no way I could face more years of staying in school. Fortunately, my parents were fine with my decision. Not only didn't they mind my leaving school, they didn't mind my continuing to live at home, either . . . as long as I found some kind of work.

My parents were lobbying for me to become an architect, which they considered a "proper" job. I considered the idea briefly, then abandoned it when I learned that it involved continuing education. I also gave some thought to a career in the film industry, though I knew even less about that than I did about the music industry. But after some deliberation, I finally decided that what I really wanted to do in my heart of hearts was to be involved in the creation of music. I realized that I was never going to get the proper training to become a professional composer or an accomplished musician, but I wanted to somehow make a contribution. I had only the vaguest of ideas about what a producer or arranger actually did, but, thanks to my experiences at the TV and Radio Show, I had a fairly clear sense of the role of the sound engineer, and that seemed to be the best fit of all my interests.

The question was, how did one go about getting such a job?

Our school had a full-time career counselor by the name of Barlow. Though I didn't know it at the time, he was to become my guardian angel. A few months before graduation day, he addressed our class assembly, advising that we begin writing letters of inquiry to prospective employers. The idea had never occurred to me; I simply had no idea how one went about securing a job, other than walking into a shop and asking the owner, or perhaps, as my father had done for me at the greengrocer's, counting on your parents' connections. Of course, my father knew no one in the record business, so that wasn't going to work this time around. Mr. Barlow had given me a potential way in. But who exactly should I be writing to?

I was pondering that question as I walked home from school one afternoon. As usual, I passed John Trapp's, the neighborhood record store, where I had so often stopped in to listen to the latest pop hits and perhaps even spend some of my hard-earned money on them. Sudden inspiration struck me: perhaps the store manager could give me advice on who I should write to.

Luckily for me, the shop was empty, and the manager seemed eager to chat. What's more, he was all too happy to share with me everything he knew about the business—which was considerable. Even though there seemed to be dozens of labels, he explained, they were all owned by just four record companies: Philips, Decca, Pye, and EMI. For example, the Parlophone label (headed, though I didn't know it at the time, by George Martin) specialized in spoken word and comedy records and was actually part of EMI. What's more, each of England's four record companies also owned their own recording "studios"—special places where the musicians went to make records, places where the recording engineer, answerable only to the producer, reigned supreme.

Eventually a customer wandered in and my crash course in the music business came to a close. Thanking the manager profusely, I literally dashed out of the store, eager to begin putting some of my new knowledge to use.

The next morning, before heading off to school, I sat down with my dad's telephone directory and looked up the phone numbers of each of the four record companies, relieved to discover that they were all based in London. I carefully dialed each number on the list and asked the receptionist for the company's address. That evening, I hunched over the small desk in my room and began my quest for gainful employment.

"Dear Sir," I carefully wrote in my youthful scrawl—making the assumption in those pre–politically correct days that there would be no women in positions of authority—"I shall be graduating from Crouch End Secondary Modern School this coming July and I am interested in working for your company, perhaps," I added hopefully, "in your recording studio. If you have any positions available, please let me know. Sincerely, Geoffrey Emerick." After carefully addressing and stamping the four envelopes, I bicycled down to the neighborhood post office and cast my fate to the winds.

For the next two weeks, I'd return home from school each day and burst through the front door in hopes that some news had arrived. Each day I would receive the disappointing answer. Finally a response came from Decca, nestled inside the self-addressed stamped envelope I had carefully included. I tore it open, heart racing . . . and then, to my dismay, saw that it contained a form rejection letter, not even properly signed. A few days later, letters arrived from EMI, and then from Philips, both with the same bad news: no vacancies, no apprenticeships being offered. I don't think I ever even got the courtesy of a reply from Pye.

As I was to learn later, it was precisely because there were only four labels and four "proper" recording studios in the entire country that each was besieged by letters from aspiring teenagers who had dreams of breaking into the business. But I didn't know that at the time: all I knew was that I had been rejected, and my hopes of a career in the music business appeared to have been dashed. For a few days, I moped around, wondering what to do next.

Then one morning my teacher announced that each of us would be meeting with the career counselor individually; my own appointment was scheduled for the next day. I began to feel some glimmer of hope: perhaps there was something he could do to help me.

"Mr. Emerick, I believe?" The voice emanated from behind a stack of career brochures piled high on an enormous oak desk. Mr. Barlow shifted slightly in his seat, lowered his glasses, and peered out at me. For a moment I felt as though I were in the presence of the Wizard of Oz.

"Yes, sir," I stammered.

"Come on in and have a seat, son. Now, tell me, are you planning on applying to university, or will you be seeking employment upon your graduation?"

"Employment, sir. And," I blurted out nervously, the words coming in a rush, "I've decided that I want to be in the record business. I want to be involved with making music; I want to work in a recording studio." He seemed taken aback, but I persisted.

"I really love listening to records and taping music off the radio," I explained, "so I think I'd be quite good at it. In fact, I've written letters to four record companies, several weeks ago. Three of them have turned me down, and I haven't heard anything from the fourth one." Carefully I produced the rejection letters from my book bag and placed them on his desk.

He perused the dog-eared letters with a look of bemusement. I could see he was quite impressed with what I had done, but at the same time he remained resistant to the idea. For the next several minutes he tried his best to convince me that a job in the Post Office installing telephones—good, steady employment, and easily attainable—was just the thing for me. But I was stubborn and could not be dissuaded.

Finally, with a sigh, he gave up. "Well, I simply don't know what it is I can do for you," he said dispiritedly. For a moment neither of us spoke. Leaning back in his chair, Mr. Barlow weighed his response. Then, finally, dubiously, "Well, I'll see what I can do. But I would still advise you to consider other options."

With that, I was dismissed. I walked out of the office feeling a curious mixture of exhilaration and dismay. I was relieved that there was still some kind of hope . . . but I was also plagued with images of a middle-aged me in a blue uniform rewiring my mum's telephone.

Over the next couple of months, I would meet with Mr. Barlow several times. On each occasion, he did his best to try to talk me into considering alternative careers, and at each I became increasingly stubborn in my convictions. Slowly I felt Barlow's attitude begin to shift from frustration to support as he recognized that this was a passion within me and not just a whim. He knew that I had my heart and mind set on becoming a sound engineer, and he no longer tried to talk me out of it.

But with graduation only a few weeks away, the clock was ticking, and deep down I was beginning to lose hope. I had no interviews, no prospects, nothing lined up if this didn't work out. I was simply determined that this was what I was going to do with my life; if our efforts failed, I had no alternative plan.

Finally, one late spring morning, my name was announced over the school's public address system and I was ordered to Mr. Barlow's office. I raced down the hall and burst into his room without even knocking.

Barlow didn't seem surprised at my sudden appearance; in fact, he looked like the cat who ate the canary. "We got lucky, my boy," he announced. "An interview has been arranged for you at EMI Studios next month. Good luck with it, and don't let us down."

He explained that he had just gotten a phone call from another career counselor who had recently been contacted by the studio manager at EMI's Abbey Road facilities because there was an entry-level vacancy. Apparently no one at this man's school had any interest in working at a recording studio, so he was ringing around to see if there was anyone else in the North London area who *was* interested. And sure enough, Mr. Barlow did know of a rather single-minded ginger-haired youth in Crouch End who was very much interested indeed.

The gods had smiled down upon me. Now it was up to me to hold up my end.

Number Three Abbey Road

It was a gray, drab summer morning—the kind of blah day that makes you want to turn over in bed and pull the covers up around your ears. But there was no sleeping late for me that day, even though my interview wasn't scheduled until nearly lunchtime. The studio was not far from where I lived, but there was no direct tube service from my neighborhood to the rather posh area where the EMI facilities were situated, so I had to leave plenty of time to ride the train all the way into central London, then change lines and ride it back out of town again. As if to underscore the significance of the event, I was awakened by my father and not my mum; he had decided to take the day off and accompany me, turning the care and running of his butcher shop over to his assistant—a rare occurrence.

Face scrubbed and hair slicked back, I pulled on my new blue suit and headed for the local tube station with my dad; though we sat side by side on the rumbling train we didn't have much to say to each other. Realizing how excited I was, he probably thought it best to keep things low-key. Frankly, I appreciated the silence—it gave me an opportunity to think about what sort of questions I might be asked and what sort of answers I could give that would land me the job.

By the time we reemerged from beneath the London streets, the sun was beginning to peek through the clouds and the temperature was starting to rise. During the short four-block walk from the St. John's Wood tube station to the imposing Victorian building at Number Three Abbey Road that housed the EMI studios, my nervous energy started to manifest itself: my wool suit began to feel decidedly itchy, and the perspiration began rolling down my back.

Finally we reached the gate to the studio's car park. For some reason I had imagined that it would be filled with Jaguars and expensive sports cars, but it looked like any other car park, jammed with Morris Minors and assorted old junkers. I was a little disappointed: perhaps this career wasn't going to be as glamorous as it seemed. My dad took one last opportunity to straighten my tie, wished me luck, and headed to a bench across the road—directly beside the now-famous zebra crossing—where he promised to wait for me.

After all these weeks and months of hoping and anticipation, it had come down to this. It was the first time I had ever seen, much less set foot in, a recording studio. I glanced up at the main entrance where my fate awaited. I couldn't decide whether the two large doors poised at the top of the short flight of steps looked welcoming or forbidding. Taking a deep breath, I climbed up the steps, then rang the buzzer.

"Yes?" barked a voice from the tinny little speaker.

My reply was rather less forceful than I intended. "Erm, Geoffrey Emerick here for my eleven o'clock interview."

"Right, come on in. You're expected."

Tentatively I pushed the door open and stepped into the reception area, where a large man in uniform was seated behind a small desk. The polished plaque carefully placed front and center read "John Skinner, Commissionaire." He was already announcing me on the telephone.

"Geoffrey Emerick, to see Mr. Waite," Skinner boomed into the receiver, brusquely motioning for me to take a seat beneath a grand picture sporting the same familiar dog-and-trumpet logo that adorned my gramophone.

I sat quietly, soaking in the atmosphere. Every wall was painted a nauseating hospital-like pale green, and the whole place seemed permeated with the pungent oxide smell of recording tape. Still, just sitting there made me feel quite important. With each tick of the clock I could feel my confidence building.

After a few moments, Skinner's phone buzzed and he instructed me to go up the stairs, first room on the left. The elegantly lettered sign on the frosted glass door read, "B Waite, Assistant Studio Manager." Timidly I knocked and was told to enter. Inside the sparsely furnished office, two men were seated behind an old-fashioned oak desk, looking rather like Mutt and Jeff: one was tall and lean, the other short and stocky. The tall man stood up and offered me his handshake.

"Mr. Emerick, I presume? I'm Barry Waite." Gesturing toward Mutt, he continued, "And this is my associate, Bob Beckett."

Beckett, who was puffing on a pipe, glanced at me distractedly from a large book he was studying intently. Judging from their white hair and bushy eyebrows, both men appeared to be in their early sixties; both wore glasses and were dressed smartly in suit and tie. For some reason I noticed how polished their shoes were. Realizing that I had neglected to polish mine the night before, I felt a blush come to my cheek.

"Sit down, Geoffrey, sit down." Waite motioned to a chair and cleared his throat. "Now then," he proclaimed, puffing his chest out, "I understand that you are interested in employment here. Mr. Beckett and I shall be asking you a few questions to see if you are a suitable candidate. Is that all right?"

For a moment I had a devilish impulse to say, "No, I'd rather you didn't." Fortunately, logic prevailed and I simply replied, "Um, yes, sir," nervously pulling my legs back under my chair in an attempt to hide my unpolished shoes.

Waite's first question to me was surprising: "Do you like Cliff Richard and the Shadows?"

"Yes, sir," I answered meekly, but all I could think was *Why the hell is he asking me such a dumb question?? Every teenager in Britain likes them; doesn't he know that?*

His next few questions made a little more sense to me: "Do you like classical music as well as pop?" "Have you ever operated a tape recorder?" "Do you know how to thread up a reel of tape?" "Do you know how to edit tape?" As I answered yes to each query, Mr. Waite dutifully jotted down my responses on his notepad, nodding thoughtfully as he did so.

Throughout all of this, Mr. Beckett was slowly disappearing behind his large book. I was later to learn that it was the studio booking ledger in which all studio and staff assignments were carefully entered; this was his primary job. Ignoring Beckett's lack of participation (not to mention the quiet but unmistakable sound of snoring beginning to emanate from behind the covers), Waite suddenly handed me his notepad, on which he had drawn a picture of a circle with a hole in it and some dimensions along the side.

"Pretend this is a plan of a pulley wheel," he said. "Can you do the side elevation of this for me?"

Doing the calculation presented no difficulty for me, even though I didn't have the vaguest idea what this had to do with recording. But I confidently drew the center line in and wrote down my answer, handing the notepad back to Waite, who examined it carefully.

"This looks correct, Bob, don't you think?" He nudged his partner, rudely awakening him in the process; it was all I could do to keep from laughing. From behind the book, Beckett grunted, probably more in protest at his sleep being interrupted than in considered agreement. With that, Waite stood up and abruptly ended the interview, informing me that I would shortly be receiving their decision by mail. A flustered Beckett was enlisted to accompany me downstairs and give me a tour of the facilities. Glancing at the clock as I said my good-byes, I noted that a mere twenty minutes had elapsed since I had first walked in the door.

Once he was fully awake, Bob Beckett turned out to be quite affable. As we began the tour and entered the first control room, he told me, "This is where you'll be working, son," which made me feel that I had done well in the interview. After all those years of imagining what a recording studio looked like, even just walking through the hallways was like a dream come true. I was particularly impressed by the cavernous size of Studio One, where, to my delight, the musicians of the London Symphony Orchestra were standing around, cups of tea in hand, as they listened to a playback over huge speakers hanging on the wall. I was even more starstruck when Beckett opened the door to Studio Two and I saw Cliff Richard and the Shadows gathered around a piano, intently rehearsing a tune with their producer Norrie Paramor. Though my heart was pounding with excitement, I did my best to contain myself as we moved from room to room.

All too soon, the visit was over and I was headed back out the front doors and into the bright sunshine. "Good luck to you, lad," John Skinner said as I passed through the reception area. Years later, he was to tell me that he clearly remembered my nervousness that day, and the sight of my father patiently waiting for me on the bench across the road.

As I made my way back across Abbey Road, discarding the itchy wool jacket and loosening my tie, my dad called out anxiously, "How did you do?"

My initial reply was a simple "All right, I guess." Then, abandoning my false air of detachment, I blurted out, excitedly, "Guess who I saw? Cliff Richard and the Shads!"

My father, who had never been especially up on pop idols, gave me a blank look. I felt a weary smile come across my face. All in all, I felt good about my chances. I thought I had done pretty well in the interview—certainly I knew that I had done the side elevation calculation correctly, though I was still baffled as to why I was asked the question—but I was also hot, exhausted, and relieved to be out of there. Without much more in the way of conversation, we trudged back to the tube station and had a lunchtime beer in a nearby pub before heading back home.

Two weeks later, I received a letter informing me that I had been given the job. My appointment was as an assistant engineer—operating the recording machines for the studio's coterie of "balance" engineers—all at the magnificent starting salary of four pounds two shillings and sixpence . . . about eight American dollars per week. I knew that I could have earned more sweeping floors in a factory somewhere, but any disappointment I had in the low wages was more than offset by my elation at landing the position. At long last, I was in . . . and on my way to becoming a sound engineer. I was over the moon!

The letter stated that I was to report for work the following Monday, at 9 A.M. sharp. That morning, face scrubbed, hair slicked back—and, this time, shoes polished—I headed off for my first day on the job. I was three months shy of my sixteenth birthday.

Most of that first day was a blur, a rush of excitement, as I was introduced to a cast of characters, many of whom would play key roles in my life for the next six and a half years. Bob Beckett, still puffing on his pipe, greeted me in the reception area as I arrived and immediately took me upstairs to meet the imperious Mr. E. H. Fowler, studio manager—the top boss at the Abbey Road facility, answerable only to the faceless suits at EMI's headquarters in Manchester Square in central London. Beckett then handed me off to assistant engineer Richard Langham, instructing me to "stick to him like glue" for the next two weeks, observing and learning the ropes. Richard immediately put me at my ease. He was only a few years older than me, and I found him to be bubbly, friendly and funny. As he took me around the various studios and mastering rooms, introducing me to everyone, it was obvious that he was well liked and popular.

There were a cadre of producers working in the three main studios that day: Norrie Paramor, who I had spotted with Cliff Richard on the day of my interview; Norman Newell, a songwriter who worked primarily with the big American artists signed to EMI's affiliate Columbia label; and gruff, blunt Wally Ridley—another old-school songwriter, who oversaw big band sessions and other top artists of the day. That day, I also met many of the facility's in-house balance engineers: brash, confident Malcolm Addey, who immediately reminded me of Groucho Marx, talking incessantly while he waggled his cigar; soft-spoken, gentlemanly Peter Bown, who specialized in show music; and Stuart Eltham, an authoritative figure who worked with light pop artists like Matt Monro. All of them appeared to be old enough to be my dad—in fact, they seemed positively ancient to me. I also met a few of the mastering engineers, who seemed isolated in their own little kingdom upstairs, sitting behind their cutting lathes and having little contact, it seemed, with the recording process at all: a venerable older gent by the name of Harry Moss, and two younger fellows—Peter Vince and Malcolm Davies. Malcolm would eventually become one of my closest friends, though we barely nodded to each other on this day.

Everyone was dressed conservatively, in suit and tie, and there were various other straightlaced chaps wandering around in white laboratory coats (the maintenance staff, as I was to learn) and brown coats (the janitorial staff). Combined with the overpowering smells—a combination of tape oxide and floor wax—and the muffled sounds of various musical genres emanating from behind closed doors, it felt almost as if I was on another planet.

Naturally enough, one of the first things Richard and I talked about was my interview; I told him the story of Beckett dozing off behind his book and he roared with laughter. It turned out that almost every employee had been asked the same nonsensical questions. Richard's theory was that Waite and Beckett didn't even really care about the answers; they were simply looking for a certain type—someone who was neat and tidy and who wasn't likely to be outspoken or opinionated. That was the EMI "look," and they weren't looking to hire anyone who was going to rock the boat.

Which is why I was surprised hear a loud, Cockney "Oy, Richard!" reverberating down the hallway, interrupting our conversation. The voice was that of fellow assistant engineer—or "button-pusher," as we were commonly known—Chris Neal, a wisecracking, spotty-faced youth who had only been hired several months before me. Even to my untrained eyes, Chris appeared to be the exact opposite of the EMI "type": though he wore the requisite tie, his collar was undone, his hair was greasy, and instead of a proper suit coat, he was wearing a tatty leather jacket. As he barreled down the hall, shouting at the top of his lungs, I could see one or two of the older employees tut-tutting and shooting him dirty looks. Sure enough, Chris's days were numbered—he was to be fired several months after I began doing sessions. In fact, the studio gossip later revealed that I had been hired precisely because management wanted him out . . . but they weren't willing to let the axe fall until they had someone else trained and ready to take his place.

"Good to meet you, Geoff," he said exuberantly, shaking my hand so hard I nearly winced. "Is Richard looking after you, then?" He turned to Richard, who appeared faintly embarrassed.

"Yeah, showing him everything he needs to know, including avoiding the likes of you," Langham replied.

Chris laughed; it was already becoming apparent to me that giving the needle was an important aspect of studio life. "Are you going to be having

Geoff with you on that pop session tomorrow evening?" he asked. "They're bloody good, those Liverpool blokes are—well worth staying late for."

Richard gave a noncommittal answer; Beckett posted the weekly work schedule in the staff common room every Monday morning, but we hadn't checked it yet. As we headed down the corridor to do so, Richard explained that Chris was EMI's self-described "resident rebel." Though he was really just an assistant engineer like we were, Chris saw himself as a bit of a talent scout, spending night after night in London's nightclubs, trying to keep his finger on the pulse of pop music. But his latest craze, Richard told me, was for this band that had come down from Liverpool for an artist test several months previously. Chris had been the button-pusher on the session, assisting engineer Norman Smith and producer Ron Richards, who worked for Parlophone label chief George Martin. Supposedly, neither Norman nor Ron had been especially impressed, but Chris had been so excited at what he was hearing that he took it upon himself to run down to the canteen and fetch George Martin, who signed them shortly thereafter. That was Chris's version, anyway. With a laugh, Richard informed me that Norman, Ron, and George himself had each subsequently made the claim that it is was *he* who had discovered this new band, who went by the very unusual name of the Beatles.

"Beatles?" I asked Richard. "What does that mean?"

"Not sure," he replied. "Maybe, as in The Crickets?" Buddy Holly and his band had been big stars in both England and America in the 1950s, and I had been a fan of theirs. Sadly, Holly had died a tragic death in a plane crash in 1959.

We finally reached the staff common room, and sure enough, Richard was scheduled to work an evening session with the Beatles the next day, assisting Norman Smith and George Martin. Our normal working hours were 9 A.M. until 5:30 P.M., with an hour off for lunch. Basic session times, Langham explained, were 10:00 until 1:00; 2:30 until 5:30; and 7:00 until 10:00. If you were scheduled for one of the late sessions, you were paid overtime . . . which is why he seemed quite happy to have been given the assignment, despite the fact that it would make for a thirteen-hour working day.

Our next stop was Beckett's office. The door was open, so we strode in without knocking, awakening the napping Beckett in the process.

"Sorry to interrupt you, Bob," Richard said with a mischevious grin, "but we were wondering if Geoff here should be sitting in with me on tomorrow evening's session."

Reaching for his glasses, Beckett scanned the book, trying to rouse himself to full consciousness. Confused, he turned to me. "Well, Emerick, how are you getting on?" It seemed like a rather incongruous question, considering that I'd been working there only a few hours.

"Fine, sir," I replied, again trying to keep myself from bursting into laughter.

"Good, son, good. Now then, what were you two saying about tomorrow's session?" Flipping the pages randomly, he seemed to be adrift. Richard repeated the question.

"The pop session booked with the Beatles, sir, that new Liverpool band that George Martin has signed. Tomorrow evening, Bob. You remember."

At last Beckett regained his composure and cleared his throat: finally, he seemed to understand what it was we were asking of him.

"Well, Mr. Emerick, I would say that it would behoove you to spend as much time as possible over these next two weeks with Mr. Langham, though you do understand that we can't be paying you overtime wages." That last bit seemed more like a statement than a question, so I looked at him blankly. "So it is your decision, Mr. Emerick. However, I would advise you to consider attending the session, even though it will be without pay."

Eager to impress, I stammered, "Yes, sir, I'll do as you say," not even stopping to consider that, with less than a full day of employment under my belt, I was already being taken advantage of.

And with that, I found myself witness to the Beatles' first ever recording session.

· 3 ·

Meeting the Beatles

I can't honestly say that the evening session was very much on my mind as I started my second day of work—the Beatles were complete unknowns outside of Liverpool at the time, so all I had to go on was Chris Neal's enthusiasm. That morning, Richard was assigned to assist on a classical session, and at one point he actually allowed me to press the Record button on the tape machine. It was a real thrill for me, and I remember thinking that it was going to be the highlight of my day.

At lunchtime, Richard and I headed upstairs to the common room, where we hungrily attacked the sandwiches we had brought from home, chatting between bites. Richard was rapidly becoming not just my trainer, but my friend, and he really seemed to be going out of his way to orient me; I never got the feeling that he viewed me as competition or a threat to his job, and I greatly appreciated that. Within a few moments we were joined by Chris, as animated and excited as ever.

"Still doing that Beatles session tonight, Richard?" were the first words out of his lips. Richard nodded in assent, mouth full of cheese and tomato, as Chris charged ahead, telling us all he knew about the band.

"They're scruffy and they wear leather jackets and they comb their hair forward," he informed us eagerly. "On the artist test, one of them even had the cheek to tell George Martin that he didn't like his tie! But they sing brilliant harmonies, just like the Everly Brothers, and they've got a true rock 'n' roll attitude."

The spectacle of Chris Neal in full flight was something to see. I was getting worn out just watching him.

Abruptly, Chris dashed off, no doubt to spread the gospel elsewhere in the studio complex. Using a corner of his napkin, Richard wiped his mouth carefully and filled me in a bit more about George Martin and Norman Smith. "They're both quite old, but they're good blokes once you get to know them," he said. "George is one of the producers on staff here, though I've never known him to do a rock 'n' roll session before. I guess he's trying to get on the bandwagon. At least he's got the sense to use Norman on the session, who's a bloody good pop musician himself."

Richard had heard good things about the Beatles' artist test, too, and not just from Chris. Apparently there was quite a buzz around the studio about them, as much for their unorthodox personalities and cheeky attitude as for their musical abilities. Clearly, they were viewed by the staff as one of EMI's top up-and-coming bands, and everyone was interested in seeing whether George and Norman could coax some hits out of them. There was also a great deal of curiosity about the fact that they were from "up north"—in those days, there was a real class divide between Londoners and those who lived outside of the capital city, especially in the grimy northern centers like Liverpool. It was almost as if England were two separate countries. Every homegrown pop star, it seemed, lived in London, which made some sense, considering that all the recording studios were located there. So having a band come in from outside of London was quite a novelty in itself, and it was apparently the source of a great deal of chatter and gossip among the studio staff. I was beginning to get the sense that something special was going to happen that evening.

First, though, there was the afternoon to get through. As Richard had no midday assignment, we had to head off to one of the editing rooms for a few tedious hours of splicing. Whenever assistants weren't working on sessions, one of our jobs was to put white leader tape in between tracks of tape copies of albums sent over from Capitol in the United States, because most of their pop records were remastered in England—which made the recordings second-generation, with the resultant additional tape hiss. That, combined with the fact that our mastering equipment wasn't comparable with what was available in the States, was the reason why English releases of American records never sounded as good as the original.

The hours flew by quickly enough, and soon people began heading out the door, their day's work done. Richard and I grabbed a quick bite of dinner at the pub down the street and then headed to the control room of Studio Two, where I was introduced to Norman Smith for the first time. He was a slight, dapper man with carefully coiffed hair, and he put me at ease immediately with a lighthearted comment about my ruddy complexion.

As I took my place beside Richard at the back of the cramped control room, I took notice of the relaxed way he and Norman joked with each other as they tested the equipment to make sure all was in working order. There was clearly a mutual respect for each other's abilities, and at that moment I realized that there was far more to the business than simply knowing the technicalities. Having an easy personality and being able to get along with people seemed just as important, and I resolved to model my demeanor after Richard's.

Studio Two was unusual at the EMI complex—in fact, unusual anywhere in the world—in that the control room was on the floor above the larger studio area where the musicians sat, overlooking it instead of being on the same level. Access between the two was navigated by a narrow flight of wooden stairs, and communications from the control room were transmitted over a pair of large speakers that hung on the far wall of the studio, directly over the emergency exit. Shortly before seven, I heard chatter coming over the open microphones, and I walked over to the control room glass to see what was going on.

My first glimpse of the Beatles was not actually all that memorable. There were seven people milling about in the studio below, but it was obvious from their unorthodox haircuts which four were the band members, although they were wearing neatly pressed white shirts and ties and not the leather jackets Chris had so admired. I assumed that the tall, lean older gentleman standing with them was their producer, George Martin, and because the other two—one of whom was a big bear of a man with glasses, and the other a rather nondescript fellow of slight build—were busily setting up the drums and guitar amplifiers, I guessed that they were the road crew.

It's almost embarrassing to admit today, but what struck me most about the Beatles when I first saw them was their skinny knit ties. In fact, I remember making a comment to Richard about them at the time, which drew him to the window to have a look for himself. A few weeks later, we both bought similar ties and wore them to work; within a short time, it seemed like everyone at EMI was wearing them.

There was still a lot of preparation to be done, so we quickly resumed our places at the back of the room while Norman continued his methodical testing.

"Doesn't he need to set up the microphones?" I asked Richard at one point. He explained that the balance engineers at EMI didn't dirty their hands doing that. Instead, they told the white coats—the maintenance engineers—which mics they wanted to use and where to place them, and it was all taken care of beforehand. Minor adjustments required during the session could be carried out by Norman or Richard, but only the white coats were allowed to change the cabling or alter signal routings. It struck me as a silly way to work, but apparently EMI had rules for everything. In a few years' time, I'd be breaking just about all of them.

After a brief period of tuning up, I began hearing music filter through the control room loudspeakers, which drew me back to the window. The four Beatles were rehearsing, with George Martin sitting on a high stool between the two singers. The song they were playing was lightweight, nothing out of the ordinary, but there was definitely an infectiousness to the beat. From behind a set of tall acoustic screens I could see their drummer flailing away. He appeared to be a very small man with a very large nose, and he didn't seem to know the song as well as the others, who kept pausing to give him instructions. As they worked their way through the arrangement, Norman hunched over the mixing console, carefully adjusting the balance of the various instruments. I was enormously impressed by the sound that he was shaping, and by the quality of the large control room speakers (known as "monitors"), which were so much better than any I had ever heard before. Their clarity enabled me to literally hear every single note of every instrument.

Finally there was a pause in the music and the door to the control room opened. In stepped George Martin. Aristocratic in bearing and elocution—he sounded almost regal to my north London ears—he said hello to Norman, then nodded to Richard before shooting me a glance.

"And who might this gentleman be?" he asked. I could feel myself blushing furiously as I stuck out my hand.

"Geoff Emerick, sir. I'm the new assistant here; I'm meant to be observing Richard."

He clasped my hand warmly. "Ah, another button-pusher to aid in the cause."

George had a sparkle in his eye and I took an instant liking to him. Without any further ado, the session began, and Richard was instructed to start the two-track machine recording. (At the time, the most advanced machine at EMI was four-track, but there were only two such machines for the three studios, and they were reserved solely for the use of established artists, not to be wasted on a new signing.) Norman Smith somberly intoned the title of the song and the take number for posterity—a process known as "slating"—and then proceeded to put the red Recording light on.

" 'How Do You Do It,' take one," he said, and there was a brief moment of silence before one of the band members did a count-in in a shaky voice and the group began playing.

Frankly, after all of the advance buildup from Chris and the other EMI staff, it was a bit of a letdown. The lead singer, who also played rhythm guitar, had a unique, nasally voice, and he sang on pitch, but without much enthusiasm, and the lead guitarist seemed to be somewhat fumble-fingered. Probably the most impressive thing about the performance was the powerful and melodic bass playing. Peeking through the window, I could see that the bass player was also singing harmony.

After just a few takes, during which George Martin used his handheld talkback mic to issue instructions, it appeared that everyone was satisfied, and the band headed up to the control room for a playback, giving me my first up-close glimpse of the Beatles. Nobody introduced them to me, or to Richard, as they made easy conversation with Norman in their odd-sounding Scouse accents. But from my perch at the back of the room, I studied their faces intently.

The lead singer, who wore thick horn-rimmed eyeglasses, similar to Buddy Holly's, had a hooked nose and a gruff demeanor. He was quite fidgety and quite funny—he kept calling Norman "Normal"—and he had a loud, hurried way of talking. In contrast, the drummer, who was indeed quite a bit shorter than the others, with an almost petite build, looked a bit dejected and didn't have much to say at all. I was also struck by how slight—almost emaciated—the lead guitarist was, and by his youth; he appeared to be only a few years older than me. Most intriguingly, he sported a black eye; I was later to learn that it was from a fight at a Liverpool club they had played at a few days previously.

And then there was the bass player. He was not only the most conventionally handsome of the four but was also the most friendly and engaging—at one point, he even nodded a hello to Richard and me. He was also clearly the most interested in how the recording sounded. Though he didn't raise his voice like the lead singer did, I had the distinct impression that he was the leader of the group. When he spoke, the others listened intently and invariably nodded their heads in agreement, and before each take, he was the one urging them on to give it their all. Looking back on it now, it's funny how most people thought of John Lennon—the hook-nosed lead singer on that first song—as the leader of the Beatles. It might have been his band in the beginning, and he might have assumed the leadership role in their press conferences and public appearances, but throughout all the years I would work with them, it always seemed to me that Paul McCartney, the soft-spoken bass player, was the real leader of the group, and that nothing got done unless he approved of it.

My main memory of that first evening with the Beatles, however, was the sheer amount of joking going on. John and Paul seemed to be doing most of it—they were oozing with confidence, and were clearly good mates. The lead guitarist and drummer, George Harrison and Ringo Starr, seemed to be taking things a lot more seriously, or perhaps they were just more nervous—it was hard to tell which.

After some conversation with Norman and another playback, George Martin announced that he was satisfied with their rendition of the song, but he wanted some handclaps superimposed. Superimposition was the equivalent to the modern-day "overdub," in which a new sound is added to an existing recording. Because the song had been recorded directly to a two-track tape (as opposed to four-track), the way this was accomplished was by loading a blank reel of tape on a second machine and putting it in record while the first machine played back, essentially making a copy of the original tape, along with the overdub. The four musicians returned back down to the studio—three of them taking the stairs, Paul taking the more unconventional route of sliding down the banister, while Richard prepared the tape machines. Because George Martin wanted handclaps only during the guitar solo, just that portion of the tape needed to be played back. Richard explained to me that it was that bit alone that would be spliced and edited into the master reel so that only one brief portion of the song would be second generation. I watched in fascination as the handclaps were added and the splicing done with brisk efficiency, and then the four Beatles trooped upstairs to hear the results.

"How Do You Do It" had been written by Mitch Murray, one of Britain's top songwriters. It had been handpicked by George Martin for the group to record—in those days, an A&R man was truly worthy of the title, choosing both the Artist and the Repertoire. Although the version recorded that night was never to be released (not until the 1994 *Beatles Anthology*, anyway), the song would later prove to be a hit for Gerry and the Pacemakers, another Liverpool band signed by Beatles manager Brian Epstein.

But once the superimposition section had been edited into the master take and played back to George Martin's satisfaction, I noticed the four Beatles shifting in their chairs uncomfortably. Clearly, there was dissension in the ranks. Lennon began the volley.

"Look, George," he said, addressing their producer bluntly, "I have to tell you, we really think that song is crap."

Martin's startled look caused him to backtrack a bit.

"I mean, it may be all right, but it's just not the kind of thing we want to do."

"Well, exactly what is it you want to do?" said the beleaguered producer.

Taking off his glasses and fixing Martin with a squinty stare, Lennon didn't mince words. "We want to record our own material, not some soft bit of fluff written by someone else."

George Martin looked faintly amused. "I'll tell you what, John," he replied. "When you can write a song as good as that one, then I'll record it."

Lennon shot him a dirty look, and for a moment there was an ominous silence.

Then Paul spoke up, politely but firmly. "Look, we're just going for a different kind of thing," he said, "and we do think we have one as good. If you don't mind, we'd like to give it a go."

George Martin exchanged wary glances with Norman. He seemed to be torn between asserting his authority and giving in. For a time he studied each band member's face, taking their measure. Finally, George broke the silence, saying softly, "All right, then, show me what you've got."

As the five of them clambered back down the stairs to the studio, Norman turned to Richard and me, shaking his head. "They've got some cheek, that lot," he said. "I reckon that's what got them this far, though."

Nose to the window, I could once again see the four Beatles rehearsing, with George Martin in their midst. George Harrison had put down his electric guitar and switched to an acoustic, which he was strumming confidently. Despite its plodding beat, there was no question that the song, called "Love Me Do," had a catchy melody. Through the open microphones, I could hear some of the conversation.

"Well, I suppose you've got the kernel of something there," George Martin was telling the group noncommittally, "but it needs something extra to make it stand out." Turning to Lennon, he said, "Don't you play a bit of harmonica, John? Can you give me something bluesy? Perhaps do a solo?"

Lennon nodded in assent, and one of the roadies headed over to an instrument case to fetch his mouth organ. As Lennon tried out a few simple licks, I realized that, for the very first time, I was getting an object lesson in exactly what a producer did, the role he played in shaping a song.

They continued rehearsing, then stopped for some more conversation. I couldn't make out exactly what they were saying, but the next time they ran the song through, I saw that Paul was singing the lead vocal instead of John—a decision of expediency, since Lennon obviously couldn't play harmonica and sing at the same time.

"Look at that, Richard," I blurted out, slightly in awe, "the other bloke is singing now!"

Norman Smith chuckled. "That's one of the real strengths in this band," he told us. "We found out during the artist test that they've got two strong lead singers, not just one. Even the guitarist sings a bit, although he's not as good as the other two."

I really liked the sound of Paul's voice; its rounder tone provided a stark contrast to John's more strident timbre. Even more impressive was the blend of their two voices, as Lennon added a low harmony part during the lines when he wasn't blowing into his harp. Chris Neal was right—they really did sound like the Everly Brothers, though their music was considerably more aggressive.

After a brief period, George Martin returned to the control room and asked Norman's opinion.

"Not bad, George, not bad," he replied. "Maybe not the instant hit that the other one was, but there's definitely something there."

The producer nodded in glum assent—clearly he wasn't convinced of the wisdom of spending time on this new song—but he ordered Richard to start the tape machine and the recording began in earnest.

The Beatles seemed to have a lot of trouble getting this one right, though—obviously they hadn't rehearsed it as much as the other song. Ringo was having difficulty maintaining a steady beat, and Paul was starting to get annoyed with him. After each take, they looked expectantly up toward the control room window, and George Martin did his best to prop them up over the talkback mic, but in his private conversations with Norman, he criticized the unsteady drumming. Finally they gave a performance that he seemed reasonably satisfied with, and following a brief conference with Norman, he called a halt to the evening's activities, not even bothering to invite the group up to the control room for a playback. The clock on the wall read 9:30, and there was still editing and mixing to do. (Though they were playing live, with no overdubs, the instruments and vocals were recorded on separate tracks to allow the engineer to balance them after the fact and, if necessary, also add echo and make minor changes to the tonal quality.)

George Martin went downstairs to say good-bye, while Norman sat down at the tape machine, displacing Richard. With bewildering speed and precision, he began editing together the best bits of the two most satisfactory takes, then moved back to the console to do a quick mix. Moments later, he dispatched Richard and me to take the mono mix tape upstairs to the lacquer cutting room so that acetate listening copies could be run off the next morning.

I didn't get to say good-bye to any of the Beatles—in fact, I hadn't said a single word to them all evening—but as Richard and I walked out together, we reviewed the events of the past several hours excitedly. Despite the abrupt way the session had ended, we had no doubt that what we had experienced that evening was something new and exciting. For all of the frustration and angst, there was still a happy energy in the room and it had translated to the recording. Richard expressed his hope that he'd get an opportunity to work with them again soon.

Secretly, so did I.

· 4 ·

Early Sessions

The remainder of my first week at EMI passed uneventfully, as I followed Richard around from session to session, some classical, some pop. Those sessions that were recorded on four-track instead of two-track were definitely less fun, because we had to sit in a separate machine room and not the control room. Looking back on it, it was an insane way to work: instead of being in the same room as the producer and balance engineer, you'd receive instructions over an intercom as to when to start and stop the tape machine. Not only could we not see what was going on in the control room and studio, we could only listen to one track at a time, which made drop-ins and drop-outs (where we'd place the machine in and out of record midway through a playback in order to replace a vocal or instrumental part) extremely difficult. Over the intercom, the balance engineer would give you just a moment's notice ("Get ready . . . drop NOW!") and you'd be expected to pull it off with precision. Years later, when I began recording the *Revolver* album, we'd insist that the four-track machines be moved into the control room, which soon became the standard way of doing things. Nonetheless, it was incredible that it took so long for the EMI management to realize the foolishness of that way of working.

To my delight, Richard and I found ourselves assigned to several more sessions that week with the George Martin/Norman Smith team. I found myself really enjoying working with them; their offbeat sense of humor and easy banter made for a very relaxed time, and helped further underscore for me how the psychological aspects of running a recording session were at least as important as the technical aspects.

During Friday lunchtime Norman walked over and joined Richard and me in the canteen. As we began to chat, I discovered that we had a great deal in common. Not only did he know a good friend of my parents, but he had also done some work with an artist named Johnny Duncan—a Crouch End neighborhood star who lived across the road from my old school.

I asked Norman about his background, and he told me that he had been a refrigeration engineer before deciding to pursue his passion for music and apply for a position at EMI. Looking around the room furtively, he confided that he supplemented his income by playing in a band, doing weddings and private parties. His main instrument, he told me, was vibes, but he also played drums. The conversation soon turned to the Beatles session we'd done earlier that week and all of the problems their drummer was having.

"Well, he's a new chap and he's just having a little trouble finding his feet," Norman explained. "He's a lot better than the bloke they used to have, anyway." Apparently, the drummer they had turned up with for the artist test in June had been so bad that he had been sacked a couple of months later. "In any event," Norman said, "George has decided to bring in a session drummer when they come in again next week, so we shouldn't have those problems again."

Richard and I looked at each other. "They're coming in again next week?"

Norman could see the enthusiasm on our faces. "Like them that much, did you?" he chuckled. "Well, I tell you what—you do the buying at the pub tonight and I'll see what I can do about getting you two in on the session."

That evening, Mr. Smith had quite a few pints indeed, courtesy of Messrs. Langham and Emerick. When we came in to work on Monday and checked the schedule, we saw that Norman had been true to his word: Richard was listed as his assistant on the Beatles session the following day. As a bonus, it was a morning session, so this time I'd actually get paid for being there.

I arrived for work extra early the next morning; I was anxious to see all the preparation that occurred before a session began. In the barnlike Studio Two, various white coats were milling about, setting up microphones as per Norman's usual specifications. I'd noticed that he always put instruments in the same areas of the studio and used the same microphones, regardless of the artist. None of the Beatles equipment had arrived as yet, but there was already a drum kit set up in the far corner, where Ringo's kit had been the previous week. I wandered up to the control room and found Norman already behind the desk, engaged in conversation with George Martin's assistant, Ron Richards, and another fellow I didn't recognize.

"Morning, Geoff," Norman said brightly. "This is Andy White, our drummer for the day."

Andy stuck out his hand; he was slight and dapper, dressed casually in a

V-neck sweater and slacks. The three men were talking about various records currently in the charts. I was quite impressed to learn that Andy had drummed on some of them.

In due course Richard arrived, followed shortly thereafter by the Beatles' two roadies, hauling in their equipment. The larger of the two—the hulking man I had observed the week prior—looked a bit perplexed. Scratching his head, he began lumbering up the stairs.

"Can anyone here tell me where I'm meant to be setting up Ringo's kit?" he asked amiably.

Ron looked a bit uncomfortable. "Well, er, actually, we won't be needing Ringo or his kit this week," he replied. "Are you the road manager?"

"One of them, mate. Mal Evans is the name." He stuck out his hand and proceeded to introduce himself to everyone in the control room, even me.

Through his thick glasses, Mal returned his gaze to Ron. "Well, Ring won't be happy to hear that, but I guess you're the governor. I'll go tell the others."

With that, he headed back down the stairs. Curious to see their reaction, I made a beeline for the control room window. Down below, I could see Mal talking to the other roadie, who shrugged his shoulders and returned to setting up the guitar amps.

A moment later, the four Beatles walked in and Mal joined them, gesturing and pointing up in our direction. Norman hadn't lifted any of the mic faders up yet, so I couldn't hear the conversation, but it was obvious that Ringo was pretty upset. The other three seemed to be placating him at first, but then began turning their attention elsewhere, strapping on their guitars and tuning up. Ringo looked around a little helplessly, at a loss as to what to do. He began heading up to the control room.

As the door opened, Norman crossed the room to greet him. "Morning, Norman," Ringo answered in a funereal tone that matched his demeanor. Looking around the room for a familiar face, he asked plaintively, "Where's George?"

A flustered Ron cleared his throat and introduced himself to Ringo. After an uncomfortable silence, he added the bad news. "I'm afraid George is going to be a bit late, so I'll be starting the session. And . . ." Another pause, another forlorn look. "Well, actually, he's asked me to tell you that we'll be using Andy here today—he's a professional drummer, hired for the session."

Ringo's face fell further still; he looked like he wanted to jump off the nearest bridge. Even though I didn't know him at all—we still hadn't spoken a single word to each other—I felt sorry for him.

Andy White, looking embarrassed, stood up. "Hello, mate," he said to Ringo, "I've heard a lot of good things about your group."

They shook hands awkwardly, then White quickly headed down to the studio. I remember being impressed by Andy's decision to leave right away, thus avoiding what could have been an unpleasant confrontation—another lesson in studio etiquette. Dejectedly, Ringo sank into a chair beside Ron and the session got underway.

The Beatles began by running through a new song, entitled "P.S. I Love You." After just a few run-throughs, White seemed to get the hang of it. I was amazed at how quickly he did so, and how well he fit in with three unfamiliar musicians—the mark of a great session player. Following some discussion, it was decided that full drums weren't necessary on the song and he was relegated to playing bongos. After a few run-throughs, Ron suggested that Ringo go downstairs and join in, playing maracas. I could sense that he was growing increasingly uncomfortable at having the sulking drummer sitting beside him, and this must have struck him as a good way of getting Ringo out of the control room.

The reunited and reinforced Beatles—considerably more polished than the previous week, I thought—soon dispatched the song and came up to the control room for a playback. They were enthused by what they were hearing, and eagerly discussed making it the A-side, but Richards dismissed them imperiously.

"It's good, but it's no A-side," he said. "We'll use it as the B-side of your first single. Now we need get back to work; George wants you to have another go at 'Love Me Do.' "

Ringo looked up hopefully, but Ron shot him down again. "I'd like you to play tambourine on this, Ringo; we'll stick with Andy on the drums."

Again, it took White only a very short time to familiarize himself with the simple song; his timekeeping was definitely steadier than Ringo's had been the previous week. The other three were playing a lot better, too, and Paul sang the lead vocal with much greater confidence. Clearly they had done a lot of rehearsing during the previous week. Even Ringo's tambourine work was impressive—it meshed nicely with each of White's snare hits, with remarkably few flams (beats that are just slightly out of time).

It took them a bit longer to get a take that Richards was satisfied with, but eventually they were summoned up to the control room. Once again, I noticed Paul listening rather more intently than the others; he was also the most conversational, chatting unself-consciously with both Norman and Ron. At one point, he and I made eye contact; he saw my head bobbing up and down in time with the beat and he nodded approvingly. Despite the fact that the other three Beatles continued to ignore me, I felt that I was starting to become a familiar face, at least to Paul.

The take approved, Ron decided to overdub handclaps throughout the entire song (not just through the harmonica solo, as they had done the previous week), and the four Beatles trooped back downstairs as Richard readied the second tape recorder. I noticed that Andy White diplomatically stayed behind. *Good move*, I thought. *Don't horn in when you're not needed.*

The superimposition took only a single run-through, and it was only noon—two songs had been completed in just two hours—so there was still another hour of time available to the Beatles.

"Have you boys got anything else you'd like to play for me?" Richards asked over the intercom.

"Yes!" came the enthusiastic reply, seemingly from all four at once.

Just then, George Martin walked in. Ron and Norman reported that all had gone well in his absence, and George got on the talkback to say hello to the band.

"Has Ron been looking after you okay?" The producer didn't wait for a reply. "Never mind; I'm here now, better late than never."

He announced that he was going to have a quick listen to what they'd done, and would then be right down to start work on the new song. After listening to a playback, George gave his approval, and Andy White was dismissed for the day. As he returned to the studio and began packing up his drums, I could see white coats moving microphones and Mal starting to set up Ringo's kit. Once George was on his way down the steps and out of earshot, Richard and Norman began discussing what had just transpired.

"I reckon that last one is a hit," Richard began.

Norman wasn't so sure. I kept my countenance . . . not that anyone asked my opinion.

"Well, it's bloody good, anyway," Richard insisted.

Norman's response was cautious. "I'll give you that much; it *is* good, but it might be a bit too ordinary. I guess we'll know soon enough." In those days, singles were often released within weeks, if not days, of being recorded, so you knew fairly quickly if you'd participated in the making of a hit or not.

Norman lifted a few faders and we were able to hear what was going on downstairs. The song being rehearsed was soulful and was sung with great feeling by John, but it had a very slow tempo and was marred by a clumsy phrase that George Harrison played over and over again on guitar, repetitive to the point of annoyance. Ringo was doing something odd, too—he was sitting behind his kit with a maraca in one hand and a tambourine in the other, all while hitting the bass drum pedal with his right foot, a ridiculous posture that caused Norman to burst into laughter and shout out to us, "Look at what that bloody drummer is up to now!"

After the first run-through, there was a great deal of discussion, and it was clear that George Martin was dissatisfied.

"Look, you've definitely got something there, boys," he said, "but I think it needs some more work, and it needs to be speeded up. I also think we need to sort out a harmonica line for John and some harmony parts for Paul."

They nodded enthusiastically and began experimenting along the lines that George had suggested, but the clock on the wall was ticking and he soon had to call an end to the proceedings. "We'll try it again next time," George assured them, and with that, the session was over.

He was true to his word. "Please Please Me" was remade by the Beatles a couple of months later, considerably sped up and with vocal harmonies and harmonica added, as per George's suggestions. According to Richard, who assisted on the session, George was so enthusiastic he got on the talkback mic and announced to the band, "Boys, you've just made a number one record." As it turned out, he hit the nail on the head—it shot to the top of the charts just weeks after it was released, giving the Beatles their first hit single.

But the version of "Love Me Do" that Andy White played on ended up being the "official" single and album version for many years; the Ringo rendition only appeared on a very few first singles, and, decades later, on the *Rarities* album and *Past Masters* and *Anthologies* CDs. It's easy to tell which is which, by the way—the one with the tambourine on it has Andy White playing drums; the one without has Ringo behind the skins.

Much later, I heard that Ringo was not only devastated that afternoon, but also harbored a grudge against George Martin for many years afterward. Ringo may have been justified in feeling slighted, but I suppose George was only doing what he felt was right. His job was to produce hit records for his artists, and in those days, as now, it was common practice to substitute session players for band members who weren't felt to be up to snuff. Andy White has the distinction of being the only outside musician to ever usurp the role of one of the Beatles on record, but it was the first and last time Ringo was supplanted from the drum chair on a Beatles recording, apart from the few times in later years that Paul—an accomplished drummer himself—took the sticks.

No one officially introduced me to the Beatles on those first two sessions, but I definitely started forming an opinion about their sound—I knew that I loved it—and about their distinctive personalities. Even with only a week's experience, I could see that their sessions were definitely looser, and more fun, than most others. Groups like Cliff Richard and the Shadows were more serious when they were in the studio, making little banter, but the Beatles were cracking jokes, chattering away, and being silly a lot of the time. They just seemed much more relaxed about things in general, and it came through in the sound of their records. I could see why Chris Neal had been raving about them . . . and I was more than a little curious as to whether the record-buying public would react the same way I did.

EMI only gave new appointees a two-week window of opportunity; by then, either you had proved that you could do the job, or you couldn't. Apparently I passed muster, because at the end of the week, I was called into Bob Beckett's office, where I was officially "graduated" to the esteemed rank of button-pusher. The following Monday morning the initials "GE" made their first appearance on the booking schedule. I was in seventh heaven. Music meant so much to me, and the idea of mingling with all these famous artists, being part of the process of making great records, set my blood tingling. I couldn't wait to get to work each morning.

My first official session as an assistant engineer was in Studio One, which had a tiny, cramped control room that could comfortably seat only three or four people, in stark contrast to the cavernous studio area that could accommodate full orchestras. The recording that day was an opera: Mozart's *Così fan tutte*, featuring Elisabeth Schwarzkopf. I loved the music, and, of course, she was a phenomenal singer, but it turned out to be a logistical nightmare. All the really important classical sessions were recorded on four two-track machines simultaneously; the tape that sounded best would be designated as the master, with the other three serving as backups. This meant that I not only had four machines to look after—keeping their heads clean and making sure the tape was threaded properly—but because this was also long before the days of electronic synchronization, I also had to start and stop each one individually. Because each machine ran on its own mechanical clock, I had to manually log all the clock timings for each take on every tape box, as well as jot down any relevant notes. I also had to be constantly aware of how much tape was left and judge when it was going to run out. The last thing you wanted was for the orchestra or singer to do a fantastic take, only to have to inform them that the tape had run out.

Then there was the physical labor of constantly changing four reels of tape. There was no backing plate, so sometimes the tape would literally start to rise up over the guideposts and fly off the machine while you were trying to spool it back as fast as you could—musicians were standing by, and time was money. You had to be very organized, and you could get into real trouble if you developed a mental block—they might want a playback of take 39 one minute, then decide to record take 62 on a completely different reel of tape, all on four separate machines. It was mentally fatiguing, like juggling ten balls at once. Little wonder that I went home with a thumping headache every night.

While I was in the midst of the *Così fan tutte* sessions, another set of operatic sessions—*The Barber of Seville*, with Victoria de los Angeles—started up, in the same studio. With two operas running at once—one session in the morning, the other in the afternoon—the maintenance engineers were kept on their toes: they had to strip everything down and then set it up all over again, differently, twice each day.

Some sessions, of course, were easier than others, but most of the people on the classical sessions were quite snooty. Because of that, I didn't enjoy doing them as much as pop sessions, which tended to be fun. But in terms of being exposed to different kinds of music, it was an incredible experience—and there were certainly some real characters in the classical world. In those days, the conductor was always referred to as "Maestro," never by name. Some of them came to the sessions dressed up in their rehearsal tuxedos; Sir Malcolm Sargent would even come to the studio in full tux and tails, adorned by a red carnation. Sir John Barbirolli conducted the *Barber of Seville* sessions; he carried a hip flask and would have a little tipple of gin between takes. Possibly because of that, he had a very pleasant personality and kept his sessions generally lighthearted.

But then there were the conductors like Otto Klemperer—authoritarian figures who absolutely commanded respect. Klemperer was like one of Frankenstein's creations. He wore thick glasses and was confined to a wheelchair. An assistant would wheel him in—Klemperer was a large, tall man, about six foot five—and the orchestra would shake when he was on the podium because they were in absolute fear of playing a wrong note. That might explain why those recordings sound the way they do: the musicians poured their hearts out because they were scared to do otherwise. If they didn't put their full fire into their playing, he'd tear them apart in front of all the other musicians. He'd embarrass the hell out of them, shouting in his booming voice, "You! Why are you even in this orchestra? If you can't play, why don't you leave?" Some of the players would actually be reduced to tears.

I noticed, too, that there was a lot of competition among the soloists about who was going to come out on top, and sometimes they would engage in heated exchanges with the conductor. As young as I was, it all seemed quite immature to me, people trying to make their presence felt by having a confrontation about something mundane in front of the entire orchestra. And quite a few of the artists were very temperamental, true prima donnas. They were generally nice to me—I was just this kid sitting at the back of the room, after all—but they were perfectionists, very demanding of their producers and musicians.

Many of the classical producers were arrogant, too. Elisabeth Schwarzkopf's producer was her husband, Walter Legge, and he could be a right pain at times. He had an Indian assistant named Suvi Raj Grubb who used to flap around Walter like a windmill. It was like a scene from a bad Peter Sellers movie. Suvi would pull Walter's chair out for him every time he'd sit down or get up, and he'd be pouring him glass after glass of Vichy water and lighting his Player cigarettes—an endless task because Legge had a habit of taking exactly two puffs before dramatically stubbing the cigarette out.

I had, of course, been exposed to overdubbing during the first two Beatles sessions, but I was surprised to learn that it was also used in operatic recordings. At times, the vocalist would be standing in an otherwise empty studio, singing along to a prerecorded tape. The reason had to do with people's availability. In those days, classical music was extremely popular worldwide, so the artists were always on the concert circuit. As a result, it could be difficult to schedule them to make an appearance in the studio on the same day as the orchestra was booked.

Although we assistants got exposed to all kinds of sessions, the balance engineers at EMI were either classical or pop. Those engineers deemed "classical" did classical music sessions exclusively, but the pop engineers—Norman, Stuart, Eltham, Pete Bown, and Malcolm Addey—would occasionally be called upon to cross the line if there was a schedule conflict. As I gained more and more experience doing all kinds of sessions, it became apparent to me that there was a tension, almost an animosity, between the classical people and the pop people at EMI; they would even tend to eat in separate areas of the canteen. The pop people were looked down upon by the classical people, even though it was the money coming in from the sales of pop records that paid for the classical sessions.

In contrast to the highbrow, high-strung, high-pressure classical sessions, some of the pop sessions I assisted on were downright hilarious. One of the first sessions I did with George Martin was for the popular, quirky Australian singer/comedian Rolf Harris. Just a few days later, I made my recording debut with the singer Bernard Cribbins. The song Cribbins was doing at the time was called "The One In The Middle"—it was a comedy B-side, just a throwaway song—and George wanted some kind of oddball sound to add comedic value. From our socializing in the pub, engineer Stuart Eltham knew that I was able to do a farting noise with my hands, and he duly informed George of that fact, so there I was, deposited into the studio and placed before a microphone, my feat captured for all posterity. It was on that session that I realized just how funny George could be—he was doubled over with laughter every time I added the rude sound effect.

And then there were the Massed Alberts, another eccentric Parlophone act produced by George. (I was later to find out that they, unsurprisingly, were a favorite of John Lennon's, too.) One memorable evening, they were in Studio Two, performing "An Evening Of British Rubbish" in front of an invited audience. At the afternoon rehearsal, one of the characters in the group had fired off a starter's pistol. It was sheer slapstick—when he fired the gun, sausages came out—but what we didn't factor in was that all the acoustic treatment in the studio ceiling (actually just seaweed hanging in fine netting; the theory was that it would absorb the damp) hadn't been vibrated in years. As the pistol went off, suddenly all this soot drifted down, turning all the chairs and the floors pitch black. Every brown coat in the EMI facility had to be recruited for a few hours of frantic sweeping and vacuuming, desperately trying to get the studio clean in time for the evening's performance.

Producers weren't allowed to request engineers, nor were engineers able to request specific assistants, but Bob Beckett still did his best to group all of us with people we liked working with. Normally if an engineer did the artist test, he carried on making records with that artist. Norman Smith had done the test for the Beatles, so he worked with them thereafter. (I later heard through the studio grapevine that Malcolm Addey had originally been asked to do the artist test for the Beatles, but declined, saying that he didn't want to "record that Liverpool shite.") Similarly, Stuart had done the artist test for Cilla Black, so he kept on working with her. Years later, after I had been promoted to balance engineer, I did a lot of her sessions, too.

By the time I'd worked with all of the staff producers, I decided that George was my favorite, mainly because of his sense of humor. Norman and Stuart were my favorite engineers; fortunately, they also happened to be the two George used most often. He didn't seem to relate well to Pete Bown, and he didn't like Malcolm Addey, who never stopped talking. Norman and

Stuart were outgoing, but they followed the unspoken rule, which was that the balance engineer—and, of course, the assistant—keep his mouth shut unless spoken to. Any unsolicited opinions were perceived as undermining the role of the producer. Whether the producer was right or wrong, the engineer wasn't allowed to say anything . . . and that's the way George Martin liked things.

Naturally, whenever I was assisting on a session, I'd be watching the engineer closely. They wouldn't actively instruct us, but if you asked why they were doing something, they'd tell you. Both Stuart and Norman were great that way. Stuart taught me a lot, especially about mic positioning, and Norman was a brilliant engineer with a keen mind. As he sat behind the mixing desk, he would often say to me, "The hit's down there, not up here." His point was that no engineer could create a hit alone: the equipment we used and the skills we developed simply provided the means for recording and enhancing a performance. Norman always claimed that he could tell whether a song was a hit or not while the band were rehearsing it in the studio.

Stuart excelled at editing and creating sound effects, but when it came to pop sessions, George would most often use Norman. My theory was that George realized that he himself was a bit out of his depth; he simply didn't know all that much about rock 'n' roll music. He had built his career on novelty and light pop records, and hadn't actually produced any rock 'n' roll acts before signing the Beatles. Even though Norman was George's age (or even older—we were never sure), he seemed to relate well to pop musicians because he was one himself. So George relied on Norman for musical, not just technical, input. More often than not, I noticed that George would relay Norman's thoughts to the band as if they were his ideas. Norman tolerated that well; he knew it wasn't his place to speak up. In those days, the producer was still very much in charge, and his methods were not to be questioned.

I was given a lot of classical sessions to begin with, simply because some of the senior assistants didn't like working with the stuffed shirts, but over the course of my first few months at EMI, it felt like I was being phased off of them. It's possible that the classical engineers slowly began to realize that I wasn't as enthused about doing those sessions as some of the newer assistants coming up through the ranks were. Soon I found myself being assigned to pop sessions almost exclusively, more often than not with George and either Norman or Stuart. Slowly but surely the camps were being drawn.

• • •

In early October—a little more than a month after I started work at EMI—
"Love Me Do" was released as a single, and by mid-December it had reached
a respectable number 17 in the British charts. "Our" Beatles were a hit, albeit
a minor one, and they were beginning to make a real name for themselves
nationally. By February, the public were clamoring for a Beatles album, and
George Martin duly began making preparations. At one point he gave serious consideration to recording them live at the Cavern in Liverpool—he and
his secretary (later to become his wife), Judy, even made a trip up there, but
deemed the venue unsuitable. Instead, the decision was made to record the
group live in Studio Two, playing their stage set straight through in a single
marathon session, as if they were doing a radio broadcast.

I harbored a slim hope that I'd get picked to assist, but Richard landed
the plum job—hardly surprising, considering that he was senior to me and
had developed a strong working relationship with both George and Norman. So I had to content myself with hearing the stories in the canteen and
in the pub, as Richard regaled us with tales of the four Beatles working
straight through their lunch break (unheard of in those days), and a hoarse
Lennon, stripped to the waist despite the winter damp and cold, nearly
shredding his voice at the end of the night with a blistering version of "Twist
And Shout." I had no means to hear the tapes—unauthorized playbacks by
staff were strictly forbidden—but based on Richard's description and my
own previous experience with the group, I hoped that some kind of opportunity would arise for me to get a preview.

Just a week or so later, I got my wish. Both Richard and Norman must
have been unavailable on this particular morning, so Stuart Eltham and I
got the assignment to work with George Martin as he overdubbed keyboards, playing them himself, onto a couple of the songs recorded for the album. None of the Beatles was present—they were out on tour—but it was a
fabulous session nonetheless, if only for the fact that I got an advance listen
of many of the album tracks.

I was completely blown away. It was the freshest music I'd ever heard, and
I remember raving to my mates about it afterward—with the "Please Please
Me" single currently topping the charts, none of us could wait for the album
(of the same name) to come out. I felt very privileged indeed to be able to
hear it well before it was released. After all, this was the number one band in
the country, and not only was I working with them, I was one of a handful of
people getting to hear the record before anyone else.

That session was my first exposure to George Martin's signature "wound-up" piano—piano recorded at half speed, in unison with guitar, but played an octave lower. The combination produced a kind of magical sound, and it was an insight into a new way of recording—the creation of new tones by combining instruments, and by playing them with the tape sped up or slowed down. George Martin had developed that sound years before I met him, and he used it on a lot of his records. Overdubbing a half-speed piano is not the easiest thing to do, either, because when you're monitoring at half speed, it's hard to keep the rhythm steady. There certainly were more than a few expletives coming from George as he struggled to get the timing down while overdubbing onto the song "Misery," on both the spread chord that opens the song, and on the little arpeggios and chord stabs that are played throughout. I was so inspired by what George was doing that I began experimenting with the same technique at home. I still had my trusty Brenell, so I'd tape some of my favorite records and then, with the tape running at half speed, I'd play over the solos on my piano. It was a fun way of spending a weekend, and it helped sharpen both my engineering and playing chops.

As I listened to the playbacks of "Misery" that afternoon, I was also struck by the way John and Paul sang the word "send" as "shend" ("Shend her back to me . . ."). Changing an "s" to an "sh" was an affectation you heard on some American records, so it helped make the Beatles sound more like their musical idols, plus it removed any kind of potential "de-essing" problems, where, if there was too much top end (treble), the sound on vinyl would distort. That was a great little vocal trick, and they used it on a lot of their songs from then on, most notably on "I Want To Hold Your Hand" ("When I / shay that shomething . . .").

Once the piano overdub was complete, George added some celeste (a bell-like keyboard instrument) to the song "Baby It's You," doubling George Harrison's guitar solo. Again, he was trying to get a new tone by blending the two instruments together—and, again, nobody had ever heard a sound like that before. Later on, he also tried adding some normal-speed piano to the song, but decided it wasn't necessary, so only the celeste made it to the record.

The following week, in the very capable hands of George Martin, Norman, and Richard, the entire first Beatles album was mixed in a single day. Mind you, since it had been recorded in twin-track mono, there wasn't much for Norman to do except balance the vocal levels against the instruments and tuck in some echo, but he did a fantastic job and it still sounds fresh and exciting.

• • •

The next Beatles session I assisted on was a mid-March harmonica over-dub on the song "Thank You Girl." Actually, it wasn't so much a Beatles session as it was a John Lennon session. He came in on his own to do it, despite the fact that he had a terrible cold. It came out in the course of conversation that he'd been home the night before and missed the band's gig: that's how sick he was. He staggered into the studio white as a sheet—he must have come straight from bed, and he had a hoarse voice. Lennon was croaking and wheezing, blowing his nose every few seconds. He was in terrible shape, but the pressures of the recording industry forced him from a sickbed and into a drafty studio. That's how little available time the constantly touring Beatles had at that point in their career.

George Martin clearly felt sorry for the unusually subdued John and pandered to him, doing everything he could to make sure Lennon was comfortable. John, as it turned out, was so foggy from his illness that he had forgotten to bring his harmonica along. There was some talk of dispatching Mal Evans to the nearest music shop to buy one, but then I remembered that my mate Malcolm Davies played a bit of harmonica to amuse himself. John shuffled up to the mastering room himself and borrowed it.

As the tape played, I noticed a ton of edits flying by. Checking the notes on the tape box, I saw that the master was made up of six different takes, which Norman had edited together a few days beforehand so that everything was ready for John's overdub. Obviously the band hadn't been able to play it all the way through, even though it sounded like a very simple song. It took John more than a dozen takes to add those little harmonica bits, too, not because he couldn't play them, but because he kept sneezing and snuffling.

Once Lennon trundled off to return to home, hearth, and cough syrup, each harmonica lick was separately edited into the master tape so that the whole recording didn't go down a generation. In theory, the balance engineers weren't allowed to do their own editing. EMI had its own editing department, and the prescribed procedure was to have the producer indicate the edits he wanted on a sheet of manuscript paper, which would be carried out by the editing staff the next day, but Norman generally ignored that edict. For one thing, he enjoyed doing edits; for another, doing them himself was the fastest, most expedient way, and, of course, everyone wanted to hear the results right away. Rules were already beginning to be broken for Beatles sessions, a reflection of how much money they were starting to generate for the label.

Listening to "Thank You Girl" today, it obviously got inadvertently sped up at some point, though we didn't have varispeed on the two-track machines in those days, so it must have happened during mastering, or when tape copies were made. Varispeed came later, with a sweep oscillator and a huge power supply that provided varying voltage to the motors. It was a technological innovation that would open the door to lots of new, exciting sounds on future Beatles recordings.

Malcolm later told me that when Lennon finally returned his harmonica, he didn't say thank you, only complained that it "tasted like a sack of potatoes." Typical! I only hope that Malcolm thought to disinfect it before playing it next, or he would have caught one hell of a cold.

Beatlemania

By early spring 1963, the Beatles were unquestionably the top band in England, with both a chart-topping single ("Please Please Me") and their debut album dominating the airwaves. Though they were to get even bigger—bigger, in fact, than anyone imagined possible—there was probably no session that underscored their popularity more than the one where all hell broke loose: the day they recorded "She Loves You."

Because of their busy touring schedule, the Beatles hadn't been in the studio for several months, so I was surprised to discover their names on the schedule sheet one early July day . . . and even more surprised to see my own name listed as the assistant, instead of Richard's. A double session was booked—afternoon and evening—and I was delighted. Not only would I get to work with them again, but, as a bonus, I'd even be getting some much-needed overtime pay.

As soon as I could, I headed for Studio Two. For some reason the smell of its freshly waxed floors (a ritual every Monday morning) always reminded me of church . . . albeit a slightly musty one. Unusually, the control room was completely empty, with no sign of either George Martin or Norman Smith. Down in the studio, Mal Evans was busily setting up Ringo's drums. I wandered in and he greeted me warmly, introducing me to the other roadie, whom I had seen several times before but had never actually spoken with. "Neil Aspinall, meet Geoff Emerick," Mal boomed.

Neil stepped forward to shake my hand, and I asked him where the Beatles were. Giving me a funny look, he replied, "The boys are out in the alleyway having their picture taken . . . that is, if the fans haven't torn them to bits yet."

He and Mal started chuckling. "I reckon your governor and his second-in-command are out there, too," Mal said, referring to George and Norman.

A few minutes later the studio door opened and the four Beatles burst in, accompanied by George, Norman, and a well-dressed gentleman I hadn't met before. Everyone seemed especially exuberant and there was lots of excited chatter about the fans outside. Lennon was making a joke about the "barbarians storming the walls," and Harrison and McCartney were comparing notes about the physical attributes of one particularly fulsome creature who had apparently invaded the proceedings before being carted off by security guards.

Everyone was so preoccupied, I was pretty much ignored; even George Martin and Norman failed to say their usual hellos. The sole exception was the well-dressed gentleman, who strode right over to me, extended his hand, and in a soft, aristocratic voice introduced himself as Brian Epstein. I had read a lot about their mysterious manager in the newspapers, but had never seen him in the studio before. Friendly though he was, Brian struck me as a bit odd. He was a quiet man, obviously upper class. He didn't come to many sessions, but he was always very polite to me when he did; however, I always got the impression that the Beatles didn't like having him around.

After a few more minutes of chat, George Martin, Norman, Brian, and I headed up to the control room to begin the work of the day. As Norman and I began testing the microphones and recording equipment, Brian and George held an impromptu meeting, discussing the morning's photo shoot as well as the upcoming month's recording schedule. By this point, Brian had a stable of artists, including Gerry and the Pacemakers and Billy J. Kramer, all of whom were signed to Parlophone and produced by George.

In those early days of Beatlemania, there always seemed to be at least a hundred girls camped outside the studio in hopes of seeing one or more of the group dash to or from their cars. How they knew when the Beatles were due to come in was a complete mystery to us—their sessions were always booked under the pseudonym, "The Dakotas" (after the band that sometimes accompanied Billy J. Kramer)—but clearly the fans had some kind of network because they'd always begin arriving an hour or so before the group did. Despite the size of the crowd, there were only ever four or five policemen assigned to control them, which always struck me as being ludicrously inadequate. On this particular day, the Beatles had, unusually, shown up several hours before the session to pose for pictures in an alleyway behind the studio, giving the girls plenty of time to call their friends, and that had swelled the crowd even more than usual. By climbing on top of the walls around the studio perimeter, the girls could see them, and the four Beatles had been waving and smiling to them throughout the afternoon, adding fuel to the fire.

That was the backdrop to the explosion that was about to occur. It all started innocuously enough. As John, Paul, and George tuned up in the studio, Norman noticed that the microphone on the bass amplifier was distorting, so he asked me to go downstairs and move it back a few inches. Out of the corner of my eye, I saw Mal and Neil go out of the studio door, no doubt heading for the canteen to fetch the first of an endless stream of cups of tea for the four musicians. On this day, though, they wouldn't be gone for long.

"FANS!!"

There was no mistaking Big Mal's booming voice as he shot back through the door, tailed closely by a breathless Neil. The four Beatles stopped what they were doing and stared at him.

"What the bloody hell are you on about?" Lennon demanded.

Before Mal could get the answer out, the studio door flew open again and a determined teenage girl sprinted in, heading straight for a bewildered-looking Ringo hunched behind his drum kit. Instinctively, Neil launched himself at her in a perfect American football–style tackle and brought her to the ground before she could reach her quarry. It all seemed to be happening in slow motion before my widened eyes.

As Mal dragged the sobbing teenager out the door, Neil caught his breath and broke the news: somehow the huge crowd of girls that had been gathered outside had overpowered the police and broken through the front door. The canteen was swarming with them, and dozens of rabid fans were racing around the EMI facility in desperate search of the Fab Four.

"It's a bloody madhouse out there," Neil shouted. "You've got to see it to believe it!"

I stood rooted to the ground, not sure what to do. Looking up at the control room, I could see George, Norman, and Brian staring down at us with great concern. Brian was the first down the steps.

"Oh dear, oh dear," he kept repeating, literally wringing his hands.

Norman was hot on his heels. "Geoff, you'd better get on the intercom and call security," he yelled at me. As I raced back up the steps, I could hear Lennon's cackling laughter reverberating off the walls.

As it turned out, there was no need to call security, because they—he—was already on the scene. John Skinner, our commissionaire, was standing there, jaw hanging open, obviously surprised to find the control room empty.

"Is everyone all right?" he asked me, looking worried. I assured him we were all in one piece, and that we had already heard the news. "Better barricade the doors until we can round them all up," he told me as he headed back to join the fray.

Curious as to what the fuss was all about, I poked my head out the door. What I saw astounded, amazed, and frightened me . . . but it also made me burst out in laughter. It was an unbelievable sight, straight out of the Keystone Kops: scores of hysterical, screaming girls racing down the corridors, being chased by a handful of out-of-breath, beleaguered London bobbies. Every time one would catch up with a fan, another two or three girls would appear, racing past, screeching at the top of their lungs. The poor copper wouldn't know whether to let go of the nutter he was struggling with and go after the others, or whether to keep his grip on the bird in hand.

As I wandered down the hallway, I could see the scene being repeated everywhere. Doors were opening and slamming shut with alarming regularity, terrified staffers were having their hair pulled (just in case they happened to be a Beatle in disguise), and everyone in sight was running at top speed. The fans were totally out of control—Lord knows what they would have done to the four Beatles if they had actually gotten their hands on them. The grim determination on their faces, punctuated by squalls of animal-like screaming, made the whole thing even more bizarre.

I returned to the studio, which seemed strangely calm in comparison, like the eye of a hurricane: things did seem to be somewhat more in control there. Neil had decided to do reconnaissance, promising to keep us informed, and a grim Mal was stationed in the doorway, literally standing there with arms crossed; he reminded me of one of the Queen's guards at Buckingham Palace. Ringo, still on his drum stool, seemed a bit shaken, but John, Paul, and George Harrison soon began taking the piss, racing around the room, giggling and screeching in imitation of the poor fan who had launched herself at him.

George Martin, flustered at first, finally regained his schoolmasterly disposition and, with a good deal of formality, announced that the nonsense was over and that the session would now begin. A somewhat calmer Brian made his good-byes to everyone, including me, and left the room timorously; I was actually kind of surprised he didn't ask Mal to escort him out. Throughout the day, Neil would periodically burst into the studio and interrupt the session to issue updated reports on the state of the fan siege.

There's no doubt in my mind that the excitement of that afternoon helped spark a new level of energy in the group's playing. "She Loves You" was a fantastic song, with a powerhouse beat and a relentless hook—Norman and I immediately agreed that it was destined to be a hit, for sure—but there was also a level of intensity in the performance that I had not heard before . . . and, frankly, rarely heard since. I still judge that single to be one of the most exciting recordings of the Beatles' entire career.

Of course, Norman Smith had a lot to do with the quality of the record, too. Clearly, he had been thinking about how he wanted to improve the sound of Beatles records, and on this session he made two significant changes. First, using an electronic device called a "compressor," he decided to reduce the dynamic range—the difference between the loudest and softest signals—of the bass and drums independently of each other; in the past, they had been compressed together because they comprised the rhythm section. Second, he specified that a different type of microphone be suspended over the drum kit—the "overhead" mic, as it was known. The result was a more prominent, driving rhythm sound: both the bass and drums are brighter and more "present" than in previous Beatles records. Combined with the group's new confidence and more intense playing (fueled, I am sure, by the adrenaline and testosterone rush they were feeling that afternoon), it was the icing on the cake.

As the group ran through their first few takes, I remember commenting to Norman on how great the drums sounded. He turned to me with a wink and said, "This old dog still has a few new tricks up his sleeve, mate." It was the kind of thing one would say to a peer, not a subordinate, and it stayed with me for a long time afterward. For the first time, I began to feel that we were operating as a team.

It didn't take the Beatles all that many takes to nail down the basic rhythm track, and John, Paul, and George Harrison overdubbed their vocals just as quickly. I was especially impressed with their tight harmony singing, and I loved the unusual Glenn Miller–like chord on the final "yeah," despite the fact that George Martin had some serious misgivings about it.

During the playback of the final recording up in the control room, all four Beatles were beaming, and Norman Smith was more hyped up and excited than I'd ever seen him before—he was actually dancing around the console in glee. From a chair in the back of the room George Martin looked on with quiet pride. "Nice job, lads," was all he said to us, but you could tell that he was elated. Everyone in the control room that afternoon was certain that "She Loves You" would be an even bigger hit than "Please Please Me" had been, and we were proven to be right—it shot straight to the top of the charts when it was finally released in late summer, their fastest-selling hit record ever . . . and, of course, it went on to sell millions when it finally reached the shores of America in 1964.

Soon enough, it was time for the evening break. During lulls in previous sessions, the Beatles would go off to the canteen to grab a cup of tea and a sandwich, but this time they were warned by Neil not to dare attempt it. At one point, a hungry and thirsty John ventured out to have a look for himself, but he quickly returned, saying, "It's not worth it; they're mad, those birds." Instead, Mal was dispatched to bring back some take-out food.

Sadly, after that day, the Beatles would never venture into the EMI canteen again; instead, they had Mal bring them cups of tea and food in. In time, Mal and Neil would actually fix up a corner of the studio as a kind of makeshift private canteen—they had an electric kettle and a table set up so they could make tea and jam butties. In many ways, the "She Loves You" session was a turning point for the group, certainly in terms of their becoming virtual prisoners of the studio; it marked the loss of their freedom at the EMI facilities and the beginning of their incarceration.

The evening half of the session was kind of a letdown in many ways. By then, most of the fans had been rounded up and the excitement had died away, and the song being recorded—"I'll Get You"—was nowhere near as good as "She Loves You." Indeed, it was destined to become the single's B-side. Still, it took quite a bit of time to record, and the session ran a little overtime. I was getting a bit concerned about how I would get home—the tubes stopped running at 11 P.M.—but George assured me that whenever evening sessions ran over, a car would be ordered for me, courtesy of EMI. I was expecting a simple sedan, but the service that the studio contracted with owned a fleet of fancy town cars, Humbers and the like. It was the first time I had ever ridden in such luxury, so it was a bonus for me. My parents were fast asleep by the time I got home, but I remember thinking how impressed they would have been if they'd seen me pulling up to our house in such a flash car.

Interestingly, no matter how late a session ran, I was never offered a ride home by any of the Beatles, not in all the years I worked with them. Nor was I ever offered a ride by Mal or Neil—it just seemed to have never occurred to any of them. If Norman had driven in and a session ran late, he would give me a lift; if not, I would have to make my own way back.

A few days after that memorable session, George, Norman, and I got together to do the final editing and mixing of "She Loves You" and "I'll Get You"—none of the Beatles were present because artists did not attend mixing sessions in those days. It marked the first time I'd seen a Beatles song all the way through, from backing track to completion, and for months afterward, whenever I heard the song being played on the radio, I'd find myself grinning from ear to ear.

W e didn't see much of the Beatles during the summer and fall of 1963, as they continued their blitzkrieg touring schedule from one end of Britain to the other. They did, however, manage to make a handful of appearances at EMI in between concert commitments, recording the songs for their second album, *With The Beatles* (which would comprise most of the songs on their debut American LP, *Meet The Beatles*). To my disappointment, Richard was back in the assistant's chair for those sessions, while I was relegated to other activities. For some reason, though, I was asked to assist George and Norman for the album's editing and mixing.

As I sat in the control room listening to the tracks, I was amazed at how much the Beatles had improved since their debut album, in terms of both their musicianship and their singing. There was a lot more confidence in their individual performances in songs like "All My Loving," "Till There Was You," and their cover of the Motown classic "Please Mister Postman"; it was almost as if they were trying to impress one another. John and Paul's songs had always been good, and I didn't see a lot of change in their songwriting ability, but they were definitely improving tremendously as a band. It must have been because of all that live touring, I supposed—not that they could ever hear themselves above all the screaming.

Sonically, everything sounded better to my ears as well. Norman had obviously done some tweaking and rethinking, probably changing around some mic placements. All in all, there was just a great spirit about that album.

My contribution to those mixes may have been minimal—all I was doing was changing tape reels and starting and stopping the tape machines—but I was learning a lot from watching Norman. I knew enough not to make comments during the session, but I do remember thinking things like *I hope Norman lifts the guitar solo up; I hope he rides the vocal here.* I was already starting to imagine how I would engineer the sessions myself, given the chance. I wasn't thinking that I could do it better than Norman—I knew that I couldn't, not at this stage—but I was starting to feel that I might take a slightly different approach to recording and mixing Beatles songs. During those sessions, I was constantly asking Norman questions about what he was doing and why he was doing it, and he was very good about answering them and being patient with me. Incredibly, we mixed that entire landmark album in just two days.

In mid-October, "The Dakotas" once again appeared on the EMI work schedule, and I was pleased to see the initials "GE" listed next to Norman Smith's name. My elation turned to frustration, however, when I arrived in the control room at the appointed time, only to be informed by Norman that the session was to be recorded in four-track. That meant I would be banished to a windowless machine room, where I could no longer view the events unfolding in the studio below. From this day forward, in fact, the Beatles always recorded in multitrack: four-track all the way through to the *White Album*, eight-track afterward. Apparently the bigwigs at EMI had decided that the band had now earned sufficient monies for the label—many millions of pounds, for sure—to be afforded the same honor as "serious" musicians, none of whom, I am certain, brought in even a fraction of the income that the Beatles did.

There were actually two, virtually identical machine rooms. Each was little more than a poorly ventilated broom closet into which was stuffed a chair, two speakers, an intercom box, a red "Recording" light, and a bulky, noisy four-track machine that threw off ungodly amounts of heat. One could work up a real sweat in there, even in the dead of winter. Luckily, they were directly adjacent to the Studio Two control room, so I could quickly nip in from time to time and see what was going on. If the Beatles had been recording in either of the other two studios, it would have been too far to walk.

There was no visual communication of any kind between the machine rooms and the control rooms and studios—all I had was an intercom system through which Norman and I could talk, and I could only monitor one track at a time. As a result, the only way I could hear studio chatter was if I were listening to the track receiving input from the vocal mics. I felt terribly isolated and removed from the action, especially after having watched the Beatles spin their magic from the control room window.

During that session, I got so antsy that I started getting in the habit of hanging about in the control room until the point where they were just about to do a take, then I'd race back out to hit the Record button. Norman and George tolerated my doing that—I guess they understood how much I wanted to be there. They'd simply say, "Okay, we're ready to try putting one down," and that would be my cue to leave. Remote autolocators (which allow tape recorders to be operated from another room and are standard equipment in recording studios today) were still a few years away. Still, it's incredible that none of our technical boffins took a look at how clumsy the whole system was and never attempted to come up with a better solution.

Despite my personal disappointment at the move to four-track, I was glad to see the Beatles again. By this point, I had done enough sessions with them that I was a familiar face; this time around, I got greetings from all four when they popped into the control room to say hello. I suppose I'd proven myself to a degree—at least they knew that I hadn't destroyed any of their tapes or accidentally erased anything. Nonetheless, there was very little personal chat. Paul made a point of asking, "What have you been up to?" but all I got from the others was a simple "All right, Geoff?"

That was good enough for me. All the same, I couldn't help but feel that my developing relationship with the group was going to be slowed by the fact that I was no longer a physical presence. I would now just be a disconnected voice coming from another room.

The afternoon's festivities began with a bit of nonsense—their first annual Christmas Record, recorded specially as a giveaway to the rapidly growing Beatles fan club. I don't remember much about it, except that there was a lot of clowning around and joking. Obviously no one was taking it all that seriously, and only a half hour or so of precious studio time was devoted to getting it down on tape. Once that was done, John announced that he wanted to have another go at "You Really Got A Hold On Me," a song that had already been recorded for the *With The Beatles* album. Perhaps, in his naivete, he thought that simply recording it on four-track instead of two-track would somehow make it sound better, but after one whack at it, the idea was abandoned, George Martin insisting that the take he already had in the can was quite good enough.

"All right, George, we give up." Lennon finally capitulated. "But you'd better come on down here and have a listen to our next number one record."

As I heard the words, I bolted out the door and headed for the control room. There was no way I was going to miss the world debut of the Beatles' next single.

I wasn't disappointed. From the very first run-through, it was apparent that "I Want To Hold Your Hand" had "hit" written all over it, and there was little George Martin could do to improve it. In fact, their first rehearsal sounded very much like the finished version on record, other than some minor changes in tempo and vocal harmony; every one of the takes they did that afternoon sounded confident, professional, and polished. Clearly, a great deal of thought and rehearsal must have gone into the song. I wondered when they'd had time to do so in the midst of their grueling touring schedule.

After the backing track was done, John and Paul did their usual fine job overdubbing the vocals. They had a real knack for close harmony singing, and they almost always sang perfectly in pitch. "I Want to Hold Your Hand" was distinguished by the attack on the vocal. Other records of the era weren't like that—they were syrupy by contrast. But John flubbed the lyrics repeatedly, which was something he did quite often, due to his poor memory and even poorer eyesight. Even if Mal or Neil taped a lyric sheet to a music stand in front of the mic, it didn't help much, because John couldn't see it properly. John and Paul knew when they got it wrong, of course—you could tell that from the guilty looks on their faces, like schoolkids, and the taunting they did of each other. But unless George Martin caught it, or thought the mistake was too obvious, they never brought it to anyone's attention. That's why the singing on some early Beatles recordings (songs like "I'll Get You," "From Me To You," even "Please Please Me") sounds a little shoddy, especially on the CD rereleases, where you can hear the individual words more clearly. I suppose there were other times when George Martin or Norman knew that a fluff had been made and let it go, on the theory that most listeners wouldn't hear it—that, plus the studio clock was always ticking: time was money. These are the kinds of mistakes that would never slip through on today's sanitized recordings . . . but I do think that they do impart character to some of those older records.

George Harrison really impressed us all that day, too. I felt that those little answering guitar licks he played in each verse provided the song's definitive hook. Norman must have agreed, because he mimed Harrison's playing the parts, face lit in a beaming smile, every time he heard them. As we listened to playbacks of various takes in the control room while the Beatles remained downstairs awaiting George Martin's verdict, I could see that he and Norman were getting more and more excited. Both of them were thinking that "I Want To Hold Your Hand" might be even bigger than "She Loves You."

The luxury of working in four-track instead of two-track gave Norman a great deal more control over the balance of the instruments. His general way of allocating the four tracks during Beatles sessions was to put drums and bass on one track, combine Lennon's and Harrison's guitars on another, and then put the vocals on a third track. The fourth track was the "catch-all" track for whatever sweetening George Martin wanted to add—handclaps, harmonica, keyboards, guitar solo, whatever. For "I Want To Hold Your Hand," George wanted the double-time handclaps to occur in each verse. As I watched the four Beatles gathered around a single mic, clowning around as they added the part, it was apparent to me how much fun they were having, how much they loved doing what they were doing.

It's always been of interest to me that Americans were introduced to the Beatles through "I Want To Hold Your Hand." What few realized was that, by the time the group recorded that single, they had already had several major hits in the British charts and were seasoned studio veterans, with over a year of making records under the watchful eye of George and Norman. Yes, it was a great song, but what made it a great record was the confidence in the performance, which came from all the experience the group had already gained in the studio. In a way, it was good that no one in the States really picked up on them before that time. "Love Me Do" or "Please Please Me"—or possibly even "She Loves You"—might not have had the impact that "I Want To Hold Your Hand" did, had any of them been America's first exposure to the Beatles. It was a stroke of good fortune that the group was at, or close to, their initial artistic peak when America first heard them.

Nonetheless, "I Want To Hold Your Hand" sounds to me today like it's got a tired energy to it rather than the "up" energy I hear in "She Loves You"—it almost sounds a little forced. Part of that might have had to do with the band being a bit weary from all the touring they had been doing, but I suspect more has to do with the fact that there weren't several hundred crazed teenage girls running around the studio that day.

There was an hour-and-a-half break between the afternoon and evening sessions, and since the Beatles and their roadies never invited us to join them in their evening meal, we used the opportunity to get away from the studio for a little while. Normally I would go round to the local pub during a break, but on this particular day Norman and I made the ten-minute walk to our favorite local restaurant, a place called the Black Tulip. I'd always order the same thing there: spaghetti bolognese. Norman, in fact, was the first person to teach me how to use a spoon to twirl spaghetti; in many ways, both in and out of the studio, he was like a father figure to me. As we were scarfing down our dinner, we talked about the session we had just done. We both enthused about what a great song "I Want To Hold Your Hand" was, but I remember telling Norman that I thought the Beatles sounded a bit tired.

"Doesn't matter," he replied. "It'll still go straight to number one, you mark my words." Norman was always a great believer in the power of a strong song. That was quite possibly the most important lesson I learned from him.

When we returned, there was an unfamiliar face in the control room. George Martin introduced the gregarious, balding gent as Dick James, the Beatles' song publisher.

"Nice to meet you, nice to meet you," he shouted boisterously, thrusting a hand in my direction.

George asked me to thread up the master take for "I Want To Hold Your Hand" so that Dick could have a listen, so I headed off to the machine room. Once I started the playback, however, I snuck right back into the control room—this was the first outsider to hear our afternoon's work, and I was anxious to see how he would react. From the instant the first guitar chords hit, it was obvious that Dick was totally blown away.

"Marvelous, marvelous," he kept repeating, slapping George on the back heartily. "Bloody brilliant, I tell you!"

Following the playback, James headed down the steps to greet the four Beatles, who were huddled around a small table drinking cups of tea with Neil and Mal. The mics were still open and the speakers were on, so I had a chance to listen in from behind the control room glass.

"Hello, Dick!" Lennon called out. He seemed pleased to see the ebullient publisher. The reception Dick got from the others wasn't nearly as pleasant.

"Is Mr. James here to count his money?" sneered Harrison. Paul simply turned his back and ignored Dick altogether, which was certainly not in character. James appeared to be oblivious to it all—he just kept chortling and waving his hands about, chatting animatedly with Lennon about this, that, and the other. Eventually, though, he seemed to take the hint and made his way out the door. Ringo remained expressionless, but Paul and George seemed glad to see him go.

In the early days, Dick James showed up often at Beatles sessions. While John always appeared to be amused by his presence, the other three generally treated him with a certain amount of scorn. Some time later, I would learn the reason for their contempt: they felt that he was making huge amounts of money off them without actually doing anything to earn it, and they frequently complained about it, and about his legendary tightfistedness (one year, he gave each of them a bottle of Brut aftershave for Christmas; another year, it was a pair of cuff links). Dick had snatched up their publishing rights—ultimately worth a fortune—based on a recommendation from George Martin. But beyond all of that, the "inner circle," consisting of the four Beatles plus Neil and Mal, always had disrespect and disregard for anyone in authority, anyone in control of the purse strings—they were basically suspicious of everybody. This included Brian Epstein, although he was far less overbearing than Dick—he'd stay in the control room and would rarely venture down into their domain—so he was not subject to as much verbal abuse. But neither of them was welcomed to Beatles sessions with open arms; that much was obvious.

The song recorded that evening—"This Boy"—was a departure for the group, and it took quite a long time to perfect. There was a lot of tweaking because it was a pretty complicated song, sung in intricate three-part harmony that George Martin—with considerable input from Paul—kept refining. George spent a lot of time at the piano with Lennon, McCartney, and Harrison, carefully checking each part they were singing and occasionally suggesting that a note be changed. Through the whole process, Ringo, who didn't sing on the track (he rarely sang harmony at all), sat at the back of the studio, smoking a ciggie and reading a comic book.

Sonically, the two recordings couldn't be more different—it's remarkable, in fact, that they were both done during the same session. "This Boy" is distinguished by its gentle clarity and separation (you can hear every note of every instrument), while "I Want to Hold Your Hand" is more of a wash of sound, a bombardment of the senses. Of course, "This Boy" is almost entirely acoustic—just bass and a little strummed guitar, played by Lennon. There are no thrashing drums, so there was no drum "bleed" on the vocal mics, which gave it a very clean sound. (The drum screens at EMI were quite primitive and hardly soundproof; they were just pieces of particle board with some burlap nailed on.) But what was most impressive about the recording of "This Boy" was that the three Beatles sang it impeccably, in perfect three-part harmony, almost every time, from first take to last. John, Paul, and George's ability to pull off complex harmony vocals was really quite astounding. You could see they'd spent a lot of time rehearsing, not just getting the notes correct, but getting their voices to blend just right. That's where all those years of playing together really paid off.

Once the vocals were recorded, however, there was another snag: Harrison's overdubbed guitar solo, which was particularly uninspired. George Martin didn't like it one bit, and insisted on substituting vocals during the middle section instead—which was a good thing, because John did an incredible job of singing them, and an even more brilliant job of double-tracking his heartfelt performance, hitting every pitch and inflection spot on. Unfortunately, the editing job Norman did later that night was not up to his usual standard, and, especially on CD, it's obvious that the middle section was recorded separately and spliced in.

At some point during a short break, I happened to be in the control room when the phone rang. Only producers were allowed to receive incoming calls while in the studio at EMI. There was a complicated system of colored lights on the wall—red, yellow, blue, and green, in various combinations—that identified who the call was for. George Martin was busy working with the boys downstairs, so I answered it, and Brian was on the line, asking to speak with George, who headed up to the control room to take the call. Judging from his end of the conversation, it appeared that they were discussing the upcoming Royal Variety Show—it had recently been announced in the press that the Beatles had been invited to play before the royal family. Brian was asking George's opinion on which songs should be performed.

"I think they should definitely do the two songs we're recording tonight," George said. "They're both absolutely terrific, and it will be a great way of promoting the next single." When the conversation ended, George got on the talkback and announced that break time was over.

"Brian says hello," he reported. "Now let's get back to work."

"Yes, sir, mein herr, sir," Lennon shouted out, emphasizing his words with a goosestep and a formal military salute. By this point, you could see they were already beginning to chafe a little, albeit good-naturedly, at George Martin's authoritarian demeanor.

Later on, when I was sent downstairs to adjust a microphone, I heard them chatting excitedly about the upcoming appearance. They were over the moon about it, even though it was obvious that they didn't care for upper-class people in general. Ever cheeky, John whispered to Paul at one point that he was going to ask the toffs in the audience to rattle their jewelry instead of applauding. Paul's reply was a taunting "I dare ya!" That was the kind of relationship they had: John was the bad boy, the rebel, and Paul—who of course wouldn't dream of saying that himself—was the instigator, the one needling him on to doing outrageous things.

It came as no surprise to me, then, that John did just that at the show a few weeks later. I heard afterward that Lennon kept winding Brian up backstage, telling him that he was going to tell the audience to rattle their *fucking* jewelry. Needless to say, Brian was absolutely terrified, pleading with John not to utter that word. I imagine that Brian was always afraid of John being too much of a loose cannon, that he would say something that would ruin their clean-cut image . . . which, of course, he did do a few years later with his remark about the Beatles being bigger than Jesus.

I always felt that Brian never got quite enough credit for the way he carefully crafted the group's image; he was very particular about the way they looked, the way they dressed, the way they presented themselves in public.

The Beatles' live television performances at the London Palladium and the Royal Command Performance that fall were the events that put them on the front page of every newspaper in England and gave them the final stamp of approval from the British public. After that, their careers would skyrocket into new, uncharted territory.

It was a gloomy, foggy evening just after Christmas 1963, and my old schoolmate Tony Cook and I were sitting in the top section of a double-decker bus, slowly weaving our way through traffic. From the streaked windows we could see the lights of the Finsbury Park Astoria ahead. The grand old theater was a splendid monument to a bygone era. With its elegant indoors fountain, twinkling stars in the ceiling, and painted castles above the balustrade, it felt more like an Arabian prince's castle than a movie theater in North London.

As kids, we'd been there many times before to see the latest potboiler or western double feature. But there was something very special in the air that night, as was evidenced by the huge crowds gathered around the front entrance. High above the marquee was a ten-foot-high blowup of four faces very familiar to me. The Beatles were performing live at the Astoria that night. It was to be the one and only time I would get to see them onstage.

Tony, needless to say, was pinching himself at his good fortune—not just because he was a Beatles fan, but because it was becoming increasingly apparent that most of the audience were girls, bundled in thick coats against the winter chill but wearing revealing miniskirts and tantalizing boots nonetheless. We disembarked the bus and made our way through the massive crowd, finally arriving at our seats in the downstairs stalls. I was thrilled to be sitting just a dozen rows or so from the lip of the stage. The arrangements had been made by George Martin, and Brian's office had provided two complimentary tickets for each of the EMI staff who had worked regularly with the group, including Norman and Richard, who attended a couple of nights later.

Comedian/singer Rolf Harris was the master of ceremonies for the 1963 Beatles Christmas Show, which was scheduled for an incredible thirty-night run, right through to mid-January. The support artists, many of whom were also familiar faces to me, had been culled from Brian's roster of acts: Cilla Black, the Fourmost, Billy J. Kramer and the Dakotas. The total show ran just three hours, with no break; the curtains would close after each performance while the stagehands set up for the next artist, each of whom used their own gear. In the meantime, Rolf came out and did his thing for a few moments; then they'd open the curtains again and a new performance would begin. All evening long, Rolf kept teasing the audience. "Here they come, here they come, they're going to be on next," he would say . . . but of course, they weren't, not until the very end.

During these lulls, the four Beatles were frequently running on and off the stage in silly costumes, doing pantomime bits. At one point, Rolf performed his hit song "Sunarise," and then he did "Tie Me Kangaroo Down Sport" along with John, Paul, George, and Ringo, albeit with changed lyrics that poked fun at their celebrity. People sometimes forget that the Beatles were the first of a new era. They weren't rock stars; there was no such thing at the time. Instead, they thought of themselves simply as entertainers, as showmen. They had all been brought up in the music hall tradition, so when Brian told them to put on tights and do corny comedy routines, they did it unquestioningly. Even John didn't seem to mind doing that kind of thing . . . not at first, anyway.

Finally, there was a huge roar from the crowd as the Beatles took the stage, clad in their signature collarless suits, slamming straight into the opening notes of "I Want To Hold Your Hand." All I heard during their entire set was twenty minutes of screaming. There was no PA system, as such—just a couple of speakers on the sides of the stage—and the whole audience was on its feet the entire time. I could tell that the group had a lot of energy—they were moving around quite a bit, hyping up the audience—but you couldn't hear a single note they were playing. There was a slight hushing of the crowd when Paul sang "Till There Was You" but it never actually went completely quiet, and all it took was a little shake of his head toward someone and the audience was off again.

The Beatles were used to the hysteria by that point. They knew what to expect, and they knew there was no point in telling the audience to shut up . . . which meant they could have performed almost anything, although I do remember that the audience went especially wild when Ringo went into the opening drum roll to "She Loves You." They were pulling out all the stops to get the crowd up—John, in particular, was doing a lot of piss-taking. Several times I saw him whispering to Paul and George, and then he'd wave his hands about and act like a spastic—a cruel but very funny routine he did frequently in the studio. I guessed he was saying to them, "Watch this." Clearly they were taking great delight in the knowledge that they could manipulate the audience any way they wanted to.

It was a real thrill for me to watch them on that stage, to see the familiar equipment—their Vox amplifiers, Ringo's drum kit, Paul's Hofner violin-shaped bass—that I had so often seen up close in the studio. It was interesting to view them from a different perspective, and being there made me realize that they really could deliver. The stark raw energy coming off that stage was the same energy that was in their records—and I suddenly realized that that was what had propelled them to the top of the charts.

When I got home that night I reflected on the fact that only a year and half previously I had still been in school, desperate to get into the recording business. Now here I was, on a first-name basis with the four musicians who had appeared on that stage; I'd been a guest of their manager, sitting in a choice seat because I had actually played a small role in the making of their records. It was quite a sobering moment; so much had happened in that year and a half. As 1963 slipped into 1964, I pinched myself at my good fortune.

How much better than this can it possibly get? I asked myself.

If only I'd had a crystal ball.

· 6 ·

A Hard Day's Night

As the last vestiges of World War II—things like rationing and national conscription—began fading away in Britain, English youth found themselves disaffected. Despite economic prosperity, there was social upheaval amid a swirl of political scandal at Number Ten Downing Street (the so-called Profumo Affair that ultimately caused both the prime minister and his secretary of state to resign in shame). The postwar baby boom had put thousands of affluent but bored teenagers on the streets and in the record stores, looking for something or someone to rally behind. We were all potential rebels without a cause . . . and our entire generation were to find their cause in the music being made by four lads from Liverpool.

At the beginning of 1964, the Beatles were the most popular band in England. By year's end, they would become the greatest cultural phenomenon the world had ever witnessed. In February of that year, they conquered America with a series of groundbreaking performances on Ed Sullivan's popular television show and a whirlwind tour; by midsummer, they were internationally acclaimed movie stars.

All of us at EMI were thrilled to witness their meteoric rise, but it had special meaning to George, Norman, Richard, and me because we were the ones who had had the closest contact with them and the greatest involvement in their musical career. Chris Neal was long gone by then, but I couldn't help but think that he, too, must have been taking great pride in their progress. Interestingly, Chris's prowess as talent-spotter was proven a second time, about a year after he assisted on the Beatles' artist test, when he tried in vain to get EMI producer John Burgess (later George Martin's partner at AIR Studios) to sign a rough-and-ready band he had seen in a Richmond club. To Burgess's eventual embarrassment, the group of scruffs, who went by the name of the Rolling Stones, would go to Decca instead and would achieve a level of fame and fortune surpassed only by the Beatles themselves.

In late January, George Martin and Norman flew over to Paris to meet up with John, Paul, George, and Ringo (who were touring, as usual) and oversee the recording of the German-language versions of "She Loves You" and "I Want to Hold Your Hand." In their infinite wisdom, EMI's executives had decided that those singles could be hits in Germany only if they were sung in the native language. It was to be the first and last time that such a pointless exercise was undertaken. By then, Beatles records would have sold in phenomenal quantities even if they'd been sung in Swahili.

At that same session, a new song—"Can't Buy Me Love"—was recorded. It had the same level of excitement as previous Beatles singles and was quickly slated to be an A-side, but first there was a technical problem to be overcome, discovered when the tape was brought back and played at our studios. Perhaps because it had been spooled incorrectly, the tape had a ripple in it, resulting in the intermittent loss of treble on Ringo's hi-hat cymbal. There was tremendous time pressure to get the track mixed and delivered to the pressing plant, and due to touring commitments the Beatles themselves were unavailable, so George and Norman took it upon themselves to make a little artistic adjustment.

As I eagerly moved into the engineer's seat for the very first time, Norman headed down into the studio to overdub a hastily set-up hi-hat from the studio drum kit onto selected sections of the song while I recorded him, simultaneously doing a two-track to two-track dub. Thanks to Norman's considerable skills as a drummer, the repair was made quickly and seamlessly, and I doubt if even the Beatles themselves ever realized that their performance had been surreptitiously augmented. Certainly it didn't affect the popularity of the record, which shot straight to the top of the charts in both England and America the week it was released.

Other than that, the Beatles did little recording in the early part of 1964. Most of their time was spent shooting *A Hard Day's Night* on the streets of London, their antics filmed for posterity under the direction of Richard Lester. Richard Langham assisted on the handful of Beatles sessions that did occur, and in our canteen and pub conversations, he assured me that their new songs were every bit as good as those we had heard before, perhaps even better.

In the meantime, I was kept busy with a variety of other assignments. For one thing, I was fortunate enough to assist Ron Richards and engineer Pete

Bown on the artist test for the Hollies. During the test, I was very flattered when Ron asked me what I thought of the band, and I was most enthusiastic—I loved their vocal harmonies and their light, delicate sound, crafted around jangly acoustic guitars. Richard Langham later took some of the wind out of my sails when he explained that the EMI producers almost always asked the assistants for their opinions of the artist under test, because they were trying to gauge the reaction of young record-buyers, and we were the most youthful employees they could turn to. Emboldened, I also took it upon myself to pass judgment on their name, too—I thought it was weak-sounding, and told Ron so, rather bluntly. Happily, my unsolicited advice was not taken and the Hollies went on to enjoy great success under their original name. They were offered a contract with EMI as a result of that test, and Pete went on to engineer most of their hit records; unfortunately, I rarely had the opportunity to work with them again.

Afterward, I did get to know Graham Nash reasonably well, just from bumping into him in the corridor or at our local pub, the Abbey Tavern, during lunch breaks (he would also sometimes be invited to Beatles sessions if the two groups happened to be recording at the same time). We discovered that we shared the same hobby—photography—and we often eagerly discussed the relative merits of different cameras and lenses. It was always interesting to me that so many recording artists—Graham, Cliff Richard, various Shadows, even Ringo—took up photography as a hobby; once the royalty checks started coming in, it seemed that they were all getting Pentaxes.

In mid-April, a Beatles session was booked at very short notice; it hadn't even been on Bob Beckett's calendar at the beginning of the week. Because Richard had already been scheduled elsewhere that day, I was given the assignment. I was later to learn the reason for the immediacy: John—always in competition with Paul for the A-side of their singles—had only just written "A Hard Day's Night" the weekend before. With the shooting for the film nearly wrapped, there was an urgent need to get the title song recorded and in the can. It would turn out to be a memorable session in many regards, not least of which because it was marred by controversy, which was unusual in those early days.

Accompanied by Neil and Mal as usual, the band rolled into Studio Two quite early that morning. Following the usual cups of tea with rounds of toast and jam, everyone got down to business. I hadn't been on a session with the Beatles for some six months, and I was impressed by how much more professional they had gotten in that relatively short span. Not only was their playing tighter, but they were acting very much like seasoned veterans in the studio, knowing exactly what they were trying to accomplish and getting it done with a minimum of fuss, very much like a well-oiled machine.

In almost no time, they blasted through several complete performances of the song, with each take picking up more energy and more refinement. Lennon and McCartney were brimming with confidence, as usual, and I remember thinking that Ringo seemed especially "on" that morning, attacking his drums with a ferocity I hadn't seen or heard before. The weak link that particular day was George Harrison, who seemed even more ham-fisted than usual as he gamely plowed his way through one mediocre guitar solo after another. But that was okay—it wasn't unusual to allocate some time at the end of a session for parts to be fixed. Sometimes we would even need to slow the tape down in order to get all the notes right.

From the band's perspective, the session was going smoothly, but there was a storm raging behind the scenes that they were blissfully unaware of. Usually, the only people in the control room while the band played in the studio down below were George Martin, Norman Smith, and whoever was assigned to be the assistant engineer—myself, Richard Langham, or occasionally one of the other EMI staff. On this morning, however, we were joined by the film's director, Dick Lester, and his presence was definitely not appreciated.

Even with my limited experience, it appeared to me that Lester was acting inappropriately; he was constantly locking horns with George Martin and butting in where he didn't belong. For some reason, he seemed to think that because the song was being recorded for his film, that gave him the right to provide musical input and direction, and that was simply not the way things were done. George was being his usual polite self, but I could see that he was getting increasingly irritated. In particular, Dick kept insisting that something "blockbuster" was needed for the opening of the film—hence John and George's crashing guitar chord that heralds the first notes of the song. But that wasn't enough for Dick, who kept making one odd suggestion after another. ("Tell them I need it more *cinematic*," he shouted to George Martin at one point.)

Despite the controversy in the control room, that morning was tremendously productive. After the ninth take—which was at a significantly faster tempo than previous ones—Lennon announced that he was satisfied, and George Martin concurred. Dick Lester, not surprisingly, called for yet another run-through, but George Martin was smart enough to keep him well away from the talkback microphone and pretended not to hear his dissent. Instead, the band members were invited to put down their instruments and come upstairs for a listen.

After a short break, Lennon went back down to the studio and effortlessly double-tracked his lead vocal—it couldn't have taken him more than ten minutes to do so—and then he was joined by Paul and Ringo. Together, the three of them put the finishing touches on their parts, Paul double-tracking his vocals, John adding an acoustic rhythm guitar, Ringo playing cowbell and bongos—all recorded together, at the same time, on a single track.

Then we were ready to attack Harrison's solo. George must have been having a bad day—or maybe Lester's increasingly annoying presence was getting to him—because he was having real difficulty nailing it. After some discussion about having Paul play the part instead (McCartney was a fine guitarist himself, and seemed always ready to jump in and show up his younger bandmate), George Martin finally decided to instead employ the same "wound-up piano" technique he had done the year previous on the song "Misery." I was told to roll the tape at half speed while George went down into the studio and doubled the guitar solo on an out-of-tune upright piano. Both parts had to be played simultaneously because there was only one free track, and it was fascinating watching the two Georges—Harrison and Martin—working side by side in the studio, foreheads furrowed in concentration as they played the rhythmically complex solo in tight unison on their respective instruments.

Once that was completed, it seemed to all of us that the song was done, but Lester kept insisting that he needed a "dreamy" fadeout in order to segue into the movie's first scene. This time, George Harrison rose to the occasion, quickly overdubbing a catchy jangling phrase on his twelve-string Rickenbacker guitar to the slightly slowed-down tape. A week or so later Norman and George Martin mixed the song (unfortunately, I was not assigned to that session) and the unforgettable title track to the Beatles' first movie was complete.

It was around this time that Ringo fell ill with tonsillitis. I learned the news from George Martin, who had gotten a call from a worried Brian. It turned out that Brian's concern was not just about Ringo's health but also about the fact that the band was scheduled to embark on a world tour in a matter of days. George had recommended session drummer Jimmy Nicol as a temporary replacement, and he apparently passed muster, because the very next morning it was an absolute madhouse at EMI. News had leaked out to the press, and scores of reporters were blocking the front entrance to the car park. Fortunately, John Skinner spotted me and escorted me in.

"What's going on?" I asked him once I got safely inside.

"It's those Beatles causing trouble again," Skinner replied with a twinkle in his eye. "They've come in to rehearse with their new drummer and it looks like all of Fleet Street has turned out to mark the occasion!" Much as I would have loved to watch on the rehearsal, I had other duties that day and was unable to come up with an excuse to peek in.

A few weeks later, I assisted on a marathon eleven-hour session where nearly the entire *Hard Day's Night* album was mixed by Norman and George. As usual, none of the Beatles were present—they were literally on the other side of the world, touring in New Zealand with a recuperated Ringo. It was a welcome assignment, but it was frustrating. Even during a mix session, I was stuck in the machine room, and I could still only monitor one track at a time, so I had no idea how Norman was manipulating and balancing the sounds. Making matters worse, on this particular session, I couldn't even go into the control room to hear the mix playback, because they were working in Studio One, which was down the stairs and quite a distance away. I simply couldn't leave my post for that length of time.

In the dining room, I probably listened to the vocal track most often, or the bass and drum track, switching between them frequently. I was trying to figure out what Norman had done, because I hadn't been present for the recording of any of the songs except the title track—either Richard or one of the new button-pushers, Ken Scott or Tony Bridge, had done the assisting on the bulk of the album. Ken would go on to engineer quite a few tracks on *Magical Mystery Tour* and the *White Album*, in addition to working on many of George Harrison's solo albums. He later told me that, much to his amazement, during the very first Beatles session he assisted on, he was invited by the band to come down into the studio and join them on a handclap overdub. George Martin allowed it—even he couldn't countermand the wishes of the group at that stage of their career—but he made a point of taking Ken aside afterward and warning him, "Don't push it." George never liked anyone in that control room to overstep his bounds; he was very old school that way.

During that mix session, I wanted more than anything to watch what Norman and George were doing, to learn how they blended everything together, to understand the approach they were taking. But given the crazy EMI way of working, that was simply impossible. In the moments between having to roll tape, I remember wishing that there were some means of routing a signal from the mixing console into the machine room so I could at least hear what they were doing. That was actually a point of contention between the assistants and the brass at EMI for some time, but they felt there was no need to accommodate us, even though it was something that could have easily been accomplished with some simple rewiring. That's one reason why I lobbied to have the multitrack machine brought into the control room later on, when I was engineering the *Revolver* sessions.

I only managed to get into the control room at the very end of the session, when Norman started sequencing the mixes, putting the album in listening order. That was the first point at which I was able to hear what had actually been done that day, and I was amazed at the way John and Paul kept coming up with great, catchy songs. There was a definite maturity in their songwriting; the new material, which included tracks like "I'll Cry Instead" and "Things We Said Today," was more in-depth and meaningful. I was struck by how well John was singing, and I also really enjoyed hearing the superb job Norman had done recording the acoustic guitars. I loved the added dimension George Harrison's twelve-string playing brought to their sound, and I was impressed with many of his guitar solos. Given the experience we'd had doing the title track, I wondered how long it took to record them. Probably the only reason George Martin allowed a less-than-sparkling solo to make it to record was that it was taking Harrison too long to get it right, and they must have just given up, settling for what they had. Most of all I remember thinking how jealous my mates would be when I told them I'd gotten a sneak preview of another new Beatles album.

When the *Hard Day's Night* movie finally opened, none of us except George Martin were invited to the premiere; I don't even think Norman got to go. I did see it later, at a local cinema with some of my mates. The music sounded quite good in the theater—they had big speakers there, and the projectionist was playing the soundtrack quite loudly—but I couldn't help but notice that some of the fade-ups were a little bit late and that some of the cues got missed altogether. Presumably the movie soundtrack had been assembled by United Artists' own audio engineers. So far as I knew, the work hadn't been done by EMI personnel at Abbey Road.

All in all, I enjoyed *A Hard Day's Night*. To me, it was a definite improvement over previous rock 'n' roll movies, potboilers like Cliff Richard and the Shadows' *Summer Holiday*. Some of the character actors were favorites of mine from their previous work—Victor Spinetti, who played the TV director, and Wilfrid Brambell, who played Paul's grandfather. The Beatles themselves were portrayed as four stereotypes in the movie, and I remember sitting there thinking to myself, "They're not really like that"—though I was probably the only one in the theater who knew that. They seemed to be playing their roles very much tongue in cheek, especially Lennon. I was quite surprised at Ringo's charismatic on-screen persona, especially in the "This Boy" scene. Up until then, I just thought of him as the drummer in the band; now I could see he had a distinct personality, that he brought something of his own to the equation. The road manager parts were completely wrong, though—the two actors were playing the fool. Neil and Mal didn't relate to the group that way; Neil didn't tell them what to do, ever, and Mal may have had a soft side, but he certainly wasn't soft in the head.

Still, it was all good fun, and it was great to see the Beatles branching out into different areas, taking on new challenges successfully, even while maintaining their lofty perch at the top of the international charts.

In the summer of 1964, I received my first promotion, to lacquer cutting. Instead of being down in the control room and studio with the artists and producers, I was now stuck in a small room upstairs, making one-off acetates so that people could listen to their day's work at home. (This was, of course, long before the days of audiocassettes or recordable CDs.) Even though the new title came with a modest raise in pay, I actually made less money than I had as an assistant because of the loss of overtime; EMI didn't keep lacquer cutters or mastering engineers on after hours. As a result, if artists were doing an evening session and wanted to listen to their work at home, they would have to wait until the next morning to get a disk. That's why it was such a big deal later on when the four Beatles got tape recorders of their own—they could take tapes home with them right away, instead of having to wait.

Fortunately, whenever Bob Beckett got stuck for an assistant on a session—if the session was booked at the last minute, or was on a weekend, for example—he would bring down one of the cutting engineers to fill in. We always jumped at the opportunity. From our perspective, it was not only a means of making up some of the lost pay, it was also a good way to keep your hand in and stay somewhat involved with the rather more glamorous work being done downstairs.

Despite the relative isolation, I didn't mind the job, really, because it gave me privacy and time to tinker with sounds in my never-ending quest to come up with things that had never been heard before. It was during one of those experiments that I first discovered phasing; I would often cut a lacquer and then play it back simultaneously with the tape so I could compare the two, but I wondered what it might sound like if I combined the two signals. Because there was no means for electronically locking the two devices together, they would drift in and out of sync, which I could control further still if I slightly adjusted the strobe varispeed on the turntable. The sound of the resultant huge, sweeping *swooosh* was incredible.

We used to get up to all sorts of pranks upstairs, out of the direct line of fire. In our idle moments, we'd have competitions to see how many songs we could cut concentrically (side by side) on a vinyl record. To fit them all into the same space, we'd have to get down to really small grooves. It was quite funny because when you then played the record, you'd hear a different song each time, depending on where you put the needle down. There was a horse-racing game mastered like that—you'd put bets on and you never knew who the winner would be. Years later the Monty Python comedy group would make a record with the same technique: their *Matching Tie And Handkerchief* album had the distinction of being "the world's first three-sided record." You never knew which B-side you'd hear on each playing.

We'd also do silly, juvenile things like make swarf bombs. Swarf was the excess vinyl material that was suctioned off as you were cutting a disc, and it was highly inflammable. We'd take the metal rings from the tape spools, stack them up to make a container, and stuff it full of swarf. Then we'd put a lid on it, stick a fuse in, and light it. There was actually a central suction machine down in the basement that used to suck up the swarf from the lathes in all the mastering rooms at the point where the needle cut the vinyl. We didn't realize it at the time, but storing all that material beneath where we were all working had to have been extremely hazardous!

Because I was cloistered away upstairs, Richard Langham had gotten in the habit of calling me on the intercom pretending to be someone else—Norman, most often, or sometimes George Martin; he imitated both their voices well. One time his practical joking nearly backfired badly on me. George Martin was on the phone asking me if I could assist on an upcoming Judy Garland session, and since the request seemed so outrageous, I assumed it was actually Richard calling.

"Bugger off, Langham!" I shouted into the phone, chortling with glee at the thought that I'd caught him out. But it really was George, and he explained that he really wanted me to do the session because he knew that Judy and her entourage would want playback lacquers immediately afterward. I could feel my face turning crimson red as I apologized profusely.

"That's okay, Geoff," he said soothingly. "I already know the kinds of things Richard gets up to. But," he added with more than a trace of sarcasm, "I don't think he does my voice particularly well . . . so you might want to get the earwax out before you come down here." *Serves me right*, I thought. *I'll get that bloody Langham if it's the last thing I do.*

I was thrilled to get a chance to meet Miss Garland, who was one of my idols. Ever since her first appearance at the London Palladium back in 1951, she'd been a star in England, and *The Wizard of Oz* was one of my favorite films. She'd lived in London on and off for many years, often booking sessions at Abbey Road when she was in town, though I'd never been lucky enough to cross paths with her before. On this particular August evening, she was in Studio Two, recording "The Land Of Promises," by Lionel Bart. Other than the fact that there was a long discussion about what key to perform the song in, I don't remember much about the recording itself—I was stuck in that accursed machine room again. After the session finished, Miss Garland's entourage were going to the local pub to celebrate, but she had decided not to join them. Instead, to my utter astonishment, Miss Garland accompanied me down the corridor and sat there while I was cutting playback lacquers of the work we'd just completed, just the two of us in this tiny room.

I was incredibly nervous, of course, but she seemed to be a really nice person, and she went out of her way to put me at ease, asking me lots of questions about my background and what my job duties entailed. At one point, she even asked me what I thought of the song she had just recorded. She was smoking like a chimney the whole time, and I was, too—I had only recently taken up the habit, more out of boredom than anything.

We were there for only an hour or so, and she made polite conversation the entire time. I had tons of questions I wanted to ask her, but I was too shy to get the words out. Instead, I simply blushed furiously and struggled to make small talk with the fabulous Miss Garland while I tried to concentrate on getting the work done. All too soon her entourage reappeared and she was whisked away. I never saw her again.

The Beatles made only sporadic appearances in the studio during the summer of 1964, but at the end of September, the mysterious "Dakotas" name began appearing with greater frequency on the booking schedule. Because they were touring solely in the UK at that point, they were able to start work in between local concert dates on what was to eventually become the

Beatles For Sale album. By that point, Richard Langham had left Abbey Road, relocating to Germany. In his place, a number of new young assistants had been hired, including Mike Stone and Ron Pender. In order to bring them up through the ranks as quickly as possible, they got the plum assignments to work with George and Norman on most of those sessions.

However, there was one very special Beatles session booked that fall, unusually, on a Sunday afternoon, and because all of the assistant engineers were off that day, it fell into my lap. I was ecstatic. It meant temporary liberation for me—out of the lacquer cutting room and back in the studio with the musicians, where all of the action was. Bob Beckett had told me the previous Monday that I'd be on that session, and I was looking forward to it all week; I was also a bit nervous about it, though not for any specific reason I can recall. Perhaps I just thought that my button-pushing chops might have gotten a bit rusty. As it turned out, I had no need to worry. Everyone was on the top of his game that day. In fact, this was to prove to be the one of the most productive Beatles recording sessions ever.

Luckily, there were no other artists booked in anywhere at the Abbey Road complex on that bright, sunny October afternoon, which gave the Beatles the freedom to leave the confines of the studio and walk the corridors for the first time since the "She Loves You" riots. There weren't even any staff around, other than a couple of maintenance engineers on call. As a result, there was a much more relaxed atmosphere than on any other Beatles session I'd ever attended . . . and that set the vibe for the great music that would be recorded that day with a remarkable economy of effort.

Because public transport was iffy on Sundays and the London traffic relatively light, Norman had decided to drive in, and he offered to give me a lift. The session was not due to begin until mid-afternoon—the Beatles were already beginning to book later and later starting times—so we arrived at lunchtime. There were already a couple of maintenance engineers in the studio setting up microphones, and Neil was there as well, fumbling with Ringo's drum hardware. This was a task that usually fell to Mal, but for some reason he wasn't there that day—they were in the middle of a UK tour, and perhaps he was dealing with something on the road for them.

Not long afterward, the four Beatles turned up. Everyone was in a jovial mood, chatting away, and I got big hellos from them all. I gathered that the tour was going extremely well; clearly they were starting to really enjoy the fame and fortune that all their hard work had brought them. There didn't even seem to be any sense of resentment that they were giving up their one off day—and a Sunday, no less—to enter the confined space of a recording studio and work. I guess recording didn't seem like work to them in those days. They obviously still liked one another's company very much and it was all just a good laugh. Nobody seemed especially tired, either. Although they'd been doing a lot of touring, they'd had the night before off, so everyone was well rested and full of energy.

As the easy banter continued—no one seemed to be in a hurry to start the session—I remember feeling very privileged to be there, to be part of such a select group. Eventually George Martin arrived and asked everyone to convene in the control room. The first order of business was to do some repair work on a new song they'd recorded just the week before, called "Eight Days A Week." As everyone settled in chairs and gathered around the console, I threaded up Norman's rough mix and the playback commenced.

I loved the song instantly. To my mind, it was an obvious single, with "hit" written all over it. As we listened intently, everyone's head was nodding in time, Ringo exuberantly tapping out the beat on his knees. As the last note died out, we all excitedly agreed that the high-energy performance captured on tape was a definite "keeper." The only problems were with the ragged beginning and overly abrupt ending, and an intense discussion ensued about how to best fix them. Paul announced that he and John had come up with an idea for an alternate beginning, doing an a cappella (unaccompanied) vocal, and George Martin, who had learned by now never to dismiss any of their ideas out of hand, said, "Fine, let's have a go." With that, they trundled off down to the studio and I was once again banished to the machine room.

Because the new intro and "outro" ending were to be spliced into a take recorded the week before, Norman had to spend some time matching sounds so that the edits would be undetectable. That was easy for Norman because he had a fixed mic setup; he always put the drums and amplifiers in the same place, and he nearly always used the same microphones and equalization. The mic positioning was mapped out in writing beforehand for the technical guys, but if things got moved during the course of the session, it didn't occur to anyone in those days to make notes—it was all pretty much down to memory. Considering all that, it's pretty amazing how well the sounds ended up matching, even though John was playing acoustic guitar and might well have moved around from take to take. Norman simply had a formula, set way of doing things—all of which changed when I later took over as engineer and experimentation became the key. It would have been a lot more work for me to match sounds for an edit piece.

Once Norman was satisfied that the sound was right, Paul, John, and George Harrison gathered around a single mic and began singing "ooos" in unison. It was interesting, but was quickly deemed too weak of a beginning for a song that was so dynamic. Rather than waste more time, George Martin decided to move things along by having the Beatles work on the outro instead. The idea they had worked out for that part was much more powerful, with Lennon and Harrison stabbing out ringing chords on their guitars, accompanied by Paul tapping out a staccato bass line on his trusty Hofner.

The problem of what to do about the ragged intro still remained, however, and as they were pondering what to do about it, Norman came up with the brilliant suggestion of simply fading in the song, instead of having everything come crashing in at full volume. Innovative for its time, this also aided in the record's success because it made it easy for radio disk jockeys to cross-fade the start of "Eight Days A Week" with another single—if they wanted to, they could even talk over the intro and plug their shows.

In all, only an hour or so was spent on those edit pieces, including the time devoted to matching sounds, and, with that, another Beatles hit was completed. Everyone's attention then turned to the first full song of the day, a cover medley of "Kansas City" and "Hey-Hey-Hey-Hey." From the way Paul was singing—nearly ripping his vocal cords apart—I was surprised that they had decided to do this song first, but after years of performing onstage, his voice was strong and could take the abuse. Notably, all the other Beatles—even Ringo, who hardly ever sang backing vocals—joined in on the chorus, doing the "hey hey hey" answering part. This medley was an established part of their live show at that point, and they really cut loose on it, playing with a confidence and a sheer, innocent joy that was positively infectious. I knew from that minute onward that it was going to be a great session. It was simply incredible to hear that much energy coming from the group so early in the day; they hadn't even had time to properly warm up. They were locked in, right from the start, and that track is the definitive proof of what a great live band the Beatles were when they were in their prime.

That session also marked the first time I started becoming a bit envious of Norman's role. In the idle moments between takes, I found myself imagining what I might do differently if I were the Beatles' full-time engineer, working in the studio with them all the time.

I also felt that a real bond began to develop between Paul and me that afternoon, and it had a lot to do with that track. Shortly after finishing the song, Paul popped into the machine room to get a little break, away from the bustle of the studio and control room.

"All right, Geoff?" he asked, sticking his head around the door.

"Yes, fine," I answered eagerly. "You know," I blurted out, hoping that I wasn't crossing a line, "that vocal was incredible—you sang that even better than Little Richard."

Paul laughed and seemed pleased. "Well, it's very nice of you to say so," he replied modestly. " 'Kansas City' is one of my all-time favorite records, actually."

It turned out we were both huge Little Richard fans, and we ended up having quite a long chat, comparing notes on different songs. He was telling me what a thrill it had been to actually meet Little Richard on tour, how outrageous he was both onstage and in real life.

Looking back, I think it was that ten-minute conversation that began the lifelong bond between us. At heart, we were both fans, and he understood that, even though he was a world-famous musician and I was just one of the backroom boys. We were only a few years apart in age, too, which helped. He could relate to me as a peer, as someone who accepted him for who he really was, not for his celebrity or fame.

The work continued at the same efficient clip. Things were moving along briskly, though we never felt hurried or under pressure. John took the vocal spotlight for their next number, a cover of an obscure song called "Mr. Moonlight." His searing vocal introduction sent shivers down my spine, even though it took him several tries to nail it.

The stumbling block again was Harrison's guitar solo—not the notes he was playing, but the odd, sped-up tremolo sound he was using, in faithful imitation of the Dr. Feelgood version that had been a minor hit a couple of years previously. Lennon thought the unconventional sound was terrific— and, personally, so did I—but George Martin insisted that it was simply too weird. After some discussion, it was decided to overdub a cheesy organ solo instead. Even though I loathed the sound, I was most impressed to see Paul playing it—up until that point, I'd had no idea that he could even play keyboards.

During one of the playbacks, I was monitoring the drum and bass track in the machine room and I heard that there was a problem with the top end. I checked the tape and saw that it looked a bit odd, so I immediately got on the intercom and said to Norman, "You need to listen to this. I think there's a problem with the tape."

It turned out that there was a manufacturing flaw in the tape, and it was affecting only the drums and bass because they were on an outside track. A white coat was duly summoned to have a look and quickly verified my discovery. Even though it interrupted the smooth flow of the session, I was viewed as a bit of a hero for that.

As the band began rehearsing their next song in the studio with George Martin, I used the opportunity to sit in the control room and relax for a few minutes. I was making small talk with Norman about something or other when all of a sudden I heard this loud, buzzing sound issue forth from the speakers.

"What the bloody hell was that?" I asked him, alarmed. My first thought was that a cable had gone bad, or that a piece of equipment had failed.

Norman chuckled. "Have a look," he said to me.

I pressed my nose up against the control room glass and was astonished to see John Lennon kneeling before his amplifier, guitar in hand.

We knew that if you brought a guitar too close to an amplifier, it would squeal, but John was using it in a controlled way for the first time. Norman later explained to me that they had discovered that sound purely by accident at a previous session, the night they recorded "Eight Days A Week." It was just serendipity: during a break, John had leaned his guitar against his amp, but had neglected to turn down the volume of the pickup. Just at that moment, for no particular reason, Paul had plucked a low "A" on his bass and, from across the room, the sound waves set John's guitar feeding back. They loved the resultant howling, so much so that Lennon had apparently been fooling around with the effect ever since. And with his new song, entitled "I Feel Fine," he was determined to immortalize the sound on record . . . years before Jimi Hendrix ever started doing it.

It was yet another indication to me that the Beatles were looking to stretch the boundaries, to go beyond the sound of just two guitars, bass, and drums. That was the brave new world I so much wanted to be a part of.

They did several takes of "I Feel Fine" that day, and every one of them had that feedback intro. I thought it was a great song, too—every bit as strong as "Eight Days A Week." Sitting in that cramped machine room, I marveled that they were recording two potential hit songs in a single afternoon. But it was the intro to "I Feel Fine" that was so exciting, so different— to me, that's what really sold the song. After all, I had gotten into recording because I was in search of unique sounds, and the Beatles had discovered this one on their own.

For most of that day, they played quite loudly, too; in fact, the Beatles often played considerably louder than other rock bands of the era. Although

their equipment was primitive by today's standards, it sounded quite forceful in the studio, and that became an integral part of their driving beat.
Lennon in particular was always turning his volume up, and then Harrison
would try to match him. That would lead to overloading problems in the
mics positioned in front of the amps (usually sensitive and expensive Neumann U 47s), at which point George Martin or Norman would tell them
both to turn down.

Lennon was also more prone to breaking strings than Harrison—he attacked his guitar harder, with less finesse—and I remember that happening
several times during the recording of "I Feel Fine," which was quite an aggressive, up-tempo song. When that would happen, he would call out, "Mal!
Mal!" Mal was usually the one who would change the guitar strings, although on this day he wasn't there, so the task fell to Neil instead. Neil was
physically a lot smaller than his fellow roadie, so everyone had a good laugh
when he walked over to take care of the problem and Lennon slowly looked
him up and down, finally exclaiming with perfect comic timing, "Cor,
you've shrunk in the wash, Mal!"

It was early evening before the song was completed, and everyone was
feeling fine indeed by that point . . . but everyone was also dying for a cup of
tea. The problem was that, being a Sunday, the canteen was locked and there
was no milk to be found anywhere. EMI, in their wisdom, didn't have the
courtesy to leave some out, even though they knew their biggest-selling
artists were going to be in the studio that weekend. Because Neil was already
on a mission to round up some fish and chips for everyone, George Martin
asked his secretary, Judy, to go out and try to find some milk, and he told me
to accompany her.

Judy and I started heading toward the Abbey Tavern because we knew the
owner and thought he might be able to rustle up a bottle for us, but as we
were walking down the street an elderly gentleman happened to step out of
his house. He said hello, we struck up a conversation, and when we mentioned what we were in search of, he was kind enough to invite us in and give
us a pint of milk to take back—even though we hadn't said a word about the
Beatles, just the fact that we were in the recording studio doing a session.

By the time we got back, the group were already hard at work on their
next song—Paul's gentle, acoustic-based "I'll Follow The Sun." It couldn't
have provided a greater contrast to everything else we had recorded that day,
and it underscored for me the incredible diversity of Lennon and McCartney's songwriting abilities. At first, they couldn't think of anything for Ringo
to do—he played drums on a run-through, but it sounded all wrong, too

aggressive and distracting; Paul wanted something more subtle. After a good deal of discussion, Paul came up with the idea of having Ringo just slap his legs in time, and that worked well. Enthralled, I watched Norman carefully position a mic between Ringo's knees; then, back in the control room, he cranked up the EQ to add some extra depth to the sound.

I loved the soft charm of "I'll Follow The Sun," and especially enjoyed the low harmony line George Martin had contrived for Lennon to sing in perfect complement to McCartney's lead vocal. But I found Harrison's simpleminded eight-note solo—not even a solo, really just the melody line—downright embarrassing. He wasn't even supposed to play that solo: for the first few takes, John did it, on acoustic guitar. Despite the overall good vibe of the day, George Harrison seemed annoyed, perhaps because he hadn't been given much to do. At one point he marched into the control room and complained loudly, "You know, I'd like to do the solo on this one. I am supposed to be the lead guitarist in this band, after all."

I thought it was a pompous thing to say, but George Martin reluctantly gave his assent, pretty much just to get the pouting guitarist out of his hair. Paul and John went along with it good-naturedly, even though nobody was satisfied with the result—you can almost hear Harrison thinking about what note to play next. He wasn't happy either, and he wanted to make another attempt at it, but a weary and slightly annoyed George Martin finally put his foot down, saying, "No, we have to move on."

Even as a seventeen-year-old sitting in the machine room who couldn't play a lick of guitar myself, I felt that George Harrison could have come up with something better than that. He seemed to be distracted, like he had something else on his mind, and I couldn't help but think that he must have been frustrated with the level of his playing that afternoon.

After their tea break—interrupted briefly by a short visit from an annoyingly ebullient Dick James—the session seemed to start coasting downhill. They had gotten all the hard work behind them and now had to knock off three more songs before it got too late, because they were due up in Scotland the next day to resume touring. In essence, the rest of the session was a live performance, very much like their debut album. First, a rejuvenated George Harrison redeemed himself with an excellent rendition of "Everybody's Trying To Be My Baby." Not only did he sing it with enthusiasm, but he played guitar confidently and well. Even his solo, performed live, was flawless.

Then with time running short, Paul moved over to the piano, where he pounded out a rollicking version of Chuck Berry's "Rock And Roll Music." The entire song, including John's scorching vocal, was performed live, with George Harrison playing Paul's Hofner bass. The only overdub was John's vocal double-track, which he reeled off in just a few minutes—he was always really good at that.

There was still one more song to be recorded—a cover of Buddy Holly's "Words Of Love," another favorite of mine. They were clearly flagging by the time they got around to it, yet John, Paul, and George sang beautiful three-part harmony, gathered around a single mic. Their vocals really imbued the track with warmth and love. It was a fitting tribute to one of the group's musical idols and the perfect way to end the evening, just short of midnight.

This had been a magical day indeed. In the space of just nine hours, we had recorded seven complete songs and done edit pieces for another, including two that were destined to become chart-topping hit singles, and there was no question of the satisfaction and goodwill emanating from all four Beatles as they headed up to the control room to say their good-byes. Ringo was first through the doorway. He clasped my hand warmly and then, tongue in cheek, thanked me for not erasing him from any of the tracks. Harrison, still glowing from his performance on "Everybody's Trying To Be My Baby," gave me a slap on the back, humming the chorus as he did so. Because the band were off to rejoin their tour in Edinburgh in the morning— a topic of conversation and a bit of a running joke all day—John couldn't resist bidding a good night in his finest Scottish accent to "wee laddie Georgie MacMartin, Norman MacSmith, and Geoffrey MacEmerick."

Paul was the last to leave. "It was nice chatting with you, Geoff—see you soon," he said amiably, giving me a thumbs-up over his shoulder as he headed out into the night.

And with that, the session was over.

The Beatles were back at EMI about a week later, mixing the tracks we'd recorded that day—one of the rare times they attended a mix session up to that point. Though I wasn't assigned to assist on the session, Paul made a point of coming into the lacquer cutting room during a break to chat with me, cup of tea in hand. As he pushed the door open, I could hear him singing "a-wop-bop-a-loo-lop," to which I dutifully answered, "a-wop-bam-boom!"

I asked him how the mixes were going, and he said fine. We then chatted for a while about what a great session it had been the previous Sunday. From that point on, Paul would pop up to my room often for lunchtime chats, always talking about some new record he'd heard or some new trick they'd come up with in the studio.

By this point, I had spent enough time with the band, and with George Martin and Norman Smith, to start to gain a real insight into what they were like as individuals. Of course, people change, and during the coming years, each of them would evolve (some, like Lennon, more radically than others), but I felt that I had a basic grasp on each of the six personalities, and on the ways they interacted with one another.

George Martin had a dry wit and a great sense of humor. Always well dressed and well mannered, he clearly enjoyed being an authoritarian figure, playing the schoolmaster to the four Beatles—who equally enjoyed their roles as prankish schoolboys. He was also very self-assured and confident. He projected the image of someone who always seemed to know exactly what he wanted. For all our differences in upbringing, training, and attitude, he and I always seemed to relate well, from the very earliest days. I suppose he initially took a liking to me because I was quiet and kept my thoughts to myself. I knew that from his point of view, there was nothing worse than having someone in the control room who was talkative and opinionated. Even after I was promoted to balance engineer, there wasn't ever a whole lot of conversation between George and me. As time went on, we got to the point where it was unnecessary—we could almost read each other's mind. But we always had a good laugh, even if the session itself wasn't going all that smoothly. As the months passed, I could sense George getting increasingly comfortable with me; despite the difference in our age and stature, he would even bum cigarettes off me from time to time.

George and Norman made for a very good working team because George had sophistication and formal training (as a classical oboist), while Norman had the musical vocabulary to relate to modern bands. George simply didn't know the vernacular of pop music. Norman might suggest to George, "Tell them to accent the backbeat," and George would dutifully relate the message. He relied on Norman for that kind of input.

From the first time we met, I found Paul to be a warm, genuine person. He didn't have airs, but he knew what he wanted, and, more important, he knew how to get his way through diplomacy and not bluster. In that way, he really did seem to be the leader of the Beatles, and not John, as conventional wisdom had it. Paul always seemed to be the one to egg the others on to play or sing better, and if George Martin got on the talkback and told them to do yet another take, it was most likely Paul who would buck the others up, saying, "Come on, let's give it our all."

It was apparent to me that Paul was the "pure" musician in the Beatles—he played so many different instruments well, and whenever he wasn't playing music, he was talking about it. As a result, the relationship he had with Norman Smith was especially strong. Norman always had a good sense of what Paul was trying to achieve musically, and I'm sure Paul realized at an early stage that his closest link to the control room was with Norman and not George.

John unquestionably was the most complex of the four. The other three Beatles had personalities that were more stable and consistent, even though they may not have shared Lennon's intellectual curiosity. When John was in a good mood—which was a lot of the time—he could be sweet, charming, caring, and incredibly funny. But he was moody, and if you caught him at a bad moment, he could be biting and nasty: you could see the anger written all over his face. The problem was that you never knew exactly which John you'd encounter at any given moment, because his mood could change quite suddenly. Fortunately, it could change back just as quickly, so if you knew he was grumpy, the best course of action was to stay out of his way for a while, until he became approachable again.

In time, I began to realize that John's mood changes seemed to always be preceded by long moments of silence. He'd get a dreamy, far-off look in his eyes and you'd think that he was pondering, ruminating. In fact, that look was probably due more to his poor eyesight then anything else. Although he wore glasses in the recording studio, they didn't seem to help much. He was often rubbing his eyes because they were tired, and he frequently had a glazed expression on his face, even before he got into drugs. As a result, there was always a funny look in his eyes, as if he were somewhere else. Perhaps everything was simply out of focus for him! Years later, I heard a story of how, as teenagers, Paul and John were walking home together late one winter night. All of a sudden, John stopped dead in his tracks outside someone's house, staring in amazement at what he was convinced was a group of people playing cards out on their lawn . . . despite the freezing temperature. Because of his bad eyesight, he couldn't tell that it was actually a nativity scene.

But underneath all the bluff and bluster, John struck me as a very insecure person. I'm not sure what he had to be insecure about, unless it was the songwriting competition he was always engaged in with Paul. Perhaps deep down he thought that Paul was more talented than he was. I also always felt that, in many ways, John was quite naive. Everything he did had an activist bent—things had to be done because they were in support of something, or against something. He tended to view the world in black and white, not shades of gray. You could never really have a relaxed, calm conversation with John over a cup of tea like you could with Paul. Everything always ended up with agitation of some kind; he was very confrontational. But he was very real, too. Even if he was being nasty, you could see that he genuinely enjoyed talking with people.

One of my few regrets is that during the entire time I worked with the Beatles, I didn't know anything about John's broken family background and all the trauma he went through as a child. I don't think even George Martin knew about it in those days. It's a shame, because if I had known, I would have understood John a bit better and perhaps he and I would have been closer.

John and Paul related to each other as peers. Theirs was not a big brother/little brother relationship (as seemed to exist between John and George), despite the fact that Lennon was a year and a half older than McCartney. They clearly had the closest friendship within the Beatles, at least at first, but they couldn't have been two more different people. Paul was meticulous and organized: he always carried a notebook around with him, in which he methodically wrote down lyrics and chord changes in his neat handwriting. In contrast, John seemed to live in chaos: he was constantly searching for scraps of paper that he'd hurriedly scribbled ideas on. Paul was a natural communicator; John couldn't articulate his ideas well. Paul was the diplomat; John was the agitator. Paul was soft-spoken and almost unfailingly polite; John could be a right loudmouth and quite rude. Paul was willing to put in long hours to get a part right; John was impatient, always ready to move on to the next thing. Paul usually knew exactly what he wanted and would often take offense at criticism; John was much more thick-skinned and was open to hearing what others had to say. In fact, unless he felt especially strongly about something, he was usually amenable to change.

There were so many differences between them, I often wondered what it was that made them such great friends, unless it was simply that opposites attract. It wasn't until years later that I learned more about their childhood and the common bond they shared of losing their mothers at an early age. Paul would, however, get annoyed whenever John would present himself as coming from a rough Teddy-boy working-class background, because he knew that was untrue. He knew that John had been brought up by his aunt

Mimi in a much more comfortable middle-class existence than either Paul or the other two Beatles had enjoyed.

During playbacks, John and Paul would often huddle together and discuss whether a take was good enough; they'd talk about what they were hearing and what they wanted to fix or do differently. John wasn't casual about making records, not in the early years, anyway. Still, it was Paul who was always striving to get things the best that they could possibly be. John certainly didn't have that attitude, but, to his credit, he was usually willing to try Paul's ideas, and he did want things to be right—he just wasn't necessarily happy about spending long hours in pursuit of perfection. He might well grumble, "We've done it to death," but if Paul was insistent, they'd do another take; inevitably, John would be the one to give in.

Many people's view of the Lennon/McCartney collaboration is a simplistic one: that Lennon was the rough and ready rocker, while McCartney was the soft sentimentalist. While that might have been partially true, their relationship went a lot deeper than that. Perhaps the most important role each played for the other was that of unbiased critic. John was pretty much the only person in the world who could turn to Paul and say, "That song is shit"—and Paul would take it. Conversely, Paul was the only person who could look John in the eye and say, "You've gone too far." They were usually diplomatic with each other—Paul might say to John, "Oh, I think you can do better than that," or something similar—but that's what it came down to. Certainly George Martin couldn't get away with that. If he dared try, they would bite his head off. There was never any doubt in my mind that Paul and John viewed George Martin as a helpmate, not as their equal.

George Harrison was always kind of a mystery to me. Although he was kind and generous with many of my EMI colleagues throughout the years, he and I just didn't have good chemistry together. He struck me as a dour, humorless man who complained a lot, and he always seemed suspicious of everyone outside of the Beatles' inner circle. He didn't interact or converse with me very much, even when we were working on one of his songs. He didn't know anything about technicalities, either—he'd just focus on the musical aspects, and discuss them with the others, or with George Martin. He might say to me, "Can you change the guitar sound a bit, Geoff?" but it wouldn't go much further than that.

George often seemed preoccupied, like he had something on his mind other than being the Beatles' lead guitarist. Maybe at a certain point he simply didn't want to be in the band anymore—certainly it appeared that he felt trapped by his fame and celebrity. He generally wouldn't join in on the joking and clowning around that would occur between takes—that was mostly between John and Paul, sometimes with Ringo involved. George was more of a loner; he was the outsider in a way. As the "bottom tier" Beatles, he and Ringo seemed to have developed a strong friendship, and I often saw him huddled with Lennon, working out guitar parts, but I rarely noticed much positive interaction between George and Paul. Paul sometimes actually seemed a bit embarrassed by Harrison's musical limitations; certainly there were many instances of eye-rolling when poor George was wrestling unsuccessfully with a solo or lead part. I imagine in those circumstances that Paul was frustrated, probably thinking that he could have mastered the part faster and played it better.

To be fair, Harrison faced an uphill battle against the massive talents of Lennon and McCartney. For one thing, he was the youngest band member and was therefore frequently treated like a kid brother, not to be taken seriously. For another, he didn't have a songwriting partner to bounce ideas off of. I always felt that at a relatively early point, Harrison simply realized that he was never going to be a Lennon or a McCartney, which might explain why he turned to Indian music—it was his own outlet, something completely separate from the others. On occasion, Lennon would lend him a hand with a lyric or chord change, but then John would quickly become distracted or bored. I never saw Paul extend himself to George that way. His attitude toward his younger bandmate seemed to be, "You shouldn't be asking me for help; you should be doing it yourself." Perhaps it was the creative and personal tension between the two that led Harrison to keep me at arm's length, because it was obvious that I had a close relationship with Paul.

Probably the thing I liked least about George Harrison was that he always seemed to be making snide remarks—not necessarily about me personally, but about the world in general. Ringo did not have that problem. In fact, he seemed to have little to say about anything; to describe him as quiet would be an understatement. In all the years we worked together, I honestly don't remember having one memorable conversation with Ringo. He was simply not outgoing, and neither was I, so we never really got to know each other. Ringo wasn't especially moody like John was, but there were days when you could tell he was pissed off about something. He could be quick-witted and charming, but he also had a very sarcastic sense of humor: you never really knew if he was being funny or if he meant what he was saying. I always felt he used sarcasm as a defense mechanism to cover his insecurity, like the way some people have a nervous laugh. But Ringo, like George Harrison, always seemed to have his guard up, and so there was a personal wall between us that I could never quite broach.

Perhaps Ringo's reticence was caused by his lack of education, due to the long periods of schooling he had missed because of the poor health he had suffered as a youngster. Perhaps he was a bit intimidated by the other three Beatles, who seemed far more worldly than him, and by the EMI staff. Lennon, for example, was always talking about current events or programmes he'd seen on TV, and Paul would, too, but Ringo never did: he was just as quiet as a mouse. Neil and Mal would frequently bring a selection of newspapers to sessions, mostly the tabloids. John always had his head buried in one, or in a book, and Paul and George would read them occasionally, too, but Ringo's taste ran more to comic books like *The Beano*.

But it was because Ringo said so little that when he spoke up and offered a musical opinion, it carried a bit more weight because the others knew that he really meant it, that it wasn't just a passing remark. If he did make any kind of comment during a session, it would most often be about the drum sounds, which he knew were critical. Funnily enough, he would often go into a near panic whenever he had to do a drum fill. You can almost hear him freezing, trying to decide what to do as he's doing it. Eventually that lack of confidence became part of his style, but there's another explanation as to why his fills were so unusual. They're not fast—in fact, he himself has likened them to the sound of someone falling down the stairs—and they're often a little laid-back, a little behind the beat. That's not because he wasn't a good timekeeper—he was—but because, unlike many of the rock drummers who came after him, he simply was not a big man physically. I would constantly be saying to Ringo, "Can you hit the snare a little harder? Can you stomp on the bass drum pedal harder?" and he would reply, "If I hit them any harder, I'm going to break the skins," but it did make a huge difference to the sound, and he did hit those drums hard. In fact, after each session that Ringo played on, there would be a big pile of wood chips around the drum kit from all the drumsticks he'd demolished. But because he was exerting so much effort, it took a certain amount of time for his arms to move up and down, hence the laid-back feel of his fills. He really did focus on making each drum hit as forceful as possible—he just didn't have the physical strength to do it quickly, as, for example, a John Bonham might.

On occasion, John and Paul could be quite rude to Ringo when he was having trouble with his fills, but once the song was recorded and done with, they would be fine with him again. Paul did coach Ringo a lot on the parts he wanted played; in fact, Paul frequently pottered around on the drums himself during breaks. All four Beatles often picked up one another's instrument, and it wasn't surprising to see even John or George Harrison fooling around behind the drums on occasion, but Paul was the only one who took it seriously.

Ringo was also very uptight and nervous when it came to singing, and with good reason: he knew that he was no vocalist, and he had to be coached and nurtured around the mic. But unless he was doing his allocated song per album, he pretty much just stayed in the drum booth. He even did most of his percussion overdubs, playing tambourine or maracas, while sitting on the drum stool. The only time Ringo would leave the drum area was when he saw John or Paul put their guitars down—that was his signal that they were taking a break. Then he'd come out and sit down with Neil or Mal.

We rarely edited together different backing tracks, so what made it to the final record was almost always a complete performance, which meant that the Beatles often had to play a song over and over again, trying to get it right. In that sense, Ringo was like a machine, drumming away for hours on end. When a session would finally finish—especially the really long all-night sessions that we started doing later in the group's career—Ringo would leave the studio totally knackered, completely drained. I was always impressed at how he'd rebound the next day, though, fresh and ready for another bout of marathon drumming. Ringo had a definite talent and style, but little imagination. I always felt, however, that he knew his limitations.

Even from the earliest days, I always felt that the artist was John Lennon and Paul McCartney, not the Beatles. That seemed obvious in the recording studio, especially with the way that George Harrison would have difficulty with trying his guitar solos and Ringo would trip over drum fills. Despite that, there was an almost mystical bond between the four of them, which extended to Neil and Mal most of the time. It was a bond that created a wall impenetrable by any of us at EMI, even George Martin. In many ways, they always had a kind of "us versus them" attitude that went beyond the fact that they were Liverpudlians and we were Londoners. They were very into being antiestablishment, and they saw us as being the establishment because we worked a proper job and had to wear suits and ties. Dealing with any of the Beatles one-on-one was pretty easy, and it generally wasn't too difficult when you were in a room with two, or even three, of them. But get all four of them together, and they would close ranks and shut you out. It was like a private club that you couldn't enter. As a result, it really was very strange working with them a lot of the time. Exciting and exhilarating, to be sure . . . but a very different kind of experience, and one that took a certain amount of getting used to.

I'd been doing playback lacquers for about a year when my mate Malcolm Davies received his big break, clearing the way for my further advancement through the ranks. One evening, over a pint at our local pub, he casually informed me that he was scheduled to do his first ever session as a balance engineer in a week's time. Malcolm had been a mastering engineer—responsible for putting the final touches on a mix as it was transferred from tape to vinyl for replication—ever since I had first started working at Abbey Road back in 1962. He'd been in the mastering room for so long, I just assumed that was where he was going to stay. I knew he loved the job, and he was really good at it, too—in fact, one of the best. In the year or so that I'd been working upstairs, he and I had become really close friends, and he'd taught me most of what I knew about the arcane art of cutting to vinyl.

But the EMI "way" was to move inexorably upward, from assistant to playback lacquer to mastering to balance engineer, whether that's what you wanted to do or not. Actually, it was a system that made a certain amount of sense insofar as you learned every aspect of the recording process. The theory was that, before you became a balance engineer, you would know what could and could not technically make it onto vinyl, what would make the needle jump and what wouldn't, and how to get a record loud. Then, as now, the object was to get your record louder than anybody else's.

So even though Malcolm was quite possibly EMI's best mastering engineer, he was required to make the move back downstairs. As it turned out, it was a role that he was spectacularly unsuited for. Nervous and high-strung, he was also headstrong—a bad combination if you have to be working closely with a strong-willed producer and an equally strong-willed artist. But no one factored that in at the time, and so, with Malcolm's promotion, I was handed the keys to his mastering room and given his position. In turn, Ken Scott, who was next in line behind me, was promoted from assistant engineer to cutting playback lacquers. For the next few years, he would be following in my footsteps, all the way to the point where he would take over for me temporarily as the Beatles' recording engineer.

Sadly, Malcolm's reign as a balance engineer ended after just a single day. He later told me the story of how, overly excited at finally being given his shot at the brass ring, he totally screwed up. Management had decided to have Stuart Eltham oversee this first session, just to make sure that all the EMI rules and protocol were followed, and Stuart was apparently not amused when Malcolm proceeded to break every one of them in his first hour on the job.

Malcolm didn't want to use the prescribed microphones. He didn't want to put them in the prescribed positions. He didn't even want to put the instrumentalists in their prescribed spots in the studio. Worse yet, he was woefully oblivious to the protestations of the producer on the session, and to Stuart's rapidly darkening facial expression. Fortunately, within days of the disastrous session, Malcolm received a job offer from producer Norrie Paramor to serve as his assistant, a job he held for a couple of years (working with people like Tim Rice and Andrew Lloyd Webber) before finally returning to Abbey Road when a vacancy again occurred in the mastering suite. Ultimately, Malcolm would, on my recommendation, be hired away by Apple and become London's top mastering engineer.

One of my most important assignments in my new position was to remaster English releases of American hits sent to us by Capitol Records in the U.S. For some reason, the Capitol executives deemed it too time-consuming to make tape copies of singles (though they did make copies of albums), so instead they'd just stick a record in a bag and send it to us. Our mastering engineers would then literally make a copy onto tape, cut out any bad clicks, and recut it back on vinyl. The job was especially demanding when Tamla Motown material came in. I was always striving to match their full, bass-rich sound, but I found that I couldn't ever do it successfully, which was quite frustrating. It took me a long while to realize that the reasons had to do with the equipment we had at EMI, which was not up to the standard of American equipment, and not because of any limitations in my ability. Still, I was constantly fighting to get that sound onto disk, and it helped sharpen my ears and my cutting chops, driving me to continual experimentation.

Though not as good as the best American facilities, the EMI mastering rooms were still quite advanced relative to those in other English studios. As a result, outside producers would often use our services, which helped further expand my horizons creatively. Occasionally Decca Records or Olympic Studios would send someone in to do a lacquer: that's how I first heard the Rolling Stones. The famous but eccentric producer Joe Meek was a frequent client, even though he had his own studio and didn't do any recording at Abbey Road. I was enthralled with the low end on his records and with their unique coloration, which I later learned was due to his home-built compressors.

Joe's tapes were distinguished by their offbeat echoes and reverbs, also the result of his self-designed equipment. The only tool we had that was roughly equivalent was EMI's acoustic echo chamber, which sounded quite good—so good, in fact, that it was rarely available for mastering, because it was almost always in use by a recording session. If a client made the unusual request that a little more echo be added during mastering, we'd most often have to resort to using EMT plate reverbs, which were considered inferior-sounding. I would later discover that the problem was that they had never been installed correctly.

I was given only a few opportunities to assist on sessions downstairs while I was mastering, though one of those occasions, with Marlene Dietrich, was quite memorable. It was a thrill to meet her, and she was pleasant with me, even bumming a cigarette at one point. But she was quite the diva, and quite temperamental with her producer, Norman Newell. Her pianist and arranger was Burt Bacharach. He was actually one of several conductors on that session, with each leading the orchestra through a different composition. Burt took the baton that night for Ms. Dietrich's cover version of the Bob Dylan song "Blowin' In The Wind," which became a big hit for her. Another arranger on that session was a very young Mark Wirtz, who later became an EMI staff producer, finding fame with a highly successful British record called *A Theme From A Teenage Opera,* on which I served as engineer. But on this evening Dietrich appeared to be outraged at Mark's youth and inexperience and she stormed out of the studio, proclaiming with great dramatic flair, "I cannot work with a child!" Fortunately, Norman was able to calm her down and she returned to resume the session. Witnessing such a tempest in a teapot from the relative safety of the control room, I found it difficult to restrain myself from a fit of the giggles.

Probably the worst thing about being promoted to mastering was that I missed out on the making of the Beatles' *Help!* and *Rubber Soul* albums. I didn't hear the *Help!* album in its entirety until after going to see the film, though I do remember Norman talking about it enthusiastically in the canteen, especially Paul's ballad "Yesterday," which he raved about. In contrast, there was almost no buzz at all in the Abbey Road corridors about *Rubber Soul.* Though everyone agreed that it had quite a few good songs and a crisp, clean sound, the general feeling among the staff that were working on it was that it was a pleasant diversion into the realm of folk and country music (Lennon and Harrison especially were heavily into Bob Dylan at this time) but not particularly noteworthy.

But all this was just idle chatter around the canteen table. To my endless frustration, I was no longer participating actively in new Beatles music. Apart from Paul's occasional lunchtime visits to the mastering room, I actually had little contact with the group for nearly eighteen months.

After a rollicking start, it now seemed as if I were out of the loop, sequestered in a tiny room well away from the action. Worse yet, given the fact that no one at EMI had ever been promoted to full engineer before the age of forty, it looked as if I might well be stuck there for decades.

Happily, things didn't quite work out that way. Thanks to Norman Smith's desire to be promoted to producer, I spent less than a year in the relative oblivion of the mastering room before being made a balance engineer. Although I had missed the excitement of being in the studio with the artists and producers, I really hadn't minded being one of the backroom boys. I actually enjoyed the learning experience and the freedom that playback lacquer cutting and mastering allowed.

Nonetheless, I was thrilled to receive the promotion, although the very term "engineering" itself seemed so wrong—to me, it conjured up images of men in white coats with oil cans. No, I'd always viewed making records as painting pictures, with the sounds of musical instruments as my palette. I think of microphones as lenses and the different frequency areas seem like colors to me: high-pitched strings as a silver shimmer, mid-range brass as golden, the low tones of a bass as dark blue. That's actually the way I hear things.

To be sure, there had been a degree of resentment and jealousy among some of the more experienced staff who were passed over for the promotion, but I just put my head down and got to work, mostly with the newer artists signed to EMI. The first big session for me was with the group called Manfred Mann. I thought they were pretty good, and I really liked their song "Pretty Flamingo"; it marked the first time I deliberately went after new sounds that had never been heard before. So I was positively elated when it climbed to the top of the British charts just a few weeks after its release. All of a sudden I was a teenage engineer with a gold record to his credit.

That gave me the confidence to expand my sonic experiments; so, quietly, cautiously, I began thinking up ways to create new sounds and new colors, despite—or perhaps because of—the very limited and primitive technology we had at hand. While I was assisting, I had pretty much adhered to the rigid rules management had passed down, but the truth was that I had never been satisfied with conventional sounds or recording techniques: they just seemed boring to me. Now, at last, I had the freedom to try the unconventional.

On one session, I decided to reverse things and put the orchestra in the acoustically deadened end of the studio, where the rhythm section usually was placed, and the rhythm section in the more "live"-sounding area. I didn't make a point of touting what I was doing—in fact, I tried to keep things hush-hush—but word got around anyway, and it caused a lot of controversy when the other engineers found out. More than a few of them got annoyed about it, too. They were coming up to me for days afterward, saying things like, "What did you do that for? We already have a place for the orchestra." They just wanted to take the easy way out; they didn't want to have to be forced to think about what they were doing or to work at creating new sounds. Maybe that's what made me stand out from the others and brought me to management's attention when it came time to find a replacement for Norman: I didn't mind hard work if the result was achieving a sound I was visualizing in my head.

When, less than six months after receiving the promotion, George Martin asked me to take over specifically as the Beatles' engineer, I was grateful for the opportunity, but I also understood Norman's wanting to advance himself. He was an older man—at least George's age, possibly older—and he certainly had sufficient musical knowledge and background to make the leap from balance engineer to producer. From his point of view, getting that promotion—attaining the final rung in the EMI career "ladder"—was all that mattered, even if it meant ending his association with the biggest act in the world. He obviously had high hopes for his new discovery, Pink Floyd, and may have sincerely believed that they would achieve even greater success than the Beatles had. (Norman wasn't completely misguided, although he parted ways with the Floyd well before their chart-topping *Dark Side Of The Moon* album. But he would go on to produce their first few albums, and would even have a hit record as an artist himself in 1973, recording his song "Oh Babe, What Would You Say" under the pseudonym Hurricane Smith.)

With the benefit of hindsight, I can equally understand George Martin's adamant refusal to allow Norman to receive the promotion *and* remain as the Beatles' engineer. There was no way George wanted another producer in the room with him when he was working with "the boys"—that would undermine his authority and place him, and everyone else, for that matter, in an extremely awkward position. George always wanted the limelight to shine on him alone. Having a peer in the control room was completely unacceptable from his point of view. Having a wet-behind-the-ears nineteen-year-old rookie engineer, on the other hand, was fine. Simply put, I presented no threat to him.

I never coveted George Martin's job, and he knew it. Having control over the sounds was my goal all along, and I was much happier tinkering with the controls of the mixing board and coming up with new sonic innovations than I would have been going through string arrangements and organizing session bookings. Fortunately, the Beatles were utterly receptive to the idea of breaking all the rules by the time I started engineering for them.

I had only two weeks to prepare myself mentally between the afternoon that George offered me Norman's seat and the first scheduled *Revolver* session, and the days flew by in a rush of excitement and nervous energy. I had immediately shared the news with my parents, of course, but they didn't have any understanding of my job and little awareness of the importance of working with the Beatles. My friends, on the other hand, were enormously impressed. Most of them were still in school or were apprenticing in "normal" jobs; all of them were in awe of my phenomenal good fortune, which we celebrated night after night at our local pub.

But it was all a cover for the growing apprehension within me. With every passing day, the tension was building. I felt as if I were in a pressure cooker.

7

Innovation and Invention:

The Making of *Revolver*

Beyond my immense relief at having passed muster and being accepted as the Beatles' new engineer, it's probably not too far-fetched to claim that recording history was made during the very first night of working on *Revolver.* Certainly the drum sound I contrived for Ringo by moving the mics in close and stuffing a blanket inside the bass drum has become the standard to this very day. Even John's vocal-through-a-Leslie trick (which in the end we used only on the very last verse of "Tomorrow Never Knows") has become a stock-in-trade whenever a producer wants a singer to sound eerily removed—or even sometimes when they just need to mask poor singing.

In the months leading up to *Revolver,* all four Beatles had been bitten by the recording bug and had gone out and bought themselves open-reel tape recorders. Paul, already developing a taste for avant-garde music, had discovered that the erase head could be removed, which allowed new sounds to be added to the existing ones each time the tape passed over the record head. Because of the primitive technology of the time, the tape quickly became saturated with sound and distorted, but it was an effect that appealed to the four of them as they conducted sonic experiments in their respective homes. They would often bring in bits of tape and say, "Listen to this!" as they tried to outdo one another in a de facto "weird sound" contest.

Inspired by the initial loop that John and Ringo had created during the first night of recording "Tomorrow Never Knows," Paul had gone home and sat up all night creating a whole series of short tape loops specifically for the song, which he dutifully presented to me in a little plastic bag when he returned for the next day's session. We began the second evening's work by having Phil McDonald carefully thread each loop onto the tape machine, one at a time, so that we could audition them. Paul had assembled an extraordinary collection of bizarre sounds, which included his playing distorted guitar and bass, as well as wineglasses ringing and other indecipherable noises. We played them every conceivable way: proper speed, sped up, slowed down, backwards, forwards. Every now and then, one of the Beatles would shout, "That's a good one," as we played through the lot. Eventually five of the loops were selected to be added to the basic backing track.

The problem was that we had only one extra tape machine. Fortunately, there were plenty of other machines in the Abbey Road complex, all interconnected via wiring in the walls, and all the other studios just happened to be empty that afternoon. What followed next was a scene that could have come out of a science fiction movie—or a Monty Python sketch. Every tape machine in every studio was commandeered and every available EMI employee was given the task of holding a pencil or drinking glass to give the loops the proper tensioning. In many instances, this meant they had to be standing out in the hallway, looking quite sheepish. Most of those people didn't have a clue what we were doing; they probably thought we were daft. They certainly weren't pop people, and they weren't that young either. Add in the fact that all of the technical staff were required to wear white lab coats, and the whole thing became totally surreal.

Meanwhile, back in the control room, George Martin and I huddled over the console, raising and lowering faders to shouted instructions from John, Paul, George, and Ringo. ("Let's have that seagull sound now!" "More distorted wineglasses!") With each fader carrying a different loop, the mixing desk acted like a synthesizer, and we played it like a musical instrument, too, carefully overdubbing textures to the prerecorded backing track. Finally we completed the task to the band's satisfaction, the white-coated technicians were freed from their labors, and Paul's loops were retired back to the plastic bag, never to be played again.

We had no sense of the momentousness of what we were doing—it all just seemed like a bit of fun in a good cause at the time—but what we had created that afternoon was actually the forerunner of today's beat- and loop-driven music. If someone had told me then that we had just invented a new genre of music that would persist for decades, I would have thought he was crazy.

A couple of weeks later, George Harrison showed up with the tamboura he had so eagerly talked of during the first night's session. Actually, he'd been talking about it almost nonstop since then, so everyone was really curious to see the thing. He staggered into the studio under its weight—it's a huge instrument, and the case was the size of a small coffin—and brought it out with a grand gesture, displaying it proudly as we gathered around.

"What do you think to that, then?" he asked everyone in sight. Not willing to trust his precious cargo to either of the two roadies, he had actually stuffed the tamboura case in the backseat of one of his Porsches, which he parked right in front of the main entrance so he could carry the instrument by hand up the steps. Once inside, he had tossed the car keys to an assistant engineer who happened to be sitting in the reception area and directed him to move it to a proper spot. That poor young man had been utterly terrified he would scratch George's car; repairing it probably would have cost him a year's salary.

But George Harrison had said that the tamboura drone would be the perfect complement to John's song, and he was right. Having seen how well Paul's loops had worked, George wanted to contribute one of his own, so I recorded him playing a single note on the huge instrument—again using a close-miking technique—and turned it into a loop. It ended up becoming the sound that opens the track. Another sonic component—the little bit of tack piano at the end—was a fluke. It actually came from a trial we did on the first take, when the group were just putting ideas down, but Paul heard it during one of the playbacks and suggested that we fly it into the fadeout, and it worked perfectly.

So much of the way that "Tomorrow Never Knows" turned out was just luck. Certainly, it wasn't planned that way or mapped out beforehand. The Beatles had come into the *Revolver* sessions completely refreshed and rejuvenated after a few months off recharging their batteries, and they connected up with me, new to the job and willing to try anything and everything. It was just magic, pure serendipity.

Most of the rest of the making of *Revolver* went just as quickly. We were firing on all cylinders creatively, and we were having a good time, but because we were constantly trying new things, it was also a lot of hard work. In fact, my strongest memory of those sessions is how utterly draining they were. Most EMI sessions weren't allowed to run past 11 P.M., but the Beatles were big enough by then that all the rules went by the wayside. They could work as late or as long as they wanted to—and we had to be there with them the whole time.

In those days, singles were probably even more important than albums. After all, the singles were the records that the radio DJs spun endlessly, thus fueling album sales. They were also far more affordable than albums—a major factor for the typical teenage Beatles fan of the era, who had limited cash to spend. George Martin's policy about Beatles singles was absolute: they had to be brand-new songs and not just reissues of album tracks. It was laudable insofar as it gave the buying public tremendous value for their money, but it also added greatly to the pressure the group was under. Not only did they have to periodically write and record musically cohesive collections of their songs, but at the same time they also had to keep cranking out commercial hits.

A few weeks into the *Revolver* sessions, George Martin received a memo from the EMI brass reminding him that a new Beatles single was soon due. John and Paul were immediately put to work. (Poor George Harrison's compositions were simply not thought good enough to be considered for singles at that point.) Whoever wrote the stronger song—with George Martin as referee—would win the prize: the prestigious A-side. The losing song would either be relegated to the B-side or be included on an album, with another, lesser song purloined to occupy the nether regions of the single. The competition was on.

One afternoon, Paul strolled into the studio, marched straight over to the piano, and confidently proclaimed, "Gather round, lads, and have a listen to our next single."

John gave Paul a sideways glance of disapproval—he never liked losing—but nevertheless joined Ringo and the two Georges for the private concert. Paul pounded out a catchy melody, instantly hummable, filled with memorable hooks. I couldn't make out the lyric entirely, but it seemed to involve book writing. Each time he would come to the chorus, Paul would stop playing and gesture to John and George Harrison, pointing out the high harmony part he planned on assigning each. By the time he finished the first run-through, it was obvious to everyone in the room that this was an instant hit. The song was "Paperback Writer," and it would indeed top the charts when it was released just a few weeks later.

But even before he got down to the brass tacks of teaching the others their parts, Paul turned to me. "Geoff," he began, "I need you to put your thinking cap on. This song is really calling out for that deep Motown bass sound we've been talking about, so I want you to pull out all the stops this time. All right, then?"

I nodded an affirmative. Paul had long been complaining that the bass on Beatles records wasn't as loud or as full as the bass on the American records he so loved. He and I would often get together in the mastering room to listen intently to the low end of some new import he had gotten from the States, most often a Motown track. Even though we had DI (Direct Inject) boxes available, I rarely used them to record Paul's bass—I still don't, as a matter of fact. Instead, I followed the standard EMI directive of placing a microphone in front of his bass amplifier. The bass sounds we were getting were decent—partly because Paul had switched from his signature Hofner violin "Beatle" bass to a beefier Rickenbacker—but still not as good as what we were hearing on those American records.

Fortunately, as Paul and John turned to George Harrison and began showing him the chords to "Paperback Writer," inspiration struck. It occurred to me that since microphones are in fact simply loudspeakers wired in reverse (in technical terms, both are *transducers* that convert sound waves to electrical signals, and vice versa), why not try using a loudspeaker as a microphone? Logically, it seemed that whatever can push bass signal out can also take it in—and that a large loudspeaker should be able to respond to low frequencies better than a small microphone. The more I thought about it, the more it made sense.

I broached my plan, gingerly, to Phil McDonald. His response was somewhat predictable: "You're daft; you've completely gone around the twist." Ignoring him, I took a walk down the hall and talked it over with Ken Townsend, our maintenance engineer. He thought my idea had some merit.

"Sounds plausible," he said. "Let's wire a speaker up that way and try it."

Over the next few hours, while the boys rehearsed with George Martin, Ken and I conducted a few experiments. To my delight, the idea of using a speaker as a microphone seemed to work pretty well. Even though it didn't deliver a lot of signal and was kind of muffled, I was able to achieve a good bass sound by placing it up against the grille of a bass amplifier, speaker to speaker, and then routing the signal through a complicated setup of compressors and filters—including one huge experimental unit that I secretly borrowed from the office of Mr. Cook, the manager of the maintenance department.

With renewed confidence, I returned to the studio to try it out for real. Paul wasn't as nontechnical as John, but this was pretty way out, even by Beatles standards. He looked at me in a funny way as I set up the big, bulky loudspeaker in front of his amp instead of the usual microphone, but he didn't say anything, and neither did George Martin, who by now was getting used to my Rube Goldberg approach to recording. They returned their attention to the rehearsals, giving me the opportunity to cautiously raise the fader carrying the bass signal. Paul's distinctively fluid bass line in "Paperback Writer" consisted mostly of notes played high up on the lowest strings, which helped round out the tone further still. It sounded absolutely huge, so much so that I became somewhat concerned that it might actually make the needle jump out of the groove when it was finally cut to vinyl. But Paul loved the sound, and it was eventually left to my mate Tony Clark to cut the master lacquer. I was glad Tony had gotten the assignment, and he did a brilliant job. If it had been one of the older guys, they would have either slashed all the bass out of it, or sent it back and told us to mix it again.

The B-side of that single was John's song "Rain." It was a good track, too, though not nearly as commercial as "Paperback Writer." I used the same bass sound on it, but it's a recording that is largely distinguished by a creative accident brought about by John's technical ineptitude. Because he and the other three Beatles owned Brenell recorders, they were able to take open-reel tapes home with them whenever they wanted to listen to works in progress. The afternoon we recorded the backing track and vocal to "Rain," John asked for a rough mix and Phil dutifully ran a copy off for him. But when he got home that night, Lennon mistakenly threaded the tape backward on his machine. Not understanding that the problem was of his making, he thought that Phil had somehow gotten it wrong. Fortunately for Phil, John liked what he was hearing.

The next day, John marched into the control room, tape in hand, and demanded that we all listen to his "incredible" discovery. George Martin tried to explain what had happened, but the ever-impatient Lennon didn't care. All he knew was that this was the sound he wanted for the song's fadeout and he was off to have a cuppa; getting it accomplished was our job. So George had me copy the track of John's singing the last verse onto our two-track machine. I then instructed Phil to turn the copy over so it would play backwards, and we flew it into the multitrack at the proper spot. Lennon was thrilled with the result. From that point on, the Beatles got backwards fever: almost every overdub we did on *Revolver* had to be tried backwards as well as forwards.

"Rain" also had an unusual sonic texture, deep and murky. This was accomplished by having the band play the backing track at a really fast tempo while I recorded them on a sped-up tape machine. When we slowed the tape back down to normal speed, the music played back at the desired tempo, but with a radically different tonal quality. It all seems very simple now—and, of course, tricks like this are easily accomplished in today's computers—but in 1966 it was a pretty revolutionary technique, one that we would repeatedly use to great effect on Beatles recordings.

I'm not a huge fan of any of the Beatles CD releases—their songs were recorded with the intention of being released on vinyl, and as far as I am concerned, that is the way they should be heard. But the "Paperback Writer"/ "Rain" single sounds exceptionally good on vinyl, not least of which because Tony Clark was able to use a brand-new piece of gear when mastering it—a huge monstrosity developed by our maintenance department that had blinking lights everywhere. It was called "ATOC," short for "Automatic Transient Overload Control," and it allowed the record to be cut louder than any other single up to that time. Unfortunately, the stereo mix of "Paperback Writer" does the song no justice. It's completely disjointed, and it isn't at all the balance that we intended. To me, the mono mix is much more exciting.

Another distinctive aspect of "Paperback Writer" is the fluttering echo at the end of each chorus, added at the mix stage. It was accomplished by routing the vocals into a separate two-track machine and then connecting that machine's output to its input. At the end of each chorus, Phil had the job of slowly increasing the record level until it just reached the point of feedback. If he went one notch too far, the echo would get out of control, so there were many attempts at doing the mix. Every time he'd go past that point, or not far enough, we'd have to stop and remix the entire song again. That's because, in the archaic EMI way of thinking, edits were frowned upon. Management didn't want anyone taking a razor to master tapes, so multitrack editing— which would allow us to join the start of one take onto the end of another— was rarely allowed in those days. Even during mixing, editing was discouraged, although it would have allowed us to create a mix in sections— something that was commonly done in most other recording studios. Somehow EMI just didn't care what was going on in the outside world: *we'd* have to get the mix right from start to finish. If we messed up the middle, or even if the very end of the fadeout wasn't quite right, we would have to start all over again; we couldn't just edit in a replacement for the bad bit. As a result, you got that adrenaline going, and the mixes themselves became performances.

We may have had to do things the hard way, but it also meant we had to put in the effort to get it right. Looking at it that way always made me feel a bit better about the long hours involved.

With the "Paperback Writer" and "Rain" recordings completed, we returned our attention to *Revolver*. Incredibly, all the tracks on the album were created in the studio before my very eyes. The Beatles had done no rehearsing beforehand; there had been no preproduction whatsoever. What an incredible experience it was to see each of the songs develop and blossom within the confines of those four walls! Almost every afternoon, John or Paul or George Harrison would come in with a scrap of paper that had a lyric or chord sequence scribbled on it and within a day or two we'd have yet another unbelievable track down on tape. Every time we did that, I would find myself thinking, *Wow, what's the* next *song going to be like?*—which gave me the incentive to make the sound even better, to try to top what we had already done.

A case in point was Ringo's showcase on *Revolver*. Almost every Beatles album had one song with a lead vocal by Ringo, despite the fact that he could barely sing. But the fans ate it up, and I have to admit there was something endearing about his voice—even if it was just the fact that you could hear him constantly straining to stay on pitch. Aware of those limitations, John or Paul would try to write him a song that had only a few notes in the melody line. For *Revolver*, Paul had composed "Yellow Submarine" for Ringo to sing.

When Paul first ran the song down on piano, it sounded to my ears more like a children's song than a pop track, but everyone was enthused and got down to work. As it happened, George Martin was out sick with food poisoning the night we began work on it; he sent his secretary, Judy, along to keep an eye on things while I took the helm. George's absence clearly had a liberating effect on the four Beatles—they behaved like a bunch of schoolboys with a substitute teacher filling in. As a result, there was a lot of clowning around that evening—silliness that George Martin would not have tolerated—and so rehearsals took up a lot more time than the session itself.

It was Lennon who finally got over his attack of the giggles and took on the role of responsible adult, admonishing the others, "Come on, it's getting late and we still haven't made us a record!" This, of course, only had the effect of sending everyone into another fit of laughter. But eventually they settled down and began recording the backing track. Then Ringo and the others added their vocals, with the tape slightly slowed down so that their voices would sound a little brighter on playback.

At a certain point, John decided that the third verse needed some spicing up, so he dashed into the studio and began answering each of Ringo's sung lines in a silly voice that I further altered to make it sound like he was talking over a ship's megaphone. The verse begins, "And we live / A life of ease," but you don't actually hear John's voice until the third and fourth lines. In fact, I had recorded him repeating the first two lines also, but a few days later,

Phil McDonald accidentally erased them—one of the few times his usually accurate drop-in skills failed him. From his station in the machine room, he got on the intercom and let George and me know of his gaffe while the Beatles were out of earshot. I could hear the distress in his voice and could sympathize—almost every assistant had made a similar mistake at one time or another.

John realized the lines were gone the next time we played the multitrack—nothing ever got by him—and he wasn't too happy about it, but rather than pin the blame on Phil, George and I quickly concocted a story about needing the track for one of the overdubs. We all tended to close ranks and protect one another at times like that, and I know that Phil was very relieved that he didn't have to face John's wrath.

After that first night of working on "Yellow Submarine," the *Revolver* sessions were suspended for nearly a week because of George Martin's illness. When we finally returned to the studio, a recovered George was back in the producer's chair . . . but, despite his return, that was to be the day the lunatics *really* took over the asylum!

Most of that afternoon was spent trying to record a spoken word introduction to "Yellow Submarine." Back in 1960, there had been a well-publicized charity walk by a doctor named Barbara Moore from Land's End to John O'Groats—the two points farthest apart on the British mainland. John, who often had his head buried in a newspaper when he wasn't playing guitar or singing, had written a short medieval-sounding poem that somehow tied the walk to the song title, and he was determined to have Ringo recite it, accompanied by the sound of marching feet. I pulled out the old radio trick of shaking coal in a cardboard box to simulate footsteps, and Ringo did his best to emote, deadpan, but the final result was, in a word, boring. Even though we spent hours and hours putting it together, the whole idea was eventually scrapped. Nearly thirty years later, we did tack the introduction back on to the remixed version of "Yellow Submarine" that was included on the B-side of the CD single "Real Love," one of two Lennon songs completed posthumously by the surviving Beatles and released in 1994.

Paul had conceived "Yellow Submarine" as a singalong, and so a few of the band's friends and significant others had been invited along for the evening's session. By then, everyone was distinctly in a party mood. Though we hadn't tried pot ourselves, Phil and I had been around enough musicians to know what it was, and we were sometimes aware of the funny smell in the studio after the Beatles and their roadies snuck a joint off in the corner, though I doubt very much if the straightlaced George Martin knew what was going on. Like guilty kids, Mal or Neil would sometimes try to cover the odor by lighting incense, but that in itself was a tip-off to us. We didn't say anything, though: if the Beatles wanted to get high during their recording sessions, it was none of our business. We were there to do a job, and we just carried on with the work at hand.

Following a long dinner break (during which we suspected more than food was being ingested), a raucous group began filtering in, including Mick Jagger and Brian Jones, along with Jagger's girlfriend Marianne Faithfull and George Harrison's wife, Patti. They were all dressed in their finest Carnaby Street outfits, the women in miniskirts and flowing blouses, the men in purple bell-bottoms and fur jackets. Phil and I put up a few ambient microphones around the studio, and I decided to also give everyone a handheld mic on a long lead so they could move around freely—there was no way I was going to try to contain that lot! The two Rolling Stones and Marianne Faithfull basically acted as if I didn't exist; to them, I guess I was just one of the invisible "little people." Patti was more gracious, going out of her way to say hello to me. She seemed shy but also very charming.

The whole marijuana-influenced scene that evening was completely zany, straight out of a Marx Brothers movie. The entire EMI collection of percussion instruments and sound effects boxes were strewn all over the studio, with people grabbing bells and whistles and gongs at random. To simulate the sound of a submarine submerging, John grabbed a straw and began blowing bubbles into a glass—fortunately, I was able to move a mic nearby in time to record it for posterity. Inspired, Lennon wanted to take things to the next level and have me record him actually *singing* underwater. First, he tried singing while gargling. When that failed (he nearly choked), he began lobbying for a tank to be brought in so that he could be submerged!

While George Martin worked at dissuading him, I began thinking of an alternative. Why not instead have John sing into a mic that was immersed in water? We had several small "spot" microphones on hand, and if one of them could be wrapped in some kind of waterproofing, perhaps it would work. George looked at me as if I were crazy, but with John imploring him to let us try it, he finally gave his begrudging approval, adding ominously that if the microphone was damaged or destroyed, it would be coming out of my paycheck. His words had a sobering effect on me—I wasn't making all that much money at the time—but it was too late to back out.

Neil was duly dispatched to fetch a glass milk bottle from the canteen and fill it with water, while Phil was sent to the mic cabinet to select the smallest microphone he could find. I was trying to figure out how to waterproof it when John called out to Mal and said, "What have you got that will work for this?"

Mal always tried to be prepared for every contingency, because if the Beatles wanted something and he didn't have it, they would give him a hard time. As a result, he carried around a doctor's bag, inside which he'd stashed all sorts of things—picks, guitar strings, fuses, flashlights, crisps (potato chips), biscuits (cookies), even household items like tissues, which he'd whip out if one of them had a cold. John must have figured that if anyone was going to have a solution to our dilemma, Mal was. He didn't disappoint. With a wink and a sly grin, the burly roadie reached into the bag, fished around for a moment, and cheerfully waved a condom aloft.

"Well done, Malcolm!" John proclaimed as the others burst into laughter. "After all, we don't want the microphone to be getting in the family way, do we?"

Fighting back an attack of the giggles myself, I wrapped the mic carefully and lowered it into the milk bottle, then placed it on top of one of the keyboards as Lennon pulled up a chair, preparing to sing into it. Then it dawned on me: *My God, if the studio manager sees this, I'll be fired on the spot.*

Just then the door swung open and none other than Mr. E. H. Fowler appeared. For some reason, he was working late that evening, and I suppose he stuck his head in to see if the lights were still on. Fortunately for me, he was a bit nearsighted. By the time he got close enough to see what we were actually doing, John had bolted from his chair, grabbed the offending milk bottle, and hid it behind his back. My heart started pounding as Fowler came closer.

"Everything all right, lads?" he asked.

"Yes, sir, Mr. Studio Manager, sir, absolutely smashing, sir," Lennon replied somberly, standing stiffly to attention. Out of the corner of my eye, I could see the others stifling their laughter—even George Martin.

"Very well, then," Fowler replied. "Carry on."

And with that, he turned on his heels and marched out of the room, satisfied that everything was under control. When the peals of laughter finally died down, we continued our sonic experiment, but the results were disappointing. Maybe it was just that the walls of the milk bottle were too thick—or perhaps the condoms of the day weren't up to the task!—but the signal was so muffled and weak as to be unusable, and the idea was abandoned. To my relief, the microphone was unharmed. It wasn't until many years later that I realized with horror that the microphone we were using was phantom

powered—meaning that it actually was a live electrical object. In conjunc-
tion with the 240-volt system used in England, any of us, including Lennon,
could have easily been electrocuted, and I would have gone down in history
as the first recording engineer to kill a client in the studio.

At the time, though, we were blissful in our ignorance. The party resumed. People began clinking wineglasses and shouting out at random;
those background screams during the second verse came from Patti Harrison, which was always ironic to me, considering how quiet she usually was.
At one point, I had to run out to the studio to see where everyone had disappeared to; I could hear voices coming over the control room speakers but I
couldn't see anyone. It turned out the party had relocated into the small
echo chamber at the back of the room. As I opened the door, I again detected the faint smell of "incense." As we neared midnight, Mal Evans began
marching around the studio wearing a huge bass drum on his chest, everyone else in line behind him conga-style singing along to the chorus. It was
utter madness.

When John ran back into the echo chamber and ad-libbed his "Captain,
captain" routine to the sound of clanking bells and chains, we were all doubled over with laughter. The ambience around his voice was just perfect, and
that was the way that all those bits happened. Although the record sounds
quite produced, it was actually spur of the moment—John and the others
were just out there having a good time. Somehow it worked, though, despite
the chaos.

Throughout the day, George Martin and I had been overdubbing various
nautical sounds from sound effects records in the EMI library. That same library was to be put to good use later that night, when it came time to add a
solo to the song. By then, everyone was too knackered—or stoned—to give
much attention to the two-bar gap that had been left for a solo, and with the
enormous amount of time that had already been spent on the track, George
Martin wasn't about to begin the long process of having George Harrison
strap on a guitar and laboriously come up with a part. Instead, someone—
probably Paul—came up with the idea of using a brass band. There was, of
course, no way that a band could be booked to come in on such short notice,
and in any event, George Martin probably wouldn't have allocated budget to
hire them, not for such a short section. So instead, he came up with an ingen-
ious solution—one that, with the passage of time, he has apparently forgotten.

In the many interviews he's given over the years, George often talks about
the idea he came up with during the *Sgt. Pepper* sessions, on the song "Being
For The Benefit Of Mr. Kite," where we raided the EMI sound effects library

and transferred over snippets of various calliopes and steam organs, which were then spliced together in a random order, some playing forwards and some playing backwards. All of that is true, and it worked brilliantly, but what George doesn't remember is that we had done the same thing with a brass band recording nearly a year earlier in order to come up with the solo in "Yellow Submarine."

Phil McDonald was duly dispatched to fetch some records of Sousa marches, and after auditioning several of them, George Martin and Paul finally identified one that was suitable—it was in the same key as "Yellow Submarine" and seemed to fit well enough. The problem here was one of copyright; in British law, if you used more than a few seconds of a recording on a commercial release, you had to get permission from the song's publisher and then pay a negotiable royalty.

George wasn't about to do either, so he told me to record the section on a clean piece of two-track tape and then chop it into pieces, toss the pieces into the air, and splice them back together. The end result should have been random, but, somehow, when I pieced it back together, it came back nearly the same way it had been in the first place! No one could believe their ears; we were all thoroughly amazed. But by this point, it was very late at night and we were running out of time—and patience—so George had me simply swap over two of the pieces and we flew it into the multitrack master, being careful to fade it out quickly. That's why the solo is so brief, and that's why it sounds almost musical, but not quite. At least it's unrecognizable enough that EMI was never sued by the original copyright holder of the song.

Looking back, I think one of the reasons I was able to come up with so many innovative sounds on *Revolver* was the sheer amount of time George Martin spent in the studio working out complex vocal harmonies with John, Paul, and George Harrison. It was a long process, but the results were always spectacular. The four of them would gather around the piano for hours on end, practicing their parts endlessly. Ringo, who rarely sang unless it was his "showpiece" song, would usually pass the time reading a magazine or playing checkers with Mal or Neil.

During those long rehearsals, I would sit in the control room by myself and have the luxury of thinking. I'd lean back, cigarette in hand, listening to endless playbacks while fiddling about with the controls, trying to achieve the sounds I heard in my head, trying to paint pictures with the Beatles' instruments and voices. With each passing day, I felt as if I were getting closer to my goal. Fortunately, I was blessed to be working with a band equally driven to breaking new ground, and with a producer willing to let me try my ideas.

We didn't know at the time that we were raising the bar for recorded music, and we had absolutely no inkling that the Beatles were to become even bigger than they already were—that seemed impossible—but we did know that we were doing good work, and we felt confident that the listening public would "get it." I'd go home each night, weary and drained, but filled with pride at all I was achieving, eager to face the next day's challenges.

Some days, of course, were better than others. There was one especially tedious session where we all wished we had never come up with the concept of backwards sounds. The song was "I'm Only Sleeping," and George Harrison was determined to play a backwards guitar solo on it. At the best of times, he had trouble playing solos all the way through forwards, so it was with great trepidation that we all settled in for what turned out to be an interminable day of listening to the same eight bars played backwards over and over and over again. Phil McDonald told me later that his arms were sore for days afterward from having to repeatedly lift the heavy tape reels off the machine and turn them over. I can still picture George—and later, Paul, who joined him to play the backwards outro in a bizarre duet—hunched over his guitar for hours on end, headphones clamped on, brows furrowed in concentration. George Martin conducted them from the window of the control room, using grease pencil marks I had put on the back of the tape on each beat as a reference. To borrow Ringo's phrase, that nine-hour session certainly was one hard day's night!

By that point, we were aided by having the tape machines and their operator, Phil McDonald, right in the control room with us. It had always been time-consuming and clumsy to communicate with the assistant engineer over an intercom, seated in a small room where he couldn't see anything, but with all the overdubs and drop-ins we were doing on *Revolver*, it was proving to be downright impossible. This in itself caused a huge palaver at EMI. When the written request to have the four-track machine relocated was submitted, the technical boys at the central office objected strenuously, saying that it couldn't be done because it would be put out of alignment if it was moved down the hall. But George Martin intervened—this was the Beatles, after all. Surely they were making enough income for the company that rules could be broken. Reluctantly, management finally agreed, and what followed was another bizarre spectacle that could have come straight out of *Snow White and the Seven Dwarfs*.

Relative to what it had been when I first began working there, the dress code at EMI had relaxed considerably by the time we began *Revolver*. As the engineer, I was no longer obligated to wear a jacket and tie. However, the technical staff were still required to wear white lab coats, no matter how ridiculous they looked, and the maintenance people—the ones who swept the floors and emptied the trash—were required to wear brown coats. So when permission was finally granted for the tape machine to be moved, there was this unbelievable scene, with four guys in brown coats wheeling it down the corridor very slowly, followed by another four guys in white coats watching intently and making notes on their clipboards in case anything un-toward happened. Marching somberly behind them, hands clasped behind their backs, were yet *another* four guys, dressed in suits—the EMI brass, making sure that the white coats were properly observing the brown coats. It was all happening at a snail's pace, and the big epic moment was lifting the tape machine over the door threshold. God only knows what would have happened to those poor guys in the brown coats if they had dropped the thing.

Most people don't realize that making a record is much like shooting a film. There are long periods of boredom and waiting around while technical details are attended to and parts worked out, interspersed with moments of creative spark. Naturally enough, my memories of the making of *Revolver* consist largely of those moments. One example was the time that George Harrison brought in some local Indian musicians from the Asian Society to play on his song "Love You To"—which I originally named "Granny Smith" on the tape box, after my favorite kind of apple, only because George never had titles for his songs. I had never miked Indian instruments before, but I was especially impressed by the huge sound coming from the tabla (percus-sion instruments somewhat similar to bongos). I decided to close-mic them, placing a sensitive ribbon mic just a few inches away, and then I heavily com-pressed the signal. No one had ever recorded tabla like that—they'd always been miked from a distance. My idea resulted in a fabulous sound, right in your face, and both Harrison and the Indian musicians commented after-ward about it.

I noticed a definite maturing in George Harrison during the course of the *Revolver* sessions. Up until that point, he had played a largely subordinate role in the band—after all, it was Lennon and McCartney's songs that had been the hits. But he ended up recording three original songs on this album—I'm not sure why he was given so much space, but it's possible that he had put pressure on Brian Epstein to put pressure on George Martin. All those discussions would have been held privately, outside of the studio, but there were definite economic considerations involved, because royalty income was directly tied to how many songs a writer got on each album. Paul and John weren't especially derisive of George's abilities as a songwriter or his explorations into Eastern music—at least, not in my presence—but George Martin always seemed a bit concerned about both the quality of Harrison's compositions and the amount of time being spent on them, which tended to make Harrison a bit self-conscious. With the benefit of hindsight, George Martin has expressed regret in some of his interviews about the short shrift that Harrison sometimes received, though it is somewhat understandable in light of Lennon and McCartney's phenomenal songwriting abilities. It's little wonder that George was often overshadowed.

I thought that George's strongest song on *Revolver* was "Taxman," and George Martin must have agreed, since he decided to put it first on the album—the all-important spot generally reserved for the best song, since the idea is to try to capture the listener immediately. Harrison didn't like paying tax, and the Inland Revenue had been after him once or twice, so he wrote a song about it, with a really clever lyric ("My advice to those who die / Declare the pennies on your eyes"). There was a bit of tension on that session, though, because George had a great deal of trouble playing the solo—in fact, he couldn't even do a proper job of it when we slowed the tape down to half speed.

After a couple of hours of watching him struggle, both Paul and George Martin started becoming quite frustrated—this was, after all, a Harrison song and therefore not something anyone was prepared to spend a whole lot of time on. So George Martin went into the studio and, as diplomatically as possible, announced that he wanted Paul to have a go at the solo instead. I could see from the look on Harrison's face that he didn't like the idea one bit, but he reluctantly agreed and then proceeded to disappear for a couple of hours. He sometimes did that—had a bit of a sulk on his own, then eventually came back. Whatever private conversations he would have with John or Paul upon his return occurred in the corridor, where none of us could hear. Sometimes Ringo would be part of the conference, but more often he would stay in the studio with Neil and Mal until the storm had blown over. Paul's solo was stunning in its ferocity—his guitar playing had a fire and energy that his younger bandmate's rarely matched—and was accomplished in just a take or two. It was so good, in fact, that George Martin had me fly it in again during the song's fadeout.

There was also a bit of stress during the recording of "Eleanor Rigby," though for an entirely different reason. After hearing Paul play this beautiful song on acoustic guitar, George Martin felt that the only accompaniment that was necessary was that of a double string quartet: four violins, two violas, and two cellos. Paul wasn't immediately enamored of the concept—he was afraid of it sounding too cloying, too "Mancini"—but George eventually talked him into it, assuring him he would write a string arrangement that would be suitable.

"Okay, but I want the strings to sound really biting," Paul warned as he signed off on the idea. I took note of what he said and began thinking of how to best accomplish that.

String quartets were traditionally recorded with just one or two microphones, placed high, several feet up in the air so that the sound of the bows scraping couldn't be heard. But with Paul's directive in mind, I decided to close-mic the instruments, which was a new concept. The musicians were horrified! One of them gave me a look of disdain, rolled his eyes to the ceiling, and said under his breath, "You can't do that, you know."

His words shook my confidence and made me start to second-guess myself. But I carried on regardless, determined to at least hear what it sounded like.

We did one take with the mics fairly close, then on the next take I decided to get extreme and move the mics in *really* close—perhaps just an inch or so away from each instrument. It was a fine line; I didn't want to make the musicians so uncomfortable that they couldn't give their best performance, but my job was to achieve what Paul wanted. That was the sound he liked, and so that was the miking we used, despite the string players' unhappiness. To some degree, I could understand why they were so upset: they were scared of playing a bum note, and being under a microscope like that meant that any discrepancy in their playing was going to be magnified. Also, the technical limitations at the time were such that we couldn't easily drop in, so they had to play the whole song correctly from beginning to end every time.

Even without peering through the control room glass, I could hear the sound of the eight musicians sliding their chairs back before every take, so I had to keep going down there and moving the mics back in closer after every take; it was comic, really. Finally, George Martin told them pointedly to stop moving off mic. In the end, the players did a good job, though they clearly were annoyed, so much so that they declined an invitation to listen to the playback. We didn't really care what they thought, anyway—we were pleased that we had come up with another new sound, which was really a combination of Paul's vision and mine.

It was during the *Revolver* sessions that I realized I simply couldn't rely on textbook recording techniques in terms of mic positioning and placement. The Beatles were demanding more, so much more, of both me and of the technology. We didn't know it at the time, but we were making tremendous advancements in the recording process.

No one had ever heard strings like that before, and neither had they heard brass the way I recorded it on "Got To Get You Into My Life." Again, I close-miked the instruments—actually put the mics right down into the bells instead of the standard technique of placing them four feet away—and then applied severe limiting to the sound. There were only five players on the session, and when it came time to mix the song, Paul kept saying, "I wish we could make the brass sound bigger."

George Martin replied, "Well, there's no way we're bringing them back in for another session—we've got to get the album wrapped up and there's no more budget for outside players anyway."

That's when I came up with the idea of dubbing the horn track onto a fresh piece of two-track tape, then playing it back alongside the multitrack, but just slightly out of sync, which had the effect of doubling the horns. I loved Paul's singing on that song, too—he really let loose. At one point while Paul was recording the lead vocal, John actually burst out of the control room to shout his encouragement—evidence of the camaraderie and teamwork that was so pervasive during the *Revolver* sessions.

Another memorable incident occurred when Alan Civil—formerly of the London Philharmonic and then the principal horn player of the BBC Symphony Orchestra—was brought in to add French horn to Paul's haunting song "For No One." Alan was under a lot of pressure doing that overdub, because it was so hard to hit the high note in the solo. In fact, most people would have never written that part for a French horn player because it was too high to play, but that was the note Paul wanted to hear, and so that was the note he was going to get. We felt that Alan, being the best horn player in London, could actually hit it, even though most horn players couldn't. Alan was reluctant to even try it; he was actually breaking out into a sweat, telling everyone it really shouldn't be done. But eventually he gave it a go and pulled it off.

Though Alan was a wreck by the time he left that session, he was well pleased with what he'd done, because it was the performance of his life. In fact, he became a star in his own right because of that, but the problem was that, from that day on, arrangers would expect other horn players to be able to do what he had done, and they were often disappointed if they gave the parts to other players of lesser ability.

The Beatles were perfectionists, and they didn't always understand the limitations of musical instruments. In particular, Paul's attitude toward outside musicians was "You're being paid to do a job, so just do it." My sense was that the classical musicians had had it so easy for so long, but that things were now changing. There was also a generational clash, because most of those outside musicians were quite a bit older than the Beatles. They were pleased to be there, pleased to have the credit on their resumes, but they didn't know how to relate to the music or the musicians—and the Beatles didn't really know how to relate to them, either. George Martin served as the middleman, as the bridge between the two generations.

"Here, There And Everywhere"—one of Paul's favorite songs to this very day, and mine, too—was distinguished by the fact that we devoted three full days to it, which in that era was a lot of time. We also planned the track layout carefully so that there was a completely separate track that we could dedicate to bass, allowing Paul to focus on each and every note when he recorded the overdub. Later on, he would sometimes spend hours working out just how to get every note in his complex bass lines to "speak" correctly.

The weeks flew by, and before we knew it, the end date was nearing. We were mixing as we went along, and the mixes were going quickly because all the sounds were there. It was mostly down to balancing instruments and vocals; we didn't have to fix many parts or add much in the way of reverb or echo, because most things were recorded right along with their effects. Incredibly, all the stereo mixes of the album were done in a single long day. Our focus was on the mono mixes, which were the real mixes as far as we were concerned, since so few people had stereo record players in those days.

Revolver also marked the first time the Beatles regularly began attending mix sessions. There are photographs of John or Paul sitting behind the console with their hands on faders, but that was just for show—I don't remember them ever actually moving any faders in those days. If I was desperate for an extra pair of hands, I might ask Paul to help out once in a while, but that didn't happen often. I once asked John to do something simple—move a fader to a certain point, or pan a vocal off to one side—and he couldn't do it. It just wasn't in his makeup.

There's something to be said for that. The four Beatles just concentrated on the music itself. They trusted George Martin and me to do our job in the control room, and they did theirs, in the studio area. That was just the way it was, that was the system. Incredibly, prior to *Revolver,* mixes weren't even given to them to approve beforehand—the first time they'd hear the final version was when the record would come out, or when they'd hear themselves on the radio. But by 1966, they were starting to assert themselves a bit more, wanting more control, more say in the sound of their final product.

Having them present during mixing slowed the process up somewhat, but they were the artists, and it was their creation. It was a plus as far as I was concerned, because it gave us more input, though it was an incursion on George's absolute power as producer. But because they'd actually played the music, they would hear things that no one else could hear—the relationship between instruments, or slightly fluffed notes or rhythms—so it was certainly useful having them there. Of course, there wasn't all that much to mix because we were only using four tracks at the time, and would continue to do so all the way up until the *White Album.* It was Paul who was usually the most involved, and his comments would generally be focused on the harmony aspects. He'd say things like, "Oh, it would be great if this note were louder." The comments I'd get from John and George Harrison would generally be along the lines of a simple "More guitar."

It wasn't until the very end, when most of *Revolver* was mixed and ready to be mastered, that someone realized that the album was a song short. The LPs of that era were a lot more concise than today's CDs, but if they were *too* short, there would be complaints—or worse yet, returns—from consumers. Not only was there a release date set, and a hungry public clamoring to hear the finished album, but the Beatles were booked to begin a European tour just days after the sessions ended, so there was no time to spare.

So on the next-to-last night, after we had all spent a full day mixing, Mal and Neil reappeared with the band's equipment and the group began frantically rehearsing John's new song "She Said, She Said." John had always been the basher in the group—his attitude was "Let's just get it done"—so it was no big surprise that we got the entire song recorded and mixed in nine hours, as opposed to the more than three days we spent on "Here, There and Everywhere." Still, he made the group run through the song dozens of times before he was satisfied with the final result. For all of that, it still sounds scrappy and rough to me, it's got the ragged feel of a track that was done in the middle of the night, under pressure. The next day we staggered in for another five hours of mixing and sequencing, and the album was done.

Incredibly, *Revolver* had been completed in just over ten weeks (we had most weekends off), with many songs taking only a few hours to get down on tape. It was always a matter of capturing the moment, and when you were working with the Beatles it had to be right. Exhausting as it was, both mentally and physically, it was a good way to work—really, the *only* way to work.

Revolver was released in August of 1966, just as the Beatles were in full swing on an international tour—a tour that would turn out to be their last. It met with immediate critical and commercial success, and the only question in the public's mind was, how on earth could they top it? Little did we know that when we reconvened in the studio in November to begin work on *Sgt. Pepper's Lonely Hearts Club Band,* we would not only be topping it, but sending all the barriers crashing to the ground.

8

It's Wonderful to Be Here,
It's Certainly a Thrill:

Sgt. Pepper Begins

John Lennon was even more agitated than usual. "Look," he said to George Martin, "it's really quite simple. We're fed up with making soft music for soft people, and we're fed up with playing for them, too. But it's given us a fresh start, don't you see?"

From the expression on his face, it was clear that George Martin didn't see.

"We can't hear ourselves onstage anymore for all the screaming," Paul interjected earnestly, "so what's the point? We did try performing some songs off the last album, but there are so many complicated overdubs we can't do them justice. Now we can record anything we want, and it won't matter. And what we want is to raise the bar a notch, to make our best album ever."

Another blank look from George Martin. I could tell what he was thinking. *Who ever heard of a band that only makes records but doesn't promote them by doing concerts?*

Lennon persisted, talking rapid-fire—a sure sign that he was starting to get annoyed. "What we're saying is, if we don't have to tour, then we can record music that we won't ever have to play live, and that means we can create something that's never been heard before: a new kind of record with new kinds of sounds."

Simultaneously, every head swiveled in my direction. All I could manage was a wan smile, but I knew then that the gauntlet had been thrown. It was down to me—not George Martin, not anyone else—to turn the Beatles' new vision into a reality.

It had been five months since I'd last seen the group, but it might as well have been five years. For one thing, they all looked so different. Garbed in colorful clothes and sporting trendy mustaches—George Harrison even had a beard—they were utterly hip, the epitome of swinging London circa 1966.

Clad in my usual "straight" suit and tie, I felt envious. *That damn EMI dress code!* John was the one who had changed the most: having shed the excess weight he'd put on during the *Revolver* sessions, he was trim, almost gaunt, and he was wearing granny glasses instead of the thick horn-rimmed National Health spectacles I was used to seeing. He also had very short, distinctly non-Beatlish hair. I'd read in the tabloids that he'd had it cut for the filming of the Richard Lester movie *How I Won the War*.

It was our first night back in the studio, and we were huddled around the mixing console, discussing how we wanted to approach the new album. I'd had no inkling of their decision to stop touring—there had been no announcement in the press because Brian Epstein was anxious to keep it quiet. I suppose he harbored hopes that they might change their mind, tempted by visions of the huge amounts of money they had been offered in recent months. But it was absolutely clear from our conversation that evening that the Beatles' minds were firmly made up. They had no intention of ever setting foot on another stage, and they seemed quite glad of it. From their description of the horrors of that last tour, I could understand why.

"Bloody Yanks," muttered Harrison.

"What are you on about?" Lennon snapped. "I was the one in the line of fire, not you."

"Well, I wasn't the one who was daft enough to compare us to Jesus," Harrison retorted testily.

Lennon shot him a dirty glance and went into a sulk. The topic seemed to depress him immensely.

John's ill-advised remark in a newspaper interview about the Beatles being "bigger than Jesus" had had far-reaching repercussions on the group's career, impacting especially on their popularity in America, to the extent where they had received death threats while on tour; some zealots were even burning their albums. It had even affected us at EMI to some degree. Earlier that fall, Brian had persuaded Lennon to record a formal apology for broadcast to American radio stations, but the problem was that John was away on holiday and unavailable to come into the studio in person. He was apparently willing to phone it in, but for some reason Brian deemed that unacceptable—not remorseful enough, perhaps? As a result, our technical boffins spent a few hurried days designing a dummy head into which John's telephoned apology would be played: the idea was that the cavities of this little plaster head would somehow make his voice more realistic, as if he were actually in the studio talking on a high-quality microphone instead of over a low-fidelity phone line. In the end, Lennon changed his mind and the apology never did materialize, but it just goes to show the lengths to which EMI would go to accommodate the Beatles; if it had been any other artist, they would never have devoted the time and resources to such a foolish idea.

In the control room, the swapping of stories continued. The band got especially animated when they began describing the indignities they had suffered in Manila: in retaliation for a supposed snub of First Lady Imelda Marcos, they had been forced to flee the country without the benefit of police protection. Things were so dicey there for a while, they said, that even Big Mal, the ex-bouncer, had gotten roughed up at the airport. They were joking a bit, but I could sense that beneath the casual banter, the four Beatles were considerably more subdued, more on their guard than they had ever been before. Clearly the events of the past months had taken a toll on them; they seemed almost robbed of their youth. No longer were they the four cuddly moptops; now they looked and acted like seasoned musicians, weary veterans of the road.

The small talk continued for some time, George Harrison's eyes lighting up as he described his visit to India. He seemed to have found a new direction for himself, and I was happy for him, even though he seemed more estranged than ever from the others. I couldn't help but notice that he was still as white and pale as always; either he'd been staying out of the sun, or he simply didn't tan.

Finally, George Martin called an end to the informal conference.

"Right then, let's get to work. What have you got for me?"

Paul started to say something, but before he could answer, John shouted out, "I've got a good one, for a starter!"

John could talk over most anyone if he wanted to, and he was never shy about jumping the queue; in fact, the first session for almost every Beatles album was devoted to recording one of his songs. A half smile played across Paul's face as he shrugged his shoulders, backing down gracefully.

As it turned out, John was correct. He did indeed have a good one for a starter.

Phil McDonald and I strained to hear what was going on downstairs. I was pleased that my partner in crime from the *Revolver* sessions was once again assigned to work with me; we had become good personal friends, and he was a reliable, if sometimes overly exuberant, assistant engineer. (In recognition of his sometimes raucous ways, John had nicknamed him "Phil The Basher.") Down in the studio, George Martin was perched, as usual, on his high stool, positioned in the midst of the four Beatles; he liked being looked up to, so he never sat in a normal chair during routining. John was standing directly in front of him, playing an acoustic guitar and singing softly. Because he wasn't close to any of the microphones we had arranged around the room, I had to push the faders up quite high to hear him.

From the very first note, it was obvious that this new Lennon song was a masterpiece. He had created a gentle, almost mystical tribute to some mysterious place, a place he called "Strawberry Fields." I had no idea what the lyric was about, but the words were compelling, like abstract poetry, and there was something magical in the spooky, detached timbre of John's voice.

When he finished, there was a moment of stunned silence, broken by Paul, who in a quiet, respectful tone said simply, "That is absolutely brilliant." Most of the time when Lennon played one of his songs through for the first time on acoustic guitar, we'd all think, *Wow, that's great,* but this song was clearly something special.

"I've brought a demo tape of the song with me, too," John said, offering to play it, but everyone agreed there was no need—they wanted to get straight into recording. The energy in the room was staggering: it was almost as if the band's creative energies had been bottled up for too long.

There was a new addition to the mound of equipment that Mal and Neil had set up in Studio Two: a cumbersome keyboard in a polished wood cabinet. It was called a Mellotron, and it was John's newest toy, brought down from his Weybridge mansion specially for the sessions. I was already somewhat familiar with the instrument because a representative of the manufacturer had been to the studio and given the EMI staff a demonstration some weeks previously. It was a revolutionary idea for its time: each key triggered a tape loop of a real instrument playing the equivalent note. There were three sets of tape loops installed, so you could have flutes, strings, or choir at the touch of a button. Some of the keys were even set up to trigger complete prerecorded rhythm sections or musical phrases instead of single notes: Lennon took great delight at hitting the lowest note, which played a corny brassy introduction, followed by an even cornier Jimmy Durante–style "Yeah!" at the end. Another key triggered a couple of measures of flamenco guitar, which John later made famous when he used it to introduce his song "The Continuing Story Of Bungalow Bill" on the *White Album.*

But it was the first time the other Beatles and George Martin had ever seen the instrument, and they were all very curious, with each taking a turn behind the keyboard, trying out different sounds. It was Paul, as usual, who discovered the musical potential instead of just the novelty value. Dialing up the flute sound, he began experimenting with the chords to John's new song. Within a remarkably short time he'd worked out an arrangement that beautifully complemented Lennon's haunting vocal line. It was pure serendipidity that the sound fitted the mood of the song so perfectly.

The Beatles weren't ever especially fast at working out parts, and this night followed the usual pattern: several hours were spent routining the song, deciding who was going to play what instrument, and figuring out the exact patterns and notes they would play. Paul was still having a whale of a time with the Mellotron, so he decided he would man it during the backing track. Ringo busied himself by arranging towels over his snare drum and tom-toms in order to give them a distinctive muffled tone. Off in a corner, George Harrison was experimenting with his new toy—slide guitar—practicing the long, Hawaiian-style swoops he planned to play on his electric guitar, punctuating John's more straightforward rhythm part. Following a long period of rehearsal, they finally decided to make a first stab at recording a backing track. It certainly was an odd sight, with Paul hunched over the large wooden keyboard and Ringo surrounded by a mass of tea towels. We spent a good eight hours in the studio that first night, and even though some of that time was spent just chatting and getting reacquainted, the only thing we got out of the session was a single take of the song which was never used.

A few days later, we reconvened at Abbey Road and work resumed on "Strawberry Fields Forever," as the song had been titled. The big breakthrough that night was Paul's coming up with the stunning Mellotron line that opens the song. Paul's inspiration really set the stage. In many ways it was a harbinger of things to come over the next several months—the perfect, unique introduction to a series of near-perfect, near-unique sessions.

All in all, three long sessions were devoted to recording that one track, which seemed like a lot at the time. John seemed to be having a lot of trouble making up his mind about how he wanted the song recorded, but with the addition of some double-tracked vocals and a few piano overdubs, it was deemed finished . . . for the moment. (Little did we know that many more hours would be expended before Lennon was satisfied.) A rough mono mix was run off and playback lacquers were ordered so the band could listen to the song at home.

Everyone's attention then turned to Paul's "When I'm Sixty-Four." Because the group was already so familiar with the song—they used to busk it onstage back when they were still playing clubs in Hamburg—the backing track was laid down in just a couple of hours. As was usual for a McCartney song, there were extensive discussions with George Martin about arrangement. Paul kept saying that he wanted the song to be really "rootie-tootie," so George suggested the addition of clarinets. The clarinets on that track became a very personal sound to me; I recorded them really close up, bringing them so far forward that they became one of the main focal points. During the mix, Paul also asked to have the track sped up a great deal—almost a semitone—so that his voice would sound more youthful, like the teenager he was when he originally wrote the song.

It was around this time that George Harrison approached me with an unusual request. "Ravi is in the next studio and they're having trouble recording his sitar," he said. "Would you mind popping over and having a look?"

Needless to say, I was surprised. I knew that he was referring to Ravi Shankar, the Indian virtuoso and George's sitar teacher, but it was perhaps the first time that Harrison had ever spoken to me directly about anything other than his guitar sound or the mix balance in one of his songs. I was flattered, though, and happy to help; frankly, I hoped that doing so might serve to reduce some of the distance between us. But I knew that I had to be diplomatic: barging in on another engineer's session was bad enough, but criticizing what he was doing while you were there was completely against studio protocol. *What the hell*, I thought, *at least I'm going in there armed with a Beatle.*

George, I am sure, had a good sense of the power he wielded, but he was actually pretty tactful: he just said to the engineer on the session, "Ravi's having a few problems getting a sound, so I've asked Geoff to come in and see what he thinks." No one other than me had ever recorded a sitar at Abbey Road before, and the engineer—one of the older, classical guys, and quite stuck-up—wasn't willing to break any of the EMI rules, so he was blindly employing the standard miking for a solo instrument . . . even though sitar was about as nonstandard as you could get. As tactfully as I could, I suggested that the engineer substitute a different mic and move it in a lot closer, just inches away. He gave me a filthy look, but with George Harrison standing behind me both literally and metaphorically, he didn't argue. Ravi loved the resulting sound, and George gave me a warm thank-you and an appreciative wink as I headed out the door.

In the midst of all this, John had been listening repeatedly to his acetate of "Strawberry Fields Forever," and he decided he didn't like it. For someone who was normally so articulate, it always amazed me how he would struggle for words whenever he tried to tell George Martin how he wanted a song arranged. This time around, he just kept mumbling, "I don't know; I just think it should somehow be heavier."

"Heavier how, John?" George asked.

"I dunno, just kind of, y'know . . . heavier."

Paul did his best to translate John's abstract notion into concrete musical form. Pointing out how well the flute sound on the Mellotron had worked, he suggested that perhaps some outside musicians be brought in, that the song be scored for some orchestral instrumentation. John loved the idea, specifically requesting cellos and trumpets.

"Do a good job, George," he instructed the still somewhat uncertain producer as he departed the control room. "Just make sure it's heavy."

Lennon didn't want to simply overdub more instruments on top of the existing rhythm track, though—he wanted to scrap the whole thing and start all over again. Unfortunately, on the night that they began doing the remake, George Martin and I were in London's West End, attending the premiere of the new Cliff Richard film *Finders Keepers*. George was quite adamant that we go, which really annoyed me. I felt our place was with the Beatles, and I felt certain that they were going to be unhappy about us taking time off so early into an album project. In retrospect, I think it may have been a psychological ploy on George's part to show them who was in charge.

It was midnight when we finally returned to the studio, only to find the four Beatles still hard at work with maintenance engineer Dave Harries, who had been recruited to start the session in our absence. In the end, only part of what he recorded ever made its way onto the final release version; George and I stayed on until nearly dawn and ended up redoing most of it.

All told, we probably spent in excess of thirty hours recording the remake of "Strawberry Fields Forever." Of course, we were constantly experimenting along the way, trying things out, some of which worked and found their way onto the final recording, and some of which didn't. We were after perfection: it wasn't a question of being 99 percent happy with something; we all had to be 100 percent happy with it. That's why everything on the album that would come to be called *Sgt. Pepper's Lonely Hearts Club Band* is so pristine and precise. For this track, John relented in his usual impatience; he was determined to carry on until the track was everything he wanted it to be. Maybe it was because of the drugs he was taking at the time, but John was definitely a lot mellower during the early *Pepper* sessions. "Strawberry Fields Forever" would receive more time and attention than any John Lennon song ever recorded with the Beatles—even more than his later masterpieces "A Day In The Life" and "I Am The Walrus."

Even when the remake was complete, adorned with all manner of exotic instruments like plucked piano, backward cymbals, and George Harrison's swordmandel (an Indian instrument somewhat like an autoharp) and then mixed to everyone's satisfaction, there was one more surprise to come.

"I've been listening to these acetates of 'Strawberry Fields' a lot," John announced a few days later, "and I've decided that I still prefer the beginning of the original version."

My jaw dropped. Out of the corner of my eye, I could see George Martin blinking slowly. I could almost detect his blood pressure rising. Ignoring both of us, Lennon continued.

"So what I'd like our young Geoffrey here to do is to join the two bits together."

George Martin let out a big sigh. "John, we'd be glad to do that," he said, the sarcasm dripping from his voice. "The only thing that stands in our way is the fact that the two versions were played in different keys and at different tempos."

John appeared nonplussed; I'm not sure he even understood why that presented a problem.

"You can do it," he said simply. With that, he turned and headed out the door.

"What do you think, Geoff?" a deflated George asked me after John had gone. My reply was noncommittal.

"I'm not sure; I guess all we can do is have a go."

Since the days of *Revolver*, we had gotten used to being asked to do the impossible, and we knew that the word "no" didn't exist in the Beatles' vocabulary. But John's request, on the face of it, appeared completely unfeasible given the technology of the time. Today, a computer can quite easily change the pitch and/or tempo of a recording independently of each other, but all we had at our disposal was a pair of editing scissors, a couple of tape machines, and a varispeed control. The problem was that as soon as you speed up a tape, the pitch also goes up; slowing down a tape has the opposite effect, slowing the tempo, but also lowering the pitch. We had our work cut out for us, but I was certainly willing to see if it was at all possible.

Fortunately, as George Martin has said many times in the intervening years, the gods smiled down upon us. Even though the two takes John wanted spliced together were recorded a week apart and were radically different in approach, the keys weren't that dissimilar—they were only a semitone apart—and the tempos were also fairly close. After some trial-and-error experimentation, I discovered that by speeding up the playback of the first take and slowing down the playback of the second, I could get them to match in both pitch and tempo.

Next, I had to find a suitable edit point, one that wasn't obvious. The idea, after all, was to make the listeners think they were hearing a complete performance. The one I picked happened to fall almost exactly sixty seconds in, at the beginning of the second chorus, on the word "going" ("Let me take you down / 'Cause I'm *going* to . . ."). Now it was a matter of figuring out exactly when to alter the playback speeds. George and I decided to allow the second half to play all the way through at the slower speed; doing so gave John's voice a smoky, thick quality that seemed to complement the psychedelic lyric and swirling instrumentation. Things were a bit trickier with the beginning section; it started out at such a perfect, laconic tempo that we didn't want to speed it up all the way through. Luckily, the EMI tape machines were fitted with very fine varispeed controls. With a bit of practice, I was able to gradually increase the speed of the first take and get it to a certain precise point, right up to the moment where we knew we were going to do the edit. The change is so subtle as to be virtually unnoticeable.

There was still one last hurdle to overcome. I found that I couldn't cut the tape at a normal forty-five-degree angle because the sound just kind of jumped—I was, after all, joining together two totally different performances. As a result, I had to make the cut at a very shallow angle so that it was more like a crossfade than a splice. It took many hours to get everything to work perfectly, but we felt justified in spending all that time because "Strawberry Fields Forever" seemed like such a landmark recording.

At the end of the evening, John popped by to see how we were getting on—I had literally finished the edit just a few moments before he arrived. As we played the results of our labors to John for the first time, he listened carefully, head down, deep in concentration. I made a point of standing in front of the tape machine so that he couldn't see the splice go by. A few seconds after the edit flew past, Lennon lifted his head up and a grin spread across his face.

"Has it passed yet?" he asked.

"Sure has," I replied proudly.

"Well, good on yer, Geoffrey!" he said. He absolutely loved what we had done. We played "Strawberry Fields Forever" over and over again that night for John, and at the conclusion each time, he'd turn to us and repeat the same three words, eyes wide with excitement: "Brilliant. Just brilliant."

Years after *Sgt. Pepper* was released, we were all amused—and somewhat horrified—to learn that some Beatles fans had gotten the idea that Paul had died in the midst of recording the album. Many of those subscribing to this ridiculous notion even thought that John was somberly intoning the words

"I buried Paul" at the very end of "Strawberry Fields Forever," during the so-called "freak-out" section. I'm sorry to disappoint anyone who ever bought into this rubbish, but Paul was, in fact, very much alive and well, and there was never any kind of plan to fool the public by scattering clues about his supposed demise. John was actually saying "cranberry sauce," not "I buried Paul," for the simple reason that we were recording around the time of the Thanksgiving holiday, and just before the take, we had all been chatting about turkey and all the trimmings, and how Americans traditionally ate such a meal at that time of year. That's the way John was—he'd often work little phrases or snatches of conversation about something he had been recently reading or talking about into the music he was recording. Certainly that was the case for his other three contributions to the *Sgt. Pepper* album: "A Day In The Life" (about the car crash that killed Guinness heir Tara Browne), "Being For The Benefit Of Mr. Kite" (from a circus poster), and "Good Morning, Good Morning" (from a television commercial for Kellogg's Corn Flakes).

At this point, we were three weeks into the album, and we'd finished only two songs. George Martin and Phil and I would chat among ourselves about how long it was taking, but we also knew that what we were getting was really good. It was a painstaking and slow process, but we had the luxury of time; we weren't under any pressure, so we could afford to spend an hour or two getting precisely the right snare sound or the optimum vocal effect. Our apparent inefficiency was a juicy topic of conversation among other Abbey Road staff, who were used to doing an album in a week. All we'd say during those canteen discussions—rather smugly, I'm afraid—was "Just wait." The lucky few who did get the opportunity to hear the tracks prior to the album's official release were absolutely gobsmacked.

To this point, George Harrison's contribution had been quite minimal: a little slide guitar on "Strawberry Fields Forever," and a line or two of backing vocal on "When I'm Sixty-Four." He had to have been doing other things during the day to occupy his mind—practicing sitar, I guessed—because he had precious little to do in the studio. Clearly, the boredom had begun setting in for George, and that was the case for Ringo, too; in later years, he's said that his strongest memory of the *Pepper* sessions was that they were when he learned to play chess. In some ways, *Pepper* was more like a John and Paul album than a Beatles album; *Revolver* and all the records that preceded it were much more of a group effort.

One major difference between *Revolver* and *Pepper* was that there was an absolute drop-dead date by which *Revolver* had to be completed, because a tour was about to begin. But with *Pepper,* the group could literally take as long as they liked, so they worked on it until they were completely satisfied; there were no other obligations to fulfill. It's possible that, behind the scenes, EMI was lobbying the group to finish it, but by this time they were so huge they were immune to any pressure. The record company simply had to wait until the Beatles themselves were ready to deliver the album.

Another change was that we began working very late nights—typically not even starting before 7 P.M.—whereas most of *Revolver* was recorded during the afternoon and early evening. Those late-night sessions, combined with the dreary London fall and winter, did make things a bit more tedious. The shift came, I suppose, because the group's lifestyle changed; they slept during the day and partied at night. By the end of the album, it wasn't unusual for sessions to start at midnight and finish at dawn, which put a strain on all of us. We sometimes suspected that Mal Evans was putting something in our tea to keep us awake, but we never found out for sure. I doubt very much if he ever dosed us with acid—it wouldn't have been very helpful to the Beatles if we were tripping in the control room!—but I suppose it's possible that he might have occasionally spiked the tea with a mild upper.

One of Paul McCartney's favorite albums of 1966 was the Beach Boys' *Pet Sounds,* and he often played it on his portable gramophone during breaks, so it wasn't altogether unsurprising when he announced that he wanted a "really clean American sound" on the next song of his to be recorded: "Penny Lane." I'd spent a lot of time mastering American records, and I was convinced that the best way to give Paul what he wanted was to record each instrument totally on its own so that there would be no leakage (or "bleed," as it was known) whatsoever. Paul's trust in me was such that he simply said offhandedly, "Okay, well, let's do it that way, then."

Ultimately, the group was to spend even more time on "Penny Lane" than they had on "Strawberry Fields Forever"—three full weeks, a huge amount of studio time in those days. Unlike any other Beatles track recorded to that point, it started with just Paul playing piano, not with the four of them playing a rhythm track together; every single part except the main piano piece was an overdub. For days, the others sat at the back of the studio watching Paul layer keyboard after keyboard, working completely on his own. As always, his sense of timing was absolutely superb: the main piano part that everything was built on was rock solid despite the fact that there were no electronic metronomes to lay down click tracks in those days. In fact, Ringo wasn't even employed to tap out a beat on the hi-hat. It was that bedrock of Paul's original piano track that gave the whole song such a great feel.

The only problem that this approach gave us was track availability. Four-track recording was a real limitation with this particular song, so we were constantly having to bounce tracks together and do reductions (which we sometimes called "premixes"). In the end, there were so many keyboards blended together, they ended up becoming a sound of their own; listening to the finished recording, it's hard to pick out individual instruments. Some of the overdubs even got buried altogether because of the density of the instrumentation and the number of bounces. Nonetheless, "Penny Lane" contains a lot of great sounds.

Apart from joining in on the backing vocals and playing a bit of rhythm guitar, John contributed very little to "Penny Lane"—he just tapped idly on a couple of conga drums. He actually liked doing that kind of thing because he could loon around; he never treated the recording process all that seriously. Overdubbing different kinds of instruments, things other than his normal six-string Rickenbacker electric or Gibson acoustic guitar, provided light relief for him: if he didn't have much to do, he'd get bored easily. The clanging fire bell, played by Ringo, came from the sound effects cupboard under the stairs in Studio Two. If the Beatles ever got stuck for an overdub, they'd head into that cupboard to find something—there was so much paraphernalia there: wind machines, thunder machines, bells, whistles—you name it. Whenever that door was opened, we knew that something fun was about to happen.

Midway through the recording of "Penny Lane," we spent the better part of an evening creating a tape of sound effects, under Paul's direction, for a live "happening" called the Carnival of Light. (A "happening" was a sixties term that embraced any kind of counterculture gathering.) It was a bit of nonsense, really, but everyone had fun doing it. Whenever the Beatles tried something really outrageous, George Martin would roll his eyes and mutter a clipped "Oh my God" under his breath. Looking back, I guess that everyone was tripping his brains out that night, but we didn't know it then. When John started shouting "Barcelona" repeatedly in one of his Goon-like voices, Phil and I were doubled over in laughter. That line, and other bits and pieces from that night's session, were later used in the sound pastiche "Revolution 9," on the *White Album*.

In contrast to John, who had only the vaguest of ideas about how he wanted "Strawberry Fields Forever" to be recorded, Paul had very definite thoughts about the instrumentation he wanted on "Penny Lane." George

Martin was tasked with creating an arrangement for flutes, trumpets, piccolo, and fluegelhorn, to which were added oboes, cor anglais (English horn), and bowed double bass. Combined with Paul's stellar bass playing and superb vocals (with backing from John and George), the track was beginning to sound full, polished, and quite finished to me.

But not to Paul's. He was still after that one last bit of magic, and inspiration came to him one night while he was at home watching a television programme featuring a performance of Bach's *Brandenburg* Concerto no. 2—coincidentally, one of the records I had discovered as a child in my grandmother's basement, and one of my all-time favorite classical pieces. The next evening, we were in the studio and Paul couldn't stop talking about it.

"What was that tiny little trumpet that fellow was playing?" he asked us. "I couldn't believe the sound he was making!"

George Martin's classical training never came in more handy. "That's called a piccolo trumpet," he said, "and the chap playing it was David Mason, who happens to be a friend of mine."

"Fantastic!" exclaimed Paul. "Let's get him in here and have him overdub it."

A few days later I found myself carefully placing a microphone in front of Mason, who was himself quite famous in the classical world as the principal trumpeter for the prestigious Royal Philharmonic Orchestra. The only problem was that no music had been prepared for him to play; instead, he had to sit there for hours while Paul hummed and sang the parts he was hearing in his head, George Martin writing the notes out by hand. By this point, it was a big deal to be asked to play on a Beatles session, and I suppose Mason felt that it was prudent to keep his countenance, though I am quite sure the lack of preparation tried his patience sorely. Eventually, though, the score was worked out to Paul's satisfaction, and he headed up to the control room to listen as we began rolling tape. True professional that he was, Mason played it perfectly the first time through, including the extraordinarily demanding solo which ended on a note that was almost impossibly high. It was, quite simply, the performance of his life.

And everyone knew it . . . except, obviously, Paul. As the final note faded to silence, he reached for the talkback mic. "Nice one, David," Paul said matter-of-factly. "Can we try another pass?"

There was a long moment of silence.

"Another pass?" The trumpeter looked up at the control room helplessly. He seemed lost for words. Finally, he said softly, "Look, I'm sorry. I'm afraid I just can't do it any better."

Mason knew that he had nailed it, that he had played everything note-perfect and that it was a prodigious feat that he could not possibly top. Quickly George Martin intervened and addressed Paul emphatically, one of the few times in recent weeks that I saw him assert his authority as producer. "Good God, you can't possibly ask the man to do that again . . . it's fantastic!"

A dark cloud gathered over Paul's face. Even though the exchange was occurring in the privacy of the control room, out of earshot of Mason and the other Beatles, George's remark clearly embarrassed and angered him. It was the kind of scene I would not witness again until partway through the making of the *White Album*, when things were to build to an exploding point.

For an uncomfortable moment the producer and his headstrong young artist glared at each other. Finally, Paul returned to the talkback mic. "Okay, thank you, David. You're free to go now, released on your own recognizance."

Handled with typical McCartney humor, the confrontation was over. Later that same day, we did a mix that was couriered to Capitol in the U.S. for pressing—George and Brian had already determined that "Penny Lane" and "Strawberry Fields Forever" would comprise the next, long-overdue Beatles single, a momentous decision that removed both songs from the *Sgt. Pepper* album. The mix was a good one, but unfortunately it was done in such a hurry that Mason's piccolo trumpet flourish at the very end of the song was inadvertently omitted. A week later, a remix was undertaken and the error was corrected. Some early U.S. pressings of the single still contained the original mix, however. As a result, they have since become quite a collector's item.

That first lot of sessions ran right through the Christmas and New Year's holidays, so the Beatles took a fair amount of time off, though there was no real break for me—whenever they weren't in Studio Two working on the album, I was engineering for other artists. Since the success of *Revolver*, I'd found myself increasingly in demand, and, not unexpectedly, I was frequently asked to impart that magical "Beatles sound" onto other records I was doing. It was a request I always declined. I felt strongly then—as I do to this very day—that every artist should stand on his own merits and find his *own* sound.

Whenever I could find the time, though, I'd listen back with great pride to those first three tracks. I knew that there was no comparison to anything that had ever come before, or since, and I knew just how revolutionary our work had been: the use of the Mellotron in "Strawberry Fields Forever," the building up of "Penny Lane" layer by layer. We were blazing new trails in recording . . . and the best was yet to come.

• • •

One mid-January evening, the four Beatles rolled up, a little bit stoned, as had become usual, but with a tinge of excitement. They had a new song they'd been working on—one of Lennon's—and they were anxious to play it for George Martin and me. They had gotten in the habit of meeting at Paul's house in nearby St. John's Wood before sessions, where they'd have a cup of tea, perhaps a puff of a joint, and John and Paul would finish up any songs that were still in progress. Once a song was complete, the four of them would start routining it right there and then, working out parts, learning the chords and time changes, all before they got to the studio. They would then get in their respective cars and be driven over to Abbey Road—although it was walking distance, they couldn't take a stroll because of all the fans—which explained why they always showed up together despite living considerable distances from one another.

The song unveiled for us this evening was tentatively called "In The Life Of"—soon to be retitled "A Day In The Life." It was in a similar vein to "Strawberry Fields Forever"—light and dreamy—but it was somehow even more compelling. I was in awe; I distinctly remember thinking, *Christ, John's topped himself!* As Lennon sang softly, strumming his acoustic guitar, Paul accompanied him on piano. A lot of thought must have gone into the piano part, because it was providing a perfect counterpoint to John's vocal and guitar playing. Ringo joined on bongos, while George Harrison, who seemed to have been given nothing specific to do, idly shook a pair of maracas.

The song, as played during that first run-through, consisted simply of a short introduction, three verses, and two perfunctory choruses. The only lyric in the chorus was a rather daring "I'd love to turn you on"—six provocative words that would result in the song being banned by the BBC. Obviously more was needed to flesh it out, but this was all Lennon had written. There was a great deal of discussion about what to do, but no real resolution. Paul thought he might have something that would fit, but for the moment everyone was keen to start recording, so it was decided simply to leave twenty-four empty bars in the middle as a kind of placeholder. This in itself was unique in Beatles recording: the song was clearly unfinished, but it was so good nonetheless that it was decided to plow ahead and get it down on tape and then finish it later. In essence, the composition was going to be structured during the recording stage. Without any conscious forethought, we were in the process of creating not just a song, but musical work of art.

Though no one yet knew what the overdubs were going to consist of, it was obvious that there were going to be lots of them, so I made the decision to record all of the instruments for that first pass on a single track, though I put Lennon's guide vocal, heavily effected with what he called his "Elvis echo," on a separate track. John loved having tape echo in his headphones ("Make it so I don't sound like me," he'd say) and I'd usually record it right along with his voice because he'd sing to the echo, which would in turn cause him to approach the song differently. The way he'd pronounce his d's and t's—really spit them out—actually triggered the tape echo better than anyone I'd ever heard. Perhaps it was down to the fact that he was a really big Elvis and Buddy Holly fan; he'd obviously studied their vocals and modeled his style on them. And, just as he was a great rhythm guitarist, he always had a great sense of rhythm in his vocals, a unique way of phrasing words.

Mal Evans was dispatched to stand by the piano and count off the twenty-four bars in the middle so that each Beatle could focus on his playing and not have to think about it. Though Mal's voice was fed into the headphones, it was not meant to be recorded, but he got more and more excited as the count progressed, raising his voice louder and louder. As a result, it began bleeding through on to the other mics, so some of it even survived onto the final mix.

There also happened to be a windup alarm clock set on top of the piano—Lennon had brought it in as a gag one day, saying that it would come in handy for waking up Ringo when he was needed for an overdub. In a fit of silliness, Mal decided to set it off at the start of the 24th bar; that, too, made it onto the finished recording . . . for no reason other than that I couldn't get rid of it.

Only one last adjustment was required before the backing track for "A Day In The Life" would be committed to tape, and that was the reversing of Ringo's and George's instrumental assignments. After the first run-through, with Harrison on maracas, George Martin turned to me in the control room and said, "He's not very steady, is he? I think I'll have him switch with Ringo," and I concurred. Ringo was a much better timekeeper, and George Harrison's concentration used to wander too much to keep a steady tempo for three or four minutes straight. I mixed the little bit of noodling Harrison ended up doing on the bongos so far in the background that it was nearly inaudible.

Normally it was Paul who did the count-in at the start of a song, even if it were a Lennon or Harrison composition, simply because he had the best sense of what would be the optimum tempo. Occasionally, however, John would count in his own songs. Whenever he did, he would substitute nonsense words: the standard "one, two, three, four" just wasn't good enough for him. On this particular cold January evening—close enough to the holidays that the Christmas trees in most homes were still up—he opted to use the phrase "sugarplum fairy, sugarplum fairy" instead, which gave us all a chuckle up in the control room. But once he started singing, we were all stunned into silence; the raw emotion in his voice made the hairs on the back of my neck stand up. Once the sparse backing track was deemed satisfactory, Lennon did take after take of the lead vocal, each heavily laden with tape echo, each more amazing than the one before. His vocal performance that night was an absolute tour de force, and it was all George Martin, Phil, and I could talk about long after the session ended.

Interestingly, even though John and Paul both had phenomenal pitch, John was quite insecure about his voice. Quite often when he'd come up to the control room and listen to a playback of his vocal, we'd have to tell John how good it was. We'd see that faraway look on his face and know that he was dissatisfied, even if it was a stunning performance; we'd have to keep re-assuring him, or he'd insist that we erase it so he could try again. George Martin would usually be the first to speak up, and then we'd all agree with him. The other three Beatles would chime in with words of encouragement, too, if they were around. But normally if John wanted to listen to a vocal playback—especially if it was just the first or second take—he'd come up to the control room on his own, and the others would stay downstairs with Neil and Mal.

The next night's session began with an intensive review of what had been laid down on tape. Our job was to decide which of John's lead vocals was the "keeper." We didn't have to necessarily use the entire performance, though. Because we had the luxury of working in four-track, I could copy over ("bounce") the best lines from each take into one track—a process known as "comping." This is a recording technique that is still very much in use today; it's rare when the lead vocal you hear on any modern record is a complete performance from start to finish. All we were really listening for when we were comping John's vocal was phrasing and inflection; he never had trouble hitting the notes spot on. Lennon sat behind the mixing console with George Martin and me, picking out the bits he liked. Paul was up in the control room, too, expressing his opinions, but George Harrison and Ringo stayed down in the studio; they just weren't involved to that extent.

With that done, it was time to reattack the problem of the missing middle section. Paul had gone through his notebook and discovered a snippet of a song—a section of an unfinished composition written months or years before—that he felt might fit, and John quickly concurred. The four Beatles, with Paul singing a guide vocal, then recorded the backing track to this new piece, which I edited into the four-track master. In what could only be described as pure serendipity, it happened to begin with the lyric "Woke up / Fell out of bed . . ." which, incredibly, perfectly fit the alarm clock ringing. If ever there was an omen that this was to be a very special song in the Beatles canon, this was it.

We now returned our attention to the main section of the song. At that point, the rhythmic accompaniment still consisted solely of Ringo's maracas and just the slightest trace of George Harrison on bongos, and John felt strongly that more was needed. Paul suggested that Ringo not just do his normal turn but really cut loose on the track, and I could see that the drummer was quite reticent. "Come on, Paul, you know how much I hate flashy drumming," he complained, but with John and Paul coaching and egging him on, he did an overdub that was nothing short of spectacular, featuring a whole series of quirky tom-tom fills.

Because John and Paul felt so strongly that the drums be featured in this song, I decided to experiment sonically as well. We were looking for a thicker, more tonal quality, so I suggested that Ringo tune his toms really low, making the skins really slack, and I also added a lot of low end at the mixing console. That made them sound almost like timpani, but I still felt there was more I could do to make his playing stand out. During the making of *Revolver,* I had removed the front skin from Ringo's bass drum and everyone was pleased with the resultant sound, so I decided to extend that principle and take off the bottom heads from the tom-toms as well, miking them from underneath. We had no boom stands that could extend underneath the floor tom, so I simply wrapped the mic in a towel and placed it in a glass jug on the floor. For the icing on the cake, I decided to overly limit the drum premix, which made the cymbals sound huge. It took a lot of work and effort, but that's one drum sound I was extremely proud of, and Ringo, who was always meticulous about his sounds, loved it, too.

With "A Day In The Life" still only partially complete, the Beatles took a ten-day hiatus so that they could attend to other duties, including shooting the promotional video for the "Strawberry Fields Forever"/"Penny Lane" single. During that time there was a significant change in our control room staff: Phil McDonald was promoted to playback lacquer cutting, and in his place came a young, fresh-faced Richard Lush. Richard had been at EMI for a year and a half at that point, and we'd worked together frequently; he'd even been with me on a handful of the *Revolver* sessions when Phil was unavailable. Richard also assisted me on my first gold record—Manfred Mann's "Pretty Flamingo"—so we knew each other fairly well. Clearly the bigwigs upstairs had a great deal of confidence in his abilities, which is why he received the assignment to work with EMI's biggest act. I always had a good rapport with Richard and a lot of respect for his abilities, and after a little initial wariness the Beatles warmed to him, too.

Richard's first encounter with Paul was particularly memorable, though it occurred when both George Martin and I were out of the room. He was sitting by the tape machine, fiddling with one of the controls when Paul wandered in. "Hello, who are you?" he asked. "I don't remember seeing you here before."

Paul was asking the question in a good-natured way, but Richard detected an undertone of suspicion, too—Phil had already warned him that the Beatles did not like seeing unfamiliar faces at their sessions. Without anyone around to vouch for him, he nervously stammered a reply.

"Erm, my name is Richard . . . I'm a button-pusher here."

Paul immediately strode across the room and got right in Richard's face.

"Oh yeah?" he sneered, assuming a puglistic stance, both fists at the ready. "Wanna fight??"

Needless to say, this very nearly caused Richard to have an unfortunate accident—one that would have certainly become studio lore had he not quickly recovered and realized that Paul's challenge to his manhood was really just a joke, just an example of Liverpudlian humor. All four Beatles were pranksters at heart. They enjoyed doing the unexpected, just to see what kind of reaction they could get out of the unwary.

I soon discovered that Richard and I shared the same irreverent sense of humor. We would even poke fun at George Martin, who took it good-naturedly most of the time. Richard would not only work with me on all the remaining *Pepper* sessions, he would pretty much become my regular assistant for the next year and a half, all the way through to the midway point of the *White Album*. Both he and Phil were excellent at their jobs, and both would go on to find success as balance engineers, Phil with the work he did on many of John Lennon's and George Harrison's solo albums, and Richard in Australia, where he was to emigrate in the 1970s.

When the Beatles next returned to Studio Two, they decided to start a new track instead of carrying on with "A Day In The Life." This was actually a pattern that was starting to develop: up until then, they'd always worked in a pretty linear fashion, more or less sticking with a song until it was done. Now it became common practice to start a track and leave it unfinished for weeks at a time before coming back to it. Working this way seemed pretty strange at first, but ultimately I became convinced that it was a good way to do things. Allowing a song to "sit" for a while—getting a bit of distance from it—invariably spawned radical new ideas, which became the hallmark of the album.

The new song was one of Paul's, and it actually ended up not only becoming the title track, but also defining the concept of the album: a performance by a fictional band that was the alter ego of the Beatles. "Sgt. Pepper's Lonely Hearts Club Band" had quite a different feel to all the other laid-back songs we'd done so far—this one was a real rocker, more like the kind of cover songs the band did in their live set earlier in their career.

There was another surprise: Paul wanted to play rhythm guitar on the backing track instead of bass—the first time I'd known him to do that. He simply told John, "Let me do the rhythm on this; I know exactly what I want." John accepted Paul's instruction without a word of protest and simply picked up a bass guitar. He didn't have any feel for the instrument, though, so we decided to record him on a separate track, using a DI box instead of a bass amp—this way, his guide bass part could be replaced later by Paul, without any problem of bleed or leakage onto any of the microphones.

In many ways, John was a paradox in terms: he was fascinated by technology, yet he was completely nontechnical. After we explained the function of the DI box, he told George Martin that he'd like to have his voice recorded that way, too. Tongue planted firmly in cheek, George explained why we couldn't do that: "For one thing, John, you'd have to have an operation first so we could implant a jack socket in your throat." Even then, Lennon couldn't quite grasp why it wasn't possible. He simply didn't like taking no for an answer.

The idea of adding various sound effects—an orchestra tuning up, the audience squirming with anticipation—came much later on; the "concept" of *Sgt. Pepper* certainly wasn't there at the start. It wasn't until the album was nearly complete and John and Paul had written "A Little Help From My Friends" that we realized the best way to segue between the two tracks was to overdub the sound of a live audience applauding, shouting and getting excited as Ringo, in his fictional persona of Billy Shears, walked onstage.

The "Sgt. Pepper" theme song was completed in a remarkably short space of time—just two days, including all vocals—despite the fact that George Harrison spent hours trying to nail down the guitar solo. In the end, Paul peremptorily replaced George's work with a stunning solo of his own, which Harrison was clearly not very happy about. But the storm quickly blew over, and everyone's attention returned to "A Day In The Life."

The first task there was to replace Paul's guide vocal in the middle section, and he and I had a long discussion about that which led to another sonic innovation. He explained that he wanted his voice to sound all muzzy, as if he had just woken up from a deep sleep and hadn't yet gotten his bearings, because that was what the lyric was trying to convey. My way of achieving that was to deliberately remove a lot of the treble from his voice and heavily compress it to make him sound muffled. When the song goes into the next section, the dreamy section that John sings, the full fidelity is restored.

Although the overdubs to the middle section were being done separately from the main body of the song, it had already been edited into the four-track master, which made Richard's job of dropping in and out a bit tricky. Paul's vocal, for example, was being dropped into the same track that contained John's lead vocal, and there was a very tight drop-out point between the two—between Paul's singing ". . . and I went into a dream" and John's "ahhh" that starts the next section. Richard was quite paranoid about it—with good reason—and I remember him asking me to get on the talkback mic to explain the situation to Paul and ask him not to deviate from the phrasing that he had used on the guide vocal. I was really impressed when Richard did that—I thought it showed great maturity to be proactive that way. John's vocal, after all, had such great emotion, and it also had tape echo on it. The thought of having to do it again and re-create the atmosphere was daunting . . . not to mention what John's reaction would have been! Someone's head would have been bitten off, and it most likely would have been mine. But Paul, ever professional, did heed the warning, and he made certain to end the last word distinctly in order to give Richard sufficient time to drop out before John's vocal came back in. Listening carefully, you can actually hear Paul slightly rush the vocal; he even adds a little "ah" to the end of the word "dream," giving it a very clipped ending.

It was at that session that a decision was finally reached about what to do to fill in the twenty-four empty bars between the main part of the song and Paul's new middle section. John had an idea—abstract, as usual—about creating some kind of sound that would start out really tiny and then gradually expand to become huge and all-engulfing. Picking up on the theme, Paul excitedly suggested employing a full symphony orchestra. George Martin liked the idea, but, mindful of the cost, was adamant that there was no way he could justify charging EMI for a full ninety-piece orchestra just to play twenty-four bars of music. It was Ringo, of all people, who came up with the solution. "Well, then," he joked, "let's just hire half an orchestra and have them play it twice." Everyone did a double take, stunned by the simplicity—or was it simple-mindedness?—of the suggestion.

"You know, Ring, that's not a bad idea," Paul said.

"But still, boys, think of the cost . . ." George Martin stammered.

Lennon put an end to the discussion. "Right, Henry," he said, his voice carrying the tone of an emperor issuing a decree. "Enough chitchat. Let's do it."

O ver the next few days, John and Paul spent a great deal of time huddled with George Martin, trying to work out exactly what they wanted to have the orchestra do. As usual, Paul was thinking musically while John was thinking conceptually. George Martin's role was to act as facilitator.

"I think it would be great if we ask each member of the orchestra to play randomly," Paul suggested.

George Martin was aghast. "Randomly? That will just sound like a cacophony; it's pointless."

"Okay, well then, not completely randomly," Paul replied. "Maybe we could get each of them to do a slow climb from the lowest note their instrument can play up to the highest note."

"Yeah," interjected John, "and also have them start really quietly and get louder and louder, so that it eventually becomes an orgasm of sound."

George Martin still looked dubious. "The problem," he explained, "is that you can't ask classical musicians of that caliber to improvise and not follow a score—they'll simply have no idea what to do."

John seemed lost in thought for a moment, and then brightened up. "Well, if we put them in silly party hats and rubber noses, maybe then they'll understand what it is we want. That will loosen up those tight-asses!"

I thought it was a brilliant idea. The idea was to get them into the spirit of things, to create a party atmosphere, a sense of camaraderie. John was not seeking to necessarily embarrass them or make them look silly—he was actually trying to tear down the barrier that had existed between classical and pop musicians for years.

As the snowball started rolling, it began to gather momentum. "How about if we use the orchestra twice in the song—not just before the middle section, but after the final chorus, also, to end the song," Paul suggested. John nodded his okay, so I set about making a copy of Mal's countdown and editing it into the multitrack tape. A little later that evening, Paul had another brainstorm: "Let's make the session more than just a session: let's make it a happening."

Lennon loved the idea. "We'll invite all our friends, and everyone will have to come in fancy dress costume," he enthused. "That includes you lot, too," he said pointedly to Richard and me.

George Martin smiled paternally. "Well, I can certainly ask the orchestra to wear their tuxedos, though there may be an extra cost involved."

"Sod the cost," John said. "We're making enough bloody money for EMI that they can spring for it . . . and for the party favors, too."

To gales of laughter from the others, Lennon began reeling off a list of what he wanted Mal to purchase at the novelty store: silly hats, rubber noses, clown wigs, bald head pates, gorilla paws . . . and lots of clip-on nipples.

While the Beatles continued their party planning, I was busy worrying about the technical aspects. Three of the four tracks of the multitrack master were already filled with overdubs, and I knew we'd be having the orchestra play at least twice all the way through, so the one remaining track clearly wouldn't be sufficient. One option was doing a mono premix, but that meant taking the recording down another generation, and we'd already done several reductions, so I really didn't want to do that. Another option was to utilize a second four-track machine for recording the orchestra, using the original tape for playback only. That would give us four additional tracks to record on, but the problem there was synchronization; we needed to find a way to lock the two machines together so that they ran at exactly the same speed—something that had never been done before, at least not at EMI.

Ken Townsend and his technical staff rose to the occasion, creating a system whereby we recorded a pulse tone on the remaining empty track of the master tape and used it to drive the motor of the second machine. That got them to run at the same speed, but there was still no automatic way of starting and stopping them both at the same time, so we resorted to a crude, but effective, way of doing that manually. I carefully placed a yellow wax pencil mark on the two tapes to mark the start point, and Richard's job was to line the two tapes up visually at the start of every take and simultaneously hit the Play button of one machine and the Record button of the other. There was still a degree of trial and error as to whether he did so successfully every time, or whether both motors kicked in at exactly the same time even if he did, but nine times out of ten it worked . . . sort of.

The session was booked in Studio One, which was the only room large enough to comfortably accommodate an orchestra, and, to further complicate matters, we had decided to use the studio's "ambiophony" system on the overdubs. This was an ongoing acoustics experiment being run by EMI's technical boffins: there were actually a hundred loudspeakers precisely mounted in the walls of the cavernous studio, and by slightly altering the delay on the signals they were being fed, the sonic characteristics of the room could actually be shaped. It was tricky to set up, and it required that I put a lot of thought and care into mic positioning, but it did yield excellent results.

We knew that we were stretching the limits of the available technology of the time, so there was a good deal of nervous apprehension between Richard and me that day. Even though the session wasn't scheduled to start until mid-evening, we were there by lunchtime, supervising the white coats as they put up microphones, fine-tuning the ambiophony system, and practicing the machine syncing. We realized quite early on that the synchronization was far from perfect. It was just a matter of keeping our fingers crossed and hoping it would work well enough often enough that we could get something usable.

Eventually the musicians began filing in, kitted in their finest evening dress. George Martin, also outfitted in a tux, flitted from one player to the next—he was on a first-name basis with most of them, and I suspect he was feeling a bit embarrassed about what it was he was going to be asking them to do that evening. Mal Evans had decked out the studio with balloons, so it all looked quite festive—unfortunately, if you listen very carefully during the orchestral climb, you can actually hear the sounds of some of them bursting in the background!

As everyone began tuning up, Mal started circulating among the musicians, handing out party favors. "Here you go, mate, have one of these," he would say amiably in his working-class Liverpool accent, rubber nose or fake boob in hand.

Most of the musicians seemed taken aback; one of them even rudely slapped Mal's hand aside. But for all of their grumbling, most of them ended up donning hats, gorilla paws, and the like, though I suspect they probably would have been a little more resistant if it wasn't for the fact that Mal was six foot four and weighed well over two hundred pounds. David Mason and Alan Civil, both of whom had been on Beatles sessions before, were two of the better-spirited participants that night; they'd gotten to know Paul, and realized he was a true artist. Dave had played on "Penny Lane" just a few weeks previously, and he did what he could to smooth things over, telling the other brass players, "It's all right, it's just a bit of fun; just go along with it."

In some ways, this session marked a transition. The lines between classical and pop music were blurring, and even though many of the orchestral players were disdainful of contemporary music, they could see the writing on the wall.

Everything was made even more special by the atmosphere that surrounded the recording—the party and the people in costumes. Richard and I sat in the control room and slowly watched the studio fill up with guests, marveling at the dozens of celebrities who appeared: Mick Jagger, Marianne Faithfull, Keith Richards, Brian Jones, Donovan, Graham Nash, Mike Nesmith of the Monkees. Brian Epstein was there, too, surveying the room worriedly; he was always so protective of his "boys." Every now and then we'd see Neil swim into the crowd, pluck out a gate-crasher, and with a certain degree of force, eject him or her from the party. He was on security detail that night, and he was clearly taking his job very seriously. Brian's assistant Tony Bramwell wandered around capturing the evening's festivities with a handheld movie camera—at one point, there had been discussion of releasing a film showing the making of the album. A few of the musicians noticed that they were being filmed and asked if they were going to be paid extra for that; one even left in a huff when he was told that he would not be receiving an additional fee.

Finally the four Beatles swept into the room, fashionably late and dressed in their Carnaby Street finest. They had promised to show up in tuxedos, but they reneged. Nonetheless, Lennon was pissed off when he saw that Richard and I weren't in evening dress or fancy costumes; in deference to the accursed EMI dress code we were simply in our normal shirt and tie. Still, John, Paul, George, and Ringo were all in a decidedly jolly mood, even more so than usual—it appeared as if they had started the party several hours earlier. They knew that they weren't going to have to play anything at the session, plus it was a Friday night, so they had the whole weekend to recover before they had to return to work.

The Beatles were very much like pop royalty in those days: they wandered around the room bestowing their attention on one subject, then the next, kind of like the royal family making a public appearance. That night, they turned the studio into their own private playroom. If they couldn't go out to party because of their fame, they'd bring the party in to them!

While the Beatles made the rounds, George Martin huddled with orchestra leader, Erich Gruenberg, explaining what it was he wanted the musicians to do. I wasn't privy to their conversation, but I could see from the arm-waving that there was trouble afoot. I wandered out into the mayhem, ostensibly to adjust a microphone, but I was actually just curious to see what the kerfuffle was all about. By the time I got there, Paul had joined the discussion.

"All we want you to do is some free-form improvisation," he was explaining earnestly to a perplexed Gruenberg.

"Not completely free-form, Erich," George interjected. "I'll be conducting, and there is a score of sorts. But we need each musician to play on his own, without listening to those around him. It's absolutely critical that each individual musician do the climb from lowest note to highest at his own pace, not playing together as a section."

This was sacrilege in the classical world. Orchestral players trained for years, even decades, to sublimate their individuality and work seamlessly as a section. A dejected Gruenberg muttered, "I don't really understand what you are asking of us, but I shall relay your instructions to the others." Waving his arms, he silenced the musicians and repeated what he had just been told.

For a moment you could hear a pin drop. Then the murmuring began. "Do *what*??" "What the bloody hell . . . ?" The general response wasn't so much outrage as it was dismay. The musicians knew they were there to do a job; they just didn't like what they were being asked to do. These were forty of the top classical musicians in England, and they certainly hadn't spent decades honing their craft in order to be told to improvise from their lowest note to the highest . . . and wear a rubber nose in the bargain. It wasn't exactly dignified, and they resented it.

Quite a bit of time was wasted as George Martin struggled to clarify things for the baffled musicians. At one point, in mid-conversation, Mal strolled over and handed George a red rubber nose. In the control room, Richard and I silently rooted for him to put it on—we thought the idea was hilarious!—but to our disappointment a distracted George just set it to one side. Paul got bored with the confusion and began wandering around the studio again, telling the beleaguered producer, "You sort it out, George."

George was getting quite irritated, not only with the musicians' recalcitrance, but with the balloons popping all around him. In addition, Paul was upstaging him a bit, talking with the musicians directly instead of through him. Paul simply had a calmer mind about things that night. Eventually George had to simply resort to the age-old reassurance: "Just trust me. Please. Just trust me."

Finally a rehearsal was called—or so the musicians thought. We had made a decision beforehand that we would roll tape for every attempt at playing the twenty-four-bar climb, whether it was a proper take or just a rehearsal. This was partially because of the technical challenges—we knew that the two machines would not run in sync every time we attempted it, so we wanted to maximize our chances—and partially because we were doing something naughty. Ever conscious of cost, George Martin had warned Richard and me not to let the musicians know we would be recording them multiple times on separate tracks, because doing so would result in massive extra charges. Instead, we were under strict instructions to make them think that each time around we were wiping the previous take and recording over it. But, of course, we weren't; over the remaining two and a half hours of the session, we actually recorded them playing that passage eight separate times, on two clean sections of four-track tape.

As the evening wore on, Paul decided to have a go at conducting, too, and despite his inexperience he did quite a good job. They took slightly different approaches: George imparted a little more instruction than Paul did, giving the musicians little signposts along the way, while Paul urged them to play more free-form. The combination and contrast between the two different styles made for an interesting sonic experience when we finally listened back to the tracks—well after the musicians had packed up and left for the night.

For most of that evening, I was closeted in the control room with Richard—the one shelter in the eye of the storm—trying to make some sense out of all the mayhem going on in the studio. It's incredible to think that such an important session—a milestone in modern music, really—was entrusted to the two of us, a couple of twenty-year-old kids! Through all the hubbub, a mellowed-out John was just wandering around in a daze. He, Paul, and George Martin popped into the control room to hear the first playback or two; other than that, they spent the entire evening in the studio along with George Harrison, Ringo, and their guests.

Ron Richards dropped by the control room for a quick listen at one point, as did many of the Beatles' friends. Frankly, it was a distraction that Richard and I did not appreciate, because we were extremely busy dealing with various technical issues. Fortunately, the control room of Studio One was quite tiny, so they could really only stand in the back; there were no chairs and no amenities. As a result, they wouldn't stay long; when they realized there wasn't much activity in the control room, they'd head back into the studio.

It was absolute chaos out there, and it was difficult ensuring that there was no extraneous noise during the recording. Everyone was told to keep quiet when the red light was on, but not all of them were able to contain themselves—there was a lot of excitement in the room, almost as if everyone there knew that they were witnessing a historic moment. One of the classical musicians had a reputation for being a real snob, and Richard and I got a kick out of watching him sit there uncomfortably, rubber nose stuck on, trying to maintain his dignity . . . but failing miserably. Actually, there was always a certain amount of animosity between the different sections of an orchestra anyway, especially if the brass players had been drinking. They were a lot looser in general, and got into the music a lot more than the string players, who tended to be a little more stuffy.

In those days, the Abbey Road staff knew that there was always something special going on whenever there was a Beatles session running. A lot of them made a point of coming in on any excuse, or if they couldn't manage that, they would hang around outside, listening through the doors. All, that is, except Mr. Fowler and Mr. Beckett, who were appalled at what their beloved studio had come to, which is why, at the height of the festivities, I was surprised to see the two of them standing at the back of the studio, looking grim and shaking their heads sadly. Probably they were thinking that Elgar—the famous conductor of the 1930s whose name had been so closely linked with the studio in classical lore—must be spinning in his grave. The two men, dressed in their usual pin-striped suits, starched white shirts, and fastidiously knotted ties, seemed like such an anachronism. *This really is a passing of the torch,* I thought as I watched them.

Fowler and Beckett stayed only a short while, though, leaving well before the final crescendo and the biggest surprise of the evening. As George Martin put down his baton and said, "Thank you, gentlemen, that's a wrap," everyone in the entire studio—orchestra members, Beatles, and Beatles friends alike—broke into spontaneous applause. It was a hell of a moment, and the perfect ending to a remarkable session.

After the orchestra left, Paul asked the other Beatles and their guests to stick around and try out an idea he had just gotten for an ending, something he wanted to overdub on after the final orchestral climax. Everyone was weary—the studio was starting to smell suspiciously of pot, and there was lots of wine floating around—but they were keen to have a go. Paul's concept was to have everyone hum the same note in unison; it was the kind of avant-garde thinking he was doing a lot of in those days. It was absurd, really—the biggest gathering of pop stars in the world, gathered around a microphone, humming, with Paul conducting the choir. Though it never got used on the record, and most of the takes dissolved into laughter, it was a fun way to cap off a fine party.

It was well past midnight when everyone crowded into the tiny control room for one last playback, the overflow of guests spilling out into the corridor, listening through the open door. Everyone, without exception, was totally and utterly blown away by what they were hearing; Ron Richards kept shaking his head, telling anyone who would listen, "That's it, I think I'll give up and retire now." But exhilarated as we all were, I could tell that George Martin was greatly relieved when the session finally ended—he had been stressed out all evening and I'm sure all he wanted to do was head home and get to bed.

As we were packing up in the wee hours, Richard and I talked about what an incredible evening it had been. "That's one session I'll never forget," Richard kept saying.

I could only summon up enough energy to quietly agree. Exhausted and elated, we felt as if we'd been part of history.

For the next two weeks, the Beatles worked on other tracks while they ruminated about how to end "A Day In The Life." By that point, it had become apparent that the monumental song would be used to close the album, so a very special ending—something far more powerful than Paul's humming experiment—was needed. The inspiration for what was finally used once again came from Paul, with eager assent from John: a huge piano chord that would last "forever" . . . or at least as long as I could figure out how to get the sound to sustain.

Attaining the massive sound was fairly easy: we would simply commandeer every available piano and keyboard in the Abbey Road complex and have lots of people playing the same chord simultaneously, then overdub them three more times, filling up a four-track tape with an abundance of audio. But the sustain was a bigger problem: even if you hit a piano chord at full volume and hold down the sustain pedal, the sound only lasts for a minute or so before fading into nothingness. Compounding the problem was the fact that tape hiss and vinyl surface noise would obliterate any low-level signal all too soon. It seemed clear to me that the solution lay in keeping the sound at maximum volume for as long as possible, and I had two weapons that could accomplish this: a compressor, cranked up full, and the very faders themselves on the mixing console. Logically, if I set the gain of each input to maximum but started with the fader at its lowest point, I could then slowly raise the faders as the sound died away, thus compensating for the loss in volume: in effect, I could counteract the chord getting softer, at least to some degree.

In between sessions, I ran a few tests with Richard and my idea seemed to work well enough, so the Beatles—or at least three of them—finally rolled up one evening to put the finishing touch on "A Day In The Life." For some reason, George Harrison wasn't there, and neither was Neil; I assumed they were doing something together. Nobody seemed surprised at their absence—the others must have known in advance—but John was quite annoyed nonetheless. In those days, all four Beatles were almost always present at all sessions, regardless of what was being recorded on any given evening. But as many hands as possible were needed, so Mal Evans was recruited to take George's place.

In preparation for the session, Richard and various brown coats had been busy moving pianos from all over the building into Studio Two, so the array that awaited John, Paul, Ringo, and Mal when they arrived was quite impressive: two Steinway grand pianos, another Steinway upright that was purposely kept a bit out of tune for a "honky-tonk" effect, and a blond-wood spinet. In addition, there was a Wurlitzer electric piano, and sequestered and screened off in the back of the studio because of the acoustic noise its bellows generated, a harmonium. Between these six keyboards, we were sure to generate a big noise indeed.

To get as strong an attack as possible, everyone decided to play standing up instead of sitting down. John, Mal, and George Martin each stood behind a different piano, while Ringo and Paul shared the out-of-tune Steinway upright; I presume they did double duty because Paul had to coach his drummer on which notes to play. Because there were four hands slamming out the chord instead of two, that ended up being the dominant instrument on the recording. John was really out of it that night, so Paul repeatedly counted everyone in. It took quite a few takes to get a keeper, because it was problematical getting everyone to hit the start of the chord at exactly the same time. Up in the control room, I would slowly raise the faders as the sound died away. By about a minute or so in, I reached full volume, and the gain was so high that you could literally hear the quiet swoosh of the studio's air conditioners.

I decided to stagger the overdubs slightly—having each start a little bit later, so that I could crossfade between them when mixing in order to get the sound to last a little longer still. On one of the overdubs, Ringo shifted position very slightly at the very end, causing his shoe to squeak. This happened, of course, just when even the sound of a pin dropping could be heard! Across Paul shot him a sideways glance, and from the look on his face I could tell that Ringo was mortified. If you listen quite closely to the song just as the sound is fading away, you can hear it clearly, especially on the CD version, where there is no surface noise to mask it.

For the last overdub, George Martin moved over to the harmonium because Paul wanted another texture, something a bit edgier. The buzziness of the harmonium fit the bill perfectly, and George did an admirable job of pumping the bellows with his feet as silently as was humanly possible. Other than placing a few screens around the harmonium, I used no acoustic treatment whatsoever—this was one time when I didn't mind leakage. I was trying to create a complete "sound" from all the keyboards, and the use of heavy compression helped glue them together further still.

Shortly after the recording was completed, George Harrison finally showed up, accompanied by David Crosby of the Byrds. John ignored Crosby but couldn't resist hurling a little sarcasm at his bandmate. "Nice of you to turn up, George. You only missed the most important overdub we've ever done!"

We all couldn't wait to hear how "A Day In The Life" would sound with all the elements in place, so it was decided to mix it right there and then, in both mono and stereo. (In those days, it wasn't uncommon to do a mix— not a rough mix, but the final one—at the conclusion of a session, in stark contrast to the complicated way things are done today, where songs are usually mixed weeks or months after a recording is complete, often with a new engineer altogether.) Ken Townsend was duly summoned—as the chief of maintenance, he was generally on call for Beatles sessions—and he and Richard began the laborious task of locking up the two four-track machines. Sod's law, with all four Beatles present and looking over our shoulders, it wasn't working a lot of the time. Often, by the time we got to the orchestral bit, they would drift noticeably out of time with one another. Everyone dealt with the problem in good humor, though—even the normally impatient John, so stoned was he that night. In the end, we were all actually laying down bets as to whether the machines were going to stay in sync or not; we'd be thrilled on the few occasions when it worked perfectly.

Even during the recording there had been minor synchronization problems. As a result, the orchestra was actually coming in at a slightly different place each time. The offset wasn't much—perhaps a half second or so—but it was enough to make their entrances a bit ragged. There was really only one track that was spot-on, hitting the cues exactly, so, during the mix, I helped out the late ones by keeping their faders down until the rest of the cacophony came in; conversely, I would slowly fade out those that ended a bit early.

That was part of the reason why the mix was so complex. The other was that I hadn't done any fader manipulation during the recording itself, because I wanted to capture the orchestral performance accurately. That meant that I had to take things to the extreme during the mix, riding the faders so as to build the sound to an incredible climax. To enhance things further still, I lowered the volume level of the orchestra at the very beginning of the passage, thus making the mix much more dynamic than the original performance was. No one sitting in that control room with us could believe how much bigger I was able to make everything sound by doing that, and everyone was extremely happy with the result.

Interestingly, a week after we did those mixes—which actually ended up being the masters used on the album—Paul decided that he wanted a different color on the ending and overdubbed yet another piano, although it was ultimately deemed extraneous and was never used. The fact that they were willing to continue to work on the track even at that point showed how committed the Beatles were to perfection by this stage of their career, and how willing they were to break all the rules. The song had already been mixed to everyone's satisfaction . . . but that didn't mean that one of us couldn't still come up with an idea to try to improve it. No one rolled his eyes, and no one—not even John—said, "Bloody hell, we've already finished that song." The spirit throughout all the *Pepper* sessions was always "If you've got an idea, let's try it."

A lot changed after "A Day In The Life" was completed. For one thing, I felt that the Beatles began working more efficiently. They took a more positive approach to the songs being recorded, because they had a better idea of the sounds we could achieve. There was still thought put into everything being laid down on tape, but there weren't always days of experimentation that might have turned a song around or completely altered the arrangement.

Going along with that was the emergence of Paul as the group's de facto producer. The sessions started running later and later—often going until dawn. At around midnight George Martin would start nodding off in the control room, and by 1 A.M. he'd usually just leave, sometimes without even saying good night. To be fair, he had a lot of other responsibilities. Even before the making of *Revolver*, he had resigned from EMI and formed his own company, AIR, an acronym for "Associated Independent Recording." (He took some of EMI's best producers with him, too.) As a result, he frequently had to be in the office first thing in the morning, and he was still producing other artists as well.

With George Martin stretched so thin and John growing ever more out of it on drugs, it was Paul who would begin playing a greater role in shaping the songs and instructing the others on what parts to play. In many ways, *Sgt. Pepper* was like two albums: the tracks recorded up to and including "A Day In The Life," and those done afterward.

9

A Masterpiece Takes Shape:

The *Pepper* Concept

Two other songs had been started while we awaited the orchestral over-dub to "A Day In The Life": John's "Good Morning, Good Morning," and Paul's "Fixing A Hole." Both were fairly straightforward rockers that could have fit in with any Beatles album released to date. After completing the backing track to "Good Morning, Good Morning," the song received a few perfunctory overdubs and then sat on the shelf for the next three weeks while an indecisive Lennon made up his mind what kind of instrumentation he wanted added.

In contrast, McCartney polished off "Fixing A Hole" quickly, although it actually was begun at another studio. George Martin couldn't get the group booked into Abbey Road on the night they wanted to record, so they moved to Regent Sound Studio in London's West End instead. Ridiculously, even though we'd recorded almost every note on the album up to that point, Richard and I couldn't go there because we were EMI employees. George Martin, on the other hand, could attend, because he was working as an independent contractor. We listened to the tapes a few days later, and while they were a bit disappointing sonically, I was impressed with the vibe: all four Beatles played together on the backing track, just like in the old days, and George Harrison played a good guitar solo, too.

Unfortunately, George's songwriting wasn't quite as impressive. His first attempt at contributing a song to the *Sgt. Pepper* album was not the well-known "Within You Without You," which ended up opening side two, but a weak track that we all winced at. It was called "Only A Northern Song," and it had minimal musical content that seemed to go nowhere. What's more, the lyrics seemed to reflect both his creative frustration and his annoyance with the way the pie was being sliced financially. (Northern Songs was the name of the publishing company set up by Dick James through which all Beatles song-writing revenues were routed.) It seemed like such an inappropriate song to be bringing to what was generally a happy, upbeat album.

Everyone in the control room shared my opinion. In our private conversations, George Martin simply said, "I'm disappointed that George didn't come up with something better," but I knew what he really meant; he was always on his guard because he didn't ever want disparaging comments to be reported back. The other Beatles were clearly underwhelmed, too. John was so uninspired, in fact, that he decided not to participate in the backing track at all.

Still, Paul, Ringo, and George ambled through quite a few takes of "Only A Northern Song"; it took a long time because nobody could really get into it, not even George himself. I think he was actually a bit embarrassed about the song—his guitar playing had no attitude, as if he didn't care. None of the takes they did that night were particularly good; in fact, it took several more hours of work the following evening before they came up with something they felt was even halfway decent. Shortly afterward, an unhappy Paul said, "Look, let's knock it on the head for the night," and they ended the session early. There was no more mention of resuming work on the song until after the mixes of *Pepper* were done and they were looking for material to give to the *Yellow Submarine* film project. It wouldn't surprise me if John and Paul had simply told George to go back to the drawing board and come up with something better.

In general, sessions where we did George Harrison songs were approached differently. Everybody would relax—there was a definite sense that it really didn't matter. It was never said in so many words, but there was a feeling that his songs simply didn't have the integrity of John's or Paul's—certainly they were never considered as singles—and so no one was prepared to expend very much time or effort on them. Often, the more time we spent on George's songs, the worse they got, whereas with John's or Paul's songs, the more time we spent, the better they got. If Harrison wanted to do one more take but nobody else was interested—and they usually weren't—that's where George Martin would step in and assert his authority. In that way, he served as the intermediary between George and the other Beatles: he would intercede if he thought John or Paul were taking the piss, not giving their full effort. Despite that, they certainly never were as focused as they were when we were recording one of their own, and that had to have spawned some degree of resentment in the lead guitarist; in many ways, he was still being treated as a junior partner.

John's next contribution to the album was a rather involved sonic pastiche called "Being For The Benefit Of Mr. Kite." In contrast to George Harrison, John Lennon always had a precise title for each of his songs, and woe betold any of us who didn't get it correct. I learned that the hard way one night when I slated a take in a hurry and mistakenly shortened the title to "For The Benefit Of Mr. Kite." John immediately corrected me in an irritated tone of voice: "No, that's '*Being* For The Benefit Of Mr. Kite.'" (A year later, midway through the *White Album* sessions, the Beatles asked me to stop doing slate announcements altogether, because it was taking them longer and longer to lay down backing tracks and they were getting agitated hearing "This is take 41" in their headphones. It must have been really off-putting to them to be constantly reminded of how many failed attempts had been made.)

The backing track to "Kite" was quite simple: Paul on bass, Ringo on drums, and John doing a guide vocal, with George Martin enlisted to play harmonium. It did take quite a few tries to nail it down, though, which caused problems for George, because the harmonium required pedaling to get air through its bellows, kind of like riding a bicycle. After playing it nonstop for hours on end, he finally collapsed in exhaustion, sprawled out on the floor like a snow angel—a sight that gave us all great amusement.

John, as usual, was full of creative ideas but was having trouble expressing them in practical terms. "What I want," he explained earnestly to George Martin and me in the control room the next day, "is some kind of swirly music, you know?" George Martin didn't know.

Lennon persisted. "I want the sound of a fairground around my voice; I want to be able to smell the sawdust and the animals. I want to feel like I'm at the circus with Mr. Kite and the Hendersons and all that."

We knew that the inspiration for "Kite" had come from a nineteenth-century circus poster hanging in Lennon's front room—he'd told us that when he first brought the song in. The lyrics were full of fanciful images from that era, so his request didn't seem all that outlandish, but he wasn't exactly giving us specific directions in how to achieve his vision, either. At one point, an exasperated John declared, "Maybe we should bring the Massed Alberts in to do an overdub." The Massed Alberts were a comedy act produced by George Martin—an eccentric brass band that dressed ridiculously and featured euphonium and tuba. "Oh, honestly!" was George's patronizing response. That was his stock expression of disapproval whenever he thought someone was talking nonsense.

Eventually, George decided that what John was thinking of was a calliope—a steam organ. Despite their enormous size, a few phone calls were actually placed to see if one was available for hire—to no avail. But as the inquiries were being made, I was starting to get an idea. "How about if we try what we did on 'Yellow Submarine'?" I suggested. "You know, cutting up some tapes of sound effects to try to create an atmosphere?"

By this point, Lennon had lost interest and was heading out of the control room in search of some new stimulation. "Yeah, fine, whatever you think."

George Martin turned to me. "I think you may be on to something there, Geoff." Richard Lush was instructed to go upstairs and search through the archives of EMI sound effects for recordings of calliopes and old organs. He came back with a stack of records and we found a few short snatches of music that seemed like they might work, so I copied them onto some fresh two-track tape. The procedure we followed next was similar to what we had done on "Yellow Submarine," only the bits of tape were longer—this time, several two- or three-second lengths were tossed up into the air and joined together randomly in order to create some thirty seconds of background sound, later overdubbed onto the very end of the song. Interestingly, just as happened in "Yellow Submarine," a lot of the pieces ended up in the correct order and had to be shifted around before it all sounded jumbled enough.

We were in Studio Three that night because our usual haunt—Studio Two—was in use by another artist. George Martin must have block-booked them in for just a month or two; it had never taken any longer to do a Beatles album, and he wouldn't have had any way of knowing beforehand that much greater amounts of time would be spent on *Pepper*. As a result, the group's gear wasn't in the studio with them; it was still being stored in Studio Two, where we would be returning for most of the rest of the album. Because they couldn't play and jam, the four Beatles were getting impatient with how long it was taking us to assemble the sounds. They were out in the studio area amusing themselves as best they could, but they kept popping into the control room, saying, "Aren't you lot done yet?" At one point John came in and he was actually quite aggravated, but Paul calmed him down, saying, "Look, it's a process and it just takes a certain amount of time. You have to expect that."

Later on, "Being For The Benefit Of Mr. Kite" was embellished with all manner of overdubs: chromatic organ runs and glockenspiel (both recorded at half speed), normal speed oom-pah-style organ (played by John), and a chorus of bass harmonicas (played by John, George Harrison, Mal, and Neil). It turned into quite a production that stretched over many weeks, and I always enjoyed hearing the final results played back.

At around this time, the sessions began getting quite trippy and psychedelic. Studio Two had these awful, filthy white walls that nobody wanted to look at during the best of times, especially not when they were being harshly lit by the large industrial fixtures hanging from the ceiling. So most of the studio lights were turned off whenever the Beatles were down there rehearsing and recording the late-stage *Pepper* songs, with the only source of illumination coming from candles, joss sticks, and a single ordinary desk lamp tilted upward so that it lit up one wall. Up in the control room, I made my own personal contribution to the atmosphere: a lava lamp and the red darkroom lamp from my childhood. Anything to counteract the dreariness! Late at night, those lamps, sitting on top of the Altec speakers, would often be the only lights on in the control room, adding to the general spaciness and weirdness of those long evenings. Sometimes we'd even turn those off and operate solely by the glow of the tubes in the tape machines.

Late-night sessions were still an unusual thing at Abbey Road; it was rare when sessions for any artist other than the Beatles were allowed to run on for so long. The bean counters at EMI had still not cottoned to the fact that it was in their interest to pamper their most important signing, so there was no milk left out for tea after the canteen staff left at 10 P.M. Everyone got so desperate for a cuppa late one night, Mal actually had to break the lock on the kitchen to get some milk. There was hell to pay the next day—you would have thought that he'd broken into the Tower of London and stolen the Crown Jewels—but after that, they arranged for him to have a key.

The next song to be worked on was "Lovely Rita." With this track, Paul began the practice of recording his bass last, after all the other parts were already committed to tape. Being able to work off of all the other elements of the track—including lead and backing vocals—enabled him to hear the song as a whole and therefore create melodic bass lines that perfectly complemented the final arrangement. He would do those overdubs in the wee hours, long after everyone else had gone home. It would be just Richard and me up in the control room, with Paul sitting on a chair out in the middle of the studio, away from his usual corner, working assiduously to perfect his lines, giving all he had to the task at hand. Richard would painstakingly drop the multitrack in and out of record, one section at a time, until every note was articulated perfectly and Paul was satisfied with the result. He, of course, was the ultimate arbiter, but he was also constantly peering up into the control room to see if we were giving him a thumbs-up or a thumbs-down.

That really was the secret to the incredibly rich, creamy bass sounds that characterize *Sgt. Pepper:* Paul's willingness to put in the long hours, free of distraction, to create harmonically intricate bass lines and then play them as well as they could possibly be played. There were nights when he would labor until dawn, keeping at it until his fingers were literally bleeding.

In turn, it was Paul's desire for perfection that enabled me to finally come up with a recording technique that yielded the ultra-smooth bass sound he and I had been pursuing for years. The key was that we would move his bass amp out of the baffles and into the center of the studio; I would then place a microphone about six feet away. With the studio empty, you could actually hear a little bit of the ambience of the room around the bass, which really helped; it gave the sound a certain roundness and put it in its own space. The sound we crafted effectively transformed the bass from a supporting rhythm instrument into a lead instrument.

There was one other unorthodox thing I would do with Paul's bass, and that occurred during the mixing stage. Most recording engineers begin a rock mix by getting the desired balance between the drums and bass—the all-important rhythm section—before adding in the other instruments and the vocals. But because Paul's bass lines are so important to the *Pepper* songs, I got in the habit of bringing the bass track in last. I'd essentially sculpt the bass sound around the other instruments so that you could hear every single nuance. Not only is everything in proper balance, but all of the individual components that go into the complete sound are carefully shaped to occupy their own sonic space and not interfere with one another.

The *Pepper* mixes were extremely complicated because there were many different instruments recorded on each track. As a result, during the three or four minutes of each song, the fader positions and EQ controls (and, in the cases of the stereo mixes, the positioning of instruments) had to constantly be changed as we went from part to part. Plus we had to work extra hard on getting balances correct in those days because we primarily mixed and monitored in mono, with everything coming out of one speaker. Back in 1967, most people's record players were mono; stereo was still largely the purview of high-end audiophiles. True Beatles fans would do well to avail themselves of the mono versions of *Sgt. Pepper* and *Revolver* because far more time and effort went into those mixes than into the stereo mixes. The stereo versions of those albums also have an unnecessary surfeit of panning and effects like ADT (Automatic Double Tracking) and flanging. Richard and I would sometimes get carried away with them because of their novelty value . . . especially if George Martin wasn't there to rebuke us. Needless to say, it was John who especially loved that kind of overkill—we'd sometimes whack

something on too severely just to see how it sounded, only to find him wink-
ing at us, saying, "More!"

"Lovely Rita" was another track where the Beach Boys influence really
manifested itself. Paul made a point of telling George Martin that he wanted
the backing vocal arrangement to emulate the way the California singing
group might approach the song. There were lots of fun overdubs on that
track, including the four band members standing around a single microphone humming through a comb and paper, each priceless Beatle comb
carefully wrapped with a single layer of the standard issue extra-scratchy
EMI toilet paper that we were all constantly complaining about. On that
same very silly night, they overdubbed the heavy breathing at the end of the
song, with John looning about and sending the others—and Richard and me
up in the control room—into fits of laughter. There were a few visitors to
the studio that evening, including Davy Jones of the Monkees, and the joss
sticks were especially prominent, ensuring that a splendid time was guaran-
teed for all.

The opportunity arose for me to make my recording debut on a Beatles
album with "Lovely Rita," but my shy nature let me down. After hours of attempting a Harrison guitar solo that never quite worked, they were stuck for
an idea, and the frustration was starting to show. I distinctly remember
standing at the top of the stairs in Studio Two and Paul's shouting up at me,
"Geoff, *you* tell us what the solo should be."

My suggestion was that they try something on piano. To my surprise,
Paul asked, "Why don't you play it?"

In a kneejerk reaction—and to my everlasting regret—I demurred; I was
simply too embarrassed to demonstrate my musical skills. Paul shrugged his
shoulders and took a stab at it, but he still wasn't a hundred percent certain
that it was a good idea, so he had George Martin play something instead.
While Paul listened up in the control room, George reeled off a honky-tonk-
style solo that was deemed acceptable, although, frankly, I wasn't too crazy
about it. But in the true *Pepper* spirit of experimentation, Paul asked me to
screw things up so the solo didn't sound like it was coming from a piano. By
that stage, I had already adopted a policy that no piano was ever recorded
the same way twice. As a result, I was miking pianos from underneath, taping mics to the soundboard—anything to get it sounding different each
time. This time around, I decided to place some sticky editing tape on the
guide rollers of a tape machine that was sending signal to the echo chamber, causing the tape to wow and flutter. The end result was an audible, and quite interesting, "wobble" in the piano sound. It was yet another

contravention of the rules that, with any band other than the Beatles, would have easily gotten me fired.

That same evening, I was witness to a bizarre scenario that seemed quite funny at the time, but could have ended tragically. For some reason, Ringo wasn't at that particular session, though Beatles biographer Hunter Davies was there, sitting unobtrusively in the back with Neil and Mal, quietly observing. John was dressed outlandishly as usual, in a festive striped blazer, but I thought he seemed unusually quiet when he first arrived. Soon afterward, he, Paul, and George Harrison were gathered around a microphone singing backing vocals when Lennon suddenly announced that he wasn't feeling well. George Martin got on the talkback. "What's the matter, John? Is it something you ate?"

The others sniggered but John remained perfectly solemn. "No, it's not that," he replied. "I'm just having trouble focusing."

Up in the control room, Richard and I exchanged glances. *Uh-huh*, we thought. *That would be the drugs kicking in.* But George Martin didn't seem to have an inkling of what was going on. "Do you want to be driven home?" he asked.

"No," Lennon said in a tiny, faraway voice.

"Well then, perhaps you'd like to get a little fresh air?" George suggested helpfully.

"Okay," came the meek reply.

It seemed to take John a long time to get up the stairs; he was moving as if he were in slow motion. When he finally walked through the doorway into the control room, I noticed that he had a strange, glazed look on his face. Gazing vacantly around the room, Lennon completely ignored the three of us. He appeared to be searching for something, but didn't seem to know what it was. Suddenly he threw his head back and began staring intently at the ceiling, awestruck. With some degree of difficulty, he finally got a few not especially profound words out: "Wow, look at that." Our necks craned upward, but all we saw was . . . a ceiling.

"Come on, John, I know a way up the back stairs," George Martin said soothingly, leading the befuddled Beatle out of the room.

Richard and I didn't know quite what to say. We'd seen Lennon out of it before, but never to this extent—and certainly never to the point where he was unable to function at a session. Down in the studio, Paul and George Harrison were clowning around, singing one of their old stage numbers in silly voices. A buzz crept into the microphone and I spent a few distracted minutes trying to track it down; finally I dispatched Richard to the studio to change the cable. As he headed down the steps, George Martin returned to the control room, alone.

Richard's presence in their midst seemed to remind Paul and George Harrison, who were still mucking about, that their bandmate was missing in action. "Where's John?" Paul asked.

Before Richard could answer him, George Martin turned on the talkback mic. "I left him up on the roof, looking at the stars."

"Ah, you mean like Vince Hill?" Paul joked. Vince Hill was a schmaltzy singer who was currently topping the charts with a sappy version of the song "Edelweiss" (from *The Sound of Music*), which Paul and George Harrison immediately began singing boisterously.

A second or two later, it dawned on them: *John was tripping on LSD and George Martin has left him up on the roof alone!* As if they were actors in an old-fashioned silent movie, the two Beatles executed a perfectly timed double take and then bolted up the stairs together, full speed, in a frantic dash to retrieve their compatriot. They knew all too well that the rooftop had only a narrow parapet and that, in his lysergically altered state, John could easily step over the edge and plummet thirty feet to the pavement below.

Mal and Neil followed closely behind, and a few tense minutes later, everyone reappeared in the control room . . . thankfully with a bewildered Lennon in tow, still in one piece. Nobody castigated George Martin for his poor decision, born, to be fair, out of naivete, but arrangements were quickly made for John to be driven home and the session ended soon afterward.

A short time later, as everyone was packing up and getting ready to leave, Norman Smith made an appearance, with the members of Pink Floyd. On this night he was dressed in a florid purple shirt instead of his usual suit and tie. Sadly, he and his protégés were given a very cool reception by Paul and George Harrison—uninvited visitors were simply not made welcome, even if they included a former workmate. After a few minutes of awkward chat, Norman headed out the door. It was the last time he popped in on any Beatles session that I was present at. Clearly, as far as they were concerned, that was a chapter that was over.

Richard and I often had a good laugh about the way the Beatles were dressing in those days. John always looked the most way-out, and his offbeat clothing frequently sported buttons with silly sayings: "Down With Knickers" was a favorite. One night he came in wearing different-colored shoes: one red and one green. We were jealous because we couldn't do things like that, even though, by this point, we were starting to wear slightly more vibrant clothes—a brightly colored tie or shirt—just to try to fit in more. John liked it when we did that, and never failed to tell us so or give us an approving look. At one session, he was giving George Martin some stick about the conservative suit and tie he was wearing, saying, jokingly, "Come on, George, why don't you join the throng?"

The genteel producer just laughed it off, replying, "I'll tell you what, John. I'll wear my funny nose tomorrow night."

John's "Lucy In The Sky With Diamonds" (which also ended up being banned by the BBC because the title words spelled "LSD") was up next, and it soon became one of my favorite tracks on the album. It was actually done very quickly—including rehearsal, it took only three nights to complete and mix. By this point the four Beatles were starting to get a little fed up with being stuck in the studio. After all, they'd been there for nearly five months and it wasn't the dead of winter anymore—the blossoms were beginning to appear on the trees outside and the weather was starting to brighten, so they were probably starting to get itchy feet. I know I was.

By now, it was evident that John's personality was changing. Instead of being opinionated about everything, he was becoming complacent; in fact, he seemed quite content to have someone else do his thinking for him, even when we were working on one of his own songs. By the spring of 1967, he was becoming increasingly disengaged, and that would more or less continue until the end of the Beatles' career. No doubt Paul was aware of the situation, and he was seizing the opportunity to step in and expand his role within the band.

That manifested itself down in the studio as they worked on this song, with John's lead vocal getting less aggressive and more dreamy with each successive take. That might have been a reflection of what he was smoking behind the screens, but Paul was clearly steering him in that direction, too. We had decided to route George Harrison's guitar through a Leslie speaker during the choruses, and because that reminded John of the "Dalai Lama" vocal effect we had used on "Tomorrow Never Knows," Mal was duly dispatched to see if he could find a rope so John could try out his theory and be swung around a microphone. From the wink Mal gave me when he returned some hours later—empty-handed—I suspect that he had spent the evening in the pub instead. He knew how absurd—and potentially dangerous—the request was, and he probably guessed that John would have forgotten all about it by the time he got back, which, of course, is exactly what happened.

A few nights later, George Martin decided that Richard and I were being overworked and gave us an evening off. It's true that we had been burning the candles at both ends—we still continued to do sessions for other artists on the days when the Beatles were not booked in—and we were now often staying behind long after George Martin would go home. Still, given the choice, I'm sure we would have both preferred to have been in on every *Pepper* session.

Malcolm Addey—he of the cigar and never-ending chatter—filled in for me that evening, as the band recorded the backing track for Paul's song "Getting Better." It was an odd choice, since I knew that George Martin didn't like working with him. Ken Townsend was recruited to substitute for Richard. Ken was really a maintenance engineer, but I suppose George just wanted a familiar face around, someone whom the group had at least met before.

I suspected that the four Beatles were annoyed that I wasn't there—there was no way they wanted a stranger engineering their sessions—and the next night, when I returned, my suspicions were confirmed.

"Glad to have you back, Geoff," George Harrison said as soon as he walked in the door. Malcolm had clearly gotten on his nerves.

When we played back the tapes of the previous evening's work in the control room, Ringo chimed in. "The drums sound a bit naff, don't you think?"

George Harrison didn't even wait for an answer. "Little wonder, considering that Malcolm didn't shut up long enough to get a decent drum sound."

I had to agree with Ringo's opinion, but I was surprised that he hadn't said anything to Addey the night before, because he usually wasn't shy about expressing his opinion if he heard something he didn't like. Perhaps he just couldn't get a word in edgewise! Malcolm had obviously utilized his own setup for recording the drums. Territorial as he was, there was no way he was going to use my configuration. I thought the snare sound was especially lacking, and it took a lot of work during the mixing stage to get the track to fit in sonically with the rest of the album.

That night, George Harrison was overdubbing his tamboura, which may have been another reason why he was in a good mood and was being unusually friendly toward me. Other than the Ravi Shankar session, pretty much the only time I interacted with him was when I was twiddling the controls of his guitar amplifier down in the studio to get sounds; often just the minutest adjustment made a huge sonic difference. The Beatles didn't have a lot of gear in the studio: apart from Ringo's drum kit, there were a dozen or so guitars and three or four guitar amps, and that was about it. But everything was tube—there wasn't a transistor in sight—and that had a lot to do with how good the guitar and bass sounds were.

It was tough trying to separate out John's and George's guitars, because they were usually recorded on the same track, in mono, so they were both coming out of the same speaker—it wasn't a simple matter of placing one in the left speaker and the other in the right speaker. Sometimes I'd spend two hours or more on each guitar, trying to differentiate between the instruments; I had to do a lot of equalization work and record each with its own echo so it would sound distinctive. A lot of the EQ adjustments were done on the guitar amps themselves instead of on the mixing console, where I only had basic bass and treble controls. Occasionally I'd patch in an external equalizer or two, but the ones we had at EMI were fairly wimpy and so had minimal effect on the sound.

Fortunately, because the Beatles were spending so much time rehearsing in the studio, I had time to make those kinds of fine adjustments and to gradually reposition microphones, moving them an inch at a time. If I said, "I can't get enough top end out of this" or "It's not a full enough sound," John or George might change to a different guitar, but I'd only ever occasionally make that suggestion—generally, I'd leave the decision of which guitar to use up to them. It would have been a lot easier if the two guitars were recorded on separate tracks, but we didn't have that luxury until the end of the *White Album* project, when the group began recording in eight-track.

After we finished the overdubs on "Getting Better"—George Harrison playing a drone on tamboura, Ringo on open hi-hat, and George Martin adding an interesting new texture by playing selected notes on a Virginal (a miniature harpsichord which he owned and brought in specially for the session)—the three of them, plus John, headed out the door; it had been a tiring session and it was well past midnight. But it was a Friday, with a whole weekend ahead to recover, so Paul decided to stay behind with Richard and me, and we dutifully pulled his amp out into the middle of the room for another long marathon of laying down the bass part. I decided to surreptitiously add just a touch of reverb to the bass that night, using the bathroom as an acoustic echo chamber. It was an effect that Paul normally didn't like, but I was looking for a little extra roundness, so I decided to try it. When he heard the playback, Paul immediately realized what I had done and screwed his face up, but he went along with it for just that one song.

For nearly a month, John had been ruminating about what kind of instrumentation he wanted on "Good Morning, Good Morning." He finally decided to add brass, but he was adamant that it mustn't sound "ordinary," and he insisted that George Martin hire a horn section comprised of old Liverpool mates instead of the top-flight session musicians we had been using. The group, who called themselves Sounds Incorporated, were nice enough blokes—actually, they were a lot of fun, which explained why Lennon liked them so much. But it took quite a long time to get a good take out of them because, throughout the session, John kept complaining that they were playing too "straight"—he had a real bee in his bonnet about that. In the end, to satisfy Lennon's demand that I take a different sonic approach, I shoved the mics right down the bells of the saxes and screwed the sound up with limiters and a healthy dose of effects like flanging and ADT; we pretty much used every piece of equipment at hand.

But first it was time for a little party. The Beatles had been cloistered in the studio for so long, they were clearly suffering from cabin fever. In addition, few people outside of our small inner circle had heard any of the *Pepper* tracks, so as everyone sat downstairs catching up with one another and reminiscing about old times, we were asked to play mixes of the completed tracks through the studio speakers.

This went on for a couple of hours, with George Martin growing increasingly annoyed. He felt we were in the studio to work, and he was cognizant of the money EMI was spending on studio time; after all, he had to work to a budget. He tolerated it for as long as he could before wandering down into the studio and saying, diplomatically, "We should be moving along now, don't you think?" What else could the man say? He never wanted to offend anyone, but, as producer, he was answerable to EMI, so he was caught in the middle. The Beatles, on the other hand, couldn't have cared less about the amount of time being spent on the record.

While George was busy being aggravated, I was studying the expressions of the Sounds Incorporated guys, trying to measure their reactions to the tracks we were playing for them. They were mesmerized! We knew that what we had been doing was exceptional, but it was gratifying to see that kind of response from people fresh to the project. From that point on, every time anyone came to visit the Beatles on a session, Richard and I hoped that we would be asked to play back something that was completed, or in progress, not just because we loved hearing the tracks, but because we enjoyed seeing the stunned looks on their faces.

Later that same evening, Paul overdubbed a lead guitar part on the song, which didn't do anything to improve George Harrison's mood. It seemed to me as if George was aggrieved a lot of the time . . . with good reason: Paul was playing a lot of his leads, and he had precious little to do. In addition, the one song he'd brought to the album had been rejected. As we got into our fourth and fifth month of recording, the preparatory meetings at Paul's house started to tail off, so the four Beatles began arriving at Abbey Road separately. Paul was almost always the first to come in, since he lived nearby, and George Harrison was often the last, so if Paul got an idea for a guitar part and Harrison wasn't around, he'd sometimes say, "Well, let's get on with it—I'll just play the part myself."

A couple of weeks later, John completed "Good Morning, Good Morning"—almost—when he added his lead vocal. It was the middle of the night by the time he finished, and I thought we were about to knock things on the head, but instead he came up to the control room and initiated a long conversation with me. Apparently he had been fretting about how to end the song—a simple fadeout was too "normal" for him, so he had come up with a concept. The idea was that as the music was fading away, the sounds of various animals would be heard, with each successive animal capable of chasing or frightening the next animal in line. John had actually thought this through to the extent that he'd written down a list of the animals he wanted on there, in order. I loved the idea, and despite the late hour Richard was sent off to the EMI sound effects library to fetch the appropriate tapes. We sat up with John until nearly dawn dubbing them on, George Martin and the others having long gone home. True, the premise kind of breaks down at the end—there's a sheep chasing a horse and a cow chasing a hen—but it's all in good fun. At that point, we had no idea that the chicken clucking at the very end would play such a prominent role in the album. That would come a little later.

"Good Morning, Good Morning" ended up with the dubious distinction of being the *Pepper* track with the largest number of overdubs, hence the most four-to-four reductions (premixes bounced between tape machines in order to open up new tracks). Despite that, it still sounds good, albeit a bit strident due to all the compensatory top end we had to add during mixing. There's a lot of ADT on John's voice, and on Paul's lead guitar—in one spot, there's a huge "wow" on the guitar where the effect almost makes it sound like the note was bent. One reason why our Automatic Double Tracking worked so well was that it had a sweep oscillator control that you could actually play like a musical instrument, allowing you to constantly vary the delay time in response to the performance.

During that mix, I also enjoyed whacking the faders all the way up for Ringo's huge tom hit during the stop time—so much so that the limiters nearly overloaded, but it definitely gets the listener's attention! Add in the flanged brass, miked in an unorthodox way, and it's all icing on the cake; take those effects off and the recording doesn't have the same magic. That song serves as a good example of how simple manipulation can improve a track sonically.

After the debacle of "Only A Northern Song," nobody was really expecting too much of George Harrison, and, quite frankly, when he came in at around this time and previewed "Within You Without You" for us, nobody was overwhelmed. Personally, I thought it was just tedious. Of course, just hearing him run it down on acoustic guitar gave very little idea of the beautiful song that it was to turn into once all the overdubs were completed, but at the time it caused a lot of eye-rolling among the other Beatles and George Martin.

As George Harrison himself later said, his heart was in India the whole time the Beatles were recording *Sgt. Pepper's Lonely Hearts Club Band*. As a result, he was a detached, reluctant participant; the only thing that brought him around again, albeit temporarily, was when we worked on "Within You Without You." George Martin must have known that he felt that way, which would explain why he was prepared to put so much time and effort into recording the song. My theory was that, while Harrison may well have felt trapped by the group's fame and notoriety, he didn't want to let the side down, either. That's why there was such a sense of relief among everyone when the track turned out so well.

The concept the two Georges had come up with was to record a rhythm track that consisted entirely of Indian instruments, and I was excited by the challenge it presented. Studio Two had a hardwood floor, so in order to dampen the sound, I normally put down carpeting underneath Ringo's drums and in the area where Beatles vocals were recorded. But this time Richard and I got out a bunch of throw rugs and spread them all around the floor for the musicians to sit on, all in an effort to make them more comfortable and make the studio a bit more homey. Mind you, the Abbey Road rugs were completely moth-eaten and dilapidated . . . but it was the thought that counted.

All four Beatles were there when the basic track was recorded, along with famed illustrator Peter Blake, who was there to talk about the *Sgt. Pepper* album cover. He mostly huddled with Paul and John while George was busy instructing the musicians as to the parts he wanted them to play. Ringo, as usual, was lost in a game of chess off in a corner with Neil. It was very calm and peaceful in the studio that evening. Harrison was surrounded by his new friends, the Indian musicians, and he was gracious and welcoming when

Peter Blake arrived; for perhaps the first time during the *Pepper* sessions, I could see that George was completely relaxed. Paul was somewhat interested in the goings-on and in how the various instruments were played—eventually he even bought a sitar himself—but John seemed quite bored, wandering around the studio aimlessly, not knowing what to contribute. Because the song was unusually long, there were quite a few glances between John and Paul when the rhythm track was being recorded, and I could tell that they were a bit dubious. *Yes, it's all very nice,* I could imagine they were thinking, *and it's all very well played, but it isn't Beatles, is it?* They never really got into it, or any of George's Indian music, for that matter, but I guess they went along with it for the sake of band unity.

Eventually the recording commenced. It was decided to first lay down a drone, with three or four musicians playing one note continuously; even Neil Aspinall was recruited to assist Harrison in playing tamboura. As the other instruments began to be layered on top of the drone, the structure of the song started to make a little more sense. I quite liked the sound of the tabla, and, as I had done on George's *Revolver* track "Love You To," I once again decided to close-mic them and add signal processing to make things a bit more exciting sonically.

A week later, a refreshed, rejuvenated George Harrison came back to the studio and oversaw the overdubbing of a couple of additional dilruba parts (a dilruba is a bowed instrument similar to a sitar, but smaller). The other three Beatles were present at the session, but boredom set in quickly, so arrangements were made to have them listen to other works in progress in another control room. Deep in concentration, George barely even noticed that the others had departed; he may have even welcomed them leaving him to work on his own. As much as I didn't care for "Within You Without You" at first, I had to admit it grew on me as we were recording it. It was to get better still with one final, very special session—the end point of the long *Sgt. Pepper* journey.

Even at this late date, there were still three more songs to be recorded, starting with Paul's gentle "She's Leaving Home." There was a bit of tension between Paul and George Martin at this session, because an outsider, Mike Leander, had been hired by Paul to do the string arrangement due to George's unavailability (George was finishing up a Cilla Black album at the time). As a result, Paul stayed up in the control room while George Martin did the conducting downstairs. Frankly, I thought it was a bit of a power play on both their parts: George was saying to Paul, "You can't expect me to drop everything I'm doing whenever you call," and Paul was letting George know that he was expendable.

The controversy had passed by the time John and Paul returned to the studio the following week to overdub their vocals. There were still two available tracks on the multitrack tape, but Paul felt strongly that he wanted certain lines double-tracked, and he also wanted the strings to remain in stereo. The only solution was to have them sing their vocals at the same time, recording each pass on a single track.

The lights in the studio were turned off to set the mood; the sole source of illumination was a table lamp next to the wall. The two Beatles, lifelong friends and collaborators, sat on high stools, facing each other, studying each other's lips intently for phrasing. Watching them, I remember thinking that John's and Paul's voices were so different yet so perfectly complemented each other's, just like their personalities and approach to music-making. It wasn't an easy vocal to nail down, either—at one point there was a long discussion about getting the right amount of emotion into the lyric. Paul was quite the perfectionist by this time, and he was really pissing John off by having him sing the same line over and over again. Up in the control room, I had to do a bit of tweaking to get the correct perspective and contrast between the two vocals.

That evening, host Brian Matthew came into the studio to interview John and Paul for the BBC program *Top of the Pops*. It was a welcome diversion from all the hard work we'd been doing, and I was quite surprised when I heard Lennon tell Matthew emphatically that there would be "no more 'She Loves You's" coming from the band and no more touring, ever. Paul and John also pretaped speeches for the upcoming Ivor Novello Awards show because they'd already decided that they wouldn't be attending in person, despite the fact that, in Britain, it was almost as prestigious as the Grammies.

We were now getting very near the end, but there was still no song for Ringo to sing. Paul and John set out to remedy that, giving their drummer a showcase with one of the very few songs they had cowritten in recent years: "With A Little Help From My Friends." There was an unusually late start for that night's session because the Beatles had spent the afternoon and early evening overseeing preparations for the upcoming album cover photo shoot. While we waited for them to arrive, George Martin, Richard, and I filled the time by dubbing on the sound effects tapes that had been previously compiled for "Good Morning, Good Morning" and "Being For The Benefit Of Mr. Kite."

Despite the late hour, all four Beatles were wide awake, excited by the events of the day; I remember them animatedly discussing the set that Peter Blake had built for them and talking about how much they loved their satin *Pepper* costumes. After hurriedly consumed cups of tea, we finally got to work. The backing track for the new song—initially called "Bad Finger Boogie" for some reason—had a real spark to it, and an inspired Ringo was really smacking his tom-toms, so I decided to take the bottom skins off again— something I hadn't done since "A Day In The Life." Ten takes were required to get a "keeper"; it was nearly dawn by that time. Richard and I watched an exhausted Ringo begin to trudge up the stairs. That was our signal, as usual, that the session was over, and we began to relax. He was at the halfway point when we heard Paul's voice call out.

"Where are you going, Ring?" he said.

Ringo looked surprised. "Home, to bed."

"Nah, let's do the vocal now."

Ringo looked to the others for support. "But I'm knackered," he protested. To his dismay, both John and George Harrison were taking Paul's side.

"No, come on back here and do some singing for us," John said with a grin.

It was always a group decision as to when a session would end, and obviously Ringo had jumped the gun a bit. Reluctantly, he headed back down the steps. "Oh no," groaned Richard. "Are we still going to be here when tomorrow's session is due to start?"

Weary to the bone, all I could do was shake my head. I was too tired to even react.

Fortunately for all of us, Ringo got his lead vocal done relatively quickly: perhaps the shock tactic of having him sing when he was least expecting it took the nervousness away, or perhaps it was just how supportive everyone was being. All three of his compatriots gathered around him, inches behind the microphone, silently conducting and cheering him on as he gamely tackled his vocal duties. It was a touching show of unity among the four Beatles.

The only problem was the song's last high note, which Ringo had a bit of trouble hitting spot-on. For a while he lobbied to have the tape slowed down just for that one drop-in, and we tried it, but even though it allowed him to sing on pitch, it didn't match tonally to the rest of the vocal—he sounded a bit silly, almost like one of the Goons. "No, Ring, you've got to do it properly," Paul finally concluded.

"It's okay; just put your mind to it. You can do it," George Harrison said encouragingly.

Even John added some helpful—if decidedly nontechnical—advice: "Just throw yer head back and let 'er rip!"

It took a few tries, but Ringo finally hit the note—and held it—without too much wavering. Amid the cheers of his bandmates and a Scotch-and-Coke toast, the session finally ended. Outside, the spring air was fresh with dew and the birds were already chirping. It looked to be a lovely, sunny day and I would get to enjoy none of it. We were all due back in the studio in less than twelve hours.

Later that night, Paul and John added their counterpoint backing vocals with ease—they had obviously rehearsed the parts quite a bit, and their voices blended so naturally—and then George Harrison added a guitar lick or two. Ringo sat up in the control room with us for most of that session, beaming like a proud papa. This was "his" song and he was quite interested in its progress, listening intently to every new overdub.

But there was still no bass on it because Paul had played piano during the backing track. So at around three in the morning, John, George Harrison, and Ringo finally headed home, accompanied by George Martin. Richard and I again hunkered down for what we knew was going to be a long night. We were right—it was a marathon, not a sprint—but it was worth every second of it. By this time, I knew exactly the kind of sound Paul was after, and I didn't do anything differently than on other *Pepper* tracks, but I do think there's something unique about the bass sound in "With A Little Help From My Friends." Perhaps it's because Paul deviated from the usual routine in that he decided to sit up in the control room with us while he played; to accommodate his wishes, Richard ran an extra-long lead down to the bass amp. Brow furrowed in deep concentration, fingers wrapped around his psychedelic-colored Rickenbacker, Paul instructed Richard to drop in and out over and over again. Determined to get every single note and phrase as perfect as it could possibly be, that night he was like a man possessed.

Sitting side by side with the ultra-focused McCartney in that cramped control room in the middle of the night, shouting out encouragement every time he'd nail a section, Richard and I truly felt privileged to be there. We knew that the work we were doing! was important, though we could hardly guess at the seismic impact it would have on popular culture when *Pepper* was finally released a few months later.

The concept that was to glue the album together had by this point been decided: all the songs would flow from one to the next, with no gap, as if the listener were present at a live performance of the esteemed Lonely Hearts Club Band. It's an approach that has been done to death ever since, but in 1967 it was a radical idea, and one that had never been applied to a rock album. The "live audience" segue between the theme song and "With A Little Help From My Friends" had worked out so well that we now had to come up with something equally spectacular for the end of the album, just before "A Day In The Life," which would be the obvious closer.

And so it was that a full month after the *Sgt. Pepper* theme was initially recorded, the four Beatles returned to the studio to reprise their performance, but with several differences. The first was that, with the end of the album in sight, everyone was really energized . . . and in a hurry to get it done quickly. Paul, in fact, was scheduled to fly to the U.S. just two days later—a trip he had no intention of postponing because it would reunite him with his girlfriend Jane Asher after several months apart.

The second difference was that, on such short notice, George Martin had been unable to book Studio Two. Other EMI artists had been bumped for the Beatles so often that they were starting to resent it; whoever had been previously booked in had obviously refused to give up their time. As a result, we were forced to use the cavernous Studio One, which was probably the least conducive place in the Abbey Road complex to recording a high-energy rock song.

Finally, we all had to come in on a Saturday. As long and as crazy as the *Pepper* sessions had been over the past four months, the Beatles had stuck rigidly to a weekdays-only schedule, usually working three to four nights a week. We'd all come to count on the weekends as a time to unwind and relax, and to get some distance from the intense work we were doing. But there was no choice in the matter, so we all trundled in on April Fool's Day for what would turn out to be a momentous session.

The acoustics of Studio One were far too reverberant for a loud rock band, so I knew that I had to make some special arrangements in advance. First, I had Richard and the maintenance engineer on duty gather up all the available tall screens and build a kind of hut, thus creating a smaller room within a room. Then I asked Mal and Neil to set up the drums and amplifiers very near one another so that there would be minimal delay on the signal that would inevitably spill between the mics, and I arranged the Beatles themselves in a semicircle so they could all see one another.

It took a lot of effort to tame that room, but it was worth it—the sound we got that day was tight and ballsy. It didn't exactly match the sound of the rest of the album, which was almost entirely recorded in Studio Two, but it wasn't awash in reverb, either, which is what would have happened if I hadn't screened off one small area for them to play in. As it is, whatever reverb exists on the "Sgt. Pepper" reprise is actually the sound of the huge room itself—there was no need to add any echo chamber when the tracks were mixed.

Everybody was really upbeat that day, and it shows. The vibe was fantastic and the energy was even higher than in the first version. It was a great rhythm track, and I could feel the excitement building from the very first moment, even in Paul's count-in, which had a tremendous energy of its own. The Beatles played the whole thing live, just two guitars, bass, and drums— the old-school lineup they had used for years—with just a single keyboard overdub. Ringo was pounding the hell out of his drums—he was even stomping on the bass drum pedal harder than usual. In fact, everyone was playing full-out. Considering that they'd all been cloistered in the studio for so long, pouring their hearts and souls into the album, it really was incredible how good and tight their playing was.

There were all sorts of nice little touches on that song; the more you listen to it, the more you hear. I always enjoyed Lennon's playful "good-bye-ee," ad-libbed right at the beginning, and, in the last chorus, where it sounds like Paul is off mic, that's just leakage from his guide vocal track onto the drum overhead mic. It was just something I could never get rid of, so we ended up not worrying about it, kind of like Mal's count during the twenty-four-bar buildup in "A Day In The Life."

With time pressure on, the entire song was completed—overdubs, mix, and all—in a single long session. The album release date was drawing near and in between takes, the band were going through contact sheets for the album cover and reviewing design ideas for the gateway sleeve and giveaways they were planning on including. At one stage, there was even a semi-serious discussion about including *Sgt. Pepper* balloons.

There was just one more session to go, and it took place less than forty-eight hours later, with Paul somewhere over the Atlantic, winging his way to America. George Harrison was the only Beatle in attendance, and the purpose was to bring "Within You Without You" to completion. As was becoming habit, it was a marathon session, running until dawn the next day, but the results were nothing short of magical.

Once again, we were in Studio One, but this time the acoustics worked for the instrumentation being recorded. George Martin was conducting the same top-flight orchestral players that worked on most of the rest of *Pepper*, but despite their expertise, the musicians took a long time to get it right; I clearly remember the look of deep concentration on their faces as they struggled to master the complex score. It was painstaking, and it certainly was a challenge to the musicians, many of whom seemed to be getting a bit frustrated as the session wore on.

The problem was that we were trying to create a blend of East meets West—conventional orchestral instruments playing over nonconventional Indian instruments. There were no real bar lines in the Eastern music, just a lot of sustained tones, most of which were playing in between the twelve notes used in Western music. That was a really hard session for George Martin—by the end of the night he was absolutely knackered. Thankfully he had the help of George Harrison, who acted as a bridge between the Indian tonalities and rhythms, which he understood quite well, and the Western sensibilities of George Martin and the classical musicians. I was never more impressed with both Georges than I was on that very special, almost spiritual night. Interestingly, from then on, many of George Martin's orchestrations began exhibiting that same kind of Indian feel, with the string sections doing slight pitch-bending. It actually put a stamp on his arrangements and gave them a unique sound.

After the string overdubs were completed and the musicians had departed, we moved into Studio Two, where George Harrison began tuning his sitar, sitting cross-legged on a throw rug we had put down for him. He only had to overdub three or four licks in the instrumental section, but some of the drop-ins were tricky, and it took hours to do. None of us ever really appreciated how difficult the sitar was to play. Despite the fact that George was quite accomplished, it did always seem to take a lot of time to get his parts recorded whenever he picked the instrument up.

Finally, with the lights down low and candles and incense burning, George tackled the lead vocal, and he did a great job. Mind you, he does sound quite sleepy on it . . . hardly surprising since he'd been up all night working on the track! Fortunately, that lethargic quality seemed to perfectly complement the mood of the song. The sun was rising as we staggered out of the studio the next morning, but I felt completely satisfied, proud of our accomplishment.

The next night, we began mixing the track. There was a fair bit of discussion about trying to cut it down to make it a bit shorter, but Harrison was adamantly opposed and we never actually attempted editing it. I suppose everyone felt they needed to let George Harrison have his way on this one. It was a very difficult track to mix, with so many time changes and so much dense instrumentation. As a result, we had to mix it in sections and then crossfade between them. For aesthetic reasons, we ended up moving a few sections closer to one another, which had the added bonus of shaving a few seconds off the running time.

We also decided to apply a lot of effects; for some reason, they seemed to suit the character of the song. There's a great deal of ADT on the vocal and on the sitar and dilruba—in fact, there's one particular phrase where the tape nearly came off the machine because Richard was wobbling it so much! When we were nearly done, John and Ringo came by to have a listen. Ringo, who had the closest friendship with George, seemed quite enthusiastic—he loved the complex rhythms. John's comment was a simple "Yeah, that's quite nice." It was hard to gauge how much they really liked it, but there's no question that they, like the three of us up in the control room, had been won over to some extent. Certainly the end result far exceeded any expectations anyone had the first day George played it for us. Listening to it today, I think it is a masterful piece of work, although it's not one of my favorite songs on the album; I find that it kind of interrupts the flow of things. That said, it certainly added a whole different flavor, and it's a good piece of music that stands up on its own merits.

Finally, at Harrison's request, we tacked on a few seconds of laughter at the end, taken from the EMI sound effects library. Personally, it was something I never liked—I felt that it spoiled the mood. George Martin tried to talk him out of it, too, but Harrison was insistent that he wanted it there, though he never really explained why. I don't think that George Harrison was ever defensive or embarrassed about the song. To the contrary, he always seemed quite confident about it and quite content on the days we were working on it. Whatever his reasons were, the laughter was added and the song was complete. I've always liked to think that "Within You Without You" actually turned out even better than George envisioned it, thanks to our combined efforts. I would imagine that he was quite chuffed with the final result.

Over the next two weeks, with Paul out of the country, George Martin and I spent a few days experimenting with the running order of the album, but mostly we just rested and recuperated from the long stretch of sessions behind us. Because most of the songs ran directly into one another, without the usual three-second gap, there was a lot of crossfading to be done, which was quite time-consuming. It was a sheer fluke the way the clucking chicken at the end of "Good Morning, Good Morning" turned into George's guitar at the beginning of the "Pepper" reprise. We were all surprised and delighted at how well that worked; I didn't even have to alter the pitch of the cluck with the use of varispeed, though I did tighten up the gap between songs by cutting out a bit of tape.

We also devoted a few days to remixing the stereo version of the album. In contrast to the way they carefully oversaw the original mono mixes, the group had expressed no interest in even being present when we did the new ones; that's how little thought we all gave stereo in those days. When Paul returned, the four Beatles gathered at Studio Two for one last night of listening. They were all thrilled with what they heard, but John and Paul felt that they wanted something additional to end the album, even after the final huge piano chord that concluded "A Day In The Life." John had read somewhere that dogs could hear higher frequencies than humans could, and requested that a supersonic tone be placed at the end to give them something to listen to. (Ironically, he didn't realize that most of the record players and speakers of the era were incapable of reproducing such a tone, so it didn't actually become audible to the world at large until the CD release some twenty years later.) That was something which could be easily enough accomplished in the mastering room, but it didn't satisfy their wish to have their two-legged fans hear something additional.

"Let's just put on some gobbledygook, then bifurcate it, splange it, and loop it," Lennon said irreverently; he always loved the sound of nonsense words. To George Martin's amusement, the four Beatles endorsed the idea wholeheartedly and raced down to the studio while Richard hurriedly put up a couple of microphones. They looned about for five minutes or so, saying whatever came to mind as I recorded them on a two-track machine. When I played the tape back for them, John identified a few seconds that he particularly liked—it consisted primarily of Paul repeating the words "Never needed any other way" for no particular reason while the others chattered away in the background—which I duly made into a loop, then flew into the ending.

And with that, *Sgt. Pepper's Lonely Hearts Club Band* was done.

All that remained was for the final mixes to be transferred to vinyl, and we had specifically requested that Harry Moss, EMI's most senior and experienced mastering engineer, be given the assignment. But George Martin and I knew that, as good as Harry was, he would probably do what most mastering engineers are trained to do: add EQ, or compression, or whatever he felt he could do to improve the sound. That was not what we wanted, however. We knew that we had come up with something very special, and we didn't want it tampered with in any way. To make our position completely clear, I wrote what I thought were three innocuous words on the tape box—"Please Transfer Flat"—and awaited Harry's cut.

Unfortunately, this was viewed as mutiny by the EMI executives. Within hours of sending the tape upstairs, I was cornered by Horace Hack, the manager of the mastering department, and he gave me hell. Red in the face with rage, he thundered, "How dare you write that on the box? How dare you try to tell my people their job?"

I thought this was ludicrous, especially considering that I had been a mastering engineer myself. Horace was quite upset, though, so I did what I could to calm him down, saying soothingly, "Look, I think you should sort this out with George Martin."

After some protracted negotiations, George worked out a compromise whereby I was allowed to be in the room when Harry mastered it—a first at EMI. (Up until then, producers and balance engineers were strictly forbidden from attending mastering sessions.) In the end, I did ask Harry to make a couple of minor EQ adjustments, but the album was essentially cut flat, as we had originally requested.

The Beatles, however, had insisted that the loop of gobbledygook be cut into the final groove in the vinyl, known as the "concentric." Their reasoning was that the automatic record players of the day would play it for a few seconds before lifting the needle off, while those people who still owned manual players would hear it drone on indefinitely until they got fed up and raised the needle themselves. It was a juvenile attempt at humor, but one that created a big technical problem for Harry. In the end, it took him nine attempts to get that concentric to work out correctly, and each time it didn't, he had to cut the whole second side of the album again. Needless to say, it was one practical joke that I'm sure Harry didn't appreciate.

The onus had been on me all throughout the *Pepper* sessions. I was constantly wracking my brains trying to come up with ways to make things sound different. John and Paul's attitude, even more than on *Revolver*, was, "We're going to play guitar, but we don't want it to sound like a guitar; we're going to play piano but we don't want it to sound like piano." We got off to a roaring start with "Strawberry Fields Forever," but I wasn't trying to match it afterward, or even necessarily better it; I was simply trying to make every track sound different, so that each song would have its own personality. As a result, I tried to take a fresh approach to every new track we recorded for

Pepper. Because we knew that the Beatles wouldn't ever have to play the songs live, there were no creative boundaries. By this time the group had enough clout with EMI that if they wanted something, by and large they got it, and there was virtually no pressure on them to deliver anything; if they didn't feel like coming in on a particular day, they didn't come in, simple as that. I don't know of any other band that ever had that kind of luxury—it probably never happened before, and it probably never will again.

In contrast to *Revolver,* there are hardly any backwards sounds on *Pepper.* The whole idea was to push the envelope both musically and sonically, and as far as the Beatles were concerned, those sounds were already old hat. In that sense, they were like kids with a new toy: once they discovered something new, they wanted to do it to death; then they got tired of it and moved on to something else. For the same reason, I never used that speaker-as-a-mic trick for Paul's bass again after "Paperback Writer" and "Rain"; in any event, it wouldn't have suited the *Pepper* and post-*Pepper* songs because it was too muddy, not defined enough. Technically, the same equipment was used to record both albums—it was all the same outboard gear, and mostly the same mics. Yet the two albums sound so different! Part of that is due to the fact that a lot of *Revolver* was recorded in the cramped confines of Studio Three, whereas most of *Pepper* was done in Studio Two, which was more spacious and had better acoustics, yielding a more pristine sound. Although the control room of Studio Three provided a more pleasant working environment because it had windows, the studio area was normally just used for solo pianos and string quartets; it simply wasn't designed to accommodate rock musicians playing loudly.

Another hallmark of *Sgt. Pepper* was that the Beatles were starting to get fed up with using the same instrumentation all the time. They wanted to advance themselves and were becoming increasingly frustrated with the same old two-guitars-bass-and-drums lineup. They were keen to introduce new tonalities: Paul's piano playing became a lot more prominent, and they relied more and more on organ and Mellotron, as well as the full spectrum of orchestral instruments that George Martin was so familiar with. We also started putting all sorts of things through Leslies—not just vocals, but guitars and pianos—and we were utilizing a lot of tape varispeeding and other manipulation techniques.

Sgt. Pepper's Lonely Hearts Club Band took more than seven hundred hours to record, spread out over four and a half months. That was a long time back in those days, though not by today's standards. For most of those hours, George Martin and I were just waiting for the band to get their ideas together. That's not to say I was just sitting around twiddling my thumbs while they were brainstorming and rehearsing. I'd fill the time constructively with constant experimentation; while they were trying out their ideas in the studio, we were trying out ours in the control room—things like unusual signal routings, different combinations of limiters and compressors, new miking techniques, even using bathrooms and other areas of the Abbey Road complex as echo chambers. We also always had to be at the ready, because at any time, without warning, they might want to record an idea and hear it back. Maybe the Beatles thought we were doing sod all until we put the red Recording light on, but that simply wasn't the case.

By 1967, eight-track tape recorders were already starting to appear in professional studios (though it would be more than a year before EMI would purchase such a machine), yet the entire *Sgt. Pepper* album was recorded in four-track. In short order, sixteen-track and then twenty-four-track would become standard recording tools, giving significantly more tape "real estate" on which to layer instruments and thus increased sonic control. But George Martin has said in many interviews that *Pepper* wouldn't have been as good had it been recorded in twenty-four-track, and I completely agree. It was because of those very limitations that we were put on the spot, forced to make creative decisions every step of the way. Necessity was the mother of invention, and that was part of the magic of the album. You had to put the right echo on, the right EQ, the right signal processing; the playing had to be right, the vocal had to be right. It made things easier in a way, because otherwise there are too many variables and too many decisions to be put off until the mixing stage.

One of the most astonishing things about *Pepper* is that, with all the tape bouncing we did—and on "Being For The Benefit Of Mr. Kite" there are actually five multitrack reductions—we never had to go back and redo any of the premixes. Never was the snare not loud enough, never was the guitar too buried, never was there something wrong with the balance. And those premixes were quite demanding, because I essentially had to imagine what might be overdubbed at a later date, so every fader move had to be carefully thought out. The Beatles were very finicky, and so was I, but because those decisions were made early—and stuck with—every overdub related perfectly to the sounds that were already there on tape.

I didn't get an engineering credit on *Pepper* when it was first released on vinyl, but I know that George Martin did try to get me one, only to be vetoed by EMI's executives on the grounds that it was against company policy. That's how little regard was given to the recording engineer then. It was a bit galling in that even Peter Blake, the guy who did the album cover got a credit and was presented with a gold disk, yet I never got one. Happily, a year after *Pepper* was released, I was honored by America's National Academy of Recording Arts and Sciences—the peers in my industry—when I was awarded a Grammy for Best Engineered Album of 1967.

With *Sgt. Pepper*, everything came together. The Beatles were looking to go out on a limb, both musically and sonically, and I was willing to climb out there with them. Somehow it all worked. The group's thought process had shifted because of the decision to stop touring and because of the drugs they were experimenting with. Everything, in fact, was changing.

10

All You Need Is Love . . . and a Long Vacation:

Magical Mystery Tour and Yellow Submarine

By the time we finished the long, grueling *Sgt. Pepper* sessions, it was almost as if we were working in a bloody factory. We all needed a few weeks off to relax, clear our minds, and get a little perspective, but that was not to be. In fact, just days after finishing the sequencing and mastering of *Pepper,* the Beatles were already hard at work on *Magical Mystery Tour* and *Yellow Submarine.*

Both projects were actually films and not albums. The main difference between the two was that the Beatles were completely uninterested in *Yellow Submarine,* which was a feature-length cartoon that Brian had obligated them to do, apparently against their wishes. As a result, it essentially became a receptacle for any song of theirs that they deemed substandard, such as George Harrison's "Only A Northern Song." "Shovel that sideways," they would say, and we knew that meant it was destined to be given over to the cartoon: they simply couldn't be bothered writing anything new for it. Making matters worse, during the summer of 1967, Al Brodax and George Dunning—the producer and the director, respectively, of *Yellow Submarine*—began sitting in on sessions in order to get the group's mannerisms down pat. If the Beatles hated the idea of the film—which they did—they doubly hated having these two guys sitting up in the control room observing them, making notes; they disliked being watched like that at the best of times, even by close friends. As a result, they treated Brodax and Dunning with utter disdain and gave them no help whatsoever.

There wasn't all that much enthusiasm for *Magical Mystery Tour* either, truth be told, except for Paul; it was his "baby," and the other three just kind of went along with it. At one point he came into the studio excitedly waving a drawing of a big circle that he had divided up like a pie, showing the various scenes he had in mind, handing out instructions to the others. It made no sense whatsoever to me, and it seemed equally incomprehensible to John, George, and Ringo, but everyone nodded bemusedly. However misguided the concept, and however poorly executed it ended up being, it was yet another sign of the Beatles wanting to branch out, to break out of the mold of just being pop stars, so I had to give them credit for that. The problem was timing: we were all so exhausted from the hard work of the past five months.

With the benefit of hindsight, it's obvious that we went back into the studio way too soon. Paul was the only one with any creative energy left, and he was determined to top *Pepper;* the others didn't seem to care nearly as much. But in the face of John's excessive drug-taking and George's spiritual journey eastward, Paul had taken control of the band's direction so firmly that the others didn't even question the wisdom of returning to work right away.

Surprisingly, most of their post-*Pepper* work was done in Studio Three, which was considerably smaller than Studio Two and therefore even more confining, both physically and aesthetically. Presumably George Martin simply couldn't book Studio Two for the times the Beatles wanted; as a result, they also began working in outside studios more and more.

Perhaps because of their drug intake, the Beatles started getting a bit complacent and lazy around this time, and their concentration was dwindling, too. Actually, it had never been all that great, especially when they were doing backing tracks. They'd get halfway through and then one of them would forget what it was they were supposed to do; that's why it would often require dozens of takes before we'd get something usable. The usual culprit was John. His mind would just wander, or else he and Paul would get an attack of giggles—most often at a certain point in the evening after they'd had a smoke of pot.

But the main problem was that we simply weren't fresh; as a result, the recordings themselves sound kind of tired. John's "I Am The Walrus" could have been a track on *Pepper,* I suppose, but it wouldn't have been a particularly outstanding one. Few of the other songs on either *Magical Mystery Tour* or *Yellow Submarine* would have fit. To some degree, the Beatles were a little too overconfident about their abilities at that point in time. They felt they could get away with recording almost anything and the public would accept it, but it wasn't as simple as that. Certainly they had no appreciation of what we had been doing in the control room during *Pepper,* of the time and effort we had devoted to creating the icing on the cake, the sounds and atmosphere.

They viewed what we were doing as normal, whereas in reality we were tearing our hair out a lot of the time!

Sadly, *Pepper* was the last Beatles album where all four band members worked like a team. There would still be good days ahead, but they would occur less frequently. The cracks were beginning to appear and tensions were starting to bubble to the surface.

The first track to be recorded for *Magical Mystery Tour* was the title song, and everyone was quite up for that session, which began, as usual, late in the evening. There was a long period of rehearsal punctuated by discussion about the various scenes they wanted to shoot for the film. Paul's vague concept—and it was quite vague at that point—was to have the four Beatles and a group of actors pile onto a coach, destination unknown, in emulation of the "bus trip to nowhere" that was so popular in England in the fifties and sixties—really just an excuse for an extended booze-up on wheels. Finally, a backing track was laid down, with Paul thumping away on the piano. Once that was done, Richard raided the EMI archives and found a tape of transportation effects recorded on location by Stuart Eltham, which I put into a loop, complete with the sounds of busses whizzing by in glorious stereo, panning from right to left.

The next night Paul showed up with a casting book that he had gotten from a film agency and everyone gathered around, excitedly picking the actors they wanted for the character roles. They were mostly choosing people they recognized from TV, plays, and films; basically, they were looking for familiar faces. Everyone had great fun going through the book, shouting out as they flipped through the pages, "Look at him! Look at her!" They were particularly amused by the photos of the fat lady who ended up playing Ringo's mother: "She's four times the size of you, Ring!" Lennon chortled with glee. One of the odder people they selected—mostly at John's urging—was someone I knew slightly: Ivor Cutler, a member of the Massed Alberts. He was a poet, a petite man dressed all in black who played a laptop harmonium, accompanying himself as he half sang, half recited his silly little couplets. Plain and simple, the guy was nuts . . . so, naturally, he was chosen.

That weekend I was at my local pub in Crouch End with some friends when someone suggested we go check out a "happening" that was occurring at Alexandra Palace, a short walk away. The event had been advertised as a "Free Speech Benefit," but it was really just a concert featuring many of the popular bands of the era, Pink Floyd among them. Rumors had persisted for days that the Beatles would be attending, and might even play a few of their new songs, although I had never heard them even discuss going, much less performing, during any of our sessions. I had to admit that I was curious, though. If they were going to be turning up at a venue in my own backyard, I wanted to be there. In the end, only a stoned, dazed Lennon made a brief appearance, kitted out in an Afghan jacket and accompanied by a few of his mates. We waved to each other across the crowded floor, but the noise and din precluded our having any kind of conversation. A short while later he disappeared into the night.

Paul had decided to add brass to the *Magical Mystery Tour* theme song, including the same kind of Brandenburg Concerto–type piccolo trumpets he had used in "Penny Lane." Since I had recorded every note of the track, I naturally assumed that I would be engineering the overdub. But EMI's executives, in their infinite wisdom, thought otherwise. Months before, I had been booked to record an eccentric group called Adge Cutler and the Wurzels doing a gig in a pub up in Somerset. Adge had recently had a number one hit in England with a singalong song I'd recorded called "Drink Up Thy Zider." Because of the success of that single, the band's management had prebooked me to record their live gig, but it happened to fall on the same evening that the brass was to be added to "Magical Mystery Tour," and despite my protests I was told in no uncertain terms by the studio management that I would be recording Adge Cutler instead of the Beatles. Incredibly, they took me off a session booked by the biggest artists in the world so that I could get on a train and record a band in a tiny pub hundreds of miles away.

Ken Townsend accompanied me on the trip, and I kept telling him that I was certain the Beatles would be ticked off that I wasn't there, especially since Malcolm Addey, of all people, was going to be taking my place. I was correct in my prediction, and I didn't hear the end of it for weeks—in fact, it's something that Paul still brings up occasionally, just to needle me. Given George Martin's reluctance to work with Malcolm, I have no idea why he was unable to pull strings and reverse management's decision. Perhaps it was just another sign that he was starting to lose control.

The gig itself was a bit of a disaster—a near riot, actually. The pub was located next door to the Nailsey Glass Works, and the local rowdies got well lubricated that night, throwing beer bottles through the windows. After quite a few drinks ourselves, Ken and I pulled a practical joke when we got back to the hotel. In those days, people would leave their shoes outside their hotel room doors to be cleaned while they slept. When we traipsed back in late that night, tipsy, it was a sight that made us laugh . . . so much so that we couldn't resist changing them all around so that, the next morning, every guest received the wrong pair of shoes.

The next evening, I was back at Abbey Road, mixing the *Magical Mystery Tour* theme song. Malcolm had done a creditable job of recording the brass, with the tape slowed down so that it would sound extra toppy when played back at normal speed, but once again the four Beatles—Harrison in particular—did a lot of complaining about Malcolm's endless chatter. Richard described the session as having been a bit strained from start to finish, with George Martin particularly on edge.

Still, their performance was quite remarkable: the Beatles played and sang with tremendous confidence, and the brass was note-perfect, with not a fluff to be heard, despite the intricacy of the part. During the mix, Richard added a lot of wobbly echo to the "roll up" backing vocals, and the piano signal was fed through a Leslie, making it quite a production. All in all, more than four days were spent on the track, and the care that went into it really shows.

It was at around this time that the warning signs began to appear. The Beatles turned up at the studio unusually late one night—near midnight—and spent some seven hours in a stoned haze, jamming endlessly . . . and pointlessly. In search of a new kind of high, Lennon had brought a big strobe light in, so at one point they turned out the lights and started running around as if they were in an old film. That lasted for about five minutes, after which everyone started complaining of a headache. All four of them were completely out of it—tripping on acid, probably—and it was the first Beatles session I'd ever attended where absolutely nothing was accomplished. Perhaps the first seeds of what was to become the instrumental track "Flying" were planted that night, but for the most part it was just them being silly, much to the annoyance of George Martin, who was constantly bumming cigarettes off me, a sure sign of his frustration. He tried to point out to John, Paul, and George that their guitars weren't even in tune, but, giggling like children, they brushed him off, saying, "That's okay, we're just doing a demo."

That in itself was a strange thing to say, since we knew all too well that anything the Beatles recorded might become part of a finished product, which was the reason we constantly rolled tape and rarely erased anything. But they were so stoned that night, we couldn't communicate with them at all. Richard Lush and I understood by this point that jamming was now the process by which they got inspiration and created new songs, but George Martin, who was not used to working this way, just didn't get it. Seven hours of playing aimlessly with out-of-tune guitars was not the way he would be running a session, but they were clearly in control now—they did as they liked. Making matters worse, George couldn't turn around and tell them off because he was scared of being fired. The Beatles were independent clients of his, so he had to tread carefully; certainly they were one artist he did not want to lose.

As midnight turned to 1 A.M., a disgruntled George Martin turned to me in the control room and said, "What am I here for, anyway?"

I had no answer. George knew that he had no function to serve on sessions like this—he was really just there to protect AIR's interest. With that, he simply got up and left, without even bothering to get on the talkback and say good night to the four Beatles, who continued jamming away in the darkened Studio Two below, oblivious.

A few hours later, a weary, bored-to-tears Richard repeated the producer's question to me verbatim, even down to George's affected upper-class accent. I had to laugh; after a moment's thought, the only response I could come up with was "You're right. Come on, let's go—this is ridiculous."

With that, we did what would have been unthinkable just a few short months ago: we walked out on a Beatles session. We didn't say a word to them, either; we just left. On our way out, we told the commissionaire that things had gotten out of hand and we were going home even though the group were still playing. We were a bit worried about how he would break the news to them and how they might react, but his response was a casual "Okay, I'll give them another half hour and then I'll go in there and tell them we're closing up and they have to leave."

The next day we couldn't wait to find out what had happened. We figured we'd get some grief about it, but nothing was ever said—the four Beatles were obviously too embarrassed to admit that we'd abandoned them. Or, more likely, too stoned to even remember.

Beyond being a mammoth waste of time and energy, those kinds of all-night sessions were starting to become a problem for the EMI management, because they were losing staff during the day—after all, we had to sleep sometime. There was also a controversy with the accounting department about the long hours we were doing during Beatles sessions. The bean counters finally realized that we were starting late in the afternoon instead of the usual nine in the morning, and they made noises about not paying us overtime anymore. There was no precedent for what we were doing—no one at Abbey Road had worked those kinds of hours before, so no one had earned the kinds of overtime pay we were earning . . . not that we got paid all that much. In the end, there was so much staff resistance that we threatened to go out on strike, and the idea was quietly dropped.

For the moment, though, I wasn't so much worried about getting or not getting overtime pay as I was about getting some extra sleep. So I was actually somewhat relieved when the Beatles couldn't get into the studio for the next couple of nights, which forced them to record "Baby You're A Rich Man"—a song which eventually served as a B-side and was used in the *Yellow Submarine* film—at Olympic Studios. Whenever they did a track at an outside studio, I usually had to do a lot of repair work to the tapes because they simply couldn't achieve the sound they were used to anywhere else. This time around, though, they actually got the entire song done—including the final mix—in a single session. It was a Lennon song, and a fairly simple one at that, but it had been a long time since they'd been so efficient. I had to admit that the results were pretty good—Olympic's chief engineer, Keith Grant, did the session himself and he knew what he was doing. In addition, Olympic's mixing console was a totally different design than ours and was capable of passing lower frequencies, so there was quite a smooth bass sound, which I thought was great.

It was around this time that the Beatles began frequenting outside studios more and more, for a variety of reasons. Perhaps they were searching for new sounds, or perhaps they simply had cabin fever and were sick of staring at the same four walls. There weren't really any amenities at Abbey Road: there were no couches or armchairs in our cramped control rooms, just a couple of uncomfortable, hard chairs. In contrast, when they went into Olympic or Trident, there would be large control rooms with plush leather sofas and comfortable chairs to sit in, all accented by low lighting and a modern decor. The only way we could get any subdued lighting in our control rooms was to turn off all the lights and open the front panels of the tape recorders; the glowing tubes inside would give out just enough light that you didn't bump into one another.

In addition, by mid-1967, every other major studio in London had an eight-track machine, and we still had only four-track, which really made us seem like we were lagging far behind. The reluctance to move up to eight-track was a reflection of EMI's staid policy of never adopting a technology before all the technical staff up at corporate headquarters had thoroughly examined it from every conceivable point of view: whenever we'd get a new piece of gear in, we weren't even allowed to use it until it had been completely disassembled and reassembled by the chief technical engineer. It was a ridiculous position to take, especially in an industry where change was beginning to happen so quickly, but the studio was never really meant to be profit-making, anyway—in essence, it was viewed as a research facility. EMI's real profits had come out of building radios and radar for military applications, not civilian use.

There was another factor that led the Beatles away from Abbey Road: the staff at other studios gave the appearance of being hipper than we were. No other recording studio in swinging London had a dress code, much less one that required the producers and balance engineers to wear jackets and ties. There was also a much more relaxed attitude toward drugs in other studios, and it wouldn't surprise me if the staff at those facilities would partake with clients, so perhaps the Beatles related to the other engineers better: there's nothing a stoner loves more than another stoner. I imagine they thought it was really cool to share a joint with the control room staff. In contrast, we must have seemed really straight and square.

But however far the Beatles would stray, they kept coming back, right up until their last album together (which they would even name after the location of the studio), for one simple reason: they couldn't get the same sound anywhere else. Unhip as we might have been, we delivered the goods. It's no coincidence that the vast majority of Beatles hits were recorded at Abbey Road.

In mid-May, George Martin took off for a two-week holiday in the south of France. The Beatles nonetheless soldiered on without him, and I was officially listed on the tape box as both producer and engineer of the two songs they recorded in his absence: Paul's "All Together Now" and an unusual collaboration between John and Paul called "You Know My Name (Look Up The Number)." Frankly, George going on vacation in the middle of these sessions did not go down well in anybody's book. We were all tired, yet he was the only one taking time off. By this point, I doubt very much if the band were crediting George Martin with their success, anyway. In fact, they probably welcomed the opportunity to get some work done without him.

I had noticed that the Beatles would often try to get a take down quickly whenever George left the room. It was kind of an in-joke, and it was always done lightheartedly, but there was an underlying message: to show him in a subtle way that they didn't really need him. Of course, when George would return and listen back to what they'd done, he'd always waffle a bit, saying something along the lines of "Well, that's interesting, but I think perhaps you need to do another take." He'd always manage to find some fault with what they'd put down on tape, because it was an insult to his ego to think that they could make a good, solid recording without his input.

But things were definitely more relaxed when George Martin wasn't around. There was always a certain protocol when he was at a session: we in the control room felt that we had to be on our best behavior, and even the Beatles seemed slightly constrained by his presence at times. When he wasn't there, we'd all let our hair down and have a bit of fun. There was just a different dynamic, and you can hear it in both of those songs, which are a lot looser, a lot more up, than anything they'd recorded in quite a while.

Lennon, in fact, made a comment at the start of the "All Together Now" session to the effect of "Well, now that the schoolmaster's out, we kids finally get a chance to play." Interestingly, the last time the Beatles had done a recording in George's absence was the song "Yellow Submarine," during the *Revolver* sessions, which was remarkably similar to "All Together Now" in both content and style. And both times, the Beatles invited friends in to sing along and create a party atmosphere. Paul obviously had worked the song out well in advance and knew exactly what he wanted: all the singing and playing is spot-on, despite the fact that it's not that strong of a song (ultimately it was relegated to the *Yellow Submarine* film). Still, it was a remarkably productive night, and it was quite an easy session, too, even though there were a lot of overdubs. A lot of it had to be played live, because they wanted the tempo to speed up from beginning to end. Paul even sang the final lead vocal—not a guide—during the recording of the backing track, while accompanying himself on acoustic guitar.

On June 1, 1967, *Sgt. Pepper's Lonely Hearts Club Band* was released worldwide to almost unanimous acclaim. For weeks afterward, it seemed that there was a new glowing review published almost daily, and George, Richard, and I read each one excitedly, taking great pride in all the hard work and effort we had put into the album. The Beatles themselves were quite pleased as well; it was a frequent topic of conversation in the studio, and they were highly amused at some of the more academically oriented reviews that praised them for a musical sophistication that they themselves were largely unaware of. Lennon in particular took great delight in reading some of those reviews out loud in his finest toffee-nosed upper-class voice, often ending the recital with a decidedly Scouse "What the fook is that twat on about?"

Ironically, during those first few days that the adulation for *Pepper* was flooding in, the group were hard at work in Studio Two on what was quite possibly the least substantive song they had ever put down on tape: "You Know My Name (Look Up The Number)." It was recorded in sections, and the sole lyric was the title phrase, repeated over and over again in a variety of genres, from straight rock 'n' roll to lounge lizard style. We all had great fun on those sessions as John and Paul dubbed on all manner of loony sound effects and sang and harrumphed in their full repertoire of comic Goon-like voices. It was such a novelty number, in fact, that it sat on the shelf for nearly two and half years before it was finally finished, at Lennon's instigation, and released as the B-side of the "Let It Be" single.

George Martin returned from his holiday when we were half done with it, and he must have felt that the inmates had been running the asylum—but I guess he also figured, if you can't beat them, join them. One night the Beatles had their friends come by to add party ambience, and to my surprise a rather sheepish-looking George marched straight down into the studio and contributed to the handclaps and crowd noise. Brian Jones of the Rolling Stones was one of the guests. He had been asked to play some guitar on the track, but he turned up with a saxophone instead. It was an instrument I didn't know he could play—in fact, I'm not so sure even *he* realized he could play it! But such was the spirit of the times that Paul and John's reaction was "Okay, well, let him blow the sax, then," which he did . . . though not very skillfully. Brian was a quiet bloke—nothing like the other Stones I had met—but he was also extremely out of it that night, so stoned that he didn't even seem to be sure of where he was.

Beatles sessions were generally very private. If the control room door ever opened and an outsider walked in, our first reaction was to stop the tape machine. Perhaps that was just us being paranoid, but that's what we'd do. Obviously we wouldn't stop the tape if we were in the middle of recording, but other than that, we'd pretty much just drop whatever we were doing and not resume work again until after the visitor had gone. If the band were down in the studio and they spotted someone they didn't know up in the control room, they'd call out, "Mal! Who's that?" Moments later he'd come up the steps and diplomatically get rid of them. Nobody ever argued with Big Mal.

I sometimes wondered what the Beatles did on the nights when they weren't working. Did they go around to one another's houses? Did they feel lost without one another? After all, they had gotten so used to being together while working in the studio every night during the long months of *Pepper*. It was likely that Paul was the one who missed the camaraderie the most, because he was always the workaholic in the group; it came as no surprise that he was the main motivator behind *Magical Mystery Tour*. People don't realize how hard the Beatles worked in the studio, and on the road. Not just physically, but psychologically and mentally it had to have been incredibly wearying. Now it was time to let off some steam. All throughout the spring and summer of 1967, the prevalent feeling in the group seemed to be: *after all those years of hard work, now it's time to play.*

For all of the fun we were having in the studio, there's no question that the Beatles really were quite unfocused at this point. Richard and I were having a great time doing these sessions, but George Martin was starting to complain a bit about the band's lack of productivity. Personally, I saw it as just a bit of harmless light relief after all the intensity that had gone into *Pepper*. The question was, how long could it last before they got bored?

For the moment, there was no time for boredom. A couple of months previously, while we were still wrapped up with the job of completing *Pepper*, Brian Epstein had made one of his infrequent visits to the studio. With a grandiloquent sweep of his hands, he called for silence.

"Boys," he announced, "I have the most fantastic news to report."

Everyone's ears perked up.

Brian paused for dramatic emphasis. "You have been selected to represent England in a television programme which, for the first time ever, will be transmitted live around the world via satellite. The BBC shall actually be filming you making your next record."

The show, he went on to explain, was to be called *Our World*, and it was a celebration of cultures around the globe. He looked around the room expectantly. I almost thought he was getting ready to take a bow. To his utter dismay, the group's response was . . . to yawn. Ringo fidgeted at the back of the room, anxious to return to the game of chess he was playing with Neil, and George resumed tuning his guitar. John and Paul exchanged blank looks for a moment. Paul didn't seem all that interested; I guess he was probably just too focused on finishing up *Pepper*.

With a distinct lack of enthusiasm, John finally said, "Oh, okay. I'll do something for that."

Brian was incensed at their casual reaction. "Aren't you excited? Don't you realize what this means to us? Don't you have any idea how much hard work and effort I put into making this deal?"

Lennon cut him off with an acidic comment: "Well, Brian, that's what you get for committing us to doing something without asking us first."

Epstein looked close to tears. At a loss for words, he stomped out of the studio in a snit. From the studio chatter that followed after he had gone, I gathered that, rather than viewing this as a coup, the four Beatles saw it as a violation of their self-declared intent to never perform live again. What's more, they resented the fact that their manager had presented it to them as a fait accompli. They were at a point where they wanted to take control of their own career.

With that, the issue was forgotten . . . until, some weeks later, during one of the "You Know My Name" sessions, Paul happened to ask John casually, "How are you getting on with that song for the television broadcast? Isn't it coming up fairly soon?"

John looked questioningly at Neil, who was the keeper of the band's diary.

"Couple of weeks' time, looks like," Neil responded after consulting his tattered book.

"Oh God, is it that close? Well, then, I suppose I'd better write something."

The "something" that John Lennon came up with—written to order, literally in a matter of days—was the song "All You Need Is Love," which not only shot straight to the top of the charts but served as the anthem for a generation, the perfect encapsulation of the naive, wide-eyed era known as the Summer of Love.

From our perspective, it seemed more like the summer of madness. One minute, we were working at a leisurely pace on two separate projects simultaneously, neither of which had a definitive end date, and the next minute the entire Abbey Road complex was thrown into an utter panic because the broadcast itself was to originate from Studio One. The project came together so fast, in fact, that George Martin was unable to book the band into any of the EMI studios, so they had to record the backing track at Olympic; once again, to my frustration, I was unable to engineer it or even attend because I was an EMI staffer.

When they got back, we hurriedly organized three sessions at Abbey Road during which we overdubbed backing vocals. Needless to say, miming to a prerecorded track was the safest course of action, but in a fit of bravado,

Lennon announced that he was going to do his lead vocal live during the broadcast, which prompted the ever competitive Paul to respond that if John was going to do that, he would play bass live, too.

It seemed to me to be a foolhardy—though brave—decision. What if one of them sang or played a bad note in front of millions of viewers? But they were supremely confident, and they could not be dissuaded by George Martin, who was adamantly opposed, but as was usual by this point, had no real authority.

In an act of further defiance, John and Paul even talked George Harrison into doing his guitar solo live, which we all knew was a tricky proposition. To my surprise, Harrison gave in without a whole lot of argument; my sense was that he was afraid of being embarrassed in front of his bandmates. Only Ringo was completely safe, for technical reasons: if the drums were played live, there would be too much leakage onto the microphones that were going to be picking up the sound of the orchestra. Ringo nodded his head solemnly when I explained that to him. I couldn't tell whether he was relieved at being absolved of the responsibility of playing live, or whether he felt left out.

The broadcast was scheduled to occur in less than a week. In the days leading up to the Sunday night broadcast, I began chain-smoking like a madman and suffered from insomnia and headaches. The other Abbey Road staffers needled me endlessly, telling me that they wouldn't change places with me for all the tea in China. I understood what they meant. I knew that I was on the hot seat: if something—anything—went wrong with the audio portion of the broadcast, the finger would be pointed squarely at me.

On the Friday evening, in the middle of a dress rehearsal, Brian Epstein came in and held a meeting with George Martin and the band in the Studio One control room, during which they debated the wisdom of rush-releasing the upcoming performance as a single. John, of course, was keen—it was his song, after all—and it didn't take much effort to talk Paul into it, either, since he knew the value of the massive publicity they would be receiving by virtue of the broadcast, thereby guaranteeing huge record sales. Only George Harrison was reluctant; presumably he was worried that he might muff his solo, even though it was only four bars long. He was finally persuaded when George Martin assured him that we could stay late afterward and do any necessary repair work. Their decision, of course, added even more pressure on me. I now had to not only do the sound for the live broadcast—the BBC truck parked outside would be receiving a feed of the monitor mix I would be creating as the Beatles and the orchestral musicians were playing live—but I had to get everything recorded cleanly on tape as well.

Adding to the chaos was John's insistence on making a last-minute change to the arrangement, which sent George Martin into a tizzy—he was doing the orchestral score and had to rapidly come up with new sheet music for the musicians, who milled around impatiently waiting for him. To his credit, George came up with a spectacular arrangement, especially considering the very limited time he had to do it in and the odd meters that characterized the song.

"All You Need Is Love" was actually quite simple when it was first presented and routined, but it grew more and more complicated as it got structured. Even though it was a Lennon composition, I noticed that Paul was taking charge to a great degree, certainly in terms of making suggestions and interfacing with the classical musicians, many of whom (like trumpeter David Mason) had worked with us before. Because George Martin wanted to remain in the control room, Mike Vickers of the band Manfred Mann was recruited to conduct.

The afternoon before the broadcast, the BBC crew rolled up and started camera rehearsals. The press was also allowed in to do a brief photo shoot, but I hardly noticed them—I was too busy focusing on the technical challenges of the live transmission; there were just so many things that could go wrong. To the group's chagrin, the photographers kept shouting out questions that had nothing to do with the upcoming broadcast. That was because Paul had done a controversial BBC interview a few days previously in which he confessed that he'd taken LSD. The other Beatles stood by him, but I could tell from the looks on their faces that day that they weren't pleased about the unwanted intrusion into what they saw as their personal lives.

We soon got word that the television director wanted to place a camera in the control room to get shots of the three of us. An obviously pleased George Martin turned to Richard and me and said, "You two had better smarten yourselves up—you're about to become international TV stars" . . . which had the effect of making me even more nervous! But we were both into clothes at that point, and during a break Richard and I excitedly discussed what we were going to wear. He owned a loud, stripey jacket that he thought would strobe in the cameras, so he planned on donning that, just for a joke. In the end, though, he was only seen in the broadcast for the briefest of moments. I opted for a simple white shirt and tie. I knew that it would simply be too hot in that control room, especially on a warm summer night, to consider wearing a jacket.

At one point during the camera rehearsals, I noticed George Harrison engaged in conversation with the television director for quite a long time. I
had no idea what they were talking about, but I did notice during the broadcast that the camera was not trained on George during his guitar solo. Perhaps he requested that specifically, either because he didn't have confidence
in his playing, or because he felt it was likely that he would replace the part
later.

There was also a bit of a flap about the vocal mics I was using, which were
quite bulky and apparently aesthetically offensive to the director. Even
though Paul and George were going to be miming their backing vocals
(which had been prerecorded, sung to John's guide vocal), Paul had requested a working microphone so that he could shout out ad-libs. The problem was that the mic I had set up blocked Paul's face on the camera angle
they wanted to use. In the end, I acceded to the director's request that a
smaller mic be substituted even though it was not the mic I would normally
have employed. I felt it was unlikely that whatever Paul ended up ad-libbing
would be of significant importance to the record, and even if it turned out
that it was, it was something we could easily overdub later.

The weekend rehearsals ground on for hours, but all too soon, it was Sunday afternoon. After completing a brief sound check, George Martin invited
Richard and me to the Marble Arch town house he shared with his wife, Judy,
so that we could relax for an hour or two before the evening's broadcast.
Judy made us lamb sandwiches, which was always a favorite of George's. It
was a nice gesture by the fraught producer, who was, like us, under a lot of
pressure. Unfortunately, I don't think it did much to steady our nerves. I just
couldn't wait for it to be over with!

When we returned to Abbey Road at around 6 P.M., the Beatles were already there, dressed in their finest Carnaby Street gear, and the tuxedoed
musicians and celebrity guests—including Brian Epstein and various rock
stars, wives, and girlfriends—were beginning to file in. There was a real
party atmosphere, similar to what we had witnessed during previous Beatles
"happenings," but Richard and I were both struck by how visibly nervous
John was, which was quite unusual for him: we'd never seen him wound up
so tightly. He was smoking like a chimney and swigging directly from a pint
bottle of milk, despite warnings from George Martin that it was bad for his
voice—advice that Lennon studiously ignored. One time as I passed by, I
heard John mumbling to himself, "Oh, God, I hope I get the words right."
On this night he was forced to rely on his memory because his ever-present
lyric sheet had to be placed off to the side due to the camera angle; if he

turned his head to consult it, he'd be singing off-mike. Paul was giving the outward appearance of being confident, but he had a strange, frozen smile planted on his face that betrayed the frayed nerves underneath. George and Ringo appeared to be the calmest of the four, though I could discern some tension in their body language as well. As the time of the broadcast drew closer and closer, you could almost sense the adrenaline as the nervous energy built in all of us.

Paul strode into the control room at one point and spent some time working on the bass sound with me. It struck me as a smart thing to do. Not only was he making certain that his instrument would come across the way he wanted it to, but getting out of the studio, away from the others and out of the line of fire, had a calming effect on both of us. It gave us both a little sanctuary where we could focus on just one specific thing and not think about the monumental technical feat we would soon be attempting to pull off.

Murphy's Law being what it is, the BBC truck lost communication moments before we went on air, so George Martin had to relay the director's instruction to "stand by" to everyone in the studio, which put added pressure on him. Just before the broadcast was due to start, George and I decided to have a shot of Scotch for luck. Richard wanted to join us, but George said, "No, you'd better not." He knew that Richard's job was absolutely critical, because he had the task of playing back the tape with the backing track from one multitrack machine while simultaneously recording the live performance on another machine. If he screwed up and put the wrong machine in record, we would have a disaster on our hands!

Just as the glasses reached our lips, Murphy struck once again. "Going on air . . . NOW!" we heard over the intercom speaker unexpectedly. According to our clock, they were forty seconds early. But there was no time to argue or debate the matter. Instinctively, George and I went into a mad scramble to hide the bottle and glasses underneath the mixing console before the camera in the control room caught us imbibing. Fortunately, we were able to complete the operation seconds before the red light went on. Considering the last-minute panic, I thought George did a remarkable job of regaining his composure, looking dapper in his *Casablanca*-like white suit. After a moment's pause while he received instructions from the BBC truck, he placed the talkback mic to his lips and said, "Ready, Geoff?"

I was . . . but while the question was being posed to me, I was also hearing the disconcerting sound of tape being spooled back; obviously Richard wasn't quite as ready as the rest of us. I tried to buy a little more time. "Ummm . . . ready, Richard?" I mumbled as slowly as I could, while my terrified assistant stared helplessly at the still rewinding tape machine. The problem was that, while the BBC television truck had been rolling the show's introductory video, we were tasked with playing back an early rough mix of the song, complete with John's guide vocal, as an underlay to what was happening on screen. Then, while Steve Race, the announcer, began introducing our segment, Richard had to spool back and quickly change reels; that was the job that wasn't quite complete when George had turned to us. It was only a matter of seconds before Richard got it sorted out and everything was indeed ready to go, but in that hot, cramped control room it seemed to take an eternity.

Finally we came to the moment of truth. George Martin called down to the four Beatles, their wives, friends, and orchestra: "Okay, stand by . . . here we go," and the broadcast commenced.

From start to finish, the entire segment was just over four minutes long, but it felt like hours. It was harrowing, to be sure, but by some miracle there were no technical problems at our end. For a few seconds during the live broadcast, the BBC did in fact lose video signal, but fortunately it was regained quickly, and in any event it wasn't our fault. The Beatles themselves gave an inspiring performance, though you could see the look of relief on all their faces as they got to the fadeout and realized that they'd actually pulled it off. John came through like a trouper, delivering an amazing vocal despite his nervousness and the plug of chewing gum in his mouth that he forgot to remove just before we went on air. Paul's playing, as always, was solid, with no gaffes, and even George Harrison's solo was reasonably good, though he did hit a clunker at the end. Unsurprisingly, despite the complicated score and tricky time changes, the orchestral players came through like the pros they were, with no fluffs whatsoever, even on the most demanding brass riffs.

Our plan—ambitious, if not a little crazy—was to try to get the final mix of "All You Need Is Love" shipped off to the factory that very night so that the record could be in the shops before the end of the week, but we knew that it would take a while for all the musicians, guests, and BBC technicians to pack up and vacate, so the remainder of the session was scheduled to occur in Studio Two. While the move was occurring, Richard and I got George Martin's permission to dash out for a brief celebratory drink at the nearby Abbey Tavern. I was drenched with sweat, both from nervous tension and the heat of the evening, and as we walked the few blocks to the pub, I kept repeating myself: "God, am I glad that's over! Get me a drink!" Richard and I were shaking with laughter and excitement as we toasted each other in the noisy pub, but we had promised George that we wouldn't be long, and that we would limit ourselves to a single shot of booze . . . with a pint chaser.

Still, we took a few extra moments for ourselves, and by the time we got back it was nearly 11 P.M. and the mix session was about to begin. George had gotten Martin Benge, the maintenance engineer on call, to thread up the tape machines in readiness. From the very first playback, the four Beatles were knocked out by what they were hearing. Harrison winced a little during his guitar solo, but Richard took the initiative and reassured him, saying, "It'll be fine; we'll put a little wobble on it and it will be great."

In the end, all we had to do was add the effect and duck the last bad note. Paul's bass playing was fine—there was no need to fix anything—and John's vocal needed only two lines dropped in in the second verse, where, sure enough, he flubbed a lyric. The only other remaining task was to redo the snare drum roll that Ringo played in the song's introduction; it had been a last-minute decision for him to do it live during the broadcast, and George Martin felt it could be done a bit better. In this day and age when recordings of live gigs are often tweaked up in the studio afterward to the point where hardly any of the actual performance remains, it might seem unbelievable, but it's the truth: the only things that were replaced on "All You Need Is Love" for the record release were the snare roll at the beginning, and two lines of the lead vocal.

The overdubs didn't take all that long to do, but we were all knackered from the events of the day, so George Martin made the decision to postpone the mix for twenty-four hours so we could all come in fresh. Rejuvenated and refreshed by a good night's sleep, we were able to complete the mix in short order, and the tape was then transferred to vinyl by Ken Scott, who was apprenticing as a mastering engineer. The single still made it out by the end of the week, only it hit the shelves on a Friday instead of a Thursday, something that didn't seem to hurt sales. "All You Need Is Love" shot straight to number one and remained atop the charts for several weeks.

After all the pressure—and ultimate triumph—of the broadcast, the Beatles decided to take most of July and August off, doing only a handful of recording dates at outside studios. At one point, Paul rang me up and asked me to join him at a session he was producing for his brother, Mike, at Dick James's small basement studio in London's West End. Paul showed up dressed in the uniform he had worn on the *Pepper* album cover, with his trumpet slung over his shoulder. If he was looking for attention, though, he wasn't to get it: it was a Sunday, and the street was completely deserted. In fact, we had some difficulty being let in. This marked the first time that Paul and I worked outside of Abbey Road . . . which I wasn't supposed to do. But it was all quite informal—the whiskey bottle came out at one point and we had a good time; I even played piano on one of the tracks. Later that night, Paul drove the three of us back home in his Aston Martin. It was quite a thrill to zip through the deserted London streets in such luxury.

Apart from that one day, I was otherwise occupied at EMI, working with other artists, continuing at the same hectic pace I had been following since my promotion to balance engineer. EMI artists were rarely allowed to work in studios outside of Abbey Road, so there was a high level of talent around, making the sessions interesting for me. One memorable project I did in the summer of 1967 was an album for the Zombies, which included their hit song "Time Of The Season." I enjoyed working with them. They meshed well as a team and were also willing to try new things, and, just as important, they wanted to carve out a sound of their own, not just be a clone of the Beatles.

All in all, it was a productive, busy time for me, and I was riding high on my successes. But there was a lot going on behind the scenes that I didn't know anything about. Tragedy was about to strike the Beatles camp, with far-ranging consequences on both their lives and their careers.

Brian Epstein always seemed like such an enigmatic figure. His visits to the studio were infrequent, and whenever he did stop by he was unfailingly polite to me and all the Abbey Road staff, though he rarely got a warm welcome from the four Beatles. But I knew nothing about his personal life, so I was shocked to hear of his untimely death from a drug overdose in late August, at the age of only thirty-seven. A few days later, Richard and I bumped into George Martin in the corridor. He was with Judy, and he was dressed to the nines, even to the extent of wearing a trilby hat. We started to poke fun at him, as we often did when we saw him wearing a new outfit, but he stopped us in our tracks when he explained, "I've just been to Brian's funeral."

It was a sobering moment. Even though I didn't know Brian all that well, it was the first time in my young life that I'd actually been acquainted with someone who had passed away. Later that evening I read in the newspaper that the family had asked the Beatles to stay away from the funeral because they didn't want the attendant publicity and hysteria. That had to have been a bitter pill for them to swallow—the very fame that Brian had helped manifest prevented them from paying their final respects.

In early September, four subdued and somber Beatles reconvened at

Abbey Road to continue the work at hand. As soon as they arrived, I walked over and offered my condolences. Ringo appeared close to tears; John seemed to be in a state of shock. George Harrison, who had only just recently begun following the practice of transcendental meditation with the Maharishi, seemed shaken but offered words of comfort.

"Mr. Epstein's body may be gone, but his spirit remains," he mumbled softly.

Of the four, Paul seemed the most composed, simply saying, "We just have to carry on, I suppose."

I didn't get the impression that Paul was any less affected by Brian's death than the others were. It just seemed to be the way he coped with loss, accepting what had happened and trying to be practical about it. In fact, years later, he reacted in a similar way to the horrific news of John's murder. I think that's simply the way Paul deals with bad news. Even when he is suffering deeply—as I'm sure he was when Brian died, and when John was killed—he tries to put on a brave face.

Looking back on it all these years later, it's obvious that Paul saw a vacancy in leadership after Brian died, and he stepped in. Perhaps that ultimately led to the band's breakup, but the fact of the matter is that someone had to. Surely Ringo and George Harrison couldn't, and between his drug use and unfocused mind, John simply wasn't capable of it at that point in his life. As I see it, Paul saved the band. After Brian's passing, they could have decided to quit while they were ahead, but he kept them going for another few years. As it turned out, they would be rocky, divisive years, but no one knew that at the time, and the Beatles still had some great music left in them. So just as Paul had assumed some of the production responsibilities from George Martin, he now filled Brian's shoes as well. Sure, he made mistakes, but he kept the greatest band in the world going at a time when they could have easily crumbled. I reckon he deserves a lot of credit for that.

There was a pallor across the session that day—we were all distracted, thinking about Brian—but there was a song to be recorded, too. It was one of John's, and, somewhat fittingly, it might well have been his strangest one yet.

"I am he as you are he / As you are me and we are all together," Lennon sang in a dull monotone, strumming his acoustic guitar as we all gathered around him in the dim studio light. Everyone seemed bewildered. The melody consisted largely of just two notes, and the lyrics were pretty much just nonsense—for some reason John appeared to be singing about a walrus and an eggman. There was a moment of silence when he finished, then Lennon looked up at George Martin expectantly.

"That one was called 'I Am The Walrus,' " John said. "So . . . what do you think?"

George looked flummoxed; for once he was at a loss for words. "Well, John, to be honest, I have only one question: What the hell do you expect me to do with that?"

There was a round of nervous laughter in the room which partially dissipated the tension, but Lennon was clearly not amused. Frankly, I thought George's remark was out of line. To me, the Beatles seemed a bit lost, as if they were looking for another place to be, a new start . . . and even in its raw state I could hear that the song had potential. Perhaps it wasn't one of John's finest compositional efforts, but with that unique voice of his and our combined creative abilities, I was sure it could turn into something good.

George Martin, however, simply couldn't get past the limited musical content and outrageous lyrics; he flat out didn't like the song. As John sang provocative lines about a pornographic priestess and letting knickers down, George turned to me and whispered, "*What* did he just say?" He couldn't believe his ears, and after the experience the Beatles had gone through with "Lucy In The Sky With Diamonds" and "A Day In The Life," I guess he was worried about more censorship problems from the BBC.

Despite George's misgivings, the Beatles were determined to work on the song, so they began running down the backing track, with John accompanying himself, unusually, on a Wurlitzer electric piano. He was not a great keyboardist at the best of times, and on this day he was especially unfocused, so he made quite a few fluffs, to George Martin's chagrin.

"Why doesn't he ask Paul to play it instead?" he asked me in the control room.

I had no answer; perhaps John was just trying to get his grief out. George became even more exasperated when it became apparent that Ringo was having trouble holding the beat steady; it was a long song, played at a laconic tempo, so it was tough going. For the first few takes, Paul played bass as usual, but then he opted to switch to tambourine, standing directly in front of Ringo, effectively acting as both a cheerleader and a human click track.

"Not to worry, I'll keep you locked in," he told his drummer confidently, once again dealing with a tricky situation that George Martin simply couldn't handle. I thought it was one of Paul's finest moments. He was trying to inject some professionalism into a session that was drifting away because the others had their minds on Brian's death. It was a classic case of him taking charge when things were beginning to unravel, and he would do that more and more as the years went on.

In the end, Ringo gave a strong performance, thanks in no small part to Paul's quick thinking; Paul always did have the most rock-solid sense of timing within the band, and Ringo had the humility to be able to accept his help when it was needed. But even listening to the record today you can hear that they're distracted, that their minds are not really on what they're doing. I distinctly remember the look of emptiness on all their faces while they were playing "I Am The Walrus." It's one of the saddest memories I have of my time with the Beatles.

I always felt that John Lennon hid some of his insecurities behind his vocal disguises and nonsense wordplay. This time, he informed us that he wanted his voice to appear to be coming from the moon. I had no idea what a man on the moon might sound like—or even what John was really hearing in his head—but, as usual, no amount of discussion with him could shed a lot of light on the matter. After a little bit of thought, I ended up overloading the console's mic preamps so as to get a smooth, round kind of distortion—something that was, once again, in clear violation of EMI's strict rules. To make his voice sound even edgier, I used a cheap low-fidelity talkback microphone. Even then, John wasn't entirely happy with the result, but, as usual, he was also impatient to get on with it.

"Okay, that'll do," he said abruptly after a brief run-through. It wasn't exactly an overwhelming vote of confidence at the time, but distortion was an effect he grew to love, and demand, on future Beatles recordings, not just on his voice, but on his guitar as well.

Ken Scott sat in on the session that night, assisting along with Richard. Ken would serve as my assistant engineer on most of the remaining sessions that week, because I was soon scheduled to take a long-overdue holiday to the Norfolk Broads, and management had decided that he would be taking my place behind the console. I liked Ken and had respect for his abilities, even though I didn't have the same personal friendship with him that I did with Richard. He asked me a lot of questions about what it was like working with the Beatles and he was quite nervous at first, but he quickly struck up a good rapport with the group—George Harrison, in particular—despite the bittersweet vibe that hung over us like a cloud.

At the time, John and Paul were both heavily into avant-garde music, especially compositions that were based upon randomness. At home, they often kept their televisions on with the sound turned off while simultaneously playing records. The next morning, they would regale us with tales of how the music often dovetailed, as if by magic, with the on-screen visuals. At one point, Paul even brought in a film projector so he could demonstrate the principle. George Martin was singularly unimpressed, but John was enthralled with the concept. As he listened to the playbacks of "I Am The Walrus," he said, "You know, I think it would be great if I could put some random radio noise on the end of it—you know, just twiddling the dial, tuning into various stations to see what we get and how it fits with the music."

George Martin made a show of rolling his eyes heavenward, but I told John that it was perfectly doable. I arranged to have a radio tuner brought down from the maintenance office so we could experiment with it. Given the studio's arcane procedures—a formal memo had to be written and approved—and the fact that the big, bulky rack-mounted tuner had to be rewired and then patched into the mixing console, it was quite an undertaking and not something we could put together quickly, which the ever-impatient John found highly frustrating. "Bloody EMI—can't even get a radio organized!" he snapped. But his face lit up when we finally got the sound going, and he had a lot of fun twiddling the dial as the multitrack tape of "Walrus" played back.

Because we knew that there was still a lot to be overdubbed onto the song, there wasn't a track free to record John's experimentations, but he ended up repeating the exercise (with Ringo twiddling the dial) when the mono mix was done a couple of weeks later. (That's the reason why "I Am The Walrus" can never be remixed: the radio wasn't recorded on the multitrack. Instead, it was flown into the two-track, live, as the mix was occurring.) Ken engineered the mono mix, but I was asked to do the stereo mix when I returned from vacation. We tried twiddling the radio dial that time, too, but the results weren't as much to John's liking as the Shakespearean play he happened to tune into during the mono mix, so we had to splice the end of the original mix in. We flanged it in order to spread the signal out in stereo, but avid listeners can still hear the image shift dramatically after the splice point, especially if you listen in headphones.

During the second night that we were working on "I Am The Walrus," Paul asked me to stay late so I could record him doing a simple piano/vocal demo of a new song he had written. When he finished, he asked me what I thought, and I gave him a thumbs-up through the control room window.

"That sounds like the start of a really good song," I said. "What's it called?"

"It's my newest one for the film—it's called 'The Fool On The Hill,'" McCartney replied proudly. I turned to Ken, who was assisting. "Just my luck," I told him. "Paul brings in a beautiful song like that and you'll get to make the record of it, not me."

Earlier that evening, we had also laid down the rhythm track for a new Harrison song called "Blue Jay Way." It was, to my way of thinking, a bit of a dirge, and, frankly, I was a bit relieved when previous commitments kept me from completing the song the next night. Later on I had a conversation with Peter Vince, who substituted for me, and he said, "Oh, it wasn't that bad," but even when the cello was overdubbed on a month later and the track was mixed with tons of special effects—sessions that I did—the song still didn't do much for me. Perhaps the main problem was that George had written and played it on organ, and he really only knew a few chords—he was even less of a keyboardist than John was.

I wrapped up my pre-vacation Beatles work with one last long session, during which they recorded the instrumental song entitled "Flying." It was really nothing more than a twelve-bar blues born out of one of their late-night jams; I simply lifted out a few minutes of the best bits, they added a number of overdubs, and the song was complete. From the outset it was always meant to be just incidental music for the film, so nobody wanted to spend a lot of time on it. Ringo's voice was the most prominent one on the chanting, and that was done deliberately because Paul wanted a different kind of vocal texture, one that wasn't so obviously "Beatlish." George Harrison's guitar had a distinctive sound, too, because I used a DI box instead of miking his amp. The end result was a mellow, jazzy tone that we felt perfectly complemented the tasty part he was playing.

Knowing that the Beatles were still hard at work at Abbey Road, I didn't really want to go on vacation, but the EMI brass insisted that I had to take the time off because it had been scheduled so far in advance. George Martin also encouraged me to go, because he knew how burned out I was. While I was away, the Beatles completed the recording of "I Am The Walrus," adding on tons of overdubs, including strings, brass, and a sixteen-voice choir making swooping noises and singing such timeless lyrics as "Oompah, oompah, stick it up your jumper" and chanting "Ho-ho-ho hee-hee-hee ha-ha-ha." Especially given George Martin's initial distaste for the song, I was quite impressed with the complex score he wrote. To my mind, it's really those overdubs that make it such a great record, because the song itself is not especially strong.

About a week later, the four Beatles and a large cast of oddball characters boarded their coach and filmed the first leg of their mystery tour, which, from what I heard afterward, ended up being more problematical than magical. At one point, they had talked about having Richard and me accompany them, but the studio brass said we couldn't go. We were both a bit upset about that, even though they really only bantered about the idea so they could have two more familiar faces on the bus for the filming; we wouldn't have been working. They did invite a number of their friends along, including a new mate of John's nicknamed Magic Alex. He would turn out to be a major thorn in my side in the years to come.

For the first few weeks while I was gone, Richard Lush continued to assist on Beatles sessions, working with Ken Scott, but then, slowly, other assistants—people like Jeff Jarratt and Graham Kirkby—were brought in; even Phil McDonald came down from the lacquer cutting room from time to time to fill in. It was starting to get to the point where, despite their exalted status as pop royalty, none of the Abbey Road staff really wanted to work with the Beatles; word had gotten around that their sessions were always extremely long, late-night affairs, and often quite aggravating. Everyone knew that if you got involved with the Beatles, you lost your social life, and for many of the younger staff—and even some of the older, married ones—that was quite unappealing, despite the prestige of working with the band and the enormous amounts of overtime pay you could earn.

Unless you had worked with the Beatles a long time, as I had, it could be difficult to accept their quirks. Ken got a taste of that early on, as he related to me some time later. The fare the Beatles ate in the studio was generally either just snack food or tea with toast and jam, prepared for them by Mal. Occasionally, though, they had dinner delivered—sometimes a curry, or steaks from a local Italian restaurant nearby; a formally dressed waiter would come in and serve their meals on silver platters. But we were hardly ever invited to join them, not even George Martin. That wasn't the way it was with other artists, who would normally bring the control room staff with them if they went out to dinner, or if food was being ordered in, they would at least ask you what you wanted. It wasn't a big issue, but dining with the artist made you feel like you were part of a team.

The Beatles simply didn't do things that way, and one evening while I was away on vacation, they sent out for food . . . and when Ken wasn't included, he started to take offense. Richard, who knew the lay of the land, defused the situation by grabbing the talkback mic and announcing, "Okay, we're going out to eat now." Without waiting for a response, he grabbed a perplexed Ken by the arm and marched him out the door. To make a point, they went to a steak house in Baker Street, a long cab ride away. When they finally got back to Abbey Road a couple of hours later, the Beatles were fine with it . . . to Ken's amazement. There was no "Where the hell have you been?" or "You're taking forever"—their reaction was just "Oh, they're here now, so let's get back to work." Richard, like me, understood that when the Beatles were recording, they just had blinders on to anything or anyone else. There was nothing meant by it; they just became very self-involved.

During the handful of sessions we had done together, Ken Scott had pretty much learned my setup in terms of mic placement, EQ, and the way I used outboard equipment. As a result, the recordings he did with the Beatles in my absence were sonically similar to mine. That made things a bit easier for me when it came time to mix the tracks he'd recorded, and it gave some continuity to *Magical Mystery Tour* despite the fact that several engineers had worked on it.

They may have no longer been performing live, but the Beatles still had great regard for their fans . . . most of the time. True, if Lennon or Harrison had been especially besieged on their way in on one particular day, they might make some kind of comment about the "bloody fans," but for the most part they were fairly tolerant. Paul, of course, was always extremely friendly and courteous toward the teenagers who would gather around the studio gates. There was, however, one occasion when the adulation really got on Lennon's nerves, and I was witness to it. Everyone was heading home at the end of a late-night session in which John was in an unusually foul mood; for some reason, I found myself at the top of the Abbey Road steps just as John's driver was trying to maneuver his psychedelic Rolls-Royce out of the car park and through the crowd of fans, who were blocking the exit. Always the practical joker, Lennon had a speaker hidden under the hood and a microphone inside the car. All of a sudden he started shouting, "Fuck off, the lot of you!"

I thought it was hilarious, and it got results, too. Startled, everyone jumped out the way and the Roller sped off into the night, the sounds of John's cackling laughter reverberating down the street.

Nonetheless, the four Beatles never seemed to forget that they owed a debt of gratitude to the record-buying public, and every year, at around Christmastime, they would make a special recording for their fan club. So with work on the soundtrack for *Magical Mystery Tour* finally complete, they spent an entire night working on a song called "Christmastime Is Here Again," which would be distributed to fan club members only. They'd obviously put a lot of thought into it beforehand, and the session was a lot of fun. Everyone was getting into the spirit of the season and Lennon rolled out his finest wee Scottish accent for an extended bit of recorded gibberish. The actor Victor Spinetti, who'd appeared with the Beatles in their previous two films (and was also a cast member for *Mystery Tour*) was at the session, too, and he was even called upon to do some singing.

Victor was also there because he was directing a play that John had written for the National Theatre, entitled *Scene Three, Act One*. He and John stayed behind with Richard after everyone else went home, and they spent a couple of hours compiling sound effects tapes for the play. I felt confident enough in Richard's abilities by that point to turn the reins over to him; I think it was actually his first time behind the mixing console, and he did just fine.

For the next month and a half, we saw nothing of the four Beatles, who were holed up in various editing rooms all over London's West End, frantically trying to cut together the *Magical Mystery Tour* film in time for its Boxing Day (day after Christmas) television transmission. They got it done, but the airing turned out to be a disaster. The public either hated what they saw, or didn't understand it, and the band were handed their first critical drubbing ever.

Part of the problem came from the fact that the film was broadcast in black and white although it was shot in color, but I think that a bigger factor was that, because of all the hype and buildup, everyone simply expected too much from it. The Beatles were musicians, not filmmakers, and *Magical Mystery Tour* was never conceived as a great work of art, just a bit of fun. Having said that, it still comes across as a bit amateurish and self-indulgent; it's really just a mishmash of ideas, no more and no less. Did the group deserve the savaging they got from the press? Probably not, but it seems to be an unfortunate human trait that we are all too anxious to tear down our idols once we have built them up. My attitude is that it was simply a starting point for Paul in his career in film. After all, you've got to start somewhere, even if you make mistakes along the way.

Abbey Road's Studio One was a cold, cavernous place even on the sunniest summer day. In the dead of winter, it was like a cross between a meat locker and an airplane hangar. But that's where I found myself on a frigid February afternoon, working with George Martin and three of the Beatles— Ringo was absent because he was scheduled to appear on Cilla Black's live television program later that evening. We would be working on George Harrison's Indian-influenced song "The Inner Light" that day, and as Mal Evans lit some candles and incense to create a vibe for George, I studied the faces of the three Beatles intently. For the first time, they had experienced failure, and they seemed quite sobered by what had happened to them; it was as if they'd been brought down a peg.

Harrison, in particular, was quite nervous about doing his lead vocal. He felt that he couldn't do the song justice, but with encouragement from Paul, he actually did a good job of it. John had little to say that day—I had the impression he wasn't too keen on the song—but he and Paul stayed on anyway, alternating between the control room and the studio, where they would sit behind George, perched up on high stools, the lights turned down low.

We had arranged to bring a TV into the studio that evening so we wouldn't miss Ringo's appearance, and it provided us all with some much-needed amusement. Neil wasn't there—he had accompanied Ringo to the BBC—but Mal busied himself with making tea and jam butties; at one point, he even broke out a bottle of Scotch and passed it around. The Beatles often would relax and unwind with a drink before going home; for those of us in the control room, that would be a sign that the session would soon be ending. They rarely imbibed while they were working, and I certainly never saw any of them drunk in the studio. Mal's bottle would usually last a few days . . . unless Richard or I got to it, which we did on occasion. The burly roadie could never fathom out why it was disappearing or why the level was going down. He used to find the most unbelievable hiding places, but Richard and I would inevitably discover it while cleaning up after the session. Even if we didn't indulge in a nip or two, we'd pour a little out, just to mess with Mal's head—it became kind of a running joke with us.

But this evening was an exception, and so, after a hearty toast to the missing drummer, we all had a good laugh as we watched Ringo go through his paces. The three Beatles reverted to their schoolkid personas and there was a lot of sniggering and piss-taking going on, especially from Lennon.

"Look at him trying to tap-dance!" John chortled as the hapless drummer did his version of a soft-shoe.

George preferred to urge his friend on, repeatedly shouting out, "Go, Ring, go!" Paul provided the least commentary; he was staring intently at the screen, analyzing Ringo's abilities as an entertainer and showman.

Once the show ended, we were back to work, this time turning our attention to Paul's energetic new song "Lady Madonna." Ken Scott had recorded the backing track the week before, but there were several more overdubs to be done that night, including vocals, saxophones, and piano. As usual, Paul was looking for a different kind of sound, so I took the same cheap micro-

phone that we had used for John's lead vocal on "I Am The Walrus" and positioned it way down in the sound holes, which yielded a muffled mid-
rangey tone. During the mix, we would heavily overdo the effects on the
vocal and the piano, too, making for a distinctive sound.

A couple of evenings later, we finished off "The Inner Light" and then we
started overdubbing onto another track that Ken had begun in my absence.
"Across The Universe" was probably the gentlest, sweetest John Lennon song
I'd heard to date, and it took me very much by surprise. At around the time
of Brian's death, the four Beatles had started studying with the Maharishi,
Mahesh Yogi, and on this night it occurred to me that perhaps meditation
had done John some good. The song represented a drastic change for him,
and it was an eye-opener for me. It was true that in recent weeks the cutting,
sarcastic John Lennon had been largely absent; we were seeing a softer side
in him, a side I didn't even know existed. I knew that McCartney could be a
rocker as well as a balladeer, but, up until this session, I'd pretty much just
thought of Lennon as a basher.

I really loved the song, and John's gentle, lyrical vocal definitely connected with me. We recorded that vocal over and over again because John
was unhappy with the job he was doing, despite the fact that we, and the entire group, were effusive in our praise. It was a problematic vocal to do because of phrasing; there were just too many words to sing, so many points at
which he had to take breaths. Because of that, John wasn't satisfied that he'd
gotten the feeling into the words that he was hoping for, and he was a bit upset about that. The song clearly meant a lot to him and he was frustrated because it hadn't come out the way he'd heard it in his head. John's
unhappiness with the vocal led to his reluctant decision to shelve the song
and work on it again at some later date, even though it was originally supposed to serve as the B-side to "Lady Madonna." Instead, "The Inner Light"
was substituted, marking the first time that a George Harrison song appeared on a Beatles single.

The legendary comedian and ex-Goon Spike Milligan (who was one of
John's idols) happened to be at the session that night as a guest of George
Martin's. He was so impressed with what he was hearing that he asked
Lennon if the track, in its current state, could be used for to help raise funds
for a charity he was involved in. A distracted, aggrieved John simply said,
"Yeah, whatever," and that's how "Across The Universe" came to be released
on a charity record for the World Wildlife Foundation. Nearly two years
later, Phil Spector was to revive the song in an effort to flesh out the *Let It Be*
album, slowing down the tape to a funereal tempo and adding a ghostly

choir in the process, but the version we recorded that night was, in my opinion, far superior. An outtake appears on *The Beatles Anthologies*, and listeners can also find an un-Spectorized (though highly digitally processed) rendition on the 2003 release *Let It Be . . . Naked.* I still feel that the best version was the original one that we recorded on that cold February evening.

The four Beatles had long been planning to travel to India to study with the Maharishi, but the trip had been postponed several times, first because of Brian's untimely death, and then because of recording commitments. But now there was a firm schedule in place, and they were due to fly out in mid-February for an open-ended stay. Their attitude was that they would go for as long as they wanted, perhaps even permanently. Personally, I didn't believe that any of them, with the possible exception of George Harrison, would end up staying in India forever, but the EMI brass knew that they wouldn't be around for the foreseeable future, so there was pressure to get their next single finished before they left so that it could be released in their absence. And because they would be out of the public eye for an extended period, it had also been decided to shoot a promotional video, supposedly of them working on the song in the studio.

With "Lady Madonna" already completed, the plan was to film the group miming to it, but when they got to the studio, an unusually assertive Lennon had second thoughts. "Oh, the hell with 'Lady Madonna,' " he said. "I've got a new song for us to do—let's film that instead." Paul was a bit annoyed, but John was like a bulldozer that day, and the decision stuck. The sounds of "Lady Madonna" would therefore accompany footage of the Beatles' recording the new Lennon song "Hey Bulldog," and nobody seemed too bothered about that. They knew that most viewers wouldn't even notice that they were in fact playing a completely different song, and they were right.

Even though it was destined to be given to the *Yellow Submarine* film, "Hey Bulldog" was a really strong song. The vibe that day was great—all four Beatles were in an exceptionally good mood because they knew they would be heading to India in a matter of days. Despite the fact that there was a film crew underfoot, it was a Sunday session, so things were quite relaxed—the Abbey Road complex was largely deserted, and the Beatles could wander around the corridors if they wanted to. At one point, Paul was helping John with the lyrics, but most of the song seemed to have been written and worked out before they got to the studio. Everyone's performance was excellent on that track: Paul's bass line was probably the most inventive of any he'd done since *Pepper,* and it was really well played. Harrison's solo was sparkling, too—one of the few times that he nailed it right away. His amp was turned up really loud, and he used one of his new fuzz boxes, which made his guitar absolutely scream.

After they got the rhythm track down, everyone was hungry, so Mal went down to the canteen—he had the key by now—and brought back some baked beans on toast, which was a particular favorite of George Harrison's. You can actually see them enjoying the impromptu meal at the beginning of the video, with everyone in high spirits. Later on, John and Paul gathered around a microphone for several minutes of barking, howling, and general clowning around. For those moments they were again the inseparable childhood friends they had once been, uninhibited and completely comfortable in each other's presence.

"Hey Bulldog" turned out so well there was some campaigning from Lennon that day for it to serve as the A-side of the single instead of "Lady Madonna." Naturally enough, Paul wasn't thrilled with the idea, but the discussion was ended by George Martin, who stated flatly that it was far too late to make the change because the record sleeves had already been printed. That may or may not have been true, but I suspect that George, like Paul, felt that "Lady Madonna" was the more commercial song.

With the trip to India looming, this was to be the last time I saw the group before the start of what would be the miserable, tension-filled *White Album* sessions; the storm clouds were gathering off in the distance. Looking back, that day may well have been the final time that all four Beatles were really happy being together in the studio. Perhaps not coincidentally, it was also the last Beatles session where neither Magic Alex nor Yoko Ono was on the scene.

11

The Day I Quit:

The Making of the *White Album*

I'd had enough.

I'd gone through six years of highs and lows with the Beatles, sharing in their incredible success with the *Revolver* and *Sgt. Pepper's Lonely Hearts Club Band* albums, and commiserating with them as they buried their young manager Brian Epstein and suffered the critics' slings and arrows following the ill-advised *Magical Mystery Tour* project. But now the bad feelings, the wrangling, the pettiness were all really starting to get to me. I was on the verge of a nervous breakdown, and I was ready to tell them I wanted out.

So much had changed since I'd last seen the Beatles just a few months previously. They had come back from their trip to India completely different people. They had once been fastidious and fashionable; now they were scruffy and unkempt. They had once been witty and full of humor; now they were solemn and prickly. They had once been bonded together as life-long friends; now they resented one another's company. They had once been lighthearted and fun to be around. Now they were angry.

I had no idea what it was they had to be angry about, but they had a definite chip on their collective shoulder when they returned to the studio in the spring of 1968 to begin work on a new album. By the time the sessions were to draw to a close that fall, they wouldn't even be able to come up with a proper title for it—they were arguing so much by then, they couldn't even agree on that. In the end, it was simply called *The Beatles,* but most people know it by the plain, unadorned sleeve it came in. The sessions for the *White Album* were far and away the most difficult and contentious ones I had ever worked on. In later years, Paul would refer to it as the "Tension Album," and I couldn't agree more.

I had followed the news of the Beatles' journey to India with great interest, though there wasn't a whole lot of publicity about it at the time. I knew that they had gone off in search of inner peace, and was surprised when it all fell apart just a couple of months later. I suppose the warning signs were there when they began drifting back to England separately: Ringo first, Paul next. It was the first time I'd known them to embark on a group activity and then splinter off as individuals.

Beyond their personal problems, there were significant business pressures on the four Beatles. In the vacuum created by Brian's death, they had decided not only to manage themselves but to start up an ambitious new company called Apple Corps, which would have both philanthropic and commercial interests. Personally, I thought that the idea of giving unknown artists a chance was laudable, at least in theory. It was a utopian vision, but it was probably doomed to failure from the outset, considering the widely varying interests and extremely limited business skills of the four principal owners. For all of their lofty goals, everything was carried out in a haphazard fashion, with no one person in charge, no one overseeing it all. Neil Aspinall, who had a background in accounting, was given an office and the task of balancing the books (which meant we'd be seeing very little of him at Beatles sessions from that point on), but he wasn't really in any position of authority at that point. Apple would ultimately swallow the Beatles whole, not only distracting them from their music but causing a slew of rifts and petty disagreements that were to escalate precipitously until the band would messily and publicly fracture into four pieces.

None of us at EMI really knew much about their private lives, but it seemed that, from the very start of the *White Album* sessions, the Beatles were bringing their problems into the studio for the first time. If there had been a rancorous business meeting in the Apple boardroom that morning, it would spill over into the overdub session that evening. If John had made a nasty crack about the Maharishi that George resented, they would have a go at each other while gathered around a microphone to do backing vocals. If Paul criticized Ringo's drumming, Ringo would get moody; if George dared question any of Paul's suggestions, Paul would get in a snit. And if any of the band members had done anything that an overly defensive John viewed as a potential slight to his new girlfriend—who sat by his side impassively the entire time they were making the album—he would be lashing out at them all with his acid tongue.

In short, the entire atmosphere was poisonous.

Making matters worse, all of us at Abbey Road were having to deal with a new studio manager, because the venerable E. H. Fowler had finally retired.

Fowler was of a different generation—he certainly never understood the pop world—but he was basically harmless. The only run-in I ever had with him was over the Grammy I received for *Pepper*. Because I had been unable to attend the ceremony in America, the statuette was delivered to Abbey Road, and Fowler simply put it in his office, without even telling me that it had arrived. It wasn't that he was mean—he was simply misguided. He felt that the award belonged to the studio and not to me personally, even though it had my name inscribed on it. I found out about it and asked that he hand it over. At first, Fowler refused to budge. Eventually, I had to get George Martin to intervene. It all ended amicably, though: there was a nice private ceremony arranged in Studio Three, with the BBC newspeople and a couple of photographers filming and snapping away while Ringo formally presented the award to me. He was the only Beatle there because the other three were still in India, and I thought it was a nice gesture. We exchanged only a few words that afternoon, but it was still one of the longest conversations I'd ever had with him.

Misguided and bumbling as he might have been, we would all come to miss Fowler, because his replacement, Alan Stagge, turned out to be a disaster. Stagge had come from IBC—a studio that specialized in orchestral work—and he was purported to be the greatest classical recording engineer in the world. He actually was quite a good engineer, but not nearly as good as he thought he was. At his very first meeting with the staff, he called everyone into Studio One and enlightened us with his new philosophy and all the changes he was intent on making. Then he concluded his little pep talk by saying, "We're all going to chip in together and make EMI even better . . . and if any of you don't agree with my plans, there's the door."

There he was, on his very first day on the job, telling all these people who'd been there for thirty or forty years that they could quit if they didn't accept his edicts unconditionally. There was a shocked silence in the room, broken by my good mate Malcolm Davies, who stood up and, with a completely straight face, said, "On behalf of the staff, I'd like to say we're all behind you, and we'd like to wish you the best of luck." Stagge bowed stiffly in acknowledgment, but we were all stifling our laughter; we knew that Malcolm was taking the piss. We realized at that moment that we were dealing with someone who didn't have a clue.

Not only was Alan Stagge clueless, he could be rude and arrogant. It was apparent within days that there was no rhyme or reason to most of his rulings; it was simply about his power. His attitude about everything was, if you don't like it, leave. There was no thought given to the importance of the engineer, or to the wishes of the producer or artist. Stagge began instituting a new system whereby the work was distributed more evenly because it seemed he felt that every engineer was interchangeable and expendable, that anyone could do any job. Yet he had no problem taking all the plum classical recording jobs for himself, which thoroughly pissed off the staff classical engineers. Even if the producer wanted someone else, it didn't matter: he was going to do the session whether they liked it or not.

Then he began doing the same with the pop engineers, shifting us from session to session for no reason other than to keep us off balance. It didn't matter that Malcolm Addey had always recorded Cliff Richard and the Shadows, or that Pete Bown had always engineered for the Hollies. Now any of us could and would be assigned to those sessions. Stagge didn't understand—or didn't care—that producers and artists wanted to maintain continuity. Many of Abbey Road's clients, to their bewilderment, soon found themselves working with two, three, or four different engineers over the course of a project, each of whom had his own sound and his own way of working.

Stagge also had little tolerance for the creative process. Oftentimes, especially after the Beatles broke the mold, pop sessions would run late into the night because someone would get a sudden inspiration and the producer would want to carry on until the idea was thoroughly explored, despite the extra expense that would be incurred. But Stagge would have none of that. If a session was booked until 10 P.M., he wanted us to end it at 10 P.M., even if the artist wanted to continue, and even if they were willing to pay the overtime costs. He actually turned up at a Pink Floyd session late one night— dressed to the nines, because he and his wife would often drop by the studio after attending an opera or classical concert—and literally pulled the plug on them.

Then he began tinkering, trying to fix things that didn't need fixing. He ordered the installation of a complicated system of fabric and sheets— almost like billowing sails—on the ceiling of Studio One because he said there was too much resonance in the high end. It altered the natural acoustics of the room to the point where, to me, the sound was ruined. Amazingly, those sheets are still up on the ceiling to this day.

Next, he changed the speakers in all the control rooms. Worse yet, the new speakers he put in were completely different from the Altecs we were used to. Stagge may have liked the way they sounded, but I hated them—

they colored everything, with way too much low end, and most of the other staff engineers felt the same way. To add insult to injury, Stagge never discussed it with any of us beforehand, which was ridiculous: the engineers who do the actual work are the *first* people you want to consult before making such a significant change to a recording studio.

The musical culture of the 1960s was decidedly different than in preceding decades; it was the young generation who were buying the records, and the artists themselves were becoming younger and hipper. Fashion was everything, especially in big cities like London, and Abbey Road had finally begun slowly changing with the times. Even though the maintenance men still had to wear white coats and the janitors wore brown coats—vestiges of Britain's rapidly evaporating class system—balance engineers and assistants were getting a little more leeway. Although we still had to wear jackets and ties, we began wearing brightly colored shirts and psychedelic ties, shedding the jackets as soon as we got inside the control room. We couldn't exactly match the freewheeling dress of our clients, but things were getting a bit looser.

Alan Stagge, of course, didn't like that. My sense is that he didn't understand the importance of artists feeling as though they could relate to the people they were working with, so without any discussion or advance warning, he announced that henceforth all balance engineers and assistants had to wear white coats, too. We hated the idea. Beyond the insult to our own sartorial taste, we knew that doing so would only alienate clients further still; I could well imagine the sarcastic remarks I'd be hearing from John Lennon if my assistant and I turned up at a Beatles session dressed that way. Fortunately, Stagge's edict only lasted one day. In an act of defiance, everyone ordered his coat twice the size it should have been, so when we put them on they were all dragging on the ground! Like a modern-day Captain Queeg, Stagge was unable to stop the mutiny . . . especially since he knew it would cost a small fortune to reorder new white coats.

All of us at the studio found the whole situation increasingly difficult to deal with, and even the newest hirees believed we had to bring things to a head. We held a staff meeting and a representative was sent to talk with Ken East, the executive at EMI's central London headquarters who was responsible for looking after the studio. Despite the fact that he had hired Stagge in the first place and was a personal friend of his, Ken took the matter seriously. In the fall of 1969—about eighteen months after he arrived—Alan Stagge finally resigned. The crisis was over . . . but by then I had already departed, as had Malcolm, Ken Scott, and many other key staff.

It's remarkable how wide-ranging an effect this one misguided individual had. Stagge estranged the staff to the point where many of us began to think about leaving, and he interrupted the teamwork aspect and flow of many recordings, quite possibly affecting their quality. Perhaps most significantly, his constant interfering and the resultant bad vibe were not going unnoticed by the Beatles, adding to the acrimony within the group and helping push them toward building their own studio instead of constantly having to deal with the hassles of working at Abbey Road. Stagge was also the reason why Malcolm Davies departed EMI, and if Malcolm hadn't gone to Apple and twisted my arm to join him, I might not have made the leap myself. It was a complicated set of circumstances, but I'm quite sure that if it weren't for Alan Stagge, a lot of things would have turned out differently.

W e started the *White Album* in the midst of all this turmoil and bad feeling, and it was not a good omen. I had been a bit on edge about starting the project anyway, because so much of the post-*Pepper* work we had done the previous year had been fraught with drama, despite the fact that things ended on a high note with the "Hey Bulldog" session. I wasn't looking forward to resuming the grueling schedule of all-nighters and the constant demands the Beatles placed on me, though I was glad to learn that Phil McDonald would once again be working as my assistant, and I was certainly looking forward to hearing John's and Paul's new songs.

Our first night back in the studio began, as usual, with small talk and catching up. "So how was India?" I asked.

It was a general question, aimed at no Beatle in particular; I was just looking to break the ice. The newspapers had reported that John and George had left suddenly because the Maharishi was suspected of having made a pass at one of the female students. It was something that I felt sure the old Lennon would have found amusing, but from the venom in his reply, it was apparent that he saw no humor in it at all.

"India was okay, I guess . . . apart from that nasty little Maharishi," he said.

Harrison looked deflated, as if it were a conversation they'd had many times before. With a deep sigh, he tried to calm his agitated bandmate.

"Oh, come on, he wasn't that bad," he interjected, earning a withering look. Lennon's bitterness and anger seemed almost palpable.

Ringo tried deflecting things with a bit of humor. "It reminded me of a Butlins holiday camp, only the bloody food wasn't as good," he said with a wink.

I glanced in Paul's direction. He was staring straight ahead, expressionless and weary. He didn't have much to say about India that day, or any other.

I sensed at that moment that something fundamental in them had changed. They were searching for something, but they didn't know quite what it was, journey to India looking for answers, and they were disappointed that they hadn't found them there . . . but it seemed to me that they didn't even know the questions. Certainly they seemed more defensive than they had ever been, more on their guard. Even though I had been working with them for more than five years at that point, I felt like they were complete strangers. For the first time, I couldn't get a read on them, couldn't fathom who they were or what they wanted. It was hardly the most auspicious way to start a months-long album project.

The rage that was bubbling inside John was the most obvious sign that something was seriously wrong. There was new tension between John and Paul, and even between John and Ringo, in addition to the often strained relationship that Paul had with George and the resentment that Ringo sometimes exhibited when Paul coached him too much on drum parts. In fact, the only two Beatles who seemed to get along during the *White Album* sessions were John and George. Perhaps that came from the experience they had shared at the ashram—after all, they were the two who had stuck it out, staying on long after Ringo and Paul had gone back home. Maybe they felt deserted by their bandmates, or betrayed. The undercurrents between the four Beatles were so complex at that point, it gave me a headache just thinking about it.

As if all that wasn't bad enough, I began hearing that very first day about a new guru they had discovered. His name was Alexis Mardas, and he had initially been a friend of John's who had now wormed his way in with the rest of the band. Magic Alex, as he was known, was a real character, living proof of the adage that a little bit of knowledge is a dangerous thing.

Alex was a smooth talker who had some vague background in electronics—he'd been a television repairman, I was later to learn—but he was way out of his depth. He seemed to have realized at an early point that John was fascinated with technology yet totally nontechnical, and in John's naivete Alex saw opportunity. His modus operandi was to get all these books and *Popular Science*–type magazines and read about new technologies. He'd then tell John about what he'd read and embellish it a little . . . but he'd present it as his original idea. Loudspeaker wallpaper? An artificial sun? John was bowled over! He didn't know any better, so he bought it, hook, line, and sinker.

Through his friendship with John, Alex had managed to sit in on a couple of sessions during the *Magical Mystery Tour* project, ingratiating himself with the other Beatles to the point where he managed to get himself invited onto the bus during the filming. He even joined them in India. I didn't notice him hanging around the studio at the time, but he was certainly noticing me, and he was taking special note of his surroundings. Whatever we were offering them at EMI, he started telling the Beatles, he could build for them smaller and better. Our ADT machine was the size of a dishwasher; he could construct one the size of a matchbox. We recorded them on four tracks; he could record them on seventy-two. We put acoustic screens around the drums; he could do that with an electronic force field. Alex had managed to successfully shake at least John's faith, if not the others, in what we were doing at Abbey Road, driving a wedge between the band and the staff.

Alex was feeding them so much misinformation, and they were so gullible, they ended up forming a complete Electronics Division within Apple . . . and then they put him in charge of it. One of his main tasks was to build them a recording studio, and all throughout the *White Album* sessions, I never heard the end of it. John and, to a lesser degree, George Harrison, kept second-guessing everything I was doing, constantly telling me, "Magic Alex says it doesn't need to be done this way; he says you should be doing it that way." I would have been willing to accept some of those comments if I thought there was any basis in reality, but I quickly became convinced otherwise. One night, I actually discovered Alex and his assistant underneath the mixing console in Studio One with a flashlight, busily studying the circuits, trying to figure out how it worked. I was livid, and I complained to Stagge, but the Beatles were so powerful they pulled strings with the EMI executives and obtained special permission for Alex to examine our equipment.

Alex never tried to engage me directly in conversation because he knew that I saw through him, and I never challenged him directly because I realized that he had gained the band's confidence to the point where doing so would be self-defeating. George Martin was as disgusted with the situation as I was, but if Alex said something particularly ludicrous, and the Beatles weren't within earshot, George would take him on from time to time. With a sarcastic smile on his face, George would ask, "Well, how exactly are you going to do that?" I noticed that Alex never gave George a straight answer—he'd just mutter through his mustache. That was his get-out: he'd mumble and pretend he was speaking in broken English, tinged with a heavy Greek accent. The funny thing was, if he did that in front of John, John would pretend that he understood what Alex was saying.

So between Alex and Alan Stagge and all the bad feelings within the Beatles camp, I had my hands full from the get-go. Making matters worse, John was exceptionally grumpy and rude the first night of recording. There was an aggressiveness I had never seen in him before; by the end of the session, he was almost psychotic. Maybe it was because of the drugs he was taking. Maybe it was all the tension of the Apple meetings, or his disappointment at being let down by the Maharishi, or the stress of his marriage falling apart. I didn't know, and, frankly, I didn't care. All I knew was that I wanted to be almost anyplace else.

But I was stuck in EMI Studio Two at Number Three Abbey Road, hunched over a mixing console with George Martin to my left and Phil McDonald behind me, and there was work to be done. As usual, we were starting the album with one of John's songs: "Revolution 1"—the slow version that would open side four of the vinyl release. Paul seemed unusually subdued that night; perhaps he was annoyed that John was dominating the proceedings so much. As the band began rehearsals, I noticed that they were playing louder than ever before; John in particular had turned his guitar amp up to an ear-splitting level. Eventually I got on the talkback and politely asked him to turn it down because there was so much leakage on all the other microphones. John's response was to shoot me a look to kill.

"I've got something to say to you," he sneered acidly. "It's your job to control it, so just do your bloody job."

Upstairs, George Martin and I exchanged wary glances.

"I think you'd better go talk to him," he said timidly.

I was boggled. *Why me? You're the producer,* I thought. But George was steadfastly refusing to get involved, so the ball was in my court. I made a point of walking down the steps leading to the studio slowly and deliberately. By the time I arrived, Lennon had calmed down a little.

"Look, the reason I've got my amp turned up so high is that I'm trying to distort the shit out of it," he explained. "If you need me to turn it down, I will, but you have to do something to get my guitar to sound a lot more nasty. That's what I'm after for this song."

The request wasn't entirely unreasonable—heavily distorted guitars were being made fashionable by artists like Cream and Jimi Hendrix—and I was about to tell him, "Okay, fine, I'll think of something . . . ," but then John couldn't resist one last jab, as he imperiously dismissed me with a wave of his arm.

"Come on, get with it, Geoff. I think it's about bloody time you got your act together."

Fuck you, John, I thought. I was incensed, but I kept my mouth shut. Weren't we supposed to be working as a team? The moment I returned to the control room, George and Phil could see just how furious I was.

"What's he on about?" George asked me.

I was so mad I couldn't even answer.

After taking a few minutes to regain my composure, I decided to overload the mic preamp that was carrying John's guitar signal. It was basically the same trick I had done to put his voice "on the moon" when he sang "I Am The Walrus." That satisfied John to some degree, but I could see that he was good and pissed off that it had taken me a period of time to get the sound sorted out. At the best of times, Lennon had limited patience, and tonight he seemed to have almost none.

Fuming and sputtering, he pushed the band to play the song over and over again, spitting out the lyrics with barely restrained venom each time. He seemed to be trying to exorcise some inner demons, screaming the words "all right" over and over again at the end of each run-through. The final take, which ended up being the keeper, ran on for more than ten minutes. By the end of it, his voice was shredded and he seemed exhausted.

"Okay, I've had enough," he hoarsely instructed us up in the control room. Ringo looked like he was about to keel over.

That first night's session was uncontrolled chaos, pure and simple, and George Martin had looked puzzled and concerned from start to finish. He and I knew that something was not quite right here, and I found myself thinking: *What am I setting myself up for?* I should have trusted my instincts.

The next afternoon, George Martin, Phil, and I were sitting in the control room having a quiet chat when John suddenly burst through the door, in a hurry as usual. Trailing closely behind was a petite Japanese woman with a camera slung over her shoulder. Ignoring us completely, John sat her down on a chair in front of the plateglass window, and then immediately dashed out of the room and into the studio, joining the other three Beatles, who were waiting patiently for the session to begin. She just sat and smiled at us, but she didn't say a word. A moment later, John burst back in; he obviously realized that he had neglected to say anything to us.

"This is Yoko," he said breathlessly, giving her a small peck on the cheek before disappearing out the door again.

That was our introduction to John's girlfriend and future wife, Yoko Ono.

For the next couple of hours Yoko just sat quietly with us in the control room. It had to have been even more uncomfortable for her than it was for any of us. She had been put in an embarrassing situation, plunked right by the window so that George Martin and I had to crane our heads around her to see the others out in the studio and communicate with them. As a result, she kept thinking we were staring at her. She'd give us a polite, shy smile whenever she'd see us looking in her direction, but she never actually said anything and she never took any pictures. After a while I started to feel sorry for her.

Eventually John plucked up the courage to bring her into the studio. Taking Yoko by the hand, he led her out of the control room and into the small recording area where the other three Beatles were rehearsing. They completely ignored her at first. To begin with, John sat her down with Mal. A little while later, he motioned her over and she plunked herself beside him . . . and that's where she stayed for the remainder of the Beatles' career.

From that point on, wherever John went, she went. If he went into the toilet, she'd walk him down the hall and wait outside, hunched down on the floor. When he came out, she'd walk with him back into the studio or control room and sit down beside him again. No one other than Neil and Mal had ever infiltrated Beatles sessions to that degree, and you could tell from the icy chill and the looks on the faces of Paul, George, and Ringo that they didn't like it one bit. Their ranks had always been so closed, it was unthinkable that an outsider could penetrate their inner circle so quickly and so thoroughly. But by his actions John was making it eminently clear that, like it or not, there was nothing they could do about it.

Once Yoko had left the control room, George Martin turned to me. Shaking his head sadly, he said, "What on earth is John thinking?"

We recognized the impact of her being there from that very first day. And from that point on, everything was different. The session the day before, struggling to get that guitar sound and dealing with Lennon's emotional catharsis, had been difficult enough, but every session from that point on would get worse and worse. Things just snowballed from then on.

John may well have been madly in love with Yoko, but there's no question that her presence at the sessions was disruptive. We all knew it, and on some level he must have known it, too, but he just didn't seem to care; bringing her into the sessions like that was almost an act of defiance. If the four Beatles ever had any discussion about her being there, it was held out of earshot, but nothing changed—she kept coming in every single day. If anything, she became even more like John's shadow; if he was sitting on one end of the piano bench, she'd be at the other end. If he slid over a bit, she'd slide with him. It really was quite uncanny how she seemed almost to anticipate his every move.

They didn't even seem to talk all that much—most of the time, John was working and she was just sitting quietly by his side. In between takes she might whisper something in his ear, or ask him if he wanted a cup of tea, but that was about it. Mind you, we noticed that she never actually made the tea, or even offered to do so; she'd simply ask Mal to make a cup. After a few days, it seemed more like she was ordering Mal around than asking him to do things, which is something I am quite sure did not escape his—or the other Beatles'—attention. Still, nothing was said; she was just there.

There was nothing unpleasant about Yoko, but we never had an opportunity to get to know her, because most of the time she wouldn't say a thing. I certainly never had any conversations with her during the *White Album* sessions beyond a simple hello or good-bye, and I don't remember her ever really talking much to George Martin or to Phil at that point either. In fact, Yoko didn't say a word to anyone except John for several days. Then one afternoon, in the middle of a backing vocal overdub, John suddenly turned to her and said, "You know, I think you should do this part."

Paul, who had been singing the line, gave John a look of disbelief and then walked away in disgust. George and Ringo, sitting a few feet away, exchanged ominous glances. Unperturbed, Lennon handed her a set of headphones and she stepped in front of the mic. For the first time, Yoko Ono appeared on a Beatles record . . . despite the fact that John was the only Beatle who wanted her on it.

I thought things couldn't get any worse, but I was wrong. A few days later, the four Beatles, plus George Martin and, of course, Yoko, were in the control room listening to a playback of a backing track when John offhandedly asked her what she thought of it. To everyone's amazement, she actually offered a criticism.

"Well, it's pretty good," she said in a tiny little voice, "but I think it should be played a bit faster."

You could have heard a pin drop. There was a look of shock and horror on everyone's face—even John's. Everyone looked at John, but he said nothing.

Infatuated as he might have been with Yoko, he must have realized that to leap to her defense would only add fuel to the fire. After a slight pause, they returned to their conversation, ignoring Yoko and what she had said. But the damage had been done, and things would never be the same again.

John seemed oblivious—or perhaps he just didn't care what the others thought. He was in love, and Yoko was going to be there beside him, offering up opinions if she wanted to, and that was that. But I could understand the other Beatles' resentment: not only was Yoko an outsider in their eyes, she had no musical background. Beyond the intrusion on their space, it was especially demeaning to George Martin, and to Paul, who was, after all John's longtime songwriting partner. Paul always had difficulty dealing with criticism, but he had such great respect for John's abilities that he would take it from him. He could even accept the occasional comment from Harrison or Ringo, but he certainly wasn't prepared to be told what to do by John's girlfriend, any more than he would have countenanced musical direction from Patti Harrison or Maureen Starkey.

That first day when Yoko spoke up and offered a musical opinion was a turning point for the Beatles. It was like John's final act of asserting himself.

In many ways, it was the beginning of the end.

Alan Stagge only tried pulling me off a Beatles session once, and it happened the third night of the *White Album* sessions, when Pete Bown was assigned to work with the group instead of me. Afterward, George Martin raised such a stink about it to Stagge's superiors that from then on the Beatles had special dispensation, and we were immune from having our team tinkered with. I bumped into Pete the next day in the corridor, and he couldn't stop talking about how drugged out and untogether the Beatles had been. I gathered that it had been a totally different experience than he had ever had with any other artist.

"Lennon told me to record his lead vocal with him lying flat on the floor," Pete said, shaking his head in amazement. "I had to get a boom stand and suspend the mic above him. Plus that odd girlfriend of his never left his side, not for one minute."

All I could say in reply was "Well, now you know what I have to go through every night."

To all the other Abbey Road engineers, the way the Beatles worked was completely alien. They had no idea that we were doing so much experimenting, all the kinds of weird things that we were trying. We didn't really talk much about what was going on in the sessions, we just kind of hinted at it—there was always an aura of secrecy around everything the Beatles were doing in the studio. Actually, I wasn't all that surprised that John had requested the strange miking, because at one point, I had tried miking him from behind his back. He got a bee in his bonnet one day about the fact that he always had to sing directly into the mic, and he kept pestering me with the same silly question: "Just tell me why the mic has to be in front of me. Why can't it be *behind* me?" Rather than go into a lengthy explanation, I just sighed and tried it out so he could hear the less-than-stellar results for himself.

Pete also told me that at one point during the session, Lennon had made a nasty remark to him—the four-track machine broke down a couple of times and a new power supply had to be installed, which caused a delay—but that he later came in and apologized, which was very unusual for him; he certainly didn't do that with me very often. Most tellingly, John had also said something to the effect of "This kind of thing won't be happening when we get our own studio set up at Apple." There was just a total distrust from him for everything we were doing, which irritated me no end. I had no doubt that a lot of that was being fomented by Magic Alex.

The *White Album* sessions were full of surprises for me. Usually, a Beatles album project would begin with the recording of one of John's songs, and this was no exception. But the second song was always one of Paul's—after all, they were the main songwriters in the band. Ringo would be allocated one song per album, and it was usually done almost as an afterthought, near the end. ("With A Little Help From My Friends" was actually the last song to be recorded for *Pepper*.) But this time around, they decided to do Ringo's song right away . . . and, even more surprisingly, it was actually a song he'd written. "Don't Pass Me By" was hardly a masterpiece—it had only three chords, no real hook, and a dreary country-tinged arrangement—but it was the second track the group decided to record.

No explanation was given, and George Martin and I were flabbergasted. The only thing we could come up with was that, behind the scenes, the others must have known that Ringo was getting a bit fed up, and they were trying to keep him happy. That seemed like the only possible reason why time and energy was being expended on a Ringo song so early on; otherwise, we would have been doing something more substantial. After all, the *Pepper* sessions had begun with "Strawberry Fields Forever" and "Penny Lane"—a stark contrast to the two relatively weak songs we were starting with here. Obviously tensions and intrigue were already in play, right at the beginning of these sessions.

Kenny Everett, the BBC disk jockey, came into the studio and did an interview with the four Beatles while they were working on "Don't Pass Me By." It was a distraction, but John got into quite a jolly mood, hamming it up for the microphone, so it did help lighten the atmosphere. The Beatles always could switch the charm on and off, and for that half hour, they became their *Hard Day's Night* characters, clowning around and acting like the lovable moptops that the public knew. It was nice to see, and I began thinking that maybe there was a glimmer of hope after all. But it didn't last for long. As soon as Kenny left, they reverted back to their miserable selves.

It was at about this time that I was first introduced to Chris Thomas, George Martin's young new assistant. All we knew about Chris was that he had simply written George Martin a letter and asked for a position as a producer's assistant, and George gave him the job, despite the fact that he had no qualifications or experience. At first, Chris just sat in the back of the control room, observing and learning. The Beatles seemed to accept him after a few days, but, frankly, I viewed him as an intruder—having yet another newcomer at the sessions was the last thing we needed. As I was soon to discover, George Martin had an ulterior motive for bringing Chris into the *White Album*.

From day one, I never had good chemistry with Chris, even though he was just a year younger than me; for the most part, I just tuned him out. At first, he was fairly respectful—he was careful not to take the producer's seat to my left, even if George wasn't there; he'd just sit by the window. But as he grew more comfortable in the situation, he began making comments. Though he would tread carefully at times, he began developing an attitude, an arrogance, that I just didn't like. I felt that he had no business being there; he had no background or training, so why should we value his opinion? George Martin and I had been doing these sessions for years, with great success, and all of a sudden Chris had infiltrated the inner sanctum, without having ever paid any dues.

Eventually, Chris and I had a real falling out. He came into Abbey Road one day with a new band, and he said to me—rather officiously, I thought— "I want the Lennon sound on the vocal and I want the Ringo sound on the drums" . . . as if it were as simple as turning a dial or pushing a button. I didn't reply, but I gave him the exact opposite of what he had asked for, and then I tried my best to never work with him again. Those were sounds I had created for Beatles records only; I wasn't about to reconstruct them for other artists. Frankly, I found it offensive that Chris even asked me to do so, especially since he had been part of our team.

One by-product of Chris's being there as surrogate producer was that the Beatles—who clearly didn't like being in one another's company anymore—were able to split up into small groups, working simultaneously in two or even all three of the studios in the Abbey Road complex. This soon became standard operating procedure for much of the rest of the *White Album*. It was as if the four band members were so much in separate spaces personally, they wanted to make their record in separate spaces physically. On those evenings, I would normally work with Paul, because I had the best rapport with him. Another engineer would accompany John or George Harrison, with the taciturn (and rarely consulted) Ringo shuttling between studios as he was needed. That was the situation on the night that we worked on Paul's first contribution to the album, the poignant ballad "Blackbird."

Neither Ringo nor George was present on that particular evening, and John wanted to begin compiling sound effects for what would ultimately become "Revolution 9," so as soon he learned that another studio was available, he decided to head off with Chris Thomas and Phil—accompanied, as usual, by Yoko. That left George Martin and me alone with Paul, which came as a blessed relief to me after all the stress of the preceding sessions; it always was a lot easier to deal with one Beatle.

Playing his left-handed acoustic guitar, Paul began running the song down, and I loved it immediately. Perfectionist that he was, he performed it over and over again, trying to get the complicated guitar part right all the way through. At one point a cameraman appeared to do a little filming for an Apple promo, and that interrupted the flow a little bit, but Paul just carried on, with his new lady friend sitting cross-legged at his feet. Paul had recently broken up with Jane Asher, and that might have been another reason why he was so subdued during the *White Album* sessions. Although she and Paul had once invited me over to their flat for dinner—I remember her making us orange soup, something I'd never had before. I suppose it's possible that Paul invited the girl along as an answer to John bringing in Yoko. But in contrast to Yoko, she didn't stay long, and George Martin had to leave early, too.

After they'd gone, Paul remarked to me that he wanted the track to sound as if he was singing it outdoors. "Fine," I said, "then let's do it outdoors."

He looked surprised, but there was a little spot outside of the echo chamber with just enough room for him to sit on a stool. I ran a long mic lead out there and that's where we recorded "Blackbird." Most of the bird noises were dubbed on later, from a sound effects record, but a couple of them were live,

sparrows and finches singing outside the Abbey Road studio on a soft summer eve along with Paul McCartney.

It wasn't until some time later that I realized that the lyric of the song was
about the civil rights movement in America; Paul never mentioned it at the
time. He was every bit as socially conscious as John; he was just more subtle
about it, not wielding a sledgehammer, as John had done with "Revolution."
They had a similar sensibility, but a total contrast in styles.

As I sat in the dimly lit control room, working peacefully with Paul on his
own, I reflected on the fact that he and John were not nearly as close as they
once had been—there was a personal distance between them, and a lot less
direct communication. In the past, Paul had had more of a tendency to influence John's songs than vice versa; it was rare when John's suggestions
would result in a major change in a Paul song—usually, he'd just be helping
finish off lyrics or contributing a middle section. But a lot of the time Paul's
suggestions would radically affect a John song. That kind of thing almost
never happened during the *White Album* sessions, however—they didn't
seem to be very interested in even getting each other's opinion, much less offering suggestions. The two of them were very much working independently
at that point—and of course George Harrison had always worked on his
own as a songwriter. That's why, as many people have observed, the *White
Album* sounds more like four solo albums than a group effort, with the rest
of the Beatles effectively acting as sidemen. At the beginning of every session, they would be asking one another, "Well, what have you got?" not
"What are *we* going to do?" It was a far cry from the camaraderie of the past.

For whatever reasons—Yoko, Apple, artistic differences—Paul and John's
creative partnership and friendship seemed to be disintegrating in front of
me. Slowly but surely, these sessions were turning into a nightmare.

In mid-June, there was a brief hiatus in the *White Album* sessions. My busy
schedule at Abbey Road precluded me from doing much dating, but I was
still a young man with a healthy interest in young women, and so I was glad
whenever I got an evening off and a chance to impress. Because I had
worked with Victor Spinetti and John months previously to compile sound
effects for a one-act play they were doing at the Old Vic (an adaptation of a
story in John's book *In His Own Write*), John had arranged for George Martin and me to attend the premiere. He'd very graciously sent me two tickets
right down in the front row, and so I invited a girl I had been seeing casually.

Her name was Mary, though I jokingly nicknamed her Plug because she worked at the electrical counter at Woolworth's.

As we made our way to the front entrance, we noticed a huge crush of fans and photographers, all straining to get a look at John and Yoko. It was one of their first public appearances together, and the curtain was delayed for a long time because they were being mobbed outside. As the crowd murmured restlessly, we began to wonder if the two empty seats next to us were theirs. Sure enough, just after the lights went down, John dashed in with Yoko by his side and they plunked themselves right down beside us. I turned to say hello and was just about to introduce Mary when I heard a loud, "Oy, John!"

Magic Alex was sitting a few rows behind us, with John's boyhood friend Pete Shotton, and they were gesturing for John and Yoko to come join them because the two seats next to them were also vacant; obviously they had sat down next to us by mistake. They got up and moved hurriedly without saying good-bye, and we didn't see either of them again that evening. Still, it was a fun night out, despite the fact that Mary didn't understand a word of the avant-garde production.

By the time the Beatles returned to the studio a week or so later, Richard Lush had finished whatever project he was working on and was able to rejoin me as my assistant. Our first night back was truly memorable: George Martin had booked all three Abbey Road studios for the complicated mix of the sound pastiche known as "Revolution 9." Unusually, Paul wasn't at the session—he had flown to the States for a few days—and Ringo wasn't around, either, so it was just John and a rather unenthusiastic George Harrison working on the track. The two of them, accompanied by Yoko, would occasionally venture out into the studio to whisper a few random words into a microphone.

Just as we had done when we mixed "Tomorrow Never Knows" two years previously, every tape machine in the facility was required for the playback of tape loops, with every available maintenance engineer once again standing around in his white coat holding pencils in place. The big difference was that on this night there was a good deal of resentment among the staff because the session was running quite late—well past midnight—and they wanted to go home. I didn't blame them; many of them had been there since nine in the morning—they didn't turn up in mid-afternoon like we did. Plus the session had to be dead boring for them because they couldn't even hear any sound; they were just standing in the various control rooms, holding pencils while the tape went round and round. Occasionally one of the loops would break and they'd have to get on the phone and let us know, which, of course, annoyed John no end.

By the time of the *White Album*, it was not uncommon for various Beatles to sit behind the mixing board alongside me; they were no longer afraid to touch the equipment. On this night John sat with me behind the console like a kid with a new toy. He was the composer and he knew what he wanted, so he manned the faders instead of me, although I served as an extra pair of hands, doing bits of panning and looking after the overall level so things didn't get out of hand and distort. The whole thing was extremely haphazard; if he'd raise a fader and there was no sound, he'd say, "Where's it gone?" A curse word might escape his lips from time to time, but that was about it. He never really lost his temper that night, though you could tell from his tone of voice that he was getting irritated. Yoko, as always, was by his side, whispering in John's ear and lifting the odd fader on occasion. Every once in a while, Lennon would shoot a glance at George Martin and me to see if we approved of what he was doing. Personally, I thought the track was interesting, but it seemed as though it was as much Yoko's as it was John's. Certainly it wasn't Beatles music.

It was around this point that George Harrison began blossoming as a record producer. He and Paul were the two Beatles most involved in discovering and nurturing new artists for the Apple label, and George had championed Liverpool singer Jackie Lomax, who became their first signing. Perhaps as an effort to escape the tedium of the *White Album* sessions, Harrison had decided to produce Jackie's debut album himself, and he asked me to engineer "Sour Milk Sea," a song George wrote for Jackie, and which ended up being Apple's first single. It was a really good session: Ringo was on drums, Paul played bass, and Eric Clapton was recruited to play guitar—the first time I'd ever met him. There was an exceptionally good vibe that night—possibly because John and Yoko weren't around—and I was quite impressed with Harrison's abilities as a producer. He seemed to know what he wanted, and he went after it with a minimum of fuss.

I had an opportunity to be a bit of a hero on that session, actually. There had been a space left to overdub Eric's guitar solo on one of the tracks, but it wasn't quite long enough—we'd have to cut off the last note of the extended solo that Clapton wanted to play—so I had to improvise something. I suggested that, instead of doing a reduction mix, we simply record the solo on a piece of clean tape and fly it in during the mix, in effect finding an extra track for him where there wasn't one.

I had the feeling I got an extra degree of respect from Harrison after that; certainly he was unusually pleasant that evening. It wasn't a particularly complex session—in fact, it was very much like a straightforward early Beatles recording—but it was a really good-sounding record for the time; the rhythm track was especially strong. This marked one of the few times I'd work alone with Harrison, and we got along fine, even though he was the producer on the project, which made me directly answerable to him.

With George, Paul, and Ringo involved in the ongoing Jackie Lomax sessions, only John—and, of course, Yoko—was present for the brass overdub and mix of "Revolution 1," which in itself was unusual because ever since the *Pepper* days, all four Beatles normally attended even mixing sessions. There were two quirks that characterized that mix. One was an accidental bad edit in the last chorus, which Lennon insisted I leave in; it added an extra beat, and he always loved weird time signatures, so it was deemed a creative accident and it became part of the song. The other oddity about the final mix was that it featured my recording debut: that's my voice hurriedly saying "Take two" just before the song begins. Because I always hated hearing my voice on tape, I had gotten in the habit of mumbling the slate as quickly as possible. John used to take the piss out of the way I rushed my announcements, so he left it in at the beginning of the song. It was done just to needle me, but at least it gave me the distinction of being one of only a few privileged outsiders who appear on a Beatles record!

A few days later, all four Beatles reunited in the studio, and John proudly played the two tracks that he had completed while the rest were away. I could see from the dark cloud that came over Paul's face that he was totally underwhelmed with "Revolution 9" when he first heard it, and there was an awkward silence after the track faded out. John looked at Paul expectantly, but Paul's only comment was "Not bad," which I knew was a diplomatic way of saying that he didn't like it. Ringo and George Harrison had nothing to say about the track at all. They looked distinctly embarrassed, and you could tell that neither one of them wanted to get caught in the middle of this.

"Not bad?" Lennon said derisively to Paul. "You have no idea what you're talking about. In fact, this should be our next bloody single! This is the direction the Beatles should be going in from now on."

Yoko, with an appalling lack of tact, managed to aggravate things further still by blurting out, "I agree with John. I think it's great." I could see that she was gaining confidence; she seemed to feel she was part of the group now. In her mind, and in John's mind, she had become the fifth Beatle.

Judging from his look of disdain, I was quite sure Paul was thinking,

You've got to be kidding, but, to his credit, he didn't rise to the bait and didn't argue—he simply said, "Well, let's listen to the next playback." Fortunately, he was reasonably pleased with the mix of "Revolution 1."

I wasn't surprised that Paul disliked "Revolution 9" as much as he did. Although he was well versed in all musical genres—in fact, he'd been into avant-garde well before John—he simply didn't see it as Beatles music, and he certainly didn't agree that it was the direction that the Beatles should go in. Later on, when they were sequencing the *White Album,* I heard through the grapevine that John and Paul ultimately had a huge row over "Revolution 9." Paul absolutely did not want it on the album, and John was just as adamant that it would be on there. In the end, of course, he got his way.

Those playbacks cast a pall on the very long, wearying session that followed, when the group began work on yet another harsh, aggressive Lennon song, which had the odd title, "Everybody's Got Something To Hide Except Me And My Monkey." I had thought that "Revolution 1" was raucous and unpleasant, but it had nothing on this track. Once again, the Beatles were playing incredibly loud down in the studio, but this time Lennon and Harrison had their volume turned up so high that Paul actually gave up competing with them. Rather than play bass on the backing track, he stood next to Ringo, ringing a huge fireman's bell, egging his drummer on. There was no microphone on him, because the thing was so loud that it bled on all the mics anyway. Physically, it was very difficult to pull off—Paul had to take a break after each take because his shoulders were aching so much.

As much as I disliked the song, I had to admit that it was the first time in any of the *White Album* sessions that there was any energy in their playing. George Harrison's lead work was crisp and efficient, much more aggressive than his usual style. The bass part Paul overdubbed on was good, too. Clearly, he was still determined to do his best, no matter what was going on between him and John.

Needless to say, by the time the track was completed, I had a splitting headache. That evening, Paul had walked into the control room on his way in and unceremoniously plunked a bottle of Johnnie Walker down on the table, saying, "This is for you, boys." George Martin looked askance—he was probably thinking: *Oh God, this is the end of the session; now Geoff and Richard are going to get pissed.* Somehow, though, we restrained ourselves until after everyone had gone home . . . at which point we drained the entire bottle.

Between the whiskey and our general sense of frustration, we did something rather naughty that night; after all the tension of the preceding weeks, we simply had to let off some steam. Giggling like the drunken fools we were, we got every last cup and saucer out of the canteen and took them into Studio Two, whereupon we smashed them up against the wall. Of course, we then had to spend another hour sweeping the floor in order to get rid of the evidence. But it was worth it. The next morning the canteen staff came in and wanted to know where all the cups and saucers had gone. Fighting our hangovers and trying to appear as angelic as humanly possible, we pleaded innocence. Whether anyone actually believed us is a matter of conjecture.

At the very next session John surprised us all with the unveiling of his lush ballad "Goodnight." Like "Across The Universe," the song showed his softer side, a stark contrast to the screamer he had belted out just the night before. It ably demonstrated the depth of his abilities as both a songwriter and a performer, which was really quite astonishing. John Lennon wasn't just a rock 'n' roller; he had a lot of facets to him. He truly was a monumental talent.

There was another surprise: John had decided to have Ringo sing the lead vocal. We were all totally caught off guard by that because we'd already recorded what we presumed was going to be the sole Ringo song on the album. It's hard to imagine that John actually thought Ringo could do a better job on it than he could—he knew as well as anyone that Ringo was no singer. Perhaps it was that he was embarrassed at singing such a gentle lullaby—maybe it wasn't macho enough for him—or perhaps he made the decision just to keep Ringo happy because he sensed some disquiet in the usually placid drummer.

John had made a demo for Ringo to take home and practice to, and it was played back a couple of times that night. (In contrast to all other previous Beatles albums, they demoed many of the *White Album* songs beforehand, gathering at George Harrison's Esher home a few days before the sessions began, though they rarely had us play back any of those tapes in the studio.) It's a shame that this particular tape has been lost to the world, and that nobody will ever hear the gorgeous way John sang his tender little song. In comparison, I really don't think Ringo did the song justice. Nonetheless, it was one of the best vocals he ever did. During the rehearsal run-throughs, John and Yoko stayed up in the control room while the other three Beatles remained down in the studio with George Martin, who played piano while Paul and George Harrison coached their drummer on phrasing and pitching. That created a unity that had rarely been present in these sessions. Just getting Yoko out of the studio seemed to lighten the atmosphere tremendously.

We were now five weeks into the making of the *White Album*. The sessions had been long and tedious, but not a whole lot had been accomplished, even by the measure of *Pepper*. And in stark contrast to *Pepper*, John had almost completely dominated the sessions to this point. George Harrison had contributed little, and only one song of Paul's—"Blackbird," performed solo—had been recorded.

That was to change in early July, when we started working on Paul's "Ob-La-Di, Ob-La-Da." It was a song John hated with a passion, and the bad feelings it engendered led to tensions that I ultimately found impossible to bear.

Most of the time, George Martin and Chris Thomas did not work together, mainly because George didn't want Chris interrupting him with his often misguided opinions. George happened to be absent on the first night the Beatles started running down "Ob-La-Di, Ob-La-Da," so Chris was the de facto producer. Initially, we all enjoyed doing the track because of its lighthearted up-tempo feel. Even Lennon got into it—at first, anyway—because it gave him a chance to clown around with his silly voices. But then it started going on and on, dragging out over three nights. Paul wasn't happy with the rhythm of the track or with the way his vocal lay. He was after a Jamaican reggae feel and he wasn't satisfied that the band had nailed it. The problem was exacerbated by the fact that even Paul didn't quite know how to lock it in rhythmically, and so he was getting pretty frustrated with himself.

Paul was something of a perfectionist by this point, but he also had to have been upset about the way John had been acting. I couldn't help but think that perhaps that had something to do with why he was so fussy about the recording of the song—maybe he did that just to annoy John, just to teach him a lesson. Throughout the preceding weeks I had noticed that John's behavior was becoming increasingly erratic—his mood swings were more severe, and they were occurring more frequently. That was definitely the case with the recording of "Ob-La-Di, Ob-La-Da." One moment he'd be into it, acting the fool and doing his fake Jamaican patois, the next minute he'd be sulking and grumbling about how the song was more of Paul's "granny music shit." You never knew exactly where you stood with Lennon at any given time, but things were definitely getting worse.

So when Paul announced several nights later that he wanted to scrap everything that had been done so far and start the song again from scratch, John went ballistic. Ranting and raving, he headed out the door, with Yoko trailing closely behind, and we thought that we'd seen the last of him that evening. But a few hours later he stormed back into the studio, clearly in a highly altered state of mind.

"I AM FUCKING STONED!!" John Lennon bellowed from the top of the stairs. He had chosen to make his entrance through the upstairs door, presumably so that he could quickly gain the attention of the three startled Beatles below. Swaying slightly, he continued, waving his arms for emphasis.

"I am more stoned than you have ever been. In fact, I am more stoned than you will ever *be*!"

I turned to Richard and whispered, "Uh-oh, he's in a right mood tonight."

"And this," Lennon added with a snarl, "is how the fucking song should go."

Unsteadily, he lurched down the stairs and over to the piano and began smashing the keys with all his might, pounding out the famous opening chords that became the song's introduction, played at a breakneck tempo. A very upset Paul got right in Lennon's face. For a moment I thought fists might fly.

"Okay, then, John," he said in short, clipped words, staring his deranged bandmate straight in the eye. "Let's do it your way." As angry as he was, I think that deep down inside Paul was flattered that his longtime collaborator had given the song any thought at all . . . even though he had obviously done so while getting out of his skull.

The remake was, I had to admit, quite good. It had a bouncier feel to it than the original version, which seemed a bit leaden by comparison, and when it was completed we all breathed a sigh of relief that we wouldn't have to be working on the song anymore. Later that night, Judy Martin stopped by the control room; she'd often stick her head in for an hour or so when we were working. She was a sweet lady from an upper-class family and she was always quite diplomatic in her dealings with us. We all got a bit slaphappy during late night sessions. Sometimes I'd turn to Richard, out of the blue, and say, "I feel like a prawn cocktail." George Martin would look at us and I could tell he was thinking, *Who's on bloody drugs? Us or them?* Even Judy would sometimes get into the spirit of things when she saw George nodding off at midnight: "Oh, teddy's stuffing is coming out," she would say, sending Richard and me into gales of laughter. I picked up on it afterward, and repeated it to George mercilessly, just to put in the needle. The Beatles weren't the only ones capable of taking the piss.

Sadly, Paul returned to his nitpicking ways the very next afternoon, announcing peremptorily that he was still dissatisfied and wanted to remake the song yet again . . . despite the fact that Ringo wasn't even there. Paul got behind the drums instead and led a clearly steamed Lennon and Harrison through another couple of run-throughs before he finally capitulated and gave up. The three Beatles then gathered around the microphone to overdub backing vocals onto the previous evening's rendition, which ended up being the version on the final album. Interestingly, all the bad feelings of the past weeks seemed to evaporate as soon as they gathered around the mic and I fed tape echo into their headphones. That's all it took for them to suspend their petty disagreements; for those few moments, they would clown around and act silly again, like they did when they were kids, just starting out. Then as soon as they'd take the cans off, they'd go back to hating each other. It was very odd—it was almost as if having the headphones on and hearing that echo put them in a dreamlike state.

Ever since the *Pepper* days, the Beatles would show up late, much later than the scheduled starting time, keeping my assistant and me waiting for hour after hour, and no one ever phoned to let us know they were running behind. Someone must have rung George Martin, because he generally knew roughly when they'd be arriving, but he never bothered to tell me, which was quite annoying. That was a contrast to every other artist, when the session would always start on time. During the making of the *White Album,* Richard and I would sit in the front reception area, waiting for them to arrive, constantly going to the front door to see if the fans were gathered outside the parking lot. If no one was there, we knew it would be at least another hour before the first Beatle would appear. Perhaps the fans were staking out Paul's house and then they'd walk over when they knew he was on his way, or perhaps they called their mates, spreading the word by phone.

While we were waiting, we'd chat about the sessions. We always hoped they'd be doing a new song that night instead of running through the same old one over and over again. That was the real highlight for us: hearing a Beatle song being debuted for the first time. John or Paul would come in and play a song on guitar or piano and they'd tell us what it was about and we'd think: *Wow, that's great.* Then we'd gradually see it changing over a period of time. Sometimes it would get better with all the endless rehearsing. Sometimes it would go downhill.

It could get incredibly boring and depressing hearing them play the same song for nine or ten hours at a stretch, especially if it was getting worse and worse as they got more drugged and went off into tangents. Interestingly, during those long jam sessions Ringo would most often be the one to take them in new directions—he'd get fed up doing the same beat all the time and he'd change it, which sometimes sparked a musical change from one of the others.

From up where we sat, we couldn't really see all that well down into Studio Two because of the dim lighting. If they were running through something for a long time and we hadn't heard anything for a while, we'd often be wondering what was going on. Sometimes we wouldn't even know if they were still down there or not; we'd just catch a little glimpse and realize, "Oh, John is still there." In fact, we sometimes wouldn't know that they'd ended a session until Ringo walked through the control room door to say good night. If he saw that we were nodding off, he'd smile and say, "Yep, we're going." Ringo would almost always be the first to go; just as they rarely arrived together these days, they usually didn't leave together.

The Beatles didn't help with loading and unloading their equipment, not even in the early days, and each had his own driver who would take him home, except for George Harrison, who sometimes drove himself in one of his sports cars. One night Mal asked me to give him a hand because the van wouldn't start—it was the same old beat-up white van they had come down from Liverpool in when they'd done their artist test back in 1962. Richard helped me push the van down the road while Mal sat in the driver's seat and jump-started it. I remember saying to him, "You've got all this bloody money now; why don't you buy another van?"

As he roared off into the night, he called out, "Go ask Neil."

Neil's move to the Apple accounting office gave Mal the luxury of hiring an assistant of his own, a redheaded kid named Kevin. Kevin did most of the heavy lifting and ran the errands, leaving Mal to look after the equipment and make the tea. Kevin was around during most of the *White Album* sessions, usually sitting down in the studio with Mal.

By this point, the Beatles had a definite anti-EMI attitude, and Richard and I and the rest of the staff, unfortunately, came under that umbrella. Nonetheless, they didn't go off and do all their recording at Olympic or Trident, studios that they kept raving about . . . but that didn't stop their constant complaining. One night Richard and I overheard them having a private conversation about us. They were saying things like "Oh, those blokes up there, they don't care about what we're doing; they don't do any more than they have to, anyway."

We were both quite hurt and upset. I thought to myself: *Fucking hell, we come in here day after day, waiting for you lot to turn up late, then we sit through hours of your stoned-out jamming in hopes that something might come out of it, and that's the appreciation we get?* Sure, it was an honor working with the Beatles and we enjoyed what we were doing, we had fun—but we were also at their beck and call just about twenty-four hours a day, and we always did everything they asked of us.

I'm not sure when they started forming the impression of "us and them." It might have started with the Abbey Road dress code, or with George Martin's infuriating habit of referring to us not by name, but simply as "the staff" whenever he was talking to the Beatles. Or perhaps it was down to communication: it was a little strange when they worked in Studio Two, where they were down in the studio and we were up a flight of stairs in the control room; those twenty steps did make them seem very far away. Yet they isolated themselves further still, putting up screens, setting up a corner of the room as a private area. We never knew exactly what was going on in there a lot of the time; you'd just see a Beatle head pop round the screen and you'd smell the joss sticks and think: *They're smoking dope again.* I'm sure that they didn't suspect that we knew, which was silly: we were all aware of their drug use, although George Martin was perhaps a bit naive about it.

By the time of the *White Album* sessions, George had really become more of a sounding board for the band than a proper producer. The big difference was that, this time around, Paul wasn't calling the shots, as he had done during *Pepper* and *Magical Mystery Tour.* In effect, it was anarchy: no one was in charge. Perhaps John thought he was, but he was incapable of producing a record, because he was too impatient and unfocused. Oftentimes, if Richard couldn't find a take fast enough, John would simply say, "Sod it, let's just do another one," even if there was a perfectly good take in the can. Things just started getting more and more chaotic. The Beatles valued George Martin's opinion—John perhaps less than the others—but they certainly didn't defer to him. If he said on the talkback, "That was good—come on up and have a listen," Paul or John would frequently overrule him, saying, "Oh, no, we haven't done it right yet."

In addition, when they were working in Studio Two, the Beatles would usually want to hear playbacks downstairs and not up in the control room. They just couldn't be bothered to walk up the stairs, and George Martin usually did not join them. That was problematic because we'd see them talking and mumbling, but we couldn't hear what they were saying—there was physically no way of playing back a track and keeping their mics open at the same time—so we didn't know if they liked what they were hearing or not.

Things got so bad during the *White Album* sessions that Richard and I actually hid behind a cupboard when the band reappeared unexpectedly late one night. They had left the studio hours before but had apparently convened in a club and then decided to head back to do more work—at four in the morning. Fortunately, I happened to spot their limos pulling into the car park and quickly told the receptionist at the front desk to say I was gone for the night. The last thing I wanted to do at the end of a long day was to enter that terrible atmosphere again.

Even lunch and dinner breaks were a cause for friction. We had become accustomed to the fact that we were never invited to join them, not that I really wanted to: Lennon had gotten into eating macrobiotic food with Yoko, and I couldn't stand the look of it, while Harrison had become very fond of curries. (To this day, whenever I think of the *White Album*, I smell Indian food!) If they were working in Studio Three, which didn't have their little set-aside tea area, they'd just eat in the control room, crowding us out. One night, Richard and I decided to head over to the local pub during a break. We were quite hungry, so we each ordered a toasted sandwich and a half pint of beer. Just as the food arrived, Mal came in and said, "John wants to record some guitar."

"We're just having our dinner," I told him. "We haven't had anything to eat yet."

"But John wants to do guitar," Mal insisted

My reply was just as forceful: "Well, he'll just have to wait."

We'd simply had enough of them by that point. We actually spent half an hour in the pub that night, which was a real luxury. Nothing was said when we got back, either. As I expected, Lennon had already forgotten that he'd even sent Mal out to fetch us.

It didn't take long for the ever-impatient John to start getting ratty and bored again, so work on "Ob-La-Di, Ob-La-Da" was suspended once more when he strapped his guitar on and started barking orders.

"Okay, we're doing 'Revolution' again," he announced.

I thought he was kidding, taking the piss out of Paul for having them do his song so many times, but George Martin quickly set me straight. They were indeed doing it again, but with a different approach.

In the early days, George Martin had picked the songs that would comprise the A-side and B-side of a Beatles single. But by this point in their career, it would be the group's decision; George might offer some input or suggestions, but it was their final call. Apparently, John and Paul had been arguing for some time about what would be the next A-side. John was pushing hard for "Revolution 1," but Paul resisted, telling John he thought it was too slow; eventually he brought George Martin in as an ally. Personally, I think Paul felt that the song simply wasn't all that good, and he was using its slow tempo as an excuse not to have it released as a single, but John had defiantly taken him up on the challenge and so was insisting that they cut it again, faster. (It would all become a moot point a few weeks later when Paul came in with "Hey Jude," which was obviously a much more commercial song. As competitive as they were, they both always wanted the strongest track for the A-side, no matter who had written it, because their royalties were split fifty-fifty regardless. The whole point was to maximize record sales, which translated into cash.)

John wanted the second, up-tempo version of "Revolution" to be even tougher and more biting than the first one. That was typical of him in those days; that was his vibe: pissed off. Ever since we'd first started work on the *White Album*, John had wanted to play louder and louder—he kept winding his guitar amp full up, but there were acoustic limitations as to how loud you could play and still capture the sound before it turned into a mess, leaking onto everything else and becoming all muddy. He didn't understand that, no matter how many times I tried to explain it to him, so he just became more and more frustrated and angry. Making things worse was the fact that, behind the scenes, Magic Alex was telling him that he would be able to play as loud as he wanted, without restriction, in the new studio he was building for them.

All that week, while we labored over the remake of "Revolution," John had been exceptionally moody. "No, no, I want that guitar to sound dirtier!" he kept demanding of me, often without even giving me a moment's space to try something out. By the end of the week, it was really starting to get to me. Fridays were usually a little more tolerable than the other nights, because I at least had the weekend to look forward to—two days away from the nastiness in the studio. But on this evening, Lennon arrived at the studio looking ready to chew someone's head off, and I was the nearest target.

"Haven't you sorted out that bloody guitar sound yet, Geoff?" he asked me almost as soon as he walked in the door.

Actually, I had an idea I wanted to try—one that I thought might satisfy

John, even though it was equipment abuse of the most severe kind. Because no amount of mic preamp overload had been good enough for him, I decided to try to overload two of them patched together, one into the other. As I knelt down beside the console, turning knobs that I was expressly forbidden from touching because they could literally cause the console to overheat and blow up, I couldn't help but think: *If I was the studio manager and saw this going on, I'd fire myself.* The ironic thing was that, years later, this ended up being precisely the guitar sound every grunge band in the world aspired to.

Lennon stood over me as I knelt there, a relentless taskmaster hammering his guitar harder and harder as I delicately moved the knobs, trying to come up with the maximum amount of overload the board could take without bursting into flames. Suddenly he ran out of patience and growled, "You know, three months in the army would have done you good." The nasty remark implied that I was just some kind of upper-class twit who had never been exposed to the real world. I felt it was particularly ironic, considering that Lennon himself had had much more of a middle-class upbringing than I ever had, was living the cloistered life of a pampered rock star, and had himself never come any closer to doing national service than the three weeks he spent filming *How I Won the War*.

I somehow managed to keep my cool and finish the session, but all weekend long I seethed and weighed my options. I didn't discuss the matter with my family, but for some time, I had been confiding in Richard and in Malcolm Davies. "I can't go on much longer," I would tell them. "I think I'm getting to the point where I've had enough."

They were both sympathetic, though Malcolm was encouraging me to tell them to fuck off, while Richard kept trying to calm me. Richard was actually as fed up as I was, but when I suggested that he walk out with me, he was noncommittal. I suppose he was worried about how leaving might affect his career.

The following Monday, I woke up feeling really down and depressed. The journey to Abbey Road seemed to take forever, or maybe it just was that I was purposefully taking the most convoluted route in order to subconsciously delay my arrival for as long as possible. Despite my best efforts, I got there eventually, and had to make the short walk across the car park and trudge slowly up the eight steps to the main entrance. Each day, I thought sadly, they were becoming more and more like John Buchan's *39 Steps*.

By this point in the recording process, the tension in the air was so thick, you could almost cut it. For weeks, I had been incensed about what had been going on, with the horrible, unsettled atmosphere, the constant bickering. Making records with the Beatles simply wasn't fun anymore.

The previous week's work was a typical study in frustration. We'd worked endlessly on just two songs: Lennon's "Revolution" and McCartney's "Ob-La-Di, Ob-La-Da," done over and over again until we were all sick to death of them. Nonetheless, here we were again, breathing in the same stale studio air, working on those same two tracks. John decided that he wanted to start things on this day by changing his raucous guitar intro to "Revolution," and that seemed to go easily enough. But once that was done, Paul made the announcement that none of us wanted to hear: he had spent much of the weekend deliberating and had decided that he wanted to sing the lead vocal to "Ob-La-Di, Ob-La-Da" yet again—probably his tenth attempt to get it to sit correctly.

I saw the grimaces flicker across the faces of George Harrison and Ringo, and I'm quite sure that none of us missed the sheer look of disgust on John's—this was a McCartney composition that Lennon openly and vocally detested. These days, the two former close friends and songwriting partners expressed little but disdain for each other's contributions; in fact, it seemed that whenever one would even bother to offer a suggestion to the other, it would be rejected out of hand, even if it was a good one. Paul and John weren't having legitimate musical differences; instead, they seemed to be saying, "I don't like what you're suggesting because I don't like you." They weren't necessarily angry at each other, but you could see that both were highly frustrated, and Yoko's constant presence certainly wasn't helping matters any. As a result, within what had once been a close-knit group, there was no longer any sense of team or unity; any camaraderie that had once been there had now simply vanished.

After setting up the vocal microphone for Paul down in Studio Two and getting a headphone mix together, Richard and I began the long, tedious process of rolling and rerolling the tape as he experimented endlessly, making minute changes to the lead vocal, in search of some kind of elusive perfection that only he could hear in his head. Sitting up in the control room between takes, I had time to contemplate matters. *What a lie we're living,* I thought sadly. The public still believed the Beatles were a band, that John and Paul still wrote together, that the four lads from Liverpool were making a group album. Nothing, in fact, could have been further from the truth. Not only were they working separately by that time, they were barely speaking to one another.

"Paul, can you try rephrasing the last line of each verse?" George Martin asked in his gentle, slightly aristocratic voice. George had sat shoulder to shoulder alongside me all these years, through the happier times of *Revolver* and *Sgt. Pepper,* but now he was struggling, out of his depth. Yet he was still trying to do his job, still trying to steer his charges toward increased musical sophistication and help push them to their best performances.

"If you think you can do it better, why don't you fucking come down here and sing it yourself?" he snarled as he whipped off his headphones and glared up at the control room.

Stunned, I looked over at George. Even he couldn't understand why Paul was still trying to redo the vocal track; in those days you simply didn't spend huge amounts of time doing that sort of fine-tuning. But as the ferocity of McCartney's verbal attack sunk in, he turned pale, clearly choking back his anger and humiliation. What happened next shocked me to the core: in sheer frustration, quiet, low-key George Martin actually began shouting back at Paul.

"Then bloody sing it again!" he yelled over the talkback, causing me to wince. "I give up. I just don't know any better how to help you."

It was the first time I had *ever* heard George Martin raise his voice in a session. The silence following the outburst was equally deafening. Richard fidgeted awkwardly at the back of the control room. He looked like he wanted to drop into a hole in the ground.

That was it for me. I took one last glance down at the studio, where McCartney was standing defiantly, arms crossed, and decided that this just wasn't worth it. I had to leave; I simply had to escape the pressure cooker. I exchanged silent glances with Richard. The look he gave me was one of concern, but with a nod of his head, he indicated that he wasn't quite ready to take the leap just yet. Not knowing what else to do, I sat at the mixing console and continued to man the controls, even though every fiber in my body was screaming, *Get out! Now!*

Somehow I saw the session through to its ragged conclusion. Paul seemed to calm down a bit, though little else got accomplished that night other than a few run-throughs of John's new song "Cry Baby Cry." Distracted and distressed, I couldn't give it my full attention, though: the only thought that kept going through my head was *I wonder if I'll ever get to finish this song.*

Finally the torturous session came to an end. Weary to the bone, I made my way home and tried to catch some sleep, but after a few hours of tossing and turning, I knew what I had to do.

The next afternoon, I walked dejectedly into the control room, where both Richard and George Martin were sitting quietly. None of the Beatles had arrived yet: they were late, as usual. I took a deep breath and at last the words came out.

"That's it, George," I announced. "I've decided I can't take it anymore. I'm leaving."

I was surprised at how resolute my voice sounded. He looked up at me quizzically.

"Leaving? Where are you going?"

The question seemed ludicrous. "I don't know, George, but I'm not doing these sessions anymore."

"What are you talking about?" he said. "You can't leave in the middle of an album."

"I can, George, and I am."

I looked over at Richard, hoping he'd make a stand with me, but he looked down at the floor, mute and despondent. As our discussion continued, I heard the sounds of the four Beatles over the control room loudspeakers; they were clattering into the studio below, accompanied as always by Yoko. Ignoring their chatter, George Martin tried sweet-talking me.

"Look, Geoff, I understand your frustration, really I do. But, honestly, you can't just walk out in the middle of a session."

Over his shoulder, I could see the four Beatles looking up from the studio below, wondering why we hadn't come down to say hello.

"No, George, I am walking out. Now. I'm not starting the session."

He looked at me in disbelief as I turned on my heels and left the control room, headed where? I didn't know. My first instinct was to go home. But instead I went to studio manager Alan Stagge's office, with a very concerned George Martin trailing closely behind. I didn't expect much in the way of sympathy, but I *was* an EMI staff engineer, and so I knew that I now needed to report to my boss and take whatever punishment was to be doled out.

Stagge's reaction to my walkout was surprisingly understated. He didn't argue with me, possibly because George Martin was so sympathetic to my plight. Instead, he simply asked me to stay on until the end of the week so they could have time to arrange for another engineer to take over.

I wouldn't, though. I was absolutely adamant that I would not return to the control room to record the Beatles ever again, and that was that. So I was given the rest of the week off, and arrangements were quickly made for Ken

Scott to be immediately brought down from the mastering room and promoted as my replacement—more like dropped in at the deep end, actually,
same as I had been a little over two years earlier.

There was an instant buzz about what I had done that spread around the
studio like wildfire, but there was no behind-the-scenes jockeying for my
position among the other Abbey Road staff. We all knew how awful these
sessions had become. As a result, no one envied me, no one wanted to be the
Beatles' engineer. There was no prestige attached to the title anymore; it had
simply become a chore.

At the conclusion of my meeting with Stagge, only one task remained,
and that was to tell the band. In the thirty minutes or so since I'd stormed
out, they had been waiting quietly at the bottom of the steps of Studio Two
to find out what had transpired.

As I headed down to face them, I could see George Harrison, Ringo, and,
surprisingly, even Paul all staring down at the ground like guilty schoolboys.
Only John Lennon had the courage to look me in the eye, and what he said
really surprised me.

"Come on, Geoff, you can't be serious about this," he cajoled. "We need
you, man, you can't just walk out on us in the middle of an album. I mean,
everyone always says what a great record *Pepper* was, even though I think it's
the biggest load of shit we've ever done."

John, I guess, was by that point viewing the rawness of the *White Album*
as his personal answer to the polish of *Sgt. Pepper,* which was largely Paul's
brainchild. He was probably attempting to flatter me, but he couldn't resist
the temptation to hurl an insult in Paul's direction at the same time. It was
yet another indication of how bad the feelings were between the two of them.

"Anyway," Lennon continued, ignoring the hurt look on Paul's face, "it's
nothing *you're* doing wrong, you know—it's just working in this shithole of
a place." He gestured with his arms and I knew exactly what he meant. There
was nothing nice about the EMI studios at Abbey Road in those days, especially for the Beatles, who were virtual prisoners of their own fame. They had
no relaxation facilities at all; for them, it was more like working in a prison.
Sure, there was a canteen downstairs, but they couldn't go there for fear of
being mobbed. Neither could they go out for a breath of fresh air, thanks to
the ever-present legions of fans waiting outside. They didn't even walk
around the corridors or go into the other studios, except on the rare occasions when there was another artist working whom they knew well and were
willing to socialize with.

So, for all intents and purposes, we were all locked in that studio each day, from the time we started until the time we finished. Sure, part of it was set up as a kind of sitting room, where they had their cups of tea and meals. But the recording area was the most awful working environment: harsh industrial lighting and bare brick walls adorned with huge mattresses stuffed with seaweed. And management was woefully oblivious to the conditions: when the Beatles had requested some better lighting around the time of the *Pepper* sessions, EMI gave us exactly three fluorescent tubes with colored gels wrapped around them, clumsily affixed to a microphone stand. Needless to say, they gave out almost no color whatsoever, but they remained, nonetheless, a mute symbol of the incompetence we had to put up with every day.

So I understood John Lennon's explanation of the band's atrocious behavior, and I was more than sympathetic, but the abruptness of my reply surprised even me.

"No, John, I *am* serious. I'm leaving. I just can't take it anymore."

And that was it. I trudged back down those eight steps and headed home. Later that evening, I would meet my friend Malcolm Davies at a pub in Muswell Hill and drown my sorrows in a prodigous booze-up. But more than feeling trepidation over my future that night, I felt tremendous relief, like someone had lifted a huge weight off my shoulders. I was glad I'd done it. *Someone* had to do something—maybe just to get the point across. But one thing seemed certain: my time as the Beatles' recording engineer appeared to be over.

· 12 ·

The Calm After the Storm:

Life After the *White Album*

Life was actually pretty good for me in the immediate aftermath of re-
signing my post. I took the rest of the week off and spent most of it fishing.
What a pleasure it was to actually see the sunshine again, to breathe fresh air
instead of stale cigarette smoke, to hear birds chirping instead of Beatles arguing! When I returned to work the following Monday, refreshed and rejuvenated, I was back on the normal day schedule. It was an arrangement that
made it unlikely that I would bump into any of the Beatles, who were still
sticking to their late night schedule, rarely showing up before mid-evening.
I wasn't particularly embarrassed about what I had done, but I wasn't especially looking forward to seeing them again, either. When I finally did bump
into them in the corridor a few weeks later, there was no problem, and I got
a friendly greeting. After that, I would pop into the control room from time
to time if I knew they were in there, just to say hello and see how things were
going. I sensed that my being there made Ken Scott a little uncomfortable,
though, so I made a point of not doing it too often.

A couple of weeks after I quit, Richard decided he'd had enough, too, and
John Smith took over for him, assisting Ken on the rest of the album, some of
which was recorded on EMI's new eight-track machine, freshly "liberated"
from the technical department for their use. John was a relatively new hiree,
but I knew him quite well because he was part of our regular Saturday-night
drinking cadre, along with Ken, Phil, and Malcolm Davies. When we'd get
together, we wouldn't talk much about how the sessions were proceeding in
my absence—I pretty much didn't want to know. The little bit of gossip I
heard indicated that things were perhaps going a little more smoothly, but
that might have been because by that point they were regularly working separately in two or three studios, and it was always easier dealing with them

when you didn't have all four Beatles in the room at once. Or perhaps my leaving had served as a wake-up call and they had made a conscious decision to curb their bad behavior.

After a while, I began hearing stories through the grapevine that the Beatles weren't always all that happy working with Ken, because he wasn't getting the kinds of sounds they were used to. They all liked Ken as a person—he had an especially close friendship with George Harrison—but even so there was discontent with some of his engineering work. Ken's lack of experience sometimes betrayed him, and I know that he wasn't ever especially popular with George Martin, because he was a little too quick to offer his opinions directly to the band instead of speaking through George, something that the producer viewed as undermining his authority.

One early August evening, I bumped into a worried-looking George in the corridor.

"Geoff, are you busy doing something right now?" he asked.

"No, I'm just on my way to dinner," I replied.

"Ah, good," he said. "Would you mind coming in and having a listen to something?"

George opened the control room door and I saw four very unhappy Beatles gathered around a flustered Ken Scott, who was tweaking the controls of a piece of outboard equipment that we called a Curve Bender. The song they were listening to was called "Hey Jude"—it was obviously one of Paul's. It was a great, catchy melody, but the recording quality was poor, with no top end whatsoever. When the playback ended, George said, "I've got a visitor here who might be able to help." Paul was the first to spot me; he broke into a big grin and gave me a wave from the back of the room.

"Ah, the prodigal son returns!" John called out brightly.

Even George Harrison gave me a warm handshake and said quietly, "Hello, Geoff. Thanks for stopping in—we really appreciate it."

"The boys recorded and mixed this track at Trident a few days ago," George Martin explained, "and we're having a bit of difficulty getting it to sound right. Would you mind having a go?"

Ken looked up from the console. "I listened to the tracks at Trident and they sounded fine," he told me anxiously, "but when we got back here . . . well, you can hear how bad it is."

Obviously something at Trident had been misaligned, and the only hope of salvaging the mix was to whack on massive amounts of treble equalization. I walked over to the console and Ken motioned for me to sit down. John Smith rewound the tape repeatedly while I worked at the controls.

Eventually we got it to sound pretty good, although the track still didn't have the kind of in-your-face presence that characterizes most Beatles recordings done at Abbey Road.

I didn't stick around for very long because I could see that my being there was embarrassing for Ken and I didn't want to overstay my welcome. I might not have even done anything that Ken himself wasn't doing—I think that all they really wanted was my stamp of approval. All four Beatles thanked me profusely as I left, and George Martin offered to walk me out. Once we got to the privacy of the corridor, he asked me if I'd consider returning to the sessions.

"No, thanks, George," I replied without a moment's hesitation. "I'm enjoying working with other artists for a change, and I'm *really* enjoying getting some sleep."

"I understand, Geoff, I understand," he said sadly. "In many ways, I wish I'd done what you did. If I didn't have a holiday coming up, I would have quit, too." We shook hands and parted ways, me heading off to a relaxing dinner, and he returning to the pressure cooker.

One of the reasons George may have hired Chris Thomas was that he knew that he had a month-long vacation scheduled and he was desperate to take it, but the crafty producer also knew that in order to do so, he had to have a representative at the sessions. Interestingly, when George did finally take off in early September, leaving Chris temporarily in charge, he decided not to let the band know ahead of time, much as he had done when I took Norman Smith's place for the start of the *Revolver* sessions. Chris, still a virtual outsider, received much the same kind of treatment from Paul that Richard Lush had endured when he had started working on the *Pepper* sessions. In answer to Paul's demand that he explain what he was doing there, Chris meekly replied that George Martin had suggested that he come in and help out with the production.

Paul's curt response was "Well, if you want to produce us, you can produce us. If you don't, we might just tell you to fuck off."

Having not been there, I don't know whether or not Chris did any actual production during the sessions he sat in on, but he apparently wasn't told to fuck off, either, so he continued to warm George Martin's seat until Martin's return in early October.

One Saturday night, Ken and John told me the full story behind "Hey Jude." The Beatles had apparently spent two full evenings working on the song at Abbey Road, one of them with a film crew present, despite the fact that a huge argument was going on between Paul and George Harrison. After that, they had decided to redo the track at Trident, perhaps thinking that a change of venue would make for a calmer atmosphere. Ken had snuck down there on the last night they were working—as an EMI staffer, he really wasn't supposed to be there at all—and heard the finished mix. When it was played back to him over their speakers at a very loud volume, he thought it sounded terrific.

The next day Ken had started the session by listening to the mix in the Studio Two control room, and he was appalled at what he was hearing; something was obviously wrong. When George Martin arrived, he asked Ken what he thought of the mix, and Ken's reply was "Well, when I was at Trident last night I was blown away, but listening to it here, it sounds like shit." Just at that moment, John Lennon walked in. George Martin, in his inimitable manner, turned to John and said bluntly, "Ken thinks the mix sounds like shit."

Not unexpectedly, that provoked an explosion from John, who stormed downstairs and informed the others of Ken's pronouncement. Ken sat at the console, mortified, watching them talking and pointing up at the control room; he was sure he was going to be fired. Finally they all came stomping up the stairs and said, "Okay, let's have a listen." It was about an hour or so later that George spotted me in the hallway and asked me to help out.

George's attempt to embarrass Ken in front of John was, unfortunately, the kind of thing he would do—he tried to make other people look subservient so that he would come off as the sole authority. Possibly he saw this as an opportunity to put Ken in his place a little bit, but I thought it was completely uncalled for.

None of this was Ken's fault anyway: all the Beatles tapes that had been recorded at Trident sounded peculiar to me because of what I suspected to be technical problems. I was vocal about my opinions, and word eventually got back to some people at Trident, who asked me to come in to talk to them about it. They made it clear that they would prefer it if I kept my opinions to myself in future. Ironically, Ken would leave EMI in about a year's time and take a job at Trident, where he was to become their star engineer. The first thing he did upon arriving was to sort out the studio's technical problems, and from that point on their tapes sounded fine.

There was one last interesting side note to the "Hey Jude" mix. Just after the start of the third verse, right between the lines "The minute you let her under your skin / Oh, then you begin," you can clearly hear Paul curse off-mic, saying "Fucking hell!" John Smith had a vivid memory of John Lennon pointing that out when they were playing the tape back.

"Paul hit a clunker on the piano and said a naughty word," Lennon glee-fully crowed, "but I insisted we leave it in, buried just low enough so that it can barely be heard. Most people won't ever spot it . . . but *we'll* know it's there."

That was just the kind of sophomoric humor Lennon was into, but I have to admit it's amusing to think that millions of fans have heard the record millions of times without ever realizing that it contains a dreaded four-letter word that was strictly taboo back in 1968.

That one time helping out on "Hey Jude" marked the last I would see of the Beatles as a group during the *White Album* sessions. A few weeks later, Paul rang me up and asked me to work with him on some tracks he was pro-ducing for a new Apple artist he had signed named Mary Hopkin. He had first spotted the Welsh singer on a television talent show, and signed her to their label on the basis of that appearance. She was really just a child then, sweet as anything, with no pretence. As we had done with his brother Mike's album, Paul and I worked well as a team whenever the other Beatles weren't around, and the sessions were pleasant, lighthearted, and a lot of fun, yielding the single "Those Were The Days," which became a huge international hit.

One afternoon, Paul brought his sheepdog, Martha, with him—the very same dog who was immortalized in his song "Martha My Dear." As she padded around Studio Three, I became quite concerned that she would get a paw caught in one of the electrical extension cords lying on the floor and re-ceive a nasty shock. Fortunately, it didn't happen, though Paul never brought her by again, which was a shame because she seemed like such a good-natured animal.

The only other Beatles-related sessions I worked on for the remainder of the year had to do with the *Yellow Submarine* album. Because I had done the mono mixes, I was asked to do the stereo versions as well. All four Beatles were present, to my surprise—in the past, they hadn't bothered being there for stereo remixes—and at one point George Harrison asked me if I could recommend a good mastering engineer for their new disk cutting room, which was being constructed in the basement of the Apple offices.

"Malcolm Davies is your man," I said unhesitatingly. I wasn't just doing a good friend a favor—he honestly was the most skilled mastering engineer I knew. Just a short time later, Malcolm was indeed hired away by Apple, the first of many EMI employees to jump ship.

I was also called upon to do the rerecording of George Martin's *Yellow*

Submarine score with a full orchestra in Studio One. This was necessitated because United Artists had bought the rights to the soundtrack, which had been recorded on their soundstage; for legal reasons, it couldn't be issued on the Parlophone LP. That's the reason why the incidental music that accompanies the film is not exactly the same as what appears on the record.

The *White Album* was released in November 1968 to mixed reviews. Some people consider it their favorite Beatles album. Personally, I think it's their least inspired effort, and I find it difficult to listen to. Of course, that may have a lot to do with my knowing the circumstances behind it. Unless you have nurtured an album, crafted it, lived with it every day, it's just a piece of plastic with some songs on it. But if you're aware of people's talents and you see them just crumble and destroy themselves, it's tough to deal with.

I didn't approach recording the *White Album* any differently, but it sounds quite unlike other Beatles albums, and I think that's because most of the sounds they were making at the time were brash, even jarring. There was little finesse; the group seemed to simply be trying to get something out of their system. Up until that time, the Beatles were always striving to get better. They didn't succeed all the time, but they were always trying; in fact, one could make a good case that they were climbing up the ladder from their very first album all the way through to *Pepper*, yet there was a definite drop-off in quality afterward.

Ken Scott told me afterward that his understanding was that the group deliberately wanted the *White Album* to be the anti-*Pepper* album, the complete opposite—even down to having a plain white sleeve instead of the ornate photograph that graced the cover of *Pepper*—but that was never discussed in the sessions I attended. It's true that John dominated the early sessions, as opposed to Paul, and maybe that was in his mind, but I don't think it was a conscious decision on the part of the band. Perhaps afterward, when they heard the ragged jumble of songs they had amassed, they decided to say that just to save face.

Given all the immense pressures they were under, it was a project that was destined to fail. On the one hand, there was John's increasingly erratic behavior and Yoko's silent but unrelenting presence; on the other, there was the stress of having to constantly deal with Apple business. Throughout the *White Album* sessions, and even when we would record *Abbey Road* a year later, Mal and Neil were constantly interrupting the Beatles in the studio, bringing them papers to sign and passing along correspondence and phone messages. If they'd had cell phones in those days, they probably would have all been on the phone all the time. That would also explain why the start of the *White Album* sessions were so scattershot—they'd come in for a few days, then not turn up for a week or so, and when they did come in, they were very unfocused.

Another factor might well have been the simple but all too true adage: familiarity breeds contempt. Our control room team—George Martin, myself, and either Phil or Richard—had been together for more than two years when I finally bailed out, and the Beatles were probably as sick of seeing our faces as we were of seeing theirs. The longer we worked together, the less respect we got from them, it seemed. We sacrificed a lot for them—our sleep, our social lives, and to some degree, our sanity—and we weren't necessarily appreciated for it. Despite the fact that they perceived us as very square, they weren't willing to concede that a lot of us actually had a good deal of training and knowledge. We may have been a bit behind the times, but Abbey Road still had the best mics, the best consoles, really good-sounding studios to record in, and people who had been taught their craft properly. Yet as time went on, the Beatles began thinking that EMI were lucky to have them. They would make comments like "We're keeping the company going"—an attitude which, in addition to all the Magic Alex nonsense, was really starting to get tiresome.

Given his status and experience, it would have been reasonable to expect that at some stage George Martin would have taken a stand, but he never did. He never confronted the Beatles about their bad attitude or the lack of respect they gave the EMI staff; he never pointed out the way we were sacrificing our personal lives and constantly coming up with innovations for them; he never made the case that we were there to help them, that we were with them, not against them. In short, George never tried to instill a sense of camaraderie, a sense of teamwork. To be blunt about it, he never displayed the right kind of leadership skills.

The reason, I think, is that he simply didn't want to give us any credit. Whether it was because of ego or insecurity, he didn't want the Beatles to get the impression that we were doing anything special. He wanted them to believe that only he was indispensible, that he was pulling all the strings and that we were just doing what he told us to do. On the rare instances when journalists were invited to come into the control room to observe the Beatles at work or take some photographs, George would clear the room—he'd tell us all to take a break until the visitors had left. He wanted the spotlight to shine on him alone. He knew that if we were sitting there, he would have to explain our role, and that would take some of the attention away from him.

Interestingly, Paul has never said anything to me about my walking out during the *White Album*. Other people have mentioned it in front of him from time to time, but all he's ever said is "Well, Geoff started the album for us, but somebody else finished it." Somehow we've never discussed it, or even joked about it. It's just a topic we avoid to this very day.

In late December I began to hear rumors that the Beatles were making preparations for their next album, which was to be recorded at Twickenham Studios because the sessions were to be simultaneously filmed. By that point, I'd had enough time to cool down. Frankly, if they'd asked me to resume working with them again, I probably would have. But I wasn't asked. The official story George Martin told me was that I couldn't do the sessions because I wasn't in the film union. In the end, independent engineer Glyn Johns, who worked at Olympic and had a union card, was hired for the project. I didn't realize it at the time, but I had dodged a bullet, because the sessions—for what would ultimately become the album known as *Let It Be*—turned out to be even more torturous and fraught with tension than the *White Album* had been, with even poorer end results.

The Beatles were so miserable recording at cold, drafty Twickenham that they decided to shift venues and complete the album at their own studio, being built for them—supposedly—by Magic Alex. Apple had taken premises at 3 Savile Row, in the heart of London's posh Mayfair district, the previous summer, and Alex had purportedly been slaving away all that time on constructing a seventy-two-track facility for them in the basement. Few artists had their own studio in those days; it was virtually unheard of. But between the lack of amenities and the strained atmosphere being engendered both by their bad behavior and by a feckless studio manager, the Beatles were getting fed up with Abbey Road, so they decided that working in their own studio provided the perfect solution. Though it was an untested and untried concept, the Beatles never were afraid to take the initiative and carve out new territory.

Alex had been mumbling excuses and overrunning his budget for months on end, but once he was put on notice that the Beatles would be starting sessions in the Apple studio in a matter of weeks, he went into overdrive. It didn't matter: no amount of motivation and hard work could make up for the fact that Alex basically did not know what he was doing. The studio he built for them was a complete and utter disaster.

For a start, there were no wiring conduits between the control room and the studio, so thick and bulky mic cables had to be run under the door and down the corridor. The speakers—sixteen of them, embedded in the walls—sounded atrocious. The mixing console barely worked at all, and what signal it did pass was distorted. Little surprise, given that it was essentially just a sheet of plywood with sixteen faders and an oscilloscope stuck in the middle, which acted as an inefficient level meter. After a day of fruitless recording tests, George Martin ordered in EMI's mobile console, which came accompanied by newly hired assistant engineer Alan Parsons. For the next few weeks, he, George, and Glyn labored over what John Lennon was to later call "the shittiest load of badly recorded shit with a lousy feeling to it ever."

Stories were beginning to filter back to Abbey Road about how dire the sessions were. It was a project that George Martin would ultimately disassociate himself from, after which Phil Spector was brought in. For all of the hassles that came from dealing with Alan Stagge, I was glad to be safely ensconced at the other end of London, far removed from all the goings-on.

One night on the news there was coverage about the rooftop concert the Beatles ended up doing at Savile Row, intended as the final culmination of the project. To my great delight, I spotted my mate Malcolm Davies up on the roof with them. By that time, he was already an Apple employee, cutting disks in their newly completed mastering room, which he, and not Magic Alex, had designed.

I was relaxing at home one Saturday morning in mid-February when the phone rang—it was Paul. After we exchanged pleasantries, he got down to business.

"I've got a proposition for you if you're interested. How would you like to come work for us at Apple? We've had a few problems with the studio Alex built for us, so we'd like you to take a look at it, let us know what you think and sort it all out for us."

From what I'd heard of Alex's folly, Paul was clearly understating the situation, but it was an offer I found intriguing, especially since I'd been getting more and more frustrated with the limited opportunity for advancement at EMI.

I hemmed and hawed. "Well . . . possibly."

"Great!" Paul said. "Why don't you pop down to Neil's office tomorrow morning and have a chat?"

Neil had his office in Wigmore Street, not at Savile Row, because that's where the main business office was located. He could be a difficult person to deal with at times—I generally got on much better with Mal—but on this early Sunday morning, with the offices deserted, he was in a good humor.

"Right then, Geoff; what will it take for you to come over and start working for us?" he asked me brightly.

I had mulled it over in my head. I knew that the job Paul was offering me would be a challenging one, and I knew from past experience that working for the Beatles would be a full-time twenty-four-hour-a-day commitment. The figure I named was what I considered fair recompense for the amount of responsibility I expected to be taking on and the long hours I expected to be working. It wasn't outrageously high, but it was a good deal more than I was earning at EMI.

A couple of days later Neil called and told me that the salary I had asked for was acceptable, but I still hedged my bets, saying that I wasn't a hundred percent sure I wanted to leave EMI, which, after all, had been my home ever since I had started my career. Over the next few weeks, I received numerous phone calls from both Neil and Peter Brown, who had been Brian Epstein's assistant and who was now the Beatles' full-time minder, encouraging me to make the jump. And I also heard almost nightly from Malcolm Davies, who was twisting my arm relentlessly. In his new position, he was being put in the middle, between the Beatles and Magic Alex, and he didn't like it one bit. "Come on over here and, for fuck's sake, sort it out," he would badger me.

But, as tempting as the Apple offer was, and as fed up as I was with working at Abbey Road, I had another iron in the fire, and I was waiting to see if it would pan out. George Martin's production company, AIR, had decided to get into the studio business, too, and he had offered me a job there. They had gotten a lease for a building in Oxford Circus, with ambitious plans for constructing a whole complex of recording facilities. It seemed to me to be a better opportunity, because it would give me a chance to work with artists other than the Beatles, although I would also still be able to work with them if they chose to continue using George as their producer.

But then George began telling me of logistical problems. Everything was falling behind schedule, and he had no clear idea of when the AIR studio would actually be able to open its doors. I began paying frequent visits to Savile Row, to see Malcolm and bring tapes of my work in for a listen, just acquainting myself with the facility and the vibe. It was a tough decision I was wrestling with: accept a challenge that would allow me not only to continue working with the most famous band in the world, but also to join my best friend, or maintain my association with the most famous producer in the world and have the opportunity to work with other artists?

While I was ruminating all this, Paul asked me to come down to Olympic Studios and lend my ear to a mix Glyn Johns was doing of his new song "Get Back." Paul was worried about what Glyn was doing because it was scheduled to be the A-side of the next Beatles single. He met me at the studio—he was the only Beatle there—and I immediately understood his concern. Olympic's control room had not two, but three speakers, and when backing tracks were being recorded, they usually put the snare drum in the center speaker alone. It was a gimmick of theirs because the snare drum was so important to the sound of rock records, but it made no sense whatsoever to me because it was critically important to know how the snare would sound when the final mix was played back over a two-speaker stereo system. Glyn didn't like being second-guessed—he was a prickly and short-tempered man—but I was there to help Paul out, and so I did my best to ensure that the snare was accurately balanced with the rest of the instrumentation. I had no official involvement in *Let It Be;* that was my sole contribution, uncredited, to the album.

Just a few days later I received a phone call from Peter Brown, telling me in breathless tones that John had just written a new song and would be coming into Abbey Road the following Monday. Would I be willing to do the session? I asked Peter rather tentatively if John was "okay" these days. He understood exactly what I was getting at; as the Beatles' designated minder, he had seen plenty of Lennon at his worst.

"Yes, he's fine," Peter assured me. "He's in really good spirits at the moment, and he's really up about the new song. And he specifically asked me if I could get you to engineer it."

How could I possibly say no to that?

The session was booked to start in mid-afternoon, and to my amazement, a chipper John actually rolled up spot on time, with Paul following just a few minutes later. It was officially supposed to be a Beatles session, but they were the only two band members to turn up that day, Paul taking the drummer's chair, playing Ringo's kit with confidence and ease. The two Beatles seemed remarkably relaxed, despite the horror stories I had heard about the rows and bad feelings engendered by the *Let It Be* sessions. On this one day, they reverted to being two old school chums, all the nastiness of recent months swept under the rug and replaced by the sheer joy of making music together.

It was even more surprising given the name and subject matter of the song being recorded that day, which Lennon proudly told me was entitled

"The Ballad Of John And Yoko." The lyrics described the circumstances surrounding their recent wedding, even crediting Peter Brown by name for having come up with the idea of them getting wed in Spain.

It was a great session, one of those magic times when everything went right and nothing went wrong. The whole record was completed in just a few hours, from start to finish, including the mix—just like the good old days. A new eight-track machine had been installed in the control room just recently, and we put it to good use that day. The eight-track recorder allowed for lots of overdubs, so John played all the guitars—lead and rhythm—while Paul handled bass, piano, percussion, and drums; they made for a great two-man band. That was one of the first times I put microphones both on top of and under the snare drum, which imparted a larger-than-life crack to the sound, the perfect complement to John's aggressive vocal. The luxury of eight tracks allowed us to do a detailed stereo mix, and, as icing on the cake, the record ended up being mastered by Malcolm at Apple.

It was so refreshing to see Paul and John in good spirits and not arguing, and the vibe of that session helped me make up my mind just a week later, when George Martin told me that there were still problems plaguing his plans for a new studio.

"Well, then," I told him, "I suppose I'd better take Paul's offer."

George was gracious and assured me that there would always be a job at AIR waiting for me if things didn't work out at Apple. Right then and there I picked up the phone and dialed Peter Brown.

"Okay, Peter," I said, my voice filled with excitement and apprehension. "I'm in."

An Anvil, a Bed, and Three Gunslingers:

The Making of *Abbey Road*

I departed EMI in the spring of 1969 to the sound of one hand clapping. As it happened, fellow engineer Peter Vince left the same day I did—off to pursue a career as a producer, assisting Norrie Paramor. Our departure decimated the Abbey Road staff, because we were the studio's two main pop engineers: Malcolm Addey had already left to try his fortunes in America, and although Stuart Eltham and Pete Bown were still there, they were getting on in years. Solemnly, Peter and I signed the personnel book and then walked out the door together. Despite the fact that we had worked on some of the biggest-selling albums of all time, no one said thank you, no one said goodbye. No one said anything, in fact.

But there was no time to look back, with or without regrets, because I had my hands full with my new job as Apple's studio manager. The Apple salad days—the days of flowing champagne, and a waiting room filled with Hell's Angels, hippies, and vagrants—were already over by the time I arrived. Allen Klein—the portly, fast-talking New York accountant that John had become so enamored of—had already taken over the running of the office by then, firing everyone he could get away with firing and forcing many of those he couldn't to resign. It was a greatly stripped-down operation, and all the remaining employees at 3 Savile Row seemed to be in a terminal state of depression and fear. Klein was clearly a force to be reckoned with, but fortunately he pretty much left me alone—he knew I had been hired directly by Paul and had the confidence of the other three Beatles, so I was virtually untouchable. Nonetheless, I found him generally unpleasant to deal with, and tried to avoid him as much as possible. Ironically, Klein's appearance on the scene spelled the end of Paul's visits to the office. George Harrison would actually be the Beatle I would have the most contact with during the four years I was at Apple.

My first official duty was to provide a formal evaluation of Alex's studio. It didn't take me long. I already knew from the visits I'd made in previous months that what he'd slapped together was completely unworkable. I wrote a memo (most of the interoffice communications at Apple were in the form of memos) saying just that, recommending that the studio be gutted and rebuilt from the ground up; there was really nothing worth salvaging. There was a lot of concern about how much money it would cost to fix Alex's mess, but I got the green light to go ahead and begin the planning stages for constructing a new studio.

I don't think Allen Klein liked Alex any more than I did; he just wanted me to confirm that Alex had nothing useful to contribute to the organization. But despite the way he'd botched things, Alex still had sufficient protection from John to hang on to his job for a while. Still, my memo obviously had some effect: just a few weeks after it was submitted, the entire Apple studio operation was taken out of Alex's hands and placed in mine. Alex's workshop was moved to the company's Boston Place facility—actually just a mews house, around the corner from Marylebone Station—and he was given the task of building modules for a new mixing console he was supposedly developing. Not surprisingly, neither the modules nor the console ever saw the light of day.

Peter Asher, Jane's brother (and also the "Peter" in the singing duo Peter and Gordon), had been an Apple executive at Savile Row before departing in the Klein era, and I was ensconced in his former office, a small, bleak room on the top floor of the musty old building. The furnishings were sparse: just an antique desk atop which sat a green banker's lamp; two run-down, creaky chairs; and a couple of bookcases that were soon stocked with technical references about studio construction and costings analyses.

I knew a lot about recording and operating recording equipment, but precious little about the technicalities. I needed a proper maintenance engineer—Alex and his assistant were obviously unqualified for the job—so I decided to hire away Ron Pender from EMI. Ron not only knew his stuff but had assisted on the *Rubber Soul* album back in 1965, so he was a familiar face to the Beatles. Thanks to Alan Stagge's onerous regime and the fact that we were offering a hefty raise, we were able to lure away Ron—and, in the years to come, many more Abbey Road employees—with ease.

In addition to my mate Malcolm Davies, there was one other ex–Abbey

Road employee already working at Apple when I arrived: John Smith, who had served as Ken Scott's assistant after I had walked away from the *White Album*. Like so many other EMI staffers, John departed after a run-in with Alan Stagge. One morning, as Stagge was reviewing the Beatles' work sheets, he offhandedly told John that Ken Scott was a "cunt" for staying late and not pulling the plug on the sessions. John was small in stature, but he had a fierce sense of loyalty. He was close friends with Ken, and he knew all too well that if Ken had dared try to end the sessions, the Beatles would have made his life a living hell, so he got right in Stagge's face and replied, "Well, if Ken is a cunt, then you're a cunt." His days at EMI were numbered after that; within weeks, Stagge had forced him out, and George Harrison had given John a job at Apple, looking after the tape library. So three of the four members of our Saturday-night gang—Malcolm Davies, John Smith, and I—were reunited once again. In the years to come, I would try—unsuccessfully—to hire away our fourth member, Ken Scott, who would instead become Trident's chief engineer.

The Beatles' disastrous *Let It Be* project had been shelved in mid-April after the group rejected the mixes done by Glyn Johns. I had no idea what their future plans were, but I knew that they had been doing some on-again, off-again sessions at Trident and Abbey Road. George Martin wasn't producing those sessions; instead, his assistant Chris Thomas was overseeing them. In May I heard through the grapevine that the group had returned to Olympic Studios with George Martin and Glyn to cut some more tracks, but I was so wrapped up in what I was doing—learning the ins and outs of studio design and construction—that I barely paid any attention. I wasn't asked to participate in any of those sessions, nor was I invited to hear any of the tracks they had been working on, which included George Harrison's "Old Brown Shoe" and the start of several other songs that eventually found their way onto the *Abbey Road* album.

One early summer afternoon I was plowing through some paperwork when the phone in my office rang: it was Paul.

"Hello, Geoff, how are you getting on?" he asked me breezily.

"Fine," I told him, "I'm just trying to sort out some of these studio costings." Naturally enough I assumed that was the reason for his call, but I was wrong.

"Never mind that, Geoff, there's something more important I need to talk to you about. We're going back into EMI this summer to record a new album, and we want you to engineer it."

Without a moment's hesitation I said, "Yeah, brilliant."

We chatted some more and I asked Paul as diplomatically as I could if everyone was getting along these days.

"Yes, things are pretty good," he replied. "We've sorted a lot of our problems out and there's going to be a better vibe in the studio this time around. We're planning on doing this album the way we used to make records, with George really producing."

It sounded almost too good to be true, but I kept my skepticism to myself. Come what may, I'd be engineering another Beatles album after all.

I was soon informed that the recording was due to start at the beginning of July, running through to the end of August. I was told to attend as many of the sessions as I could without abandoning my other responsibilities, though it was made clear that the Beatles didn't want the planning of the studio to interfere with the making of the new album. A few days later, George Martin phoned, welcoming me back, but adding ominously that my presence might cause some "problems" with the EMI staff. Outside engineers had never been allowed to work at Abbey Road before, and already there were mutinous rumblings. Even when an outside engineer came in just for a visit, there was hostility. One day, Glyn Johns popped in to hear a playback, and judging from the reaction of the staff, you would have thought the studio was under siege. It was down to insecurity and self-preservation, people in fear of losing their jobs.

Even though I had been a faithful employee of the studio for more than six and a half years, I was now viewed as an interloper, and there was tremendous resistance, especially from some of the old-timers, to my being allowed to engineer the sessions. Eventually a high-level meeting was held at Manchester Square, where a compromise was hammered out: I would be allowed to work on the album, provided a staff engineer was present as well. But—and this was apparently very important to the EMI bigwigs—my name would not be permitted to be inscribed on the tape boxes or work sheets; only the staffer's name could appear.

When I was told about the arrangement, I had a good laugh. First of all, I couldn't care less whether or not my name was on the tape boxes; I hadn't ever gotten a credit on a Beatles album before, and I wasn't expecting one this time either. (Much to my surprise, the eventual record sleeve did actually say, "Thanks to Geoff Emerick." It wasn't exactly an engineering credit, but at least it was an acknowledgment.) Second, I welcomed the idea of another engineer being there because I knew just how much work lay ahead of me regarding the building of the new Apple studio. Having another qualified engineer there would take a lot of the pressure off me and allow me to leave early, or turn up late, if meetings and other planning responsibilities dictated.

I was even more pleased when George informed me that he had pulled strings to get my old friend Phil McDonald assigned as the balance engineer for the entire project. Phil may not have had a great deal of experience or finesse, but he knew what he was doing, and because he had largely apprenticed with me, I was confident that the sounds he would get on tape would not differ significantly from mine.

The only area of concern was the potential for interference. Too many cooks can indeed spoil the broth, especially in the confinement of a cramped control room with demanding artists all around you. But my fears were allayed with one simple phone call.

"Look," Phil told me, "I'm sure you don't want me in the room with you while you're engineering any more than I want you in the room with me while I'm working, so let's just work in shifts. If you have to come in late, I'll begin the session and split when you arrive. If you have to leave early, I'll come in later and take over."

I was amazed—and impressed—at how mature Phil was being about the whole thing . . . until I discovered his real motivation some time later. It turned out that Phil The Basher was really more like Phil The Conniver: he had a new girlfriend who had a flat near Abbey Road, and he merely viewed this as an opportunity to spend increased quality time with her . . . hours that presumably would be all the more pleasurable because he would be billing them to EMI.

I spent the summer dividing my time between recording the Beatles and meeting with surveyors and architects. The session hours were far more civilized than they had been at any time since *Revolver*—we generally started in mid-afternoon and were done before midnight—but it was rare when I was able to attend an entire session from start to finish. Sometimes Phil would start things off and I'd come in halfway through. Other times I would begin the session and he would wait in the front hallway reading a newspaper until it was time for me to head out and get back to Apple studio business.

There was also a lack of continuity in the assistant engineers who worked on the sessions. My old compatriot Richard Lush was still working at Abbey

Road, but he had decided that he'd had enough of working with the Beatles and opted not to participate at all. Taking his place at the back of the room were two new youngsters: Alan Parsons, who'd done some work on *Let It Be,* and John Kurlander. Both ended up enjoying tremendous success: Alan formed his own group, the Alan Parsons Project, and was the engineer for Pink Floyd's huge hit album *Dark Side Of The Moon*; and John stayed on at Abbey Road through to the mid-1990s, eventually becoming their chief engineer before moving to America and winning numerous awards for his soundtrack work on films such as the *Lord of the Rings* trilogy.

Kurlander, who had worked with me on the "Ballad Of John And Yoko" session, proved to be an exceptionally able assistant, with an eye for detail that made my job a lot easier. One afternoon we got to chatting and he said that when he was told by management that his next assignment was to assist for the Beatles, his immediate reaction was "Why me?" The group still hadn't shed their reputation of being difficult to work with; no one wanted to be assigned to their sessions, despite the prestige.

But in contrast to the mayhem that was the *White Album*, the atmosphere during the making of the *Abbey Road* album was quite muted. Everyone seemed to be walking on eggshells, trying not to offend. For the most part, Paul was less officious, and John less acerbic. Yoko was still there every day, but by this time the Beatles were so used to her being around that she was like part of the furniture . . . for the most part. Ringo was Ringo, though he seemed to have a little more of an "I'm a star" attitude. Perhaps the biggest change was in George Harrison, who was far more confident and self-assured than ever before. Both of the songs he contributed to the album—"Something" and "Here Comes The Sun"—were melodic and well crafted, virtually on a par with the work of Lennon and McCartney, and he seemed to know it.

Looking back, it seems to me that the Beatles were all on their best behavior because they were determined to turn in a good album after the disaster that was *Let It Be*. Magic Alex's name rarely came up, because they knew by then how badly he'd botched their studio. And there were few conversations about the studio planning work I was doing for them concurrently at Apple, although George Harrison occasionally asked me a question or two, mostly about the budget.

Yet things weren't a hundred percent rosy during the making of *Abbey Road*. There were still some arguments, but they were few and far between and they seemed to blow over fairly quickly. Perhaps the explanation lay in the fact that all four Beatles were rarely in the room at the same time. It seemed that they were deliberately trying to stay out of one another's way; if one of them was doing an overdub, the others would generally go home. That hadn't been the case when we were recording previous albums, where everyone would hang around and give input and support. It was apparent that they weren't working as a team anymore, but that seemed to be what it took for them to coexist in the studio together.

The first day I arrived, George Martin greeted me with a look of deep concern. "John's been in an accident," he announced in a clipped tone of voice. "A car crash up in Scotland, with Yoko. He's not too badly injured, thank goodness, but they're both in hospital and won't be here for at least a week." While I digested the sobering news, George looked away and muttered sarcastically, "What a fine way to start the project."

As it happened, the first week of the *Abbey Road* sessions were quite peaceful without John and Yoko's presence, though a bit tentative because of equipment problems. The new mixing console had a lot more bells and whistles on it than the old one, and it gave me the opportunity to put into practice many of the ideas I'd had in mind for years, but it just didn't sound the same, mainly because it utilized transistor circuitry instead of tubes. George Harrison had a lot of trouble coming to terms with the fact that there was less body in the guitar sound, and Ringo was rightfully concerned about the drum sound—he was playing as hard as ever, but you didn't hear the same impact. He and I actually had a long conversation about that, which was quite unusual, but after a good deal of experimentation I came to the conclusion that we simply couldn't match the old Beatles sound we had become used to; we simply had to accept that this was the best we could achieve with the new equipment. Personally, I preferred the punchier sound we had gotten out of the old tube console and four-track recorder; everything was sounding mellower now. It seemed like a step backward, but there was nothing we could do—there was an album to record and we simply had to get on with it.

Fortunately, the music the Beatles were making at that point in their career lent itself to that sound. The new sonic texture actually suited the music on the album—softer and rounder. It's subtle, but I'm convinced that the sound of that new console and tape machine overtly influenced the performance and the music on *Abbey Road*. With the luxury of eight tracks, each song was built up with layered overdubs, so the tonal quality of the backing track directly affected the sound we would craft for each overdub. Because the rhythm tracks were coming back off tape a little less forcefully, the overdubs—vocals, solos, and the like—were performed with less attitude.

The end result was a kinder, gentler-sounding record—one that is sonically different from every other Beatles album.

Interestingly, it was at only the second session for the album that Paul, accompanying himself on acoustic guitar, recorded "Her Majesty," the song fragment that ended up concluding *Abbey Road*. Later that same day, after Ringo and George Harrison arrived, the three Beatles recorded the backing track for "Golden Slumbers"/"Carry That Weight." The two songs were joined together even at that early stage because Paul had already come up with the idea of linking up several short snippets into a medley of sorts. No one was sure how John would react, but we got on with the work anyway. There seemed to be an assumption that he would go along with it, and that this time around, in contrast to the *White Album*, he wouldn't be calling all the shots.

Over the next few days, as we all anxiously awaited John's arrival, the three Beatles continued work on "Golden Slumbers"/"Carry That Weight" as well as Paul's newest vaudeville-influenced song, "Maxwell's Silver Hammer." Ringo even joined in on singing some harmonies, presumably doing parts that would have otherwise been given to John. Everyone just wanted to get on with the work at hand, Lennon or no Lennon.

Paul was in high spirits during the early *Abbey Road* sessions—he even got back into the habit of sliding down the Studio Two stairway banister when departing the control room, just as he had done during their very first session back in 1962—but he did spend a lot of time working on "Maxwell," which irritated George Harrison a bit. One afternoon, they got into a heated argument about it and I started to think, *Uh-oh, here we go again*. But it died down relatively quickly, and the tension was broken when it came time to do the anvil overdub on the choruses. There was no thought given to finding a way to approximate the effect: Paul wanted the sound of an anvil being struck, so Mal was dispatched to track one down. I have a clear memory of him dragging it into the studio, struggling under its weight as the rest of us laughed our heads off. Both he and Ringo had a go at hitting it. Ringo simply didn't have the strength to lift the hammer, so Mal ended up playing the part, but he didn't have a drummer's sense of timing, so it took a while to get a successful take.

Unlike *Pepper*, the Beatles weren't looking for the impossible on *Abbey Road*; there was little of the "make sure this guitar doesn't sound like a guitar" kind of thing. Nonetheless, there was a good deal of discussion about Paul wanting the bass on "Maxwell's Silver Hammer" to sound like a tuba, to make the recording sound old-fashioned. We accomplished that by having him articulate the bass like a tuba by sliding into the notes instead of hitting them spot on. A fair amount of time was expended on getting that sound, but Ringo and George Harrison made a point of absenting themselves, so there was no one to raise an objection. At this late stage of the Beatles' career, it seemed that the best way for them to approach making a record—perhaps the only way—was for each band member to work on his own.

We'd been receiving daily reports on John's and Yoko's progress as they slowly recuperated at home, and early on the morning of July 9, George Martin had gotten a call from Mal Evans saying that Mr. and Mrs. Lennon were at long last on their way into the recording studio. As the afternoon wore on, there was a great deal of anticipation as to what kind of shape John would be in and what his mood would be. Everyone was concerned about his well-being—it was a bad accident, and he was lucky to be alive—but there was also an unspoken worry about how John and Yoko's presence would affect the relatively good vibe of the sessions so far.

Suddenly, without warning, John and Yoko materialized in the studio doorway, like two apparitions dressed in black. After a moment's hesitation, we all rushed over to see if he was all right.

"Yes, I'm okay," Lennon reassured us softly. As everyone gathered around anxiously, he appeared to brighten. "I've brought the car with me, too," he blurted out unexpectedly, explaining that he'd arranged for the hire car in which he'd had the accident to be crushed into a block and towed down from Scotland. The tow company had been instructed to bring it to the Abbey Road parking lot first so we could all have a look before it would be taken to John's mansion in Tittenhurst Park, where it would eventually serve as an interesting if somewhat gruesome lawn sculpture. Talking animatedly with his fellow Beatles, Lennon appeared to forget about Yoko for a moment. Clearly annoyed, she tugged at his sleeve and let out a small moan, gaining his attention.

"I'm afraid that Mother is still not too well, though," he said, suitably chastened. Even during the *White Album* sessions John had started referring to Yoko that way, which I always found a bit creepy.

Yoko started to say something, but before she could get a word out, the door burst open again and four men in brown coats began wheeling in a large, heavy object. For a moment, I thought it was a piano coming in from one of the other studios, but it soon dawned on me that these were proper deliverymen: the brown coats they were wearing had the word "Harrods" inscribed on the back. The object being delivered was, in fact, a bed.

Jaws dropping, we all watched as it was brought into the studio and carefully positioned by the stairs, across from the tea-and-toast setup. More brown coats appeared with sheets and pillows and somberly made the bed up. Then, without saying a word, Yoko climbed in, carefully arranging the covers around her.

I'd spent nearly seven years of my life in recording studios, and I thought I'd seen it all . . . but this took the cake. George Martin, John Kurlander, Phil, and I exchanged wary looks; out of the corner of my eye I could see that Paul, Ringo, and George Harrison were as gobsmacked as we were. Lennon walked over to the bed.

"Are you okay?" he asked solicitously.

Yoko mumbled an affirmative. Lennon turned to us.

"Can you put a microphone up over here so we can hear her on the headphones?" he asked. Dumbfounded, I nodded to John Kurlander and he began setting up a boom stand, suspending the microphone above the supine Mrs. Lennon's face.

For the next several weeks, Yoko lived in that bed. Her wardrobe consisted of a series of flimsy nightgowns, accessorized with a regal tiara, carefully positioned to hide the scar on her forehead from the accident. As she gained her strength, so too did she gain her confidence, slowly but surely starting to annoy the other Beatles and George Martin with her comments. She spoke in a really tiny voice, and she always referred to the Beatles in a peculiar, impersonal third-party way: "Beatles will do this, Beatles will do that," never failing to leave off the "The." That used to really irritate Paul. On occasion, he'd even try correcting her: "Actually, it's *the* Beatles, luv," but she persistently ignored him.

It wasn't as if Yoko was just lying in that bed resting quietly, either—there was a long line of visitors there by her bedside paying supplication, almost all the time. Various Beatles would be recording in one end of the room, and she would be lying there at the other end, chatting with friends, making her presence all the more obvious—and aggravating—to the rest of the band. George Martin had returned on the premise that it was going to be like the good old days, but we had never had a Beatle wife in bed in the studio with us in the old days. That probably explained why he seemed so depressed and frustrated during those weeks.

There was a distinct change in the atmosphere after John and Yoko arrived, although personally I felt it had more to do with Lennon being there than his bedridden wife. He was grouchy and moody, and he flatly refused to participate at all in the making of "Maxwell's Silver Hammer," which he derisively dismissed as "just more of Paul's granny music." The day after John arrived, the group were recording the backing vocals for the song, with both George Harrison and Ringo joining Paul at the mic as an impassive John simply sat in the back of the studio and watched them. After a few uncomfortable moments, Paul strode over and invited his old friend and collaborator to join in. I thought it was a nice gesture, an olive branch. But an expressionless Lennon simply said no, I don't think so. A few minutes later, he and Yoko got up and went home. With nothing to contribute, John just didn't want to be there.

During the first few days they were back, John and Yoko spent most of their time huddled in a corner whispering to each other, or they would go down the hall to the producer's office—the "green room"—and make phone calls. It didn't come as a huge surprise to me; I just took it as par for the course. At one point George Martin said to me, "I wish John would get more involved," but to my knowledge he never did or said anything to try to get the recalcitrant Beatle to participate more. John was definitely very odd by this point, and his involvement in all the *Abbey Road* sessions would be sporadic. For the most part, if we weren't working on one of his songs, he just didn't seem interested.

One of the new faces at the *Abbey Road* sessions was Paul's recent bride, Linda. She'd occasionally stop by the studio for an hour or two and take some photographs, but she was careful to never wear out her welcome. On occasion, she'd sit by Paul's side at the piano, but that would only happen if he was working on his own, and not if any of the others were there; Paul clearly disapproved of Yoko being in the studio, and he didn't want to seem like a hypocrite.

All the other Beatles—even John—had a cordial relationship with Linda, but I never saw her reach out and try to start a conversation with Yoko beyond saying hello or good-bye; clearly there was some tension between the two Beatle wives. If Paul and Linda were in the control room and they saw John and Yoko start heading up that way, they would leave, deliberately taking the outside stairs so they wouldn't even have to pass one another on the steps. The two couples definitely were drawing a line in the sand, and they seemed to be going out of their way to avoid a confrontation.

Linda was amiable, outgoing, and friendly, and I took an immediate liking to her. Like Paul, she was naturally diplomatic: if there was any kind of problem going on down in the studio, she'd just say, "Oh, I think it's time for me to go," and that would be the last we'd see of her for a while. Linda and I were to develop a strong friendship over the years to come. She was someone I always respected, and whose company I always enjoyed.

While John and Yoko slowly recuperated and returned to full strength, the other Beatles got on with finishing up songs they had begun back in the spring: George Harrison's lush ballad "Something"; Ringo's "Octopus' Garden," his first composition since the *White Album*'s dismal "Don't Pass Me By"; and Paul's rocker "Oh Darling." Work also continued on "Here Comes The Sun," a Harrison song that, for once, was brimming with optimism.

A lot of time and effort went into "Something," which was very unusual for a Harrison song, but everyone seemed aware of just how good a song it was, even though nobody went out of his way to say so. That's just the way the Beatles were: compliments were few and far between—you could always tell more about the way they were thinking by the expressions on their faces. In the end, it became Harrison's most famous and popular composition, and it marked the first time a song of his was featured on a Beatles A-side, selling millions and earning the respect of singers like Frank Sinatra . . . although for years Sinatra was convinced that Lennon and McCartney had written it.

George was clearly still holding a grudge against Paul, and it seemed that he got some degree of revenge during the recording of "Something." I couldn't help but notice that Harrison was actually giving Paul direction on how to play the bass, telling him repeatedly that he wanted the part greatly simplified. It was a first in all my years of working with the Beatles: George had never dared tell Paul what to do; he'd simply never asserted himself that way. But for all that, George was once again very nervous when it came time to do the vocal. No matter what we did to create a vibe—turning the lights down low, lighting incense—he just couldn't get comfortable. It was a difficult song to sing, but in the end he did a magnificent job, and he turned in a remarkably good guitar solo, too. It was interesting: George never seemed to get cold feet doing backing vocals, but whenever he had to do a lead vocal, he'd lose his confidence.

Just as he had done back in the *Revolver* days when he introduced Indian instruments to Beatles records, George was responsible for some of the more unique sonic textures on *Abbey Road*. Many of them came from his newest toy: a massive Moog synthesizer. It was a foreboding black object the size of a bookcase, littered with dozens of knobs, switches, and patch cords. Mal grunted and sweated as he dragged the thing in, packed up in eight huge boxes. The Moog people had given a demo at EMI some months prior, so I wasn't altogether unfamiliar with the device, but it took forever to set up and get just a single sound out of it. Harrison sure loved twiddling those knobs. I have no idea if he knew what he was doing, but he certainly enjoyed playing with it.

The other new tonality George brought to the album was slide guitar, which he frequently asked to have patched through a rotating Leslie speaker; it became his signature sound on *Abbey Road* and on many of his subsequent solo albums. It seemed to me that Harrison's progress as a musician was more linear than that of the other Beatles. He wasn't an especially good player at the beginning of their recording career, but he kept getting better and better until in the end he was quite a formidable guitarist. The fact that he went off on an Indian tangent, getting familiar with music that contains so many different polyrhythms (and so many more notes than are used in Western music), had to have helped his playing, which no longer was European- or American-influenced. For all intents and purposes, his approach to guitar became Eastern, which gave him a distinct sound that characterized many late-period Beatles recordings.

Despite the fact that John was still moping around, saying little and contributing next to nothing, we had great fun doing overdubs on "Octopus' Garden." Paul and George were both in high spirits on the days we were working on it, and together they chipped in, putting as much effort into it as if it were one of their own songs. For once, Ringo sang the lead vocal with confidence, and he even got the inspiration—recycled from "Yellow Submarine"—to blow bubbles into a close-miked glass of water. As the songwriter, Ringo acted as the de facto producer for the track, and in one of our rare conversations, he asked me if I could make the vocals in the middle section sound as if they were being sung underwater. It was one of the few times during the *Abbey Road* sessions that I was challenged to come up with a new kind of sound, and I jumped at the opportunity. After some experimentation, I discovered that feeding the vocals into a compressor and triggering it from a pulsing tone (which I derived from George Harrison's Moog synthesizer) imparted a distinctive wobbly sound, almost like gargling. It was weird, almost like something out of a cheesy science-fiction movie, but Ringo loved the result.

It was at around this time that Paul started getting in the habit of coming in early every afternoon, before the others arrived, to have a go at singing the lead vocal to "Oh Darling." Not only did he have me record it with fifties-style tape echo, he even monitored the backing track over speakers instead of headphones because he wanted to feel as though he were singing to a live audience. Every day we'd be treated to a hell of a performance as McCartney put his all into singing the song all the way through once and once only, nearly ripping his vocal cords to shreds in the process.

George Martin would frequently announce triumphantly, "That's it; that's the one," but Paul would overrule him, saying, "No, it's not there yet; let's try it again tomorrow." For all that—and he took many whacks at the song, over many days—I never sensed any real frustration in Paul, even though he was obviously having trouble getting the vocal the way he wanted it in his head. He knew what the ultimate goal was, and he knew that he was going to get it eventually. Besides, ever the consummate showman, he simply enjoyed singing it.

Frankly, I think the reason Paul did those vocals each day before the other Beatles arrived was so he wouldn't have to face their disapproval or withering remarks—he wouldn't even play them each day's attempt to solicit their opinion. Perhaps he had learned his lesson from "Ob-La-Di, Ob-La-Da," when he had sung the vocal over and over again in front of everybody, pissing his bandmates off mightily in the process.

There was one other factor, and that was pride. Paul's ego prevented him from ever giving John a stab at singing the lead on "Oh Darling," despite the fact that it was a song that was probably better suited to Lennon's voice. Even though John was standing by in the studio, apparently ready, willing, and able—in later years, he admitted publicly that he would have loved to have sung that lead—Paul was determined to give a Lennon performance all by himself. To a great degree he succeeded . . . but what a shame it was that, by the time the Beatles got to record the song, they were unwilling to ask one another for help. Such was the vibe of the *Abbey Road* sessions.

"Okay, lads, I'm ready. Time to let yer hair down and do some rock 'n' roll."

It was nearly three weeks into July, and two weeks after the prodigal son had returned to the studio when we finally heard those words from a fully recovered John Lennon. He was about to run the Beatles through a new song—the second of his to be recorded for *Abbey Road* (they'd done some work on "I Want You (She's So Heavy)" before the summer sessions had commenced)—and we all waited with bated breath to see what he'd come up with. "Come Together" may not have been a masterpiece, but it was a catchy, hooky tune, and even though it clearly owed a lot to Chuck Berry, its abstract, somewhat risqué lyric had that distinctive Lennon stamp. The first time he played it for us, chugging away on his acoustic guitar, it was a lot faster than the final version that made it to the album. It was Paul who suggested it be done at a slower tempo, with a "swampy" kind of sound, and

Lennon went along with it uncomplainingly; he always took well to constructive criticism.

John was in a pretty good mood that day, too—he seemed to come to life when we were working on one of his own songs, rather than one of Paul's or George's. True, all three of them exhibited a lack of patience if it wasn't their song—there was always a definite drop-off in interest whenever any one of them was working on another Beatle's composition—but John was consistently the most flagrant offender.

Despite Lennon's improved frame of mind, there were clearly still underlying tensions and old wounds that hadn't healed. The band kept breaking into long, pointless jam sessions, as they had done frequently during the *White Album* sessions, and I could see that John was treating Paul in an offhand manner, despite the fact that Paul came up with the electric piano lick and swooping bass line that pretty well define "Come Together." John even made a point of playing the piano line, once he'd looked over Paul's shoulder and learned the part. That would have never happened in the old days: both men knew that Paul was the better piano player, and he normally would be manning the keyboards even if they were recording a Lennon song.

John not only sang the lead, but also did all the backing vocals on "Come Together" by himself. He didn't ask either Paul or George to join in, and neither of them volunteered. Harrison didn't seem to care one way or the other, but I could see that it was getting to Paul. Finally, in some frustration, he blurted out, "What do you want me to do on this track, John?"

John's reply was a diffident "Don't worry, I'll do the overdubs on this."

Paul looked a bit hurt, then angry. For a moment I thought there was going to be an explosion. Instead, he contained himself, shrugged his shoulders, and simply walked out of the studio—one of the few times he ever left a session early. Paul had to have felt humiliated, but rather than having a fight or an argument about it, he chose to just get up and leave, without any dramatics. The next day, he returned, and nothing further was ever said about it.

We happened to be working on "Come Together" just as *Apollo 11* was about to land on the moon, and I raced home late that night after the session ended so I could watch Neil Armstrong's historic first step on my newly acquired color TV. To my disappointment, the broadcast from the moon was in black and white.

The studio chatter the next day was not just about the moon landing, though. Abbey Road's technical staff had been tinkering for some time with a new system they called "compansion," which was meant to be their answer to Dolby noise reduction. It had recently gotten its first trial at an orchestral session in Studio One, but it had been an abject failure. In fact, it caught on fire just as the conductor's baton came down, filling the control room with smoke and sending the staff running out the door. I cried with laughter as the story was related to me—yet another grand EMI experiment gone awry.

George Martin would walk into the control room every day with several newspapers and a great big bar of Cadbury's chocolate for the three of us. Food was always very proprietary among the Beatles. Mal would get everybody his own thing, and there was no sharing, no eating family-style; no one was allowed to try anyone else's food. That principle applied to us, too—we knew never to help ourselves to any snacks they had laid out in the studio. But in their minds, the reverse was not true: anything they found in the control room was fair game as far as the Beatles were concerned. So whenever they'd head upstairs for a playback, George Martin would snatch the Cadbury's chocolate bar off the console and hide it underneath.

One afternoon we were working through lunch, as usual, and John Kurlander was sitting at the back of the control room, holding a bag of crisps (potato chips) in one hand and rewinding the tape with the other. He was still fairly new to Beatles sessions and so he kept munching away even as the Beatles began walking up the stairs toward us. But George Martin knew that they'd grab any food in sight, so just as the door was about to open, he yelled, at the top of his lungs, "Quick, hide the crisps!" Kurlander was so surprised, he nearly jumped to the ceiling . . . but he managed to instinctively pull the bag away just as Lennon started to grab at it.

That odd attitude toward food actually triggered one of the strangest altercations I was to witness during the otherwise generally placid *Abbey Road* sessions. We were working on the backing track to "The End"—the song designed to conclude the album's long medley—when the four Beatles trooped upstairs to listen to some playbacks. Yoko stayed behind, stretched out languorously in the bed, wearing the usual flimsy nightgown and tiara.

As we were listening, I noticed that something down in the studio had caught George Harrison's attention. After a moment or two he began staring bug-eyed out the control room window. Curious, I looked over his shoulder. Yoko had gotten out of bed and was slowly padding across the studio floor, finally coming to a stop at Harrison's Leslie cabinet, which had a packet of McVitie's Digestive Biscuits on top. Idly, she began opening the packet and delicately removed a single biscuit. Just as the morsel reached her mouth, Harrison could contain himself no longer.

"THAT BITCH!!!"

Everyone looked aghast, but we all knew exactly who he was talking about.

"She's just taken one of my biscuits!" Harrison explained. He wasn't the least bit sheepish, either. As far as he was concerned, those biscuits were his property, and no one was allowed to go near them. Lennon began shouting back at him, but there was little he could say to defend his wife (who, oblivious, was happily munching away in the studio), because he shared exactly the same attitude toward food.

Actually, I think the argument was not so much about the biscuits, but about the bed, which they had all come to deeply resent. What Harrison was really saying was "If Yoko is well enough to get out of bed and steal one of my biscuits, she doesn't need to be in the bloody bed in the first place." It almost didn't matter what the argument was about. By this stage, whenever the four of them were together it was like a tinderbox, and anything could set them off . . . even something as dumb as a digestive biscuit.

But the tempest in a teapot (or should I say biscuit packet?) blew over quickly enough, and everyone returned to the business at hand. Paul was trying to talk a very reluctant Ringo into doing a drum solo toward the end of the long medley.

"You know how much I hate solos!" Ringo kept saying, same as he did when we were working on "A Day In The Life."

"Well, just do a *token* solo then," Paul said half jokingly.

Ringo looked to Lennon and Harrison for support, but, for once, they were siding with Paul. Eventually Ringo capitulated and performed the only drum solo—if you discount his little fills at the end of the 1963 B-side "Thank You Girl"—ever to appear on a Beatles record.

Even after extensive coaching from Paul, Ringo still wasn't sure what he was going to play, and I could see that he wasn't the least bit confident that he could pull it off, either. We had to do a lot of takes, and each take was quite different. The final solo he played was actually considerably longer than what eventually made it onto the album—with input from Paul and George Martin, I edited it down significantly, using only the best bits.

One of the benefits of working in eight-track was that we were able to record Ringo's solo in stereo, spread over two tracks, allowing the listener to hear different tom-toms and cymbals in each speaker. That was very unusual for a Beatles song: drums were almost always recorded in mono, even after we made the move to eight-track. The new mixing console also provided many more inputs than the old one, so I was able to put a dozen or so mics on Ringo's kit, as opposed to the three or four that I had used previously.

Having more mics gave me finer control over shaping the sound, though it also provided the potential for more technical problems (such as signals canceling each other out), so I had to be extremely careful about mic positioning and creating the proper balance. I would often wander into the studio and literally put my ear in different places, listening to the difference in sound if I were a quarter inch versus a full inch away from the drumskin, or the way the tonality of a cymbal changed if you listened to the edge of it instead of the top. For me, that was always the key to mic positioning: doing lots of listening out in the studio.

Working in eight-track also gave us the luxury of occasionally removing the cymbals from Ringo's kit altogether so that he could overdub crashes later. That was because having to play them in real time would sometimes affect his timing—by the time Ringo hit the cymbal, he'd be late getting back to the drum.

That night, just before leaving, Paul sat down at the piano and started playing a new song. He explained that it wasn't one he wanted to do for the album. Instead, he planned on giving the song to a new group that Apple had recently signed, a band called Badfinger. It was quite late and Paul was tired, so he asked me to set up all the sounds for him so that he could come in fresh first thing the next morning and record it straightaway. I knew that I'd be a little late coming in the next day because I had a meeting scheduled at Apple, so Phil ended up doing the actual recording. The song turned out to be the million-seller "Come And Get It," and Phil told me afterward that Paul knocked off the demo in under an hour, while John and Yoko sat quietly in the control room, offering no input or assistance.

But by the time I arrived, an agitated John was deeply involved indeed. More specifically, he was having a row with Paul and George Martin.

"We've already done the concept album," he argued, presumably referring to *Pepper.* "Why do we need to do another one?"

"Look, John, we're just trying to think symphonically," George replied. "We're trying to create a complete work out of song fragments."

John was derisive at first, saying, "You're taking yourselves too seriously," but when Paul invited him to contribute some compositions of his own to the medley, he seemed to capitulate.

"Well, I might have one or two that could fit," he said sheepishly.

I exchanged glances with Paul. I'm sure we were both thinking the same thing: *He's just been waiting to be asked.*

A few days later we recorded the backing tracks to Lennon's "Here Comes The Sun King" and "Mean Mr. Mustard," both recorded together in a single pass. There is a slight gap between the two songs, so they could have easily been recorded separately, but knowing in advance that they would be sequenced in that order, John made the decision to play through both of them in one go, which made it a little more of a challenge to the band's musicianship. But they pulled it off—it really was a group effort, and all four Beatles played with energy and enthusiasm, each making his own unique contribution to the sound and arrangement. Even Ringo came up with a strong idea, draping his tom-toms with heavy tea towels and playing them with timpani beaters in order to give John the "jungle drum" sound he was after.

John was actually in a pretty good mood throughout the entire session. I could see that he was a bit looser, a little more recovered from his injuries, and a lot less worried about Yoko, who was no longer lying in the bed, though it remained, unmade, in a corner of the studio, a mute reminder of the weirdness we'd had to deal with over the past weeks.

The vibe was so good that, this time around, Paul was invited by John to participate in both songs, which seemed to lift his spirits greatly. They even disappeared behind the screens at one point for a puff on a joint, just the two of them, and when they came out they had a fit of giggles as they sang the pseudo-Spanish gibberish at the end of "Here Comes The Sun King"; in fact, they found it impossible to get through a take without dissolving into laughter.

Things weren't quite so pleasant when we returned the following week to tackle John's "Polythene Pam," which ran into Paul's "She Came In Through The Bathroom Window," again recorded together, one into the next. John was unhappy with Ringo's drumming, commenting acidly at one point that it "sounded like Dave Clark," which was clearly not meant as a compliment. He was so impatient at Ringo's inability to come up with a suitable part that he finally said, "Sod it, let's just put one down anyway."

But Ringo was upset that John was unhappy with his drumming, and he spent a good deal of time working on it with Paul even after the backing track was done. Finally, he said to John, "Why don't we just record the backing track again? I think I've got a part you'll like now," but Lennon waved him off.

"I'm not playing the bloody song again, Ring. If you want to redo the drums, go ahead and overdub them."

That night, Ringo did just that. Fortunately we were working in eight-track, so I was able to record the new drum track without erasing the old one. It took many hours to do, but Ringo eventually pulled it off, managing to play the new drum part from start to finish without losing the beat . . . and those were the days before we had click tracks, so his only reference was the original drum track, which we fed to him through headphones.

For all of the kerfuffle, they were fun tracks to record, and the ensemble playing was superb. Sitting up in the Studio Two control room, I commented to George Martin that it sounded like old-style Beatles, like the four of them playing together as a band circa 1963. "You're right," George said sardonically. "You'd never guess that the four of them actually can't stand each other."

The next night, Paul overdubbed his bass on "Polythene Pam," and at one point he overshot the note on one of his glissandos. Instinctively, he said, "Oops, let me drop that in and fix it," but we all spontaneously overruled him, saying, "No, it's great! Leave it in"—even George Martin got into the spirit of things. When someone made a mistake like that and the others liked it, we'd often actually make it louder when we'd mix the song so as to accentuate it. Sometimes we'd even double-track the mistake with different instruments so it would be even more obvious. It was all about playing a joke on the fans, giving them a treat, something to talk about. That's what we did on "Polythene Pam": Paul's overshoot actually became a feature.

The medley was now nearly complete, and it was decided to do a test edit to see how all the various components fit together. That session was a long one—for the first time since the *White Album* days, we worked late into the night—but everyone was really upbeat and quite pleased with the results. There was only one little bit of contention, and it had to do with the cross-fade between "You Never Give Me Your Money" and "Here Comes The Sun King." John didn't like the idea of there being such a long gap between the two songs, but Paul felt strongly that the mood needed to be set for the listener before "Sun King" started. In the end, Paul got his way—John merely shrugged his shoulders and feigned disinterest. At first, a single held organ note was used for the crossfade. Later on, when it came time to sequence the finished mixes, Paul arrived with a plastic bag of tape loops (just as he had done when we worked on "Tomorrow Never Knows" years before) and we used several of them—including recordings of crickets and bells—instead.

At around midnight, while we were busy working, we had an unexpected visitor—a London bobby. The local constabulary would regularly patrol the area around the studio because of the constant fan presence, and the EMI security guards had gotten quite friendly with them. Occasionally, if there was a lull and we were down in Studio Two with the Beatles, we'd look up into the empty control room and see that John Skinner had brought one of the policemen by to have a look. We'd occasionally get a bit worried if joints were being passed around, but they were really just interested in getting a cup of tea and catching a glimpse of some famous pop stars. But on this night, the policeman happened to pop in on his own, unannounced, and I could see that it threw quite a scare into John, who'd already been the victim of a drug bust. He was trying to contain his nerves, but after the bobby left, Lennon gave Mal a right bollocking: "It's your job to keep people out of here!" he shouted at the hapless roadie.

That same night, the fate of Paul's little snippet entitled "Her Majesty" (which he had recorded with Phil at the start of the *Abbey Road* sessions) was settled. Originally, it was placed between the songs "Mean Mr. Mustard" and "Polythene Pam," but Paul didn't like it there and told John Kurlander to edit it out. John's editing skills weren't quite up to snuff at that point, and he accidentally cut it one beat too early, on the last crashing note of "Mustard." He was about to correct the problem when a tired Paul said, "Never mind, it's only a rough mix."

Kurlander knew that EMI had strict rules about ever throwing anything away, so he did the proper thing—he kept the mix of "Her Majesty" and stuck it onto the end of the test edit, after about twenty seconds of red leader tape. Red leader tape is used by engineers to mark the end of a song, but when Malcolm Davies cut the test lacquers at Apple the next day, he either missed seeing the leader tape fly by, or decided to include the song anyway, because he wasn't sure of our intent. Paul loved it! When it came time to sequence the final album, he insisted that we do it the same exact way, having "Her Majesty" close the side after a twenty-second gap—similar to the bonus "hidden" cuts that are sometimes included on today's CDs. The only thing Paul had us do was cut the very last note off. I guess he figured that since "Her Majesty" was starting with the last note of "Mean Mr. Mustard," she might as well not have a last note of her own.

George Martin had been lured back with the same promise that Paul had made to me: "We'll do it like in the old days." It was a nice thought, to be sure, but things didn't quite work out that way. For starters, there was Yoko and the bed. Then there was the newfound confidence that had developed in all of them—even George Harrison and Ringo—and their years of experience making records, all of which meant that George Martin still had to take a backseat . . . most of the time.

One of the exceptions was John's beautiful song "Because." Everyone agreed that the song was begging for big, lush harmonies—just the kind of thing that was George Martin's forte. Delighted to be contributing at last, he spent many long hours with John, Paul, and George Harrison gathered around the piano while he worked out their complex parts note by note.

First, though, a backing track had to be recorded, and George Martin was heavily involved in that as well. John had written the song on guitar, gently picking individual notes rather than playing chords, but he felt that something more was needed.

"Why don't I double your line exactly on harpsichord?" George suggested, and Lennon quickly agreed. "Yeah, great, that will help make it a little more classical-like, too."

I was never quite sure what he meant by that last remark until years later, when John revealed in an interview that he had based the song's accompaniment loosely on the languid arpeggios of Beethoven's *Moonlight* Sonata.

So George Martin headed down into the studio, along with John and Ringo, while Paul and George Harrison stayed up in the control room. Ringo's job was to act as a timekeeper, a human click track; he was merely to tap out a steady tempo on hi-hat, for reference purposes only. Hunched over their instruments, deep in concentration, they labored for a long time on that backing track. It wasn't really their fault: Paul, who was acting as surrogate producer, was pushing them too hard that night, having them do take after take, playing way past their peak. When the exhausted trio finally came up to the control room to have a listen, they realized that they had laid down a perfectly good take an hour before. John didn't say anything, but he shot an embarrassed Paul a dirty look. Fortunately, they seemed too tired to make an issue out of it.

The following Monday everyone returned to the studio fresh and rejuvenated from a weekend off, ready to tackle the vocals. The only problem was that George Martin had worked out nine harmony parts for the Beatles to sing, but we only had five tracks to record them on. That was resolved easily enough when it was decided to have John, Paul, and George Harrison sing their three-part harmony together live, instead of overdubbing each part one at a time, and then have them do two additional passes in order to add on the remaining six parts. It was as much an aesthetic as it was a technical de-cision, because their voices had always meshed so well naturally.

It was mid-afternoon, but the lights in Studio Two were dimmed way down low for atmosphere. The four Beatles—Ringo was there, too, provid-ing moral support—were gathered in a semicircle, the sparse backing track playing softly in their headphones. To start with, everyone was standing up, but it quickly became apparent that this was going to be a time-consuming process, so they were soon sitting, on regulation EMI hard-back chairs, not stools. To get the phrasing spot-on, Paul was making hand gestures, con-ducting the others. It would take more than five hours to get those vocals done, and though John's patience was sorely tried that afternoon, no one gave up. Perfection was the goal, and nobody was prepared to accept any-thing less.

George Martin took his place next to me in the control room, listening intently. Yoko was up there with us, too, but she never said a word the entire afternoon. John, Paul, and George Harrison each had his own mic, but they were all being recorded on a single track, so I was focused on doing the bal-ance. To keep the purity of the sound, I had decided to use no signal pro-cessing whatsoever—no compressors or limiters. That meant that I had to manually "pot" the sound to smooth out the peaks and valleys—moving the faders up and down as it was being recorded—carefully following the dy-namics of each word, each syllable. Fortunately, I'd had plenty of time to learn those moves during the long hours of vocal rehearsals.

The three Beatles sang "Because" over and over and over again that after-noon; they probably did each pass twenty or thirty times. Pitching was not a problem—they rarely sang out of tune, and they were good at remembering their parts—but it wasn't easy to get the phrasing precise, starting and end-ing each word at exactly the same time. Even John was unusually patient that day, though he rebuked Paul once or twice, at one point snapping, "Jesus Christ, give me a break already . . . I wish I hadn't written the bloody thing!"

But John kept at it, as did George Harrison, who, to my surprise, never uttered a word of complaint. They knew they were doing something special and they were determined to get it right. There was no clowning around that day, no joking; everyone was very serious, very focused. Their goal was to be able to sing each pass all the way through from start to finish—it was almost a matter of pride—but everyone was starting to get so weary, we ended up having to do a few drop-ins. Actually, we couldn't do too many even if we wanted to, because the breaths between phrases would make any drop-ins apparent. That day I saw the four Beatles at their finest: there was one hundred percent concentration from all of them—even Ringo, sitting quietly with his eyes closed, silently urging his bandmates on to their best performance—all working in tandem to get that vocal nailed, spot on. It was a stark example of the kind of teamwork that had been so sorely lacking for years. It's tempting to imagine what the Beatles might have been able to accomplish if they could only have captured and sustained that spirit just a little longer.

I was so enamored of the sonic results of not using compressors or limiters that I even decided to mix the entire track without them. That was a first for any record I'd ever made; in fact, it was quite probably a first for *any* major pop recording done since the cumbersome devices were introduced in the early fifties. Yet every word, every syllable is crystal clear on the final mix, due to the time and effort we all expended on getting the song recorded right in the first place.

The next couple of days were spent doing overdubs and putting finishing touches on a number of songs. The focus quickly shifted to the song entitled "The End," which we assumed was going to be the album closer, so it was quite important. There were quite a few empty bars to fill after Ringo's drum solo—Paul had left them bare in a spirit of "we'll think of something eventually," just as we had done with the middle section of "A Day In The Life"— and there was a long discussion about what to add on top to flesh it out.

"Well, a guitar solo is the obvious thing," said George Harrison.

"Yes, but this time you should let *me* play it," said John jokingly. He loved playing lead guitar—he'd often mess about doing lead parts during rehearsals—but he knew that he didn't have the finesse of either George or Paul, so he rarely did so on record. Everyone laughed, including John, but we could see that he was at least half-serious.

"I know!" he said mischievously, unwilling to let it go. "Why don't we *all* play the solo? We can take turns and trade licks." Long guitar solos with dueling lead guitarists were becoming the vogue at the time, so it was a suggestion that clearly had merit.

George looked dubious, but Paul not only embraced the idea but upped the ante further still: "Better yet," he said, "why don't all three of us play it live?"

Lennon loved the idea—for the first time in weeks I saw a real gleam in his eye. It didn't take long for John's enthusiasm to rub off on George Harrison, who finally got into the spirit of things.

Mal was immediately sent out into the studio to set up the guitar amps, while the three Beatles stayed in the control room, listening to the backing track and thinking about what they were going to play. Paul announced that he wanted to take the first solo, and since it was his song, the others deferred. Ever competitive, John said that he had a great idea for an ending, so he was going to go last. As always, poor George Harrison was overshadowed by his two bandmates and got the middle spot by default.

Yoko, as usual, was sitting by John's side in the control room while they were having this discussion, but as Lennon got up to walk out into the studio, he turned to her and said gently, "Wait here, luv; I won't be a minute." She looked a little shocked and hurt, but she did as John asked, sitting quietly by the control room window for the remainder of the session. It was almost as if he knew that she would put a damper on things and spoil the atmosphere if she were in the studio with them. Something inside told John that to get this to work, he needed to be doing it with just Paul and George, that it would be better for Yoko not to be by his side this one time.

Maybe that was the reason, or perhaps it was because on some subconscious level they had decided to suspend their egos for the sake of the music, but for the hour or so that it took them to play those solos, all the bad blood, all the fighting, all the crap that had gone down between the three former friends was forgotten. John, Paul, and George looked like they had gone back in time, like they were kids again, playing together for the sheer enjoyment of it. More than anything, they reminded me of gunslingers, with their guitars strapped on, looks of steely-eyed resolve, determined to outdo one another. Yet there was no animosity, no tension at all—you could tell that they were simply having fun.

While they were practicing, I took great care to craft a different, distinctive sound for each Beatle, so it would be apparent to the listener that it was three individuals playing and not one just person taking an extended solo. They were each playing a different model guitar through a different type of amplifier, so it wasn't all that difficult to achieve. I had Mal line the three amps up in a row—there was no need for a great deal of separation because they were all going to be recorded on a single track. Because there was little overlap between each two-bar solo, I knew that I could balance the levels afterward simply by moving one fader.

Incredibly, after just a brief period of rehearsal, they nailed it in a single take. When it was over, there was no backslapping or hugging—the Beatles rarely expressed themselves physically like that—but there were lots of broad grins. It was a heartwarming moment—one of the rare times I could say that in recent months—and I made a point of congratulating each of them when they came into the control room to have a listen. I was so blown away by Harrison's playing in particular that I made a point of saying "That was really brilliant" as he walked through the door. George looked a bit surprised, but he gave me a nod and a gracious thank-you. It was one of the few times when I felt like I had connected on a personal level with him.

I guess there's also the possibility that, as they were performing the solo, they realized they might never get to play together again; perhaps they were viewing that moment as a poignant farewell. It was the first time in a long time that the three of them were actually playing together in the studio; for most of the *Abbey Road* sessions, it was just one or two of them, plus, sometimes, Ringo. In addition, they knew that this track would be closing the album; it seemed to have been already decided that "The Big One," as we were calling the medley, would comprise side two of the album, in contrast to side one, which would contain individual songs, opening and closing with Lennon compositions.

For me, that session was undoubtedly the high point of the summer of 1969, and listening to those guitar solos still never fails to bring a smile to my face. If the good feelings engendered by that one day had only been present throughout the entire project, there's no telling how great *Abbey Road* might have been.

· 14 ·

And in the End:

The Final Stroll Across Abbey Road

For several weeks, the four Beatles had been engaged in animated discussion about what to call the new album. There had been lots of suggestions—*Four In The Bar* and *All Good Children Go to Heaven* among them—but the name that seemed to have the most support was *Everest,* in honor of the brand of cigarette I was smoking at the time. It was a name that also conjured up an image of climbing the highest mountain. Perhaps in their minds that served as a metaphor for the difficult task they were undertaking—recording one last album together. The name also lent itself to a compelling visual image: the four Beatles posing in front of—or even on top of—the magnificent peak.

The idea was bantered around for a couple of weeks, with Paul getting increasingly excited about making a trip to Tibet, and Ringo growing increasingly unhappy; John and George Harrison seemed to blow hot and cold. The Beatles' drummer suffered from a chronically finicky digestive system, and so he never enjoyed travel; he probably didn't fancy the prospect of having to pack another suitcase full of tinned baked beans, as he had done when they had gone to India.

As the deadline for printing up the album sleeve drew near, John and George Harrison began to balk at the idea, too, taking Ringo's side. They just couldn't see having to make such a long journey for the sake of a photo shoot.

"Well, if we're not going to name it *Everest* and pose for the cover in Tibet, where are we going to go?" a frustrated Paul asked one afternoon.

John and George Harrison looked flummoxed. Finally, Ringo chirped in.

"Fuck it; let's just step outside and name it *Abbey Road,*" he joked.

And that, believe it or not, is how the album got its name. It had nothing to do with how much they loved the studio, despite what the Abbey Road executives have claimed for decades. In point of fact, they hated the place. It was simply because they were unwilling to travel any farther than they had to.

And so it was that on a blistering hot August morning, the day after completing "The End," the Beatles got dressed up—John in his white suit, George Harrison in denim, Paul barefoot—and stepped outside, walking back and forth across the Abbey Road zebra crossing a few times while a photographer snapped a couple of dozen photos. The police obligingly blocked off the traffic at both ends of the street for a few minutes so the band members didn't have to worry about getting hit by an oncoming car, and there were only a handful of fans present, because in recent years the Beatles had rarely made an appearance at the studio before mid-afternoon. As a result, the photo shoot went quickly, and everyone found himself with a few hours to kill before the session was due to start. George Harrison and Mal spent their free time at the nearby London Zoo, while Ringo went shopping; Paul invited John round to his house for a spot of tea and, one would hope, some friendly conversation.

Later that day, we continued the work at hand, with Paul and Ringo overdubbing guitar and tambourine on "Oh Darling" while George set up the Moog synthesizer at John's request and twiddled the knobs as the great behemoth spit out white noise, tacked onto the end of "I Want You (She's So Heavy)." We ended the session fairly early; there was a summer weekend ahead, and we all had plans. I was going fishing.

I had gotten into fishing when I was just a kid, and it's something I still love to do. I've always found it to be a great stress reliever—for me, one day's fishing is like a week's holiday. It's almost a Zen thing—you're just focusing on the float in the water, chasing the thoughts from your mind, and it's quite exciting when the float starts bobbing, because you don't know what's underneath there. I'd often spend Sundays fishing up in Alexandra Palace to unwind, and I'd even go during the week if a session was starting late.

One afternoon, I had gotten sunburned out on the lake, and when we got to the studio that evening Lennon was quite concerned. He went out of his way to tell me, "Oh, you've got to be careful of the sun. I know all about that because you've got the same fair skin as my aunt Mimi." He could be very solicitous that way . . . if he was in a good mood. I explained that I had gotten the burn while fishing, and all of a sudden he began peppering me with questions: What sort of bait do you use? How do you know when the fish are biting? What do you do when one of them is caught? Lennon always wanted to absorb everything around him, and he could get interested in almost any subject.

By the end of our brief conversation, he eagerly announced that he wanted to try it for himself. I told him that Malcolm Davies was a fisherman, too, and plans were made for us to all go out together one afternoon. Needless to say, it never transpired, and a week later John had forgotten about the whole thing, although a year or two later he did invite Malcolm and me up to Tittenhurst for a couple of days of fishing . . . but on a weekend he was going to be away. We took him up on the offer, and had a grand time, but we never actually saw John with a fishing rod in his hand. As with most things Lennon, the concept was more important than the execution.

The remainder of the week was a busy one, overdubbing and tidying up several tracks and starting the mixing process; the days of mono had long since passed, so only stereo mixes were done (that had been the case ever since the *White Album*). There were occasional tensions, but overall there was a good vibe, perhaps because everyone was seeing the light at the end of the tunnel.

So far, every instrument on *Abbey Road* had been played by one of the four Beatles—in contrast to *Sgt. Pepper*, *Magical Mystery Tour*, and the *White Album*—there had been no outside musicians involved at all. That was fine with John, but not with Paul or George Harrison, both of whom wanted orchestral instruments added to a few of their songs. Accordingly, George Martin wrote some arrangements and booked London's top players for a single marathon session. Unfortunately, EMI had still not installed an eight-track tape recorder or large-scale console into the Studio One control room, so we were forced to set up a complicated system of audio tie-lines and closed-circuit television that allowed the musicians to be seated in the larger Studio One while we recorded them in the control room of Studio Two.

The day was broken up into two parts: an afternoon session, overdubbing parts onto the "Golden Slumbers"/"Carry That Weight" and "The End" sections of the medley; and an evening session, when we'd be adding orchestra to George Harrison's "Here Comes The Sun" and "Something." Following the pattern that had been established for much of the album, the only Beatle at the afternoon session was Paul, and the only one at the evening session was George Harrison. Phil McDonald, however, was there with me for the entire day—working in two studios at once really complicated things, and we needed the extra pair of hands. George Martin did the conducting while each Beatle essentially produced his own session. Thankfully, there were no major technical mishaps and everything worked smoothly.

The only hitch came when George Harrison announced that he wanted to redo the guitar solo on "Something." We were perfectly willing to accommodate him, but the problem was that there was only one track available, and we needed to use that for the orchestra. The only solution was for him to play it live, right along with the orchestra, so we could record them simultaneously on the same track. I was enormously impressed when he nonchalantly said, "Okay, let's do that"—it took a lot of nerve and self-confidence to be willing to put himself under that kind of pressure. George had to play the solo correctly all the way through, without punch-ins, because the sound coming from his guitar amp would leak onto the other mics, and he wouldn't get a lot of whacks at it, because it was costing quite a lot to have that orchestra there. But he managed to play the intricate solo with ease, and by the end of the long night both his songs were completed and ready to be mixed.

The remainder of the week was spent doing final mixing and sequencing. Despite the presence of most of the Beatles most of the time, everything went uneventfully, until the day it came to tackling John's "I Want You (She's So Heavy)." Lennon was so enamored of the white noise that George Harrison had overdubbed from his Moog synthesizer that he actually had Ringo supplement it by spinning the wind machine secreted in the Studio Two percussion cupboard. As we sat in the control room mixing the track, he started becoming almost obsessed with the sound. "Louder! Louder!!" he kept imploring me. "I want the track to build and build and build," he explained, "and then I want the white noise to completely take over and blot out the music altogether."

I looked over at John as though he were crazy, but he paid me no mind. Over one shoulder I could see Yoko smiling a taut little smile, her tiny teeth gleaming in the light. Over the other, I could see a dejected Paul, sitting slumped over, head down, staring at the floor. He didn't say a word, but his body language made it clear that he was very unhappy, not only with the song itself, but with the idea that the music—Beatles music, which he considered almost sacred—was being obliterated with noise. In the past, he would have said something—perhaps just a diplomatic "Don't you think that's a bit too much, John?"—but now Paul seemed too beaten down to argue the point with a gleeful Lennon, who seemed to be taking an almost perverse pleasure at his bandmate's obvious discomfort.

To Paul, it must have been like "Revolution 9" all over again. John was deliberately distorting Beatles music, trying to turn the group into an avant-garde ensemble instead of a pop band. I looked around the room. Ringo and George Harrison seemed to be into what John was doing—they had their eyes closed and were swaying to the beat. It was just Paul looking miserable, staring down at the floor. His isolation from the others never seemed more apparent.

The white noise was a great effect, though the way that it just kept building and building rubbed me up the wrong way, both sonically and aesthetically. But it was John's song, and it was going to be done John's way, no matter what Paul or I—or anyone, for that matter—thought. Yet for all of his certainty about the concept, John remained indecisive until the last minute about which version of "I Want You" he even wanted me to mix—there were several backing tracks that had been recorded at Trident back in April, two of which had received overdubs. In the end, Lennon had me edit together two of them; the splice comes right after his last "She's so . . ." It was like working on "Strawberry Fields Forever" all over again, but this time around, thankfully, both takes were in the same key and at the same tempo.

And then there was the matter of how the song would end. When they recorded the backing track, the Beatles had just played on and on, with no definitive conclusion, so I assumed I would be doing a fadeout. John had other ideas, though. He let the tape play until just twenty seconds or so before the take broke down, and then all of a sudden he barked out an order: "Cut the tape here."

"Cut the tape?" I asked, astonished. We had never ended a song that way, and an abrupt ending like that didn't make any sense unless the track was going to run directly into another one. But that wasn't the case here, because it had already been decided that "I Want You" was to close side one of the album. My protestations had no impact on John: his decision was absolute.

"You heard what I said, Geoff; cut the tape."

I glanced over at George Martin, who simply shrugged his shoulders, so I got out the scissors and sliced the tape at precisely the point John indicated . . . and that's the way side one of *Abbey Road* ends. At the time, I thought he was out of his mind, but due to the shock factor it ended up being incredibly effective, a Lennon concept that really worked.

During the *Abbey Road* sessions, it never occurred to me that we were working on the last Beatles album. No one had said anything to that effect, and, frankly, the idea seemed inconceivable to me. Of course I realized that they were growing apart and arguing a lot, but they were also still making great music together . . . and they were clearly still a going commercial success. Even in our private conversations, the only thing George Martin would say was that he didn't feel they were giving a hundred percent, that it wasn't like the *Pepper* days, but that much was obvious. My sense was that they would take some time off and sort their differences out and that in another six months we'd be back doing another album. I had witnessed firsthand the nastiness that plagued the *White Album* sessions, and heard stories about the horror show that was *Let It Be*, yet they had come back to do more good work even after those awful experiences.

Perhaps I was just being a bit naive, or perhaps I simply didn't want to believe that it was over. But if I didn't have a clue, one was soon to be provided to me. During the last day or two of working on *Abbey Road*, all four Beatles were preoccupied with looking through the contact sheets of the cover photo shoot. Paul, ever the organizer, carefully marked the ones they liked the best and there were long discussions about which one to pick. Each band member had a different favorite, but they all seemed to want a shot of them walking *away* from the studio, not toward it. That's how much they had come to dislike being there.

All four Beatles were on hand for the final mix session for *Abbey Road*, and it turned out to be the last time all four of them would ever be in a recording studio together. Incredibly, the same unseen hand that propelled me toward a lifetime career as an audio engineer ensured that I was present for their first ever proper recording session . . . and for their last.

If, as George Harrison said, all things must pass, then *Abbey Road* was a pretty good way for the Beatles to take their final bow. Following a rocky start, with John first absent and then recuperating and moody—and notwithstanding the spectacle of a Beatle wife holding court in a bed installed in a corner of the studio—they found a way to turn it into a band effort . . . despite the fact that the four of them were rarely in the room together. (Lennon, in fact, doesn't appear at all on several of the album's tracks.) Yet the mood improved as the sessions wore on, and there were some good moments, moments where they managed to suspend the tensions and make music the priority once again. More important, they found a way, however fleetingly, to once again be four old friends.

Ever since John's virtual abdication during *Pepper*, Paul had gotten increasingly assertive in the studio, but, for the most part, he was on his best behavior during the *Abbey Road* sessions. Even though he was still constantly striving to achieve perfection, he wasn't being as patronizing as he had been in recent years. He was aware of the promise of a "better vibe" he had given me and to George Martin, and he did his best to honor it and contain his emotions, even if it meant walking on eggshells. On some level I'm convinced he knew that if he lost his cool in front of us, it was all over.

Everyone—even Lennon—was trying his best to keep the tinderbox from exploding, yet I felt that all that self-discipline took a lot of the edge off the music, too. *Abbey Road* is far mellower and more "organic"-sounding than any other Beatles album; it stands apart from their other recordings, with a totally different attitude. Nonetheless, it turned out to be one of their best-selling records, and it earned me my second Grammy for Best Engineered Album.

Perhaps the biggest problem we faced was the way the four band members had grown apart, both musically and personally. Paul was the only one of the four who seemed to care about being a Beatle anymore, which made him increasingly isolated from the others in the studio, just as he had withdrawn from taking an active role in Apple. Under Yoko's influence, John had already moved on to "conceptual" art, like his *Two Virgins* album and the solo work he was doing with the Plastic Ono Band. He was also, as I was later to learn, hooked on heroin during the time we were recording *Abbey Road*, which would account at least in part for his wild mood swings. (Typically, Lennon even wrote and released a song—"Cold Turkey"—about the experience.) Ringo just seemed tired and burned out from all the marathon sessions of the past two and a half years. Uncharacteristically, he lost his temper once or twice during the making of *Abbey Road* and even walked out for a couple of days, just as he had in the late stages of the *White Album*.

And then there was George Harrison, who didn't really find himself until *Abbey Road*. Not only had his guitar playing improved tremendously, but for the first time, he had come into the studio armed with songs that were every bit as good as John's and Paul's, and he knew it. With his increased confidence, he began asserting himself more, taking a distinct "I don't give a shit" attitude. At one point Paul was trying to make a suggestion about adding a part on "Here Comes The Sun" and Harrison interrupted him sharply, saying, "No, I think the song is fine as it is."

When Paul persisted, Harrison cut him off with a flat, "Look, I don't have to listen to you." That kind of exchange probably wouldn't have happened in the earlier days. It was clear that George was very much trying to stand on his own two feet, and no longer felt that he had to bother hiding his resentment at Paul's telling him what to do. In the past, he'd put up with it on

Paul's songs—in fact, he'd even put up with it when Paul tried to tell him what to play on his *own* songs—but those days were over. He simply wasn't about to let that happen anymore.

In short, the Beatles had become four individuals. Ever since *Pepper*, things were always so much better if they weren't all there at the same time. Paul might start a session off by doing a bass or guitar overdub on his own, and everything would be fine. Then the others would start arriving and the goodwill would slowly dissipate; as each Beatle would come in, their attitude would be "Okay, I'm here now, so let's do what *I* want to do." As opposed to the support and camaraderie that characterized early Beatles sessions, each would grow resentful if the spotlight wasn't actively shining on him. As a result, any little thing could set any of them off at any time. It was odd, though, how that rarely happened when there were two, or even three of them interacting; there was just some kind of bad chemistry when all four of them were in a room together.

By the time we were recording *Abbey Road,* they knew it, too, and they would coordinate their schedules so that the only times the four of them came into the studio would be on the days when they had to lay down a rhythm track, or when we were mixing. And when that happened, the wall between them and us would inevitably go up, and even George Martin became very much like part of the crew.

Abbey Road is chock-full of intricate harmonies and vocal arrangements that George Martin worked on assiduously, and he was responsible for the orchestral scoring and conducting. But possibly his greatest contribution to the sessions was that he acted as a buffer. By that point, John couldn't care less what George Martin thought, and neither could Harrison, but Paul was clearly trying hard not to let his longtime producer down, so he toned things down a notch and kept a lot of his thoughts to himself. If George Martin hadn't been there, the four Beatles probably would have gone at it hammer and tong. There weren't even any outside musicians there, like Billy Preston, who had sat in on much of *Let It Be,* to defuse the situation.

He may have still been officially in charge of Beatles sessions, but George Martin wasn't really in control any longer, and he hadn't been for some time. He'd never made a point of being down in the studio with them while they were recording; apart from the very first run-through, or when they were working out harmonies at the piano, he'd always be sitting with us in the control room. That was a good thing—they had to have some space—but it served to isolate him from them as well. When they'd come up into the control room for a listen—and, unlike most other artists, they always seemed to want to listen back to *every* take—Paul would be asking George Martin if a vocal was good or bad, but I couldn't help but notice that at the same time he'd be looking at me to see whether I gave a nod of approval or whether I was grimacing to show that I thought it wasn't up to snuff. John, on the other hand, never looked to me for nonverbal signs of approval or disapproval—if he wanted to know what I thought, he'd just come right out and ask me.

There was another key factor that made *Abbey Road* unique, and that was that, unlike previous Beatles albums, it was being created amid daily life. The group's attitude wasn't "Okay, I'm going to lock myself in a studio for seven weeks and I'll pay all my bills and deal with everything else when the project is done"—which is the way most recording artists do it. No, this time around, they were determined not to allow the album to interfere with their personal lives, or with Apple business, so the approach was "We'll do a few hours of recording, then we'll have a meeting with the plumber, then we'll do a vocal overdub."

As a result, there were lots of distractions, and lots of visitors on a daily basis, and not just to Yoko's bedside. Other musicians, artists, and celebrities were constantly filing in, sometimes trying to sell something or get Beatle approval for a project, sometimes just to hang out. As a result, those of us in the control room would be doing a lot of waiting around while everyone socialized. That kind of thing had gone on to some extent during the *Pepper* and *Magical Mystery Tour* sessions, too, but the guests wouldn't come into the control room; they'd come in the downstairs entrance and sit with the Beatles in their little private screened-off area. Often George Martin would look down there and ask us, "Who's that sitting with them?"

Not that anyone got in who wasn't invited: there was a whole social calendar with strict appointment times that were rigorously enforced by Mal and Neil. By the time they were working on *Abbey Road,* the Beatles might well spend the first three or four hours of a ten-hour session just chatting with friends and acquaintances. Perhaps they did this purposely—maybe they felt that having more of an open house atmosphere would force them to be on their best behavior. Sometimes the theory worked; other times it didn't: if an argument were to break out, it might just as easily happen in front of guests as in private.

Sadly, there were to be no more Beatles sessions. But I didn't know that at the time; all I knew was that, with *Abbey Road* wrapped, I had to return my focus to Apple. I had a studio to build.

Fixing a Hole:

The Apple Years

My directive was brief and to the point: get on with it. After years of putting up with the peeling paint and bare walls of Abbey Road, the four Beatles were desperate for their own recording studio. They simply didn't want to have to go through the whole process of booking studio time anymore—if one of them wrote a song in the middle of the night, they wanted to be able to walk right in and record it. They had always resented having to wait a week, or even a day, to get into the studio when inspiration struck, and they felt that, as EMI's biggest-earning act, they had the right to bounce other people who had dared to book times *they* wanted. But, as willing as the studio management was to try to accommodate them, they had other artists to serve as well, and to a large degree the Beatles had worn out their welcome.

To my amazement, Magic Alex was still considered a friend of the band, despite all the money he had wasted on building them a useless studio—in fact, I was chastised by Paul in one phone conversation when I made some ill-advised comment about Alex's ineptitude. I often wondered why they were so fond of Alex; nobody else found him all that likable, and most people around the Beatles saw right through him. The mixing console he had constructed for them had been put in storage while I was doing the *Abbey Road* sessions. In the end I sold it to a secondhand shop in Edgeware Road for the staggering sum of five pounds—probably twice what it was worth. At least he was now out of my hair, ensconced in Boston Place, essentially doing busywork. There, he would wander around wearing a white lab coat, looking like some mad scientist—an image he carefully cultivated—supposedly working on a new mixing console while actually spending his time fabricating useless things like little plastic boxes with red and green lights in them that blinked on and off in response to sound, essentially just small color organs. The ever-naive Lennon was so impressed that he ordered Alex to build several hundred of them, both large and small. Ultimately, they would sit in storage, abandoned and unused.

One of the last of Magic Alex's fantastic promises was that he was going to construct a flying saucer. The catch was that it was going to be coated with a magic paint that would render it invisible. Incredibly, he was taken seriously. Days before he was to unveil these great new inventions for his four wealthy benefactors, there was a fire in his workshop. Not long after that, he disappeared from the scene.

Number three Savile Row was a five-story Georgian town house that had originally been constructed as a residence, but it had been utilized as office space for decades before the Beatles purchased it. The basement had been used for storage; it was essentially just a corridor with several small rooms off of it, and Alex had done only minimal construction down there. In fact, he had stupidly plunked the recording area directly next to the building's heating plant, so that you'd hear loud thumps and wheezes coming from the room next door whenever the boiler switched on. Obviously the whole thing had to be completely gutted out and rebuilt from scratch, which was going to be a very expensive proposition. Soundproofing the basement was also going to be costly, because one of the London tube lines ran nearby; its subsonic rumbles and rattles would be much harder to contend with than anything that went on in the building itself. As we delved further into the project, it actually began looking as if it was going to be cost-prohibitive to build the studio at Savile Row, so I started looking for another site altogether. It never panned out, however, so we went ahead with the construction at Apple headquarters.

By the time I started my employment at Apple, Klein was already ruling with an iron fist and so Paul was staying completely away from the Savile Row offices. But John and Yoko were around quite a lot, and Harrison generally came in one or two days a week; Ringo was there somewhat less often, at least in the beginning. John and Yoko took over former Apple Records honcho Ron Kass's old office on the ground floor, and there was a large communal room on the second floor that was painted all in white, which quickly became the main gathering place for hangers-on; George Harrison also used it as his office on the days he would come in. I was spending most of my time either down in the basement or in site meetings with architects and surveyors, so I didn't see a lot of the Beatles even if they were in the building.

Early on it became apparent to me that none of the Beatles were taking any heed of the memos I was generating, so I just went ahead with the studio planning on my own. I had very little contact with Allen Klein; I dealt mostly with his assistants, people like Peter Howard, his second-in-command, and Terry Mellis, his chief accountant. I was happy with that arrangement, because there really wasn't anything I liked about Klein. He could only see in terms of dollar signs, and I found his habit of saying "ka-ching!" whenever he'd hear a Beatles song especially disconcerting.

The short, round business manager would arrive every morning in one of Lennon's cars, either the Mercedes or the Rolls—somehow he'd talked John into getting the use of them—dressed in an ill-fitting polo-neck sweater and shapeless trousers. He'd spend most of the day up in his office, yelling at people on the phone. Fortunately, he was flying back and forth to New York a lot of the time, so he wasn't around all that much, and that was fine with most of the Apple employees because we didn't want to see him anyway. It was Peter and Terry who really ran the shop. They were both English, but Klein also had a stable of faceless, nameless associates from his New York ABKCO office who would hang around from time to time. Klein pretty much stayed out of my hair, although as work on the studio proceeded, there were a lot of contractors to be paid, and it was sometimes tough getting his people to write checks.

At first, Allen seemed to take a liking to Malcolm Davies; Malcolm was the only member of our studio team who spent any significant time with him. But the relationship soured when Klein sent his assistant Tony King to ask Malcolm for an acetate of a Beatles single being cut downstairs, and Malcolm told him to fuck off—rightfully so, because the rule was that test pressings of their product could only be released directly to the four Beatles. Fortunately, by that time Malcolm had not only earned a reputation as the best mastering engineer in London but had developed a close friendship with Lennon. Those were probably the only things that saved his job.

Apple was not in its psychedelic heyday under the Klein regime—we had to fill out time sheets and materials requisitions, so it wasn't all peace and love—but there was still a lot of hustle and bustle in the Savile Row offices. The phones were constantly ringing and there was a steady stream of visitors dropping off tapes and trying to get an audience with one of the Beatles. It wasn't exactly an all-day party, but there was certainly a looser atmosphere than you'd find in most other places of business. There were two girls whose only job was making sandwiches and refreshments, and there was a fellow who would come around the offices once a week to take the liquor orders. Adding to the surreal atmosphere was the closed-circuit TV system designed by Magic Alex that continuously played eight-millimeter film loops of *Mag-*

ical Mystery Tour on dozens of small televisions in white plastic enclosures throughout the building.

The purpose of Klein's bloodletting had been to stop the money going out the front door, but everyone knew that the money was going to be coming in from the basement. Though the studio wasn't open yet, it was viewed as a sound investment, and the Apple mastering room had already gained a solid reputation as one of the best in the world, thanks to Malcolm's skill, both as an engineer and as the room's designer. He had hand-selected the equipment, and had specified that rubber shockmounts be placed underneath the lathe in order to insulate the platter from spurious vibrations—both from the street and the nearby underground railway—which could degrade the sound.

Working with Malcolm was an ex-musician named George Peckham, who had at one time been a guitarist with a Liverpool group called the Four-most. Peckham was a nice guy, a lot of fun, and quite the ladies' man. Under Malcolm's tutelage he also became one of the most in-demand mastering engineers in London. At the time, there were few independent mastering rooms in London other than Apple and Trident, so Malcolm and George were kept extremely busy. They mastered practically every hit record of the era, and it got to the point where they were actually turning people away.

So we had our little team assembled: me, Ron Pender, Malcolm, George, and John Smith, who looked after the tape library and did tape copying. Many of the Apple staff viewed our crew with suspicion, and a lot of them thought of me as being Paul's spy, which was particularly ironic considering how little contact I actually had with him during the years I worked there. The Apple staff upstairs may have viewed us as the little rats in the basement, but we knew that we were ultimately going to be the ones to bring in the money to cover their paychecks. Soon we would become even more disliked. Once the demolition and construction started, we would be responsible for bringing chaos into their everyday lives.

But we kept to ourselves, and the Beatles trusted us. We prided ourselves on being straight arrows, on being completely honest and upfront. We knew that if any one of us had been accused of doing anything untoward, it could have spelled the end of the entire project. And we never forgot that Alex was the person we were following. Under his watch, the job had gotten a bad reputation, and we were determined to clean it up.

My goal was to build the best, most modern studio in the world. The problem was that I was trying to construct it in a building that was hundreds of years old. Nonetheless, after a long series of meetings with architects and surveyors, it was determined that what we wanted to do was feasible, although it was going to be expensive. Once the budget was approved and all the paperwork was in place, the demolition phase commenced.

First, though, the mastering room had to be moved to Boston Place because there was no way it could continue operating amid the noise and dirt of the basement being gutted; masonry and wreckage were going to be flying all over the place. Boston Place quickly became a place of refuge for me: all my friends were there, and I much preferred their company to the people working upstairs at Savile Row. There was an elderly couple who had a flat above the mastering room; the wife would spend most afternoons leaning out the window watching the comings and goings on the street, and she always had a friendly wave for me. They were nice people, too—always cheerful, never complaining. Given the raucous music constantly being played below them at high monitoring levels, it probably helped that they were somewhat deaf, too.

On the other hand, we were never especially popular with our neighbors at Savile Row, especially after the demolition started. Located in London's posh Mayfair district, the street is world-renowned as tailors' row, where celebrities and royalty alike have their suits made; all the big designers, people like Tommy Nutter, had their workshops and showrooms there. Most of the business owners in the area had been horrified when the Beatles first opened the doors of Apple to every eccentric in London. Now they also had to contend with workmen and noise and dirt everywhere.

Despite the protestations, the jackhammers and sledgehammers were soon going at full tilt, and the basement was quickly reduced to little more than a pile of debris. Neither Ringo nor John and Yoko ever popped down to see what we were doing, but George Harrison made an impromptu appearance one day, standing atop the rubble and asking me where the various rooms where going to be situated. I almost mistook George for a workman at first, because he had a long beard and was dressed really scruffy, looking much like he did on the cover of *All Things Must Pass*, complete with boots and a big, floppy hat.

While the demolition was going on, I was in a nonstop series of meetings with architects and manufacturers to decide on the studio layout and the equipment we wanted to bring in, as well as the finer points of the interior design, fabric and the like. The Beatles were not involved in those meetings at all; they left those decisions up to me. As far as I was concerned, it was simply a matter of finding whatever was most suitable. I knew that I was not expected to cut corners, despite what Klein's people might want.

In late September, my focus was once again diverted when George Martin rang me up and said, "We're doing Ringo's album." That's how I found out that Ringo wanted me to engineer his debut solo record, *Sentimental Journey*; he never spoke with me about it directly. I guess he just wanted to have a familiar face around; that's how they all were. Because we were doing the recording at EMI, Phil McDonald was the "official" engineer of record, but we really played tag team, as we had done for during the making of *Abbey Road*.

The sessions ran on and off for about six months—we'd do a few days at EMI or Wessex Studios, then not work on it again for weeks at a time. Ringo sang all the tunes on the album, but he didn't play drums because it wasn't a rock record; it was a collection of prewar standards, conducted by George Martin and orchestrated by a variety of arrangers, including Quincy Jones, Elmer Bernstein, and Maurice Gibb of the Bee Gees; Paul even did one of the arrangements. Ringo was clearly enjoying himself on the sessions— it was a project he had long wanted to do ("Something for me mum," he told me)—but it often took a long time to get a vocal done. He'd sing two lines and then we'd stop—George Martin kept having to say to Ringo, "Another one, please." Despite all that, Ringo seemed quite confident; he wasn't nearly as nervous as he had been when called upon to sing on Beatles records.

He and I also had considerably more interaction than we'd ever had on Beatles sessions, and he was a good deal friendlier with me than he'd ever been before, although that invisible wall never quite came down. Ringo was just uptight all the time, or perhaps it was just an act to keep me at a distance. The problem was that I never knew if I was talking to the actual person underneath the veneer or not. He always seemed uncomfortable carrying on a conversation. He'd take it only so far and then he would inevitably back off, breaking things off in some abrupt or even nasty way. Ringo may have come across as lighthearted and jolly in his public appearances—or whenever there was a film camera rolling—but I never found him to be very genuine, or much fun to be around.

The first session for *Sentimental Journey* was at EMI, recording the orchestra for "Night And Day." Because I was no longer an employee, the Abbey Road staff did as little as possible to help; some of them even went out of their way to make my life more difficult. That very first night the maintenance engineer assigned to the session decided to stage his own little protest at the idea that an outsider was operating the console. I was well aware of the EMI policy, which stated that only maintenance engineers were allowed to touch the patchbays, so when I wanted an alteration made to the setup, I made the appropriate call upstairs. Normally they would respond within a minute or two—they knew that studio time was quite expensive—but this time no one appeared, even after repeated calls.

Neither Neil nor Mal was at the session that night, so I dispatched my assistant, John Kurlander, to try to find the missing maintenance man. Kurlander finally found him hiding in one of the stalls in the bathroom—he only managed to flush him out by banging on the doors and shouting, "I know you're in there; come on out!" The fellow hid for nearly twenty minutes, holding up the session and an entire orchestra, before he finally came out and sheepishly did what we requested. He never apologized for his unprofessional behavior, either.

Ringo wasn't the only Beatle who called on me to help with recording chores. Freshly recovered from his heroin-induced lethargy, John was starting to become active once again. In late December he asked me to go into Abbey Road with him to help mix and edit two songs that had been sitting on the shelf for a long time: "You Know My Name (Look Up The Number)," which had been recorded back in the *Magical Mystery Tour* days, and "What's The New Mary Jane," which was recorded during the *White Album* sessions. John was determined to see these two tracks come out as a single despite the fact that they were hardly representative of the band at their best. Fortunately, he was later overruled by the other Beatles. The original recording of "You Know My Name (Look Up The Number)" was long and rambling—way too lengthy to fit on a single—so we spent a lot of time editing it down. Despite the presence of two EMI assistant engineers, I did the actual cutting myself; I was always pretty good at editing and rarely had my assistants cut the tape.

"What's The New Mary Jane" was particularly bad; it was actually more of a chant about getting stoned than a proper song. I had the distinct feeling that Yoko was really behind the making of that track, and that John was finishing it up just to keep her happy. She was taking the whole thing quite seriously—in fact, everything seemed to be a matter of grave importance to her—but John kept grinning at me conspiratorially as we were working on it. Judging from some of the off-color jokes he was making, he was in a really good mood that day, acting like his old self again.

A week or so later I was back in the EMI control room, reunited with George Martin, Phil McDonald, and Richard Lush. Our task was to run off stereo mixes of "Lady Madonna," "Rain," "Hey Jude," and "Revolution" for a U.S. Capitol release, a greatest-hits album entitled *Hey Jude*. Those four tracks had only ever been mixed in mono, and I was glad that the record company was giving us the opportunity to run off new mixes from the original multitrack tapes instead of subjecting them to the pseudo-stereo processing that marred so many early Capitol releases.

One afternoon John Lennon was hanging around in the Apple mastering room with Malcolm and John Smith when I popped in to say hello. We were all in a rather silly mood that day and we got John Smith, whom Malcolm and Lennon had nicknamed "Smithy," to demonstrate his bizarre laugh, which always reminded us of the old children's record "The Laughing Policeman." As it turned out, that had been one of Lennon's favorite childhood records, too.

"That's fantastic," he said excitedly. "Let's go into EMI and record a modern version of it, with Smithy's laughter overdubbed on top."

We thought it was just another of Lennon's whims that would be forgotten in a day or two, but much to our surprise he went ahead and booked time at Abbey Road, inviting us all to come along. Phil McDonald was requested as engineer, and it seemed as if we were actually going to be making a record with a Beatle. But somehow the plans went awry, because when we turned up at Studio Two at the appointed time, there was a BBC film crew waiting. John and Yoko had apparently come up with an alternative "concept." They had decided that instead of recording "The Laughing Policeman," we were all to put on red rubber noses (probably the same ones Mal Evans had given out at the "A Day In The Life" orchestral session two years previously), line up at a microphone, and whisper the first thing that came into our heads. Lennon had arranged for cases of booze to be brought in, and we soon all got out of our minds, making total fools of ourselves. The entire bizarre session was duly captured by the film crew and scheduled for broadcast on the BBC television program *Panorama*.

The session ran on for hours, with everyone getting drunker and sloppier by the minute. Sometimes John and Yoko joined in with us; other times they just sat in the back of the room, eating macrobiotic food, observing us impassively as we flailed around on the studio floor. When it came time for me to whisper something into the microphone, I drew a total blank, then suddenly blurted out, for no reason whatsoever, the immortal words "Bill Livey's head."

Bill was the chief technical engineer at Abbey Road—he was really high up in the chain of command. He was a perfectly nice guy, but he was also perfectly bald. The poor guy had told all his friends and family that this BBC program was going to be about the studio where he worked, so they were all gathered together in his house watching this . . . then I come on camera and say, "Bill Livey's head," giggling like an idiot. A couple of days later, the studio manager came up to me in the corridor and said, "You really need to apologize to Bill." I did write him a letter of apology, and fortunately he took it in good spirits, but it was an episode I was never able to quite live down.

At the end of the session, after John and Yoko had gone, John Smith and I were looking at the remains of their meal and I stupidly said, "Who on earth would actually eat all this shit? It looks horrible!" We'd all had a lot to drink, and I didn't realize that the tape recorder was still running; we had open mics all around the room because the BBC people wanted to capture all the studio chatter. The tapes were supposed to be sent over to the BBC the next morning to be edited with the film footage, but there was no way I was going to let them out with my insult on there—I'd seen Lennon lose his temper over far lesser offenses. In fact, I was sufficiently inebriated that I couldn't be sure *what* I had said during the course of the evening. Frantically, I asked John Smith to go through all the tapes and cut out all my swearing and embarrassing moments. To his everlasting credit, he did—in fact, he sat up the whole night doing just that. I was scared to death when the broadcast came on, but fortunately Smithy had done an excellent job of saving my behind.

A couple of weeks later, Lennon asked me to record a live gig he and Yoko were doing at the Lyceum Theatre. It seemed like a straightforward enough assignment: the EMI mobile unit had been hired, with Pete Bown sent along to do the engineering. My job was to oversee and produce the recording, and I asked John Smith to come along as my assistant. But when we got to the gig, we discovered that, in true Lennon fashion, it was anything but straightforward. For one thing, the theater had a revolving stage . . . and nobody had bothered to tell Pete. He had plugged in all the mics as usual, but as the stage began moving, one by one all the leads started coming out. He was totally freaking out—perhaps the first time I ever saw him lose his cool.

There were a series of artists performing that evening, and when it was finally time for the Plastic Ono Band to take the stage, Lennon strolled on, dragging this huge pillowcase behind him. As John Smith went out there and began positioning the vocal mic, Lennon gave him a sly wink and nodded his head toward the pillowcase, indicating that he wanted it miked up, too. Smithy looked down and, to his amazement, there was Yoko sitting calmly inside. He had no idea what to do, so he just stuck a mic on a boom stand and moved it nearby. For all we knew, he had miked her bum!

That was one of the first times they did their "bagism" act on stage. At certain gigs, a bag would be dragged out onstage, although neither of them was actually in it, but on this particular night it was definitely Yoko. Not only had Smithy looked inside to confirm that, but there was no mistaking her unique shrieking.

That holiday season, I attended the first of many Apple Christmas parties. For months beforehand, many of the office staff had been pinching boxes of the newly released *Abbey Road* album to give away as Christmas presents, but I informed all of my staff that we weren't going to take a thing out of that building: not an album, not a paper clip, nothing. That wasn't in our nature anyway, but we took a certain amount of pride in knowing that we weren't going to join in the plundering that was going on all around us, even under the Klein regime. Behind the switchboard was a room filled with stacks of gold disks the Beatles had been awarded over the years, just piled on the floor—a pile that somehow grew smaller and smaller as the months wore on. At one point, Klein's people actually ordered an inventory of the entire building. You'd think they'd want an independent person to do it, but they hired the husband of one of the accountants! I was livid when I heard about that, and I confronted the woman, asking how she could possibly bring her husband in when we were supposed to be doing an independent inventory. She simply shrugged her shoulders; that was just the way they did business.

The most memorable thing about the 1969 Christmas bash was that it nearly marked the end of Apple . . . literally. The demolition phase of the studio project had been completed by then, although the construction had not yet begun. As you gazed out the window from the second floor, where the party was being held, you looked straight down into this pit, this great gaping hole where the basement had once been. The contractors had put in just enough support beams for a hundred people jumping up and down and dancing—that's how many had been invited—but two hundred had turned up. As the festivities went on into the wee hours and the room got more crowded, I began to get increasingly concerned.

As carefully as I could, I began walking around, having a quiet word in everyone's ear, saying, "Um, I think we should get out of here—the floor's about to cave in." Amid the din and the free-flowing booze, nobody paid me much mind—they just assumed I was kidding around—but I wasn't. Actually, I was scared to death that the whole building was going to collapse, taking all of us and assorted Beatles and Beatle wives with it. Somehow it didn't happen, but I can't help but think that if one more uninvited guest had shown up, my place in Beatles history would have been quite different.

Shortly after the New Year, John and Yoko took off for a few weeks' holiday. While they were gone, Paul, Ringo, and George Harrison convened at Abbey Road to record George's song "I Me Mine." They had been filmed rehearsing the track at Twickenham when they were working on *Let It Be,* and the director insisted that the scene be left in because it showed John and Yoko waltzing around the studio; that gave Harrison all the excuse he needed to insist that the song be placed on the album as well. I was up to my neck in site meetings, so I was unable to engineer the session, but Paul rang me up and said, "Why don't you pop by anyway? It should be fun."

As soon as I could get away, I headed up to EMI and stuck my head in for an hour or two. It was the first time I'd seen Paul in months, and he looked a bit subdued, but all in all there was a pretty good vibe that day. George Harrison was every bit as confident as he had been during the *Abbey Road* sessions, and the three Beatles seemed to be getting along pretty well, having a good time playing and singing together.

When John returned at the end of the month, I received a memo informing me that my presence was required at Abbey Road for an upcoming Plastic Ono Band session, where the new Lennon song "Instant Karma" was to be recorded. The producer was one of my heroes: the legendary Phil Spector. Phil McDonald, as usual, was standing by as the "official" engineer, but on that particular day I was free of Apple commitments and ready, willing, and able to record the entire session. It didn't quite work out that way.

I knew of Phil Spector's reputation, of course—the eccentric American was legendary in the music business not just for his "wall of sound" but for his temper tantrums and unnerving habit of carrying a gun—but this was the first time I'd actually met him in person.

I was a bit delayed getting to the session, but from the moment I arrived, I knew that I was in for a new experience. The first clue was the presence of two nasty-looking bodyguards standing outside the control room door. Even John and Yoko didn't have their own bodyguards; these bruisers were obviously Spector's. As I walked in, I saw Spector hovering over Phil McDonald's shoulder, looking distinctly unhappy. I walked over and introduced myself. He mumbled a quick hello in response, then scuttled off nervously. That was actually the last conversation we had that day; he never said another word to me.

Soon the musicians began filing in: John, Yoko, George Harrison, Billy Preston, bassist Klaus Voorman (a friend of John's and George's from the Hamburg days), and drummer Alan White (who later found fame as a member of the band Yes). I walked into the studio to say hello, and stayed out there as everyone began running through the song, listening intently to the sound and supervising the maintenance guys as they moved mics around. By the time I got back into the control room, the two Phils were embroiled in an argument. Every few moments, Spector would grab the big volume control on the right of the console and crank the sound all the way up. Then Phil The Basher—who, despite his loosey-goosey approach, had a reluctance to monitor at high levels—would clasp his hands over his ears and start shouting, "No, no, no! It's too loud!!" Spector would then turn the sound down a bit . . . for a few moments, after which he'd crank it up once more and the whole dispute would start all over again.

I was amazed. Although we had come a long way since the Norman Smith days of "engineer as king," it was still studio protocol at Abbey Road that the producer not actually touch the console—it was considered meddling. Instead, he was supposed to *ask* the engineer to make changes. That's what the engineer was there for, after all; he was the knob-twiddler: one person, one job. And you certainly didn't lean over the board and whack the volume way up, because that was a sure way to blow a very expensive pair of speakers.

I never actually said anything to Spector, but I suppose the look on my face spoke volumes. As the rehearsal continued, I took over from Phil McDonald at the console and started to shape the sounds. I was getting on with my work, generally ignoring Spector, who appeared to be pouting at the back of the room . . . whenever he wasn't marching over and turning up the volume, that is. After a while he went out into the studio; through the glass, I could see him talking to John. A moment later, the control room door swung open and John walked in, alone.

As always, Lennon didn't mince words.

"You're making Phil a bit uncomfortable," he said. He didn't appear angry or upset; he was just acting as a messenger.

I was just as blunt with him. "Fine. In that case, I'll leave," I said, and I did.

And that was that: the one and only time I ever worked with the estimable Mr. Spector.

I didn't ask what I'd done wrong, or what I'd done to offend—I could see that I was making Spector edgy, and I knew that Phil McDonald was perfectly capable of doing the session. Frankly, I was glad to get out of there. I had other things to get on with, and I had no desire to be around the bad vibes. I certainly admired Phil Spector for his past achievements, but the person I was seeing that day was just a bundle of nerves who didn't seem deserving of his vaunted reputation. He certainly wasn't in control at all.

Nonetheless, both Lennon and Harrison ended up hiring Spector to finish off *Let It Be* and produce many of their solo projects, and Phil McDonald would become John's and George's personal engineer. It wasn't surprising. By that time, there was a lot of tension between Paul and both John and George, and I had always been viewed as being "Paul's guy." Phil McDonald was not only a good engineer, he was someone that John and George could relate to, because he'd been on so many Beatles sessions for so long.

John Lennon had always been impatient, and he was always taking the piss, trying to see how far he could push things. But by this point in his career, his patience had almost completely evaporated; his attitude was "Do anything, just get it out." "Instant Karma" was the most extreme example of that. They never did a proper mix, only a rough, and Phil Spector even marked the tape box, "Do Not Use," but Lennon said, "To hell with it; issue it. It'll do. Who will know?" John cared a lot about his records on an emotional level, but technically he didn't give a damn. He simply didn't understand how good a record could sound, given a little bit of time and attention. But he did understand one thing: it was a product that featured a couple of Beatles, so no matter how bad it sounded, it wouldn't sell a copy less.

In mid-February, the *Sentimental Journey* sessions resumed, and one evening, we took a break to watch John mime "Instant Karma" on *Top of the Pops*. I was trying hard to read Ringo's blank facial expression: How must it have felt for him watching his bandmate appearing on his own, as a solo artist? Neither John nor George Harrison had any involvement in Ringo's album, so perhaps the fractures ran deeper than I even thought.

For all of the time and effort that went into *Sentimental Journey*, there was a certain lack of attention to detail that bewildered me. One night Ringo came in to overdub his vocal onto the backing track we'd recorded for the song "Dream." Within minutes we realized that it wasn't anywhere close to being in a key he could sing in; incredibly, nobody had bothered to check beforehand. George Martin was in a panic. In the end, we had to speed the track up a great deal so that Ringo could sing it, which made the instruments sound very odd. We were all worried about the audio quality, but Ringo said, "It's fine. They'll never know." He was right, too: to the best of my knowledge, no reviewer ever picked up on how strange the track actually sounds.

One of the huge disadvantages of working for Apple was that there were no set hours: the Beatles just assumed I was on twenty-four-hour call. Late one Sunday night, Mal Evans phoned me at home and said, "George is doing a session at Trident and he'd like you to come over and help out."

It was nearly midnight and I didn't really want to get out of bed, but I went anyway, just to keep the peace. By the time I arrived at the session, it was nearly 1 A.M.; Harrison gave me a curt hello and immediately offered me a bowl of curry—the last thing I wanted to be eating at that hour of the morning. George was in the studio producing Ringo, recording "It Don't Come Easy," with Ken Scott engineering—a track that gave Ringo his first hit single.

Apparently Harrison had wanted a certain guitar sound that Ken just couldn't get for him, so he had instructed Mal to call me in. I did what I could to help, as unobtrusively as possible, and then made my way back home. George Harrison really was quite a talented producer—he knew what he wanted, and he was a very different person when he wasn't on Beatles sessions. Perhaps that was because he didn't have to contend with being second-guessed by Paul, or John . . . or Yoko.

There were, to be sure, some very funny moments during my time at Apple. One Saturday night our little crew, consisting of Malcolm, Phil, Ken, John Smith, and me, had gone to a pub in Swiss Cottage and were standing out in the road at around midnight trying to hail a cab. All of a sudden we saw a white Mercedes glide by. It came to an abrupt stop and the driver wound his window down; it was George Harrison. He looked at us weaving unsteadily.

"Oh, pissed again, I see," he said, deadpan.

Then he simply wound the window back up and drove away. It was a distinctly Pythonesque moment. No wonder George later became so involved with the famed comedy team.

My social life, however, was still severely limited. There was a girl at a local pub with the unlikely name of Lana Turner, and John Smith tried to hook me up with her, but things didn't work out between us. I did, however, manage to have a couple of memorable dates with one of the secretaries at the architect firm, a girl named Annette. The first time we went out, I booked us a table at a fairly posh restaurant. Annette was enormously impressed; on a secretary's salary, she was clearly not used to fine dining. Somewhere between the appetizer and the entrée, she excused herself to go the ladies' room. I waited patiently for the longest time, but after about twenty minutes I began to get concerned, so I asked an attendant to go look for her. A few minutes later she was led back to the table, dazed and bleeding from a small wound on her forehead; somehow, she'd managed to walk into a glass door and knock herself out. Needless to say, not much came of that relationship.

But it was hardly all fun and games—in fact, it was bloody hard work getting that studio designed and built. There was absolutely nothing straightforward about the project; at one time or another we encountered every problem you could possibly encounter. For one thing, physical access at Savile Row was extremely limited. Not only was it a very small premises to begin with, but we were building a room within a room, and so we had to hire extra-thin workmen to fit in the void between the walls. The noise coming from the underground train that ran nearby was another huge problem, forcing us to float everything on special shock-absorbing pads. Designing the air-conditioning system was a nightmare; building an echo chamber was problematic because of leakage; there were delays, cost overruns, constant aggravation.

Yet it was an experience I would not trade for anything, because I gained so much invaluable knowledge and training. I had to learn how to read drawings and architectural blueprints; I got a crash course in acoustics, in electrics, in air-conditioning design, in every aspect of construction and demolition. Perhaps the greatest testimony to the fine job our architects and designers did came late one night when John Smith was working in the studio on his own. As he headed out the door at around 3 A.M., he found the entire street cordoned off, swarming with cops. A policeman came rushing up to him, saying "What the fuck are you doing here?" It wasn't until he was spirited away for questioning that he was informed that an IRA bomb had gone off right next door, while he was working. He never felt a vibration, never heard a thing: that's how solid the construction was.

By mid-March, I'd heard through the grapevine that Phil Spector was hard at work on *Let It Be*, huddled with Pete Bown up in one of Abbey Road's small remix rooms. None of the Beatles attended those mix sessions, having long ago walked away from the project in disgust. One afternoon I got a phone call from Peter Howard, Allen Klein's second-in-command.

"Phil Spector is doing a fabulous job on the album, you know," he began. I grunted noncommittally as Peter continued his gushing. "Well, it's sounding terrific, let me assure you. In fact, he's going to be overdubbing strings and choir onto some of the tracks next week, and Allen would consider it a personal favor if you would attend."

"Why?" I asked. Klein had to have been well aware that Phil Spector didn't want me at his sessions, as had been made clear when I'd started work on "Instant Karma."

"I really don't know," Peter said. "He'd just like you to be there."

I said I'd try to pop by, and as I hung up it occurred to me why Klein was so anxious to have me there looking over Spector's shoulder. It appeared to me that, like most of the Apple staff, Klein was convinced I was Paul's "spy," despite the fact that I'd had almost no contact with McCartney the entire time I'd been working there. Klein knew that Paul did not want Spector touching the tapes, though he'd been overruled by the other three Beatles. But Klein was still trying to win Paul over, so it was in his interest to have Paul hear that the eccentric producer was indeed creating a masterpiece out of the ragged recordings. What better way than to invite Paul's spy to sit in on the session? Klein was obviously gambling that I'd be impressed and would tell Paul how great everything was sounding.

So it was with a somewhat jaundiced eye that I went to Abbey Road on April Fool's Day, 1970, accompanied by Malcolm Davies, whom I'd invited for moral support. By the time we arrived, the session was already in full swing . . . and it was immediately evident that something was terribly, terribly wrong. Spector approached me a bit sheepishly and gave me a perfunctory greeting. He knew I was there at Klein's request, so there was nothing he could do about it, even though he obviously wasn't happy to see me. Klein himself stood silently at the back of the room, flanked by two of his New York "associates," all three of them wearing matching sunglasses, cashmere polo-neck sweaters, and ostentatious gold chains. They were trying to look intimidating, but I thought they just looked ridiculous. It was all I could do to stifle a laugh.

"This sounds like crap; what kind of bullshit studio is this, anyway?"

The whiny, high-pitched voice was Spector's, and his invective was directed at a harried-looking Pete Bown. I sized up the situation: Spector was trying to make his presence felt by being obnoxious—a strategy that never works in the confines of a recording studio. Diplomacy obviously wasn't Spector's strong point; he was storming around, not only shouting at Pete, but at the orchestral players—the finest in London—telling them, "You call yourselves musicians? You can't even play this right!" He was totally alienating everyone in sight. I suppose it was an important session for him, and he was obviously very nervous, but he really was blowing it.

The assistant on the session was a totally mortified Richard Lush. "This is nothing; you missed the worst of it," he whispered to me.

Apparently the musicians were furious because they had been asked to play on three tracks instead of the two they were booked for, yet they weren't being offered any extra pay. Spector's response had been to blow his top, screaming, "You'll do what I tell you to do, and you'll like it!" which had triggered an impromptu walkout. As the seriousness of the situation began to dawn on Spector, he had turned to Pete Bown for help because he knew that Pete was on a first-name basis with all these musicians . . . at which point the beleaguered and embarrassed engineer had just slipped out the door and gone home for a while. It sounded like something straight out of a Three Stooges film.

Pete had only just come back a few minutes before Malcolm and I arrived, and some kind of truce had been declared. Now Spector was pacing between the studio and the control room, alternating between trying to placate the still angry musicians and trying to get Pete to add more echo and reverb than was humanly possible. As I watched the circus unfold, I realized to my horror that Spector had reduced the Beatles' performance down to one or two tracks so that he could have five or six tracks for orchestral and choir overdubs, as if they were more important than the group's playing. At one point he wanted even more tracks. When Pete told him he had none to spare, Spector had the unmitigated gall to actually wipe one of Paul's vocals— erasing it forever—in order to free up another track for one of his many choir overdubs. I was aghast.

Things went from bad to worse. Just as the musicians finally calmed down enough to start rehearsing "The Long And Winding Road," Spector turned around and said to Richard, loudly enough for us all to hear, "I hope Paul likes this, because I've changed the chords."

I couldn't believe my ears. Spector was not just remixing Beatles music, he was actually *altering* it. As the orchestra ran through the score, Spector started demanding that Pete record them louder, and Pete politely refused, explaining that the meters were already pinning. Pete Bown was an excellent engineer, a consummate professional, and he wasn't about to start overloading an orchestral overdub for Phil Spector—or anyone else, for that matter; quality orchestral recordings were his specialty, and he took pride in his work.

I looked around the room. The only Beatle present was a clearly embarrassed Ringo. The insanity kept building and building until Spector finally lost it completely, waving his arms and screeching, "I must have more echo! I must have more reverb!"

That was the straw that broke the camel's back for Ringo, who grabbed Spector by the arm and told him to step outside for a private chat. When they came back in, Spector was a little better behaved, so I have to assume that Ringo told him to cool it, but he was still running amok. Actually, that really impressed me; it was one of the few times I'd seen Ringo assert himself and take charge. As the only Beatle there, he probably felt that the task of enforcer fell on his shoulders by default.

It was one of the most ludicrous sessions I ever attended, and all I could think was how glad I was to not be engineering it. Phil Spector's whole modus operandi was to push people to the limit. He wasn't necessarily inept; he was just extreme, but that most certainly was not the way I liked to work. I turned and walked out the door, disgusted and relieved all at the same time.

On April 10, 1970, Apple released the solo album Paul had long been working on up in his home studio in Scotland. Accompanying the record was a press release announcing formally that the Beatles had split up.

I can't say I was surprised at the news, but I wasn't expecting it either. There had been rumors flying around the Apple offices about them breaking up for some time, but I had never paid them much mind. I was obviously aware of the fact that there had been hostilities within the band for years, and I knew that there were constant meetings going on between Klein and Paul's in-laws, the Eastmans, but I had no idea what was being discussed at those meetings. Certainly I had no clue that John had told the others he was quitting right after the *Abbey Road* sessions.

I suppose it's poetic justice that it was John—ever impatient, often irascible John—who finally forced the issue. With Yoko egging him on, Lennon's attitude was "We've been pop stars and done all the simple stuff; now we really should be taken seriously as artists." As far back as 1966, he had been forging new paths with "Tomorrow Never Knows" and "Strawberry Fields

Forever"; in 1968, he had been arguing that "Revolution 9" should be a single. That was his vision of where he wanted to take the Beatles. Paul was every bit as stubborn as John, and every bit his equal in terms of talent and songwriting ability. The only problem was that he wanted to take the group in exactly the opposite direction. In the face of such massive talent—and such massive ego—it's no surprise that George Harrison felt overwhelmed and simply wanted to leave; I had the sense that he'd wanted out as far back as the pre-*Revolver* days.

By the end, it's fair to say that the four Beatles hated one another, for a variety of reasons. It's actually understandable, considering all the time they'd spent together, stuck in hotel rooms and recording studios for year after year; no wonder they couldn't wait to get away from one another. When the announcement was made, I couldn't help but reflect on the fact that it had been almost four years since they'd done their last tour. For four years, they had been doing nothing but recording in that dank, depressing place known as Abbey Road.

What was it that actually broke up the band? Perhaps Klein was a factor. Paul couldn't stand him, and as time went on, even the others grew embarrassed that he was representing them. Still, it's hard to believe that business differences alone could have ended the close friendships that the four Beatles had developed for more than a decade. John and Paul, in particular, had literally grown up together.

And I honestly don't think it was Yoko, either, though her constant presence clearly irritated the others and perhaps acted as a catalyst to speed up the process. There's no denying that Yoko was good for John—at that time in his life, he needed stimulation, someone to get his creative juices flowing. As far-out as some of their ideas were, she had given John the confidence to take control of his career again instead of simply bowing to Paul's wishes, as he had done during the *Pepper* and *Magical Mystery Tour* sessions. It was that self-confidence that gave him the strength to walk away from his life as a Beatle.

No, I always felt that the main reason for the breakup were irreconcilable artistic differences. John, Paul, and George Harrison simply wanted to follow different paths. John wanted to make art; Paul wanted to continue doing pop music; and George just wanted to pursue his Eastern interests. Sadly, inevitably, there was no common ground anymore, only a common history.

John may have been the one who brought things to a head, but it was Paul who finally ended it. After eight months or so of nasty, public sniping in the newspapers, he made the difficult decision to sue his former friends and collaborators, filing the formal legal papers on December 31, 1970.

The phenomenon known as the Beatles was officially over.

Lawsuit or no lawsuit, life at Apple went on. Construction work on the studio continued at a steady pace well into 1971, and I was spending a lot of time consulting with technicians, because we wanted the recording area to sound acoustically like Abbey Road's Studio Two. But our room was going to be considerably smaller, so the best we could do was to design the acoustics to re-create the same decay time. I was quite pleased with the results: in the end, the room sounded much larger than it actually was.

Adding to the pressure on me was the fact that I was beginning to embark on a new career as a record producer, even while I was overseeing the building of the studio. Paul had produced Mary Hopkin's first single "Those Were The Days," but then he seemed to lose interest in working with her, so I asked him if I could take over. I did a number of sessions with her at Trident in 1969 and 1970; a few of the tracks got released, but shortly afterward she was dropped by the Apple label.

The other artist I began working with was the band Badfinger, who had been brought to Apple's attention by Mal Evans. Unlike Neil, Mal had no training in anything other than looking after the Beatles. With the demise of the band, Mal was at loose ends; he simply didn't know what to do with his life, so he decided to become a talent scout. He had met Badfinger's manager, Bill Collins, at a gig somewhere, and they had developed a close friendship— or so Mal thought. Bill was a strange guy; to me he seemed very paranoid, constantly protecting his position, and extremely manipulative. Mal became a huge fan of the band and eventually persuaded Paul to not only sign them, but to produce and write a song for them—"Come And Get It"—which became a huge hit.

As a talent scout, Mal was a success. Badfinger clearly had musical ability, and, like the Beatles, they were blessed with not one, but two lead singers and songwriters: Pete Ham and Tom Evans. Then Mal made the mistake of overestimating his abilities. He'd hung around in the recording studio with the Beatles long enough that he thought he knew how to produce records, but he really didn't. As he had done with Mary Hopkin, Paul quickly lost interest in producing Badfinger, but this time the torch was passed to Mal instead of me . . . and he was clearly in over his head. The band needed guidance—they were really just boys, and they were heavy drinkers to boot—and I don't think Mal guided them very well. With no musical background, he couldn't contribute creative ideas or input. Instead, he just relied on the engineers he was using—Ken Scott and Richard Lush—to do their job. As a result, the Badfinger tracks he produced were lackluster and deemed unreleasable by the Apple record people. No amount of enthusiasm and urging from Mal could get them, or any of the Beatles, to change their minds, and so the tapes just sat on the shelf.

Aggravating the situation was the fact that the group had added a new member—Joey Molland—who seemed to me to be just as paranoid and manipulative as Bill. They soon fell in league with each other, and the next thing Mal knew, he was being called on the carpet by Allen Klein. The poor guy . . . all he had done was introduce the group, who were nobodies at the time, to the most famous recording artists in the world and gotten them a record deal. Now he was being forced out, not just because he hadn't been a very good producer, but because Bill Collins thought that Mal was out to take his job as manager!

It was a nasty, embarrassing meeting, and while Bill and Mal stamped their feet like angry bulls, Klein laid down the law: I was to be the band's new producer. It was a great opportunity for me—I really liked the band and believed in their music—but in retrospect I can see that Bill used me to force Mal out. In July and August of 1970 I took Badfinger into EMI, and, with my old assistant John Kurlander doing the engineering, I produced their *No Dice* album, which was met with critical acclaim. One of the tracks on the album was Pete and Tom's "Without You," which ended up becoming a massive hit when it was later covered by Harry Nilsson.

In early 1971, I brought Badfinger back into the studio, working both at EMI and at the newly opened AIR facility, and we recorded a few more tracks, but there were all kinds of internal and external pressures being brought to bear, and our work ended up being shelved. Later on, George Harrison took over as the band's producer; then, when he got fed up, the American musician Todd Rundgren was brought in. Rundgren even did some sessions with them at the Apple studio in early 1972—traumatic, emotionally charged sessions during which, at one point, Pete Ham slammed his expensive Martin guitar down on the floor in disgust, shattering the exquisite instrument to pieces. A few dribs and drabs from those sessions were eventually released, along with some of the tracks I had done earlier, but the band never had a hit again.

The Badfinger story is a heartbreaking one of Machiavellian proportions, which culminated in the tragic suicides of both Pete and Tom. It was a classic example of how good things can go so badly wrong.

With the construction phase coming to an end, I turned my attention to outfitting the studio. We didn't have the wide range of equipment choices there are today, but Ron Pender and I still spent considerable time exploring the options that were available. The first and largest item to consider was the mixing console. My preference was for a custom-made Neumann console (made by the same German manufacturer of the world-famous microphones). It was way ahead of its time—it had every bell and whistle we would ever need—and we had extensive conversations with their designers in Berlin, but Klein balked at the cost, so there was a long delay while we went back and forth, waiting for an answer.

I was getting enormously frustrated: we were in the process of building the best-looking and best-sounding studio in the world, and we were stuck for a mixing desk because Klein wouldn't okay the expense for the one we wanted; obviously he was stalling for time. The memos I circulated to the three ex-Beatles who were at Apple—John, Ringo, and George Harrison—were being totally ignored, and I was starting to feel completely cut off from my own project. One evening Ron and Ken Scott came over to my house for dinner and I was moaning about the situation.

"Why don't you call Paul?" Ken suggested.

It was something I'd been thinking about, but dreading. I'd had no contact with Paul at all since the beginning of the year; he hadn't even told me he was doing a solo album. Most of it was recorded at his home studio, but he did do a few tracks at EMI, with Tony Clark engineering. I assumed that he didn't ask me to do the sessions because I was an Apple employee, and he simply didn't want any involvement with the company at all—he had cut himself completely off. So I was wary about calling him; I just felt that the last thing he wanted was to get involved in Apple business. But it seemed like it was the only thing I could do to try to get some resolution, and with Ken and Ron urging me on, I dialed his number.

After a few rings, Paul answered the phone himself. To my relief, he was quite friendly. After some small talk and catching up, I explained the situation and said, "Look, do you think we can get an answer on the mixing console?"

Incredibly, Paul's response was "What's wrong with the console that's already there?" That's how out of touch he was.

I had to explain once again why Alex's console was useless and why we needed a new one. Finally, he said, "I'll see what I can do," but as far as I know nothing happened.

We eventually settled on a less expensive Helios console, which not only had a very clean, crisp sound but was significantly smaller than the Neumann desk, freeing up valuable space in the small control room. In the end, I was quite satisfied that we had indeed built a world-class studio. The proof would come when we opened our doors to clients, but I was confident that Apple would stand up to the very best of our competition: Trident, Olympic, EMI, and even AIR.

As spring turned to summer, the Apple studio began to take shape, and the basement at 3 Savile Row took on a distinctly professional ambience. There was muted lighting everywhere, and all the walls were fine wood, the floors polished parquet. The reception area, just to the left of the downstairs entrance, was decorated opulently, with elegant Regency furniture and solid brass fittings on the wall. Directly opposite was the disk-cutting room; the maintenance room and toilets were located down the corridor. A bit farther on was the studio control room and a separate entrance to the studio itself; opposite was the tape copying room. The only thing missing was a staff room, but the local café served that function quite nicely.

A great deal of thought and effort had gone into the interior design. Having learned from the mistakes of Abbey Road, I was determined to make Apple studios a pleasant place to work, a space that would encourage rather than discourage the creative flow. The control room walls were done in a soft blue fabric, while those in the mastering room were covered with a purple and mauve zigzag fabric evocative of sound waves; the tape copying room featured a blue fabric with a circular design that vaguely resembled disks. The studio ceilings were covered with angular panels that were specially designed to give the appearance of height. The walls were also covered in panels, and there had been a lot of discussion about what color to paint them. Finally one of our designers came up with a brilliant idea: we could use lighting to change the color. Lamp recesses were duly built along the floor so that the walls could be underlit; by sliding in different colored gels, you could literally make the studio any color you wanted.

Our opening party was held in August 1971. George Harrison was the only Beatle in attendance; the other three simply couldn't be bothered. He and his wife, Patti, spent most of the night wandering around the room chatting amiably with the press people on hand. There were perhaps a hundred people there in total, including Badfinger and a few other Apple artists, along with several of our colleagues from EMI, Trident, and Olympic, who were busily examining our equipment and designs, looking for ideas to pinch. Both George Martin and Ken Scott were invited but neither of them could make it: George was busy that night at AIR, and Ken was working with David Bowie, recording abroad. Other than Klein and Peter Howard, only a handful of the upstairs Apple people joined the festivities; the basement was considered our domain and they rarely crossed the informal line of demarcation. Truth be told, working in the only profitable division of Apple gave those of us down in the studio a slight feeling of superiority to the bean counters and gofers who populated the upper floors.

One of my first decisions was what rate to charge. We all felt that our studio was just a little bit better than any other in London, so I set our hourly rate 10 percent higher than any other studio in town, even more than Trident and EMI. That gave us a little touch of exclusivity, and it worked: within weeks, the room was heavily booked, to the point where we even had to prebook hours for necessary maintenance work. The mastering room, now moved back to Savile Row, continued to be booked solid as always, and the fact that you could walk out of the control room directly into the disk cutting room that same night and walk out with an acetate was a real bonus: all the facilities were under one roof, which in those days was quite unusual.

The irony was that the studio was originally supposed to be for the Beatles' own use exclusively, but as it turned out, it became a commercial enterprise that was so much in demand, they had a hard time getting in themselves . . . which is why the others followed Paul's lead and started building home studios of their own. George Harrison got mightily pissed off at one point because he couldn't book the time he wanted. Phil McDonald, with whom he had a good relationship, had to go upstairs and smooth things over with him.

Despite that hiccup, George maintained a fairly steady presence at the Apple studio, recording parts of his *Living In The Material World* and *Dark Horse* solo albums there, as well as a Nicky Hopkins record. Later, when the famous American songwriters Jerry Leiber and Mike Stoller came over to produce the debut Stealers Wheel album (which included the hit song "Stuck In The Middle With You"), Harrison would frequently pop in to see how we were getting on. His attitude seemed to be "Apple is my company so I should be staying on top of things." I engineered that album and found Leiber and Stoller to be great to work with.

George could, however, be infuriating on occasions. Every now and then he would get into his Hare Krishna thing, and he'd walk around with this little white bag that resembled a sling; he looked as if he'd broken his arm. You'd go up to him and ask him a question, any question: "Do you want to do your vocals now?" or something like that—and he'd start to answer you but then begin mumbling away, chanting his mantra. It seemed as if he had to chant this mantra every so often, no matter what, so one minute you might find him being attentive, the next minute—maybe even mid-sentence—he'd be chanting. We used to speculate that he had an alarm clock in that little bag. How else would he know when it was time to chant?

For all of Harrison's eastern allegiances, it was Lennon who came across most like a guru during the Apple days, espousing obscure philosophies and constantly telling us to do this or that because Yoko had said the stars were aligned correctly. John was close with Malcolm and so he spent a fair amount of time hanging around with him in the mastering room. Ringo might have popped his head in once or twice also, but the only time Paul ever came in was late one night when he showed up, unannounced, to cut a disk with George Peckham. Peckham had a habit of collecting newspaper clippings about the Beatles and putting them up inside his cupboard door. Unfortunately, one of the clippings he had posted contained something derogatory about Linda McCartney, and as luck would have it, Paul happened to open the door and discover it.

There was an awkward silence, but professional that he was, Paul finished the session without saying anything. The next day he had a quiet word with Malcolm about what had happened, because Malcolm was ostensibly in charge. He didn't make a big issue out of it, but he was clearly upset. That was the last time Paul ever set foot in Apple, and he never spoke to George Peckham again.

We frequently accepted outside bookings, but most of our clients were Apple Records artists. One of George Harrison's new signings was the Von Eaton brothers—Lon and Derrek. They were a couple of American blokes, and they were quite pleasant to deal with, but their problem was that they couldn't match the feel of the demonstration tape that had gotten them their record deal in the first place. It's actually a common enough occurrence—in recording studio parlance, it's a phenomenon known as "chasing the demo."

Artists, especially inexperienced ones, are often much more relaxed when they're making a rough recording at home that they know will never be released. But when they get into a professional studio and the pressure is on, they sometimes freeze up and give a less inspired performance. Harrison started out producing the brothers' album, with me doing the engineering, but then he got fed up and frustrated, so he had his old friend Klaus Voorman take over as producer. I knew him from as far back as the *Revolver* days, when he'd come into the sessions to talk about the album cover he was designing. He and I just didn't click, though, so I begged off from the project and turned the reins over to another engineer.

As word spread, a steady stream of artists began coming into the Apple studios: Jack Jones, Harry Nilsson, even Roger Daltrey of the Who. At one point, Leo Sayer booked time to do an album, produced by former teen idol Adam Faith. Things got a bit crazed one night and Adam fired a starter's pistol off in the studio, right by engineer John Mills's head—something that was completely out of character for him. Mills nearly sued Adam for damaging his hearing after that.

My schedule began getting as packed as it had ever been during my EMI days, with one artist after another requesting my services. I did an album with the all-girl group Fanny, which was produced by Richard Perry. Then there was *Painted Head* by folk-rock singer Tim Hardin, produced by ex–Shadows drummer Tony Meehan. One of the tracks on that album featured one particular note that just seemed to be the most incredible sounding bass note ever recorded. It was so good, in fact, we used that track as a reference for many years afterward, whenever we were trying out loudspeakers. The bassist on the session didn't do anything special—he just kind of touched the string—and neither did I, but somehow it made the room shake.

Working at Apple was fun and it was exciting, but it was also extremely tiring. By this point, I had put in nearly a decade as a recording engineer, including the two long years I had spent overseeing the construction of the new studio. I was starting to become a bit burned out. In the back of my mind, I knew that this particular chapter in my life was soon going to be coming to an end. The writing was on the wall, and new horizons were starting to beckon.

We had always been divorced from what was going on upstairs at Apple, and I wanted it that way. The people I had hired to work down in the studio area were a solid team; we meshed well together, and our division was making a lot of money for the company, which pretty much ensured our job security. But once the storm had passed—once the construction phase was over and the studio was open—we were able to see things around us a lot more clearly. There was simply no escaping the fact that the four Beatles were in litigation; the base upon which the entire enterprise was standing was shaky ground. Apple was supposed to be a Beatles company, but they didn't exist anymore, so where did that leave any of us?

It seemed as if Apple had no real direction, and there was nothing on the horizon that indicated any kind of movement in the foreseeable future. The company was caught in the middle of the legal wrangling between McCartney on one side, and Klein and the other three Beatles on the other side. Artists were getting dropped from the Apple label, and the Beatles were working painfully slowly at their home studios: without Beatles product, the record division had little to do. It was all getting quite discouraging, and I began casting about for other opportunities. I was pretty open about it, too: George Martin had made a standing offer to come work at AIR if I was ever unhappy, and I made no secret about that.

The biggest problem with Apple was that you'd get one Beatle giving you the green light to go ahead with something, and then another one would come in and say no, don't do it. Not only was it frustrating, it often cost money hanging around waiting for them to come to a consensus. During the time when I was getting desperate for a decision on the mixing console, I called George Harrison's secretary and scheduled a mid-afternoon meeting with him. An hour after the appointed time, there was still no sign of him, so I phoned downstairs.

"I thought we were going to have a meeting," I said.

"We can meet, but I'm not going to come up to your office; you've got to come down here" was Harrison's churlish reply. I wasn't playing any kind of power game, so I didn't really understand his attitude. I just thought he was going to pop up and have an informal chat in private, not in the big common white office where everyone was always eating sandwiches and gossiping.

In all the years I worked with him, I never saw George Harrison actually lose his temper, but he could be very abrupt with people. Still, he and I had a good working relationship—at one point, he even invited Ken Scott and me down to Friar Park to get our opinion on building a home studio there. But it really wasn't George Harrison who served as the catalyst for my leaving Apple; nor was it John and Yoko, who were already living in America. It was Ringo.

With John and Paul completely gone from the Apple scene, and George slowly getting his home studio together, Ringo began appearing in the offices with greater frequency and asserting himself with greater confidence. He had signed two artists to the Apple label—the classical composer John Tavener, and singer Chris Hodge—and seemed to be enjoying his new role as starmaker. At one point, Malcolm tendered his resignation because things weren't getting done and supplies weren't being ordered, and it was Ringo who sat him down and persuaded him to stay; he took charge of the situation, and Malcolm was quite impressed.

I couldn't say that I shared Malcolm's opinion. Some months previously, Ringo had gotten into the stainless steel furniture business with a partner. Personally, I thought the furniture they were building was cold, modern, and without any character or comfort whatsoever; it certainly didn't fit at all with the ambience of the Apple studio. Yet without saying a word to me or to anyone else, their crew turned up one day and ripped everything out of the studio reception area, replacing all the fine Regency-style furnishings with their own pieces, essentially turning our studio into a showroom. I thought it was a rude, arrogant thing to do.

Then came the final straw. One morning in early 1972, our studio architect rang me up and said, "Guess what? Ringo wants to put a film scoring suite above the studio."

I thought it was a crazy idea, but Ringo was an ex-Beatle, and Apple was there to serve Beatle whims, so we got the surveyors and contractors in and the conclusion they reached was that it could not be done without knocking the entire building down, from the ground floor on up. I thought that was the end of it; surely no one in his right mind was going to actually do that.

But that's exactly what they did. In the summer of 1972, just a year after we finally opened the studio, the entire upstairs Apple staff was moved to office premises in St. James Street, where Neil and the other accountants had long been ensconced in order to be as far away from Klein as possible. After all the blood, sweat, and tears we had poured into creating a world-class studio, it was all being torn apart. Suddenly there was daylight above us, and no way out of the basement apart from a ladder; when you looked up from the reception area, all you saw was gaping sky. We had spent a huge amount of money building a beautiful echo chamber and that was ripped out, too. The entire Apple operation was thrown into utter chaos, and we were trying to operate a commercial enterprise in a basement that no longer had much of a building above it.

The ultimate irony was that Ringo's folly never got built. After the demolition was completed but before any money could be sunk into the construction, Allen Klein suddenly disappeared from the scene, his management contract having expired at the end of March 1973. None of the Beatles—not even John, his greatest ally—opted to renew it, and they all pretty much gave up on Apple at that point. The company was placed in Neil Aspinall's hands, not that it mattered much: each of the four ex-Beatles already had his own management, his own career completely separate from the company. Rumors of yet another staff purge began circulating; the dismal atmosphere was getting worse by the day. By July, I'd had enough. Everything was disintegrating in front of my eyes, and I was determined to walk away before the whole thing crumbled.

Without any hesitation, and without any regrets, I went to see George Martin and told him I was ready to take that job at AIR. Malcolm Davies took over running things after I left, but he soon had to shut down the studio for lack of business, and only the disk-cutting room and tape copying room remained. By May 1975, the entire Savile Row operation was completely closed down.

The dream, as John Lennon once said, was over.

· 16 ·

Drainage, Lizards, and Monsoons:

The Making of *Band On The Run*

AIR Studios was located on the top floor of a beautifully ornate Regency building directly overlooking Oxford Circus, in the very center of London. Underneath us was the posh Peter Robinson department store. The space occupied by our three studios and film mixing suite had once been the store restaurant, where the elite would take their tea and cucumber sandwiches after a busy day's shopping. But it was actually pretty well suited for a recording complex: it had high, vaulted ceilings, with neoclassical frescoes everywhere . . . and, of course, it had its own kitchen.

George Martin's standing offer of a job was made in good faith, and to his credit he honored it when I was ready to make the move, despite the fact that he already had a full complement of engineers on staff. The studio had been open since October 1970—a good nine months before we had been able to get Apple completed—and so George had had plenty of time to hire some of the best and brightest engineers in London. Bill Price had been brought over from Decca and made chief engineer, and all the administrative staff were already in place; the studios were booked solid and everything was operating like a well-oiled machine. There clearly was some resentment among some of the staff when I was suddenly plunked in there, so I knew that I had to tread carefully. I'm sure that it caused an awkward situation for George, but he ultimately sorted it out.

I'd only been at AIR for a couple of weeks—just barely time to get acclimated and do a handful of sessions—when I received a phone call from Linda McCartney. We made small talk for a while and got caught up, then she put Paul on the line.

"Hello, Geoff. I hear you've moved," he said cheerfully. "I've got another project for you, if you're interested."

"Sure," I replied, without waiting for any particulars. Whatever it was, I welcomed the opportunity to be working with Paul again.

"You might not want to say yes quite so fast," he laughed. "You're going to have to pack your bags; we're going to record our next album in Lagos."

I had a vague idea where Lagos was—I knew it was in Africa, at least—and in my head I conjured up images of lions, tigers, and zebras. It seemed exotic and exciting, so I quickly assented and the details were worked out. As soon as I got off the phone, I consulted an atlas. To my horror I realized that I had just committed to spending two months in the West African country of Nigeria, hundreds of miles from the Serengeti Plain.

Why had Paul called after all this time? It seemed fairly obvious: as long as I was an Apple employee, he wouldn't hire me, simply because he wanted to have nothing whatsoever to do with the organization. But once he heard that I had left, he wasted no time in getting back in touch. He and I always had a good rapport and worked so well as a team, plus Paul, like the other three Beatles, always liked having a familiar face around.

But why Africa? That was a tougher question to answer. Perhaps it was simply that Paul was looking for someplace exotic to record, someplace warm and sunny. George Harrison had recorded some of his Indian music at an EMI studio in Calcutta, so Paul knew that the company owned studios around the world; there had actually been a map in the studio manager's office at Abbey Road with pins indicating the location of each one.

We can all be a little naive at times. In later interviews, Paul explained that he envisioned "lying on the beach all day doing nothing and recording at night." Instead, we would be getting open drainage, lizards, and monsoons.

Nigeria had once been part of the British Commonwealth, but a visa was still required for entry. To my horror, when I rang the consulate I was informed that I was required to first pay a visit to London's Tropical Disease Hospital in order to have yellow fever, typhoid, and cholera shots—diseases that were rampant in the undeveloped country. As he jabbed me in the arm with the painful vaccines, the doctor also casually mentioned that I'd have to take malaria tablets the whole time I was there. I actually got a mild dose of yellow fever as a result of the vaccinations—much like a bad flu—and it lasted for about five days. This was already starting to seem like a really bad idea.

Things weren't going any more smoothly for Paul up in Scotland, as I was to soon learn. He had convened his band, Wings, for a series of prepro-duction meetings in late July, but the rehearsals were apparently quite con-tentious. By early August the bad feelings had built to the point where, at the very last moment, his drummer and lead guitarist quit. That left rhythm guitarist Denny Laine as the only remaining member: Wings had been re-duced to a trio.

For no particular reason, Paul and I hadn't spoken since our initial phone conversation, so I had no idea of the problems he was dealing with, and he had no idea about the reservations I was starting to have about the wisdom of the entire enterprise. It had originally seemed like such an excit-ing adventure, but in the days before we were due to depart, my nerves were beginning to get frayed. Beyond the fact that I didn't know anything about the living conditions in Lagos, I had no idea what the studio had in the way of equipment, so I didn't know what kinds of hurdles I'd be facing technically—no advance research had been done, which, in hindsight, was really quite foolish.

The bottom line was that I didn't really want to go, but I didn't want to let Paul down, either. I had my anxiety pretty much under control in the weeks leading up to the start of the project, but then I started getting stage fright. The night I was due to fly out, Malcolm Davies and John Smith came along for moral support. We all gathered at one of the pubs in Victoria Station (where I'd soon be catching the train to Gatwick airport) for a bon voyage drink, despite the fact that I was hardly in a celebratory mood.

"What am I getting myself into?" I kept asking them. There were thun-derstorms raging outside, which did nothing to make me feel any better about getting on that plane.

"Leave it to you to pick the worst possible weather for flying in," Smithy said, grinning from ear to ear. "That plane of yours will be bouncing from thundercap to thundercap."

Malcolm urged me to buy extra flight insurance—with him listed as beneficiary. True friends, both of them.

Somehow I forced myself to continue the journey, and all too soon I was strapped in my seat, a reluctant passenger on the midnight British Caledon-ian flight to Lagos. Smithy was correct—the long flight was extremely tur-bulent, making the hours pass even more slowly. I didn't get a wink of sleep, either, despite the many Scotches I was ordering. But on one of her visits to my seat, the stewardess had a surprise.

"This is for you, sir," she said, handing me a glass of champagne. "It's from one of the first-class passengers."

Looking up, I saw a grinning Denny Laine standing behind her. We hadn't met before, but I recognized him from photographs—between his long hair and colorful garb, it was obvious that he was a musician.

"You must be Geoff," he said, offering me a warm handshake as he settled into the empty seat beside me. We commiserated about what an awful flight it was, and then I asked him if Paul and Linda were sitting up front with him as well.

"No, they'll be flying out in a day or two," he explained. "They thought we should be the advance party and suss out the situation first."

Over the next few hours he filled me in with the details of the difficult rehearsals and the last-minute resignations of his fellow band members. By the time we landed, I decided that I liked Denny—he was easygoing and a good conversationalist, and I started to feel a little better about things. It turned out that he and I would be sharing one of two villas that had been rented, along with two roadies; Paul, Linda, and their kids would be staying at the other one.

The studio had arranged for a car to meet us at the airport, and when we finally arrived at the villa after a short but bumpy ride, I was anxious to have a look around the property, but then my exhaustion suddenly hit me. Without even bothering to unpack, I fell straight into bed, but between the heat and my excitement I wasn't able to sleep very much. When I finally got up, Denny was nowhere to be seen, so I decided to head over to the studio and get my first peek at the facilities. I rang the number we had been given and asked if a taxi could come pick me up. Good thing I did, because it turned out to be more than an hour's drive away. Every so often, I'd see some poor soul hobbling slowly down the road, wrapped in bandages and sheets. Watching me carefully in his rearview mirror, the driver answered my unspoken question.

"Those are lepers," he explained calmly.

Lepers!

As we pulled up to the address I had been given, my heart sank further still. *Surely this can't be it*, I thought. But it was. EMI Lagos was actually no more then a large shed. My heart began to sink. I was greeted at the door by a smiling, friendly face: it was Odion, the studio manager—I never found out if that was his first name or his last name. He introduced me to the assistant who had been assigned to the project. He had only a single name, too: Monday.

Thankfully, the interior wasn't quite as unimpressive as the exterior. It wasn't brand spanking new, but it wasn't too run-down either. In many ways, all the EMI studios were fairly standardized; it was almost like the Mc-Donald's concept, where the theory is that a Big Mac should taste the same wherever you buy it. The directive came from EMI headquarters in England as to what equipment each of their studios around the world should provide. The difference was that outlying studios often had older, secondhand gear because company policy was to send discarded equipment from Abbey Road to the studios in third world countries. As a result, the console at the Lagos studio was actually pretty decent—it was the standard EMI console, a smaller version of what they had at Abbey Road—and the monitors were exactly the same ones I had gotten used to during my years at EMI. As I was wandering around inspecting the facility, Monday brought in an old cardboard box.

"What's this?" I asked.

"These are our microphones," he replied. I looked inside: a few dozen mics were strewn about haphazardly; not one of them was stored inside its protective case. There were a couple of decent Neumanns in there, but the rest of the microphones were run-of-the-mill, inexpensive models, and none of them looked like they were in particularly great shape.

Sixteen-track recording was state-of-the-art in 1973, but I knew it would be too much to expect to find that in the Lagos studio. With some trepidation, I asked to see the multitrack machine. It was eight-track, which was fine—I could deal with that—but then Monday went on to explain that it only had four "sync" amps. These were the electronic components that allowed you to listen to prerecorded tracks off the record head. What that meant was that I could only ever play back four tracks when we were overdubbing. Yes, I could choose which four tracks I wanted the musicians to hear—the sync amps could be swapped around easily enough—but it was still quite a limitation, and quite a nuisance.

I was amazed: hadn't any other artist ever complained about this? Neither Odion nor Monday seemed to understand why I thought it posed a problem. It turned out that every other artist who had ever come into the studio just performed live, with the various instruments spread over the eight tracks—they had literally never done overdubs. Since he had no experience, I obviously couldn't leave the drop-ins and drop-outs to Monday, so I would end up doing them all myself. I simply gave him the job of threading up the tape reels and starting and stopping the machine.

I walked out of the control room and had a look at the studio. It was a decent size, and there was the required amount of cabling and mic stands, but there was no drum booth—in fact, there were no acoustic screens whatsoever. It took a while for me to explain what acoustic screens were and why we needed them. I was starting to get a bit exasperated, but Odion was eager to please.

"No problem, man," he said. "We'll get a carpenter in to make them."

When we arrived the next morning, a crew of workmen were indeed hard at work building screens. We all mucked in helping them so that we could start the sessions—at one point even Paul picked up a saw and began sawing wood. By the third day or so, they were all done . . . except that the carpenters had left an empty hole in the middle of each screen! They couldn't understand the concept, couldn't understand why the screens had to be filled in with a sheet of glass in order to block the sound. Eventually a glazier was located and they were completed, but there was a little drama there for a while, and we lost a few days of recording time as a result.

The heat in Lagos was oppressive, so air-conditioning was a necessity in the control room; without it, the equipment would constantly be overheating. It was reasonably cool in there, but the air-conditioning in the studio was considerably less efficient, and it was often uncomfortably warm. The strangest thing about the Lagos facility was that there was a door at the back of the studio that led directly into the pressing plant. When you opened it, you saw a couple of dozen shirtless guys standing ankle deep in water, pressing records in this small, steaming, hot room. There was a corrugated roof overhead, but you could clearly see daylight in there, so it was only partly roofed, to keep the worst of the rain out and let some of the hot air escape. It was incredibly noisy in there, too, though there was sufficient soundproofing so that the din didn't actually interfere with our recording.

For all of the technical limitations and bizarre surroundings, we managed to get a good sound out of that little studio. To this day, I don't know quite how we did it, but *Band On The Run*, as the album came to be known, turned out to be somewhat of a landmark recording. I'm convinced, in fact, that it wouldn't have sounded any better if we had done it entirely at a state-of-the-art London studio—all of which goes to show that the music is all that counts.

I have no love for lizards or snakes or insects. Never have, probably never will. Unfortunately, those are three things that Nigeria has in abundance, which probably tempered my view of what I am sure is an otherwise lovely country. By the second day I was there, I hated the place.

It actually all started the day I arrived. When I finally gave up on my attempt at taking a nap, I wandered into the kitchen to have a poke around, just to see if the cupboards were stocked with anything edible. I opened the door to the pantry and nearly jumped out of my skin: somebody had stored their collection of dead spiders there, all stuck on a big polystyrene whiteboard with pins. When I went to sleep that night and pulled the covers back, I found that Denny had discovered the collection as well, and had put several of the dead spiders in my bed, as a practical joke. Suddenly I didn't like Mr. Laine quite so much . . . but luckily I'd seen the spiders beforehand, so I didn't react nearly as severely as he'd obviously hoped I would.

The next morning I woke from a deep, refreshing sleep, and in the warmth of the sun everything seemed a lot brighter. *This place isn't so bad*, I was thinking as I gazed out the bedroom window. At least the villa was gorgeous, the company tolerable, the impending project full of promise. Just then, this huge lizard popped up from the tall grass, staring right at me. It had a big red head and a green neck . . . it was terrifying! I didn't know if it was dangerous or poisonous; I didn't know what to think. Then I began looking around the bedroom and realized that I was sharing my space with a family of translucent "jelly lizards," scuttling all over the walls, ceilings, and floors.

Within minutes I was on the phone to Odion, telling him that I wanted to be moved to a hotel. One night in that villa was quite enough for me.

Of course, the hotel wasn't that great, either. It was largely bereft of lizards, but it was plagued with an infestation of giant cockroaches. I first became aware of them when I was in the bathroom and I heard a swishing sound. My first thought was that the toilet handle was stuck, so I went to investigate. To my horror I saw a huge nest of swarming cockroaches rustling around in a trap behind the toilet bowl—that was the source of the noise.

The damn things were the size of dinner plates, and they were a real nuisance. You couldn't drink the water in Lagos because it came out of the taps a revolting yellow color, so instead of taking a glass of water to bed at night in case I woke up thirsty, I kept an open bottle of Coke by the bedside. One morning I happened to take a look inside and it was full of big cockroaches; I had taken a swig of it in the middle of the night, too. In my frustration I actually dropped the heavy bottle on one cockroach, from a height, to try to kill it. Incredibly, the bottle landed upright on the huge insect and started moving; it was obviously going to take more than a large glass bottle to kill them. A small elephant gun, more likely.

Everyone else opted to stay at the villas, so it was lonely at the hotel at times, but I still felt it was worth it. For one thing, it was a lot closer to the

studio, so my commute was shorter. The traffic jams were horrendous in Lagos, and people had a disconcerting habit of driving over the verge in the
middle and going the wrong way down the opposite side of the road until
that, too, got jammed up. But everyone seemed used to sitting in traffic jams
for long periods of time. There were even street vendors selling travel-sized
board games to the people in the cars, just to keep them occupied while they
sat there.

Another advantage of staying at the hotel was that it had a dining room
that was open fairly late, so at least I could get a proper meal of some sort after the session ended. The food wasn't great, but it was edible and probably
better than anything I could have fixed for myself at the villa; in any event,
the last thing I felt like doing after a long day's work was cooking myself a
meal. Of course, like anyplace else in Lagos where food was present, the hotel dining room was plagued with insects. One night, someone at a table at
the other end of the room called the waiter over. I was watching with fascination, curious as to what the problem was. The waiter strolled over and
lifted up the tablecloth . . . and then, to my astonishment, he ducked under
the table on his hands and knees. The next thing I heard was this big banging
sound—the waiter had taken his shoe off and was killing a giant cockroach
that was crawling around on the floor.

That was what life was like in Nigeria—things like that were an everyday
occurrence. I kept my malaria pills in a box on the breakfast table so I'd remember to take them every morning, and I took salt tablets with me wherever I went because it was so easy to get dehydrated. Not that there was all
that much sun—we actually landed in Nigeria just at the start of monsoon
season. It was incredibly hot and humid, and there was pouring rain and red
mud everywhere. There were open drains, too, which led to a huge problem
with mosquitos. One of the roadies was getting eaten alive by them, though
for some reason they weren't going after me especially. I guess it's possible
that they were taking pity on me, considering the endless battles I was engaged in with the cockroaches.

"Glad you're here with me, Geoff. We're off on another adventure, aren't we?"

Those were Paul's first words to me when we finally met up at the studio.
Though we'd spoken on the phone a few times, I hadn't seen him in person
for years—we hadn't done any socializing at all while I was at Apple—and I
hadn't worked with him since the *Abbey Road* sessions back in 1969. He was

a changed man, not so much physically but emotionally. He'd clearly matured, yet in many ways he was back to his old self, the chipper, optimistic person he had been during the *Revolver* and *Pepper* days, and I could see in his face that there was a lot less tension and stress in his life. Paul was still filled with confidence and still very much in charge, but this time around there was no John Lennon to stand up to him or disagree with anything he was saying—he wasn't answerable to anyone. Working with Paul on solo projects was actually very much like the time I had recorded "Blackbird," or any of the tracks I did with him when the other Beatles weren't around. Like George Martin, he and I had been working together so long that we could almost read each other's mind—in fact, we never even had a conversation about what I had gone through at Apple. Paul never asked me any questions about what had gone on there, and still hasn't, to this very day.

At that first session, Linda greeted me with a big hello and a big hug. She hadn't changed at all since the *Abbey Road* sessions. We chatted for quite a long time, and I asked her how she was enjoying the life of a musician on the road.

"Well, I know that I'm not exactly a musician, and I hate being up on that stage," she said self-effacingly. "Still, the touring is a lot of fun, and at least we get to spend a lot of time with each other and with the kids."

They had brought their daughters—James hadn't been born yet—to Nigeria with them; the kids were never left behind, which I always found admirable. Paul and Linda were very involved parents, and as a result their kids were exceptionally well behaved. The girls used to collect the lizards in the garden and keep them in a big cage; they were always showing their collection off to anyone who would have a look. I would feign terror, though it wasn't really all play-acting.

From day one, I had found Linda to be an easy person to get along with— she was down to earth, with no airs, no pretensions. She was a quick study, too: during the *Band On The Run* sessions, she started to learn how to read the expressions on my face. If she thought her singing was a bit out of tune, she'd just peer into the control room and would know how to interpret a certain look from me. To me, Linda was always an integral part of the band's sound. If you take her voice out of the vocal harmonies, it's just not Wings anymore.

Denny was clearly the third wheel, but Paul nonetheless had regard for his abilities and opinions. If Denny made a musical suggestion, Paul would consider it seriously and incorporate it . . . if he liked what he was hearing. It wasn't like John talking to Paul, where they really did consider each other to be equals, but the two men clearly had a mutual respect, and I didn't pick up on any tensions between them during the Lagos sessions. Denny also seemed to have a good, solid friendship with Linda, and he got along great with the kids, too.

Although it undoubtedly inspired the title track, Paul and Linda never talked much about the musicians who had quit on the eve of the sessions. It was Denny who was actually most resentful that the other members of Wings hadn't turned up. His attitude was "Screw them, let's muck in and make a good album without them." He seemed determined to impress Paul, and to not let the team down. Denny was the putative guitarist in the band, but that didn't stop Paul from playing many of the solos and the difficult bits himself. Harmonies occasionally presented a problem for Denny. He would sometimes have difficulty singing in tune, which would try Paul's patience and create minor technical problems for me: scattered throughout the harmony track would be the sounds of a frustrated Denny mumbling, "Fuck!" off-mic, just loud enough to be heard. It would sometimes take me hours to edit out the offending bits.

Paul didn't exactly treat Denny like a sideman, but he also never hesitated to tell him what he thought. Overall, however, the three members of Wings worked well as a unit. The conditions were bad, but the vibe was great. We always did have fun during those sessions.

Paul was never one for working on weekends, so we quickly settled into a five-day-a-week schedule, which made things quite relaxing. Because it was so hot during the day, and because there was limited air-conditioning in the studio, we didn't start the sessions until mid-afternoon. On occasion, Paul and Linda and the kids, plus Denny, would spend their mornings swimming at a country club near the airport and then have lunch together. I never joined them; I would just sleep late and putter around in the hotel before heading over to the studio an hour or two ahead of starting time. We usually ended our sessions by midnight, but we sometimes went through the night, even until dawn a couple of times, especially toward the end of our stay.

But the very first week we were there, things definitely did not go according to plan: one evening, while taking a stroll with Linda, Paul got mugged at knifepoint. While his wife shrieked, "Don't kill him! He's Beatle Paul!" he calmly surrendered his wallet, camera, and watch, but that wasn't good enough for his assailants, who demanded his bag, too. Paul was smart enough not to argue, but it was a devastating blow, because inside were all his demo tapes and notebooks containing the words and music for the songs he'd written for the album.

The next day, Paul told us all what had happened.

"You're lucky you're a white man," Odion said. "If you were black, you would have been killed. Everyone here believes that white people can't tell us apart. If they thought you could have identified them to the police, they would have finished you off."

Paul blanched visibly; Linda looked as if she was about to faint. But he was always one to try to make the best of a bad situation.

"I think I can remember how most of the songs went," he told us. "And those that I can't remember . . . well, I guess I'll have to write some new ones."

That was how easy it was for Paul to compose music and lyrics. If he needed to, he could literally knock off a song in an hour or two, as he had done when he wrote "Picasso's Last Words" at Dustin Hoffman's request during a dinner party.

The songs "Jet," "Mrs. Vandebilt," and "Mamunia" were ones that he remembered in their entirety, but much of the rest of the album was written on the fly, in Lagos. The title song, "Band On The Run," had been written just before Paul and Linda left for Nigeria, so he was able to recall that one pretty well, too. Its lyrics were tweaked a bit while we were there, and so they were evocative of the unique situation Paul found himself in: abandoned by his bandmates, trapped in a recording studio in a strange and threatening land. Little wonder he felt a tinge of paranoia.

The mugging was a wake-up call for all of us, but it had happened in a dangerous area on the outskirts of town. Both the hotel and studio were near the center of Lagos, so I generally felt safe, at least during daylight hours. The general manager of the pressing plant was English, and he would pick me up and take me to the studio every afternoon. At night, they'd have a car waiting to drive me back to the hotel.

The sessions generally ran very smoothly, with few hiccups of either a technical or artistic nature. There was a bit of a kerfuffle at one point because somehow Ginger Baker, the drummer in Cream, had gotten the impression that we were going to record the album at his Nigerian studio, ARC. There were lots of phone calls flying back and forth, but Paul was adamant that he had never promised to work anywhere but at the EMI studio. Just to smooth things over, he agreed to a compromise: we would spend a day at Ginger's place and see what it was like. We ended up doing most of the song "Picasso's Last Words"—which was intentionally recorded to resemble a

Picasso painting, with lots of seemingly unrelated song fragments stuck together—at ARC, although we added a lot of overdubs later when we returned to London, editing them together, along with snatches of other tunes on the album, to try to make one cohesive piece out of it. Ginger's studio was fairly well equipped, and he did his best to try to sell us on the idea of booking it for the rest of the album—he even lent a hand to the recording, playing some percussion at one point. But Paul had made a commitment elsewhere and he intended to honor it, so we only spent the one day there before returning to EMI.

Paul played all the drums on *Band On The Run*, and he always loved getting behind the kit. Truth be told, we really didn't miss having a drummer in the band at all. Most backing tracks would begin with him and Denny playing together on drums and rhythm guitar, or sometimes they'd both play acoustic guitars. Then the songs would slowly be built up, layer by layer. Linda almost never played keyboards during the backing track, so we would overdub her parts on afterward, with both Paul and Denny doing the guitars, and all three of them singing backing vocals.

And, of course, Paul sang lead and played bass on the entire album. He had been a great bass player even from the earliest days, and his technique and musicality just kept getting better and better as the years went on. Nonetheless, it seemed to me that he reached a plateau with *Sgt. Pepper*, when he was willing to stay late, hour after hour, getting every note to speak perfectly. It was almost as if he reached the absolute heights of what a bass player could do on *Pepper*; he went from great to superlative back to great again. But *Band On The Run* was like his resurgence. Paul's bass playing was so strong that we mixed it prominently throughout the album, once again propelling his performance into the limelight.

As the sessions went on, the hours grew longer, so relaxation time on the weekends became increasingly important. One Sunday a local official took us out on a boat trip to an island, where he had arranged for a buffet spread of all the local delicacies. I was always a picky eater—most of the time I just had the chicken in the hotel—so I approached the buffet table cautiously. Amid all the unfamiliar foods piled high on the table, one stood out immediately: a platter of sliced giant snails. They actually looked cartoonish, like the silhouette of a snail, which was quite funny, but also quite nauseating. Needless to say, I didn't try them. In fact, I didn't touch anything that day, making vague excuses about having a touchy stomach. I never did add the fact that it was the sight of their food that caused my discomfort.

Another evening I was invited to Odion's house for a home-cooked meal. His wife had gone to great trouble to cook a stew, but the meat in it—of unknown pedigree—was so tough that I couldn't swallow it no matter how much I chewed. Eventually I made an excuse to go to the bathroom, where I promptly spit it out. He and his wife were very personable and chatty, but they were very much on their guard about talking politics.

It seemed as if there was never a dull moment recording *Band On The Run*—every productive, fun session seemed to be counterbalanced with something bad happening. The biggest scare came the afternoon Paul fell ill. It was a Friday and we'd only just started the session, but everyone was in a good mood and looking forward to the weekend. Paul was standing in front of the microphone, laying down a vocal with his usual aplomb when all of a sudden he started gasping for air. Within seconds, he turned as white as a sheet, explaining to us in a croaking voice that he couldn't catch his breath. We decided to take him outside for some fresh air, which probably wasn't the smartest thing to do, because once he was exposed to the blazing heat he felt even worse and began keeling over, finally fainting dead away at our feet. Linda began screaming hysterically; she was convinced that he was having a heart attack. I shouted at Monday to run inside and fetch the studio manager. Odion dashed out and quickly assessed the situation; we were pleading with him to call an ambulance, but he coolly explained that he could get Paul to the local hospital in his car a lot sooner than any ambulance could. Paul was starting to come around by this point, but we lifted him off the ground and gently deposited him in the backseat. Then Linda and one of the roadies piled into the car and they went roaring down the street.

In the silent aftermath, Denny and I looked at each other. Was Paul indeed having a heart attack? What on earth was going to happen next? We went back into the studio, worried and deeply concerned, and tried to fill the time by doing a guitar overdub, but our minds weren't really on what we were doing. A few hours later we got a call from Linda saying that Paul was okay, that he had been released from the hospital and was on his way back to the villa. And, she told us, he was stubbornly insisting that he would be back in the studio on Monday at the normal time.

When we all returned to work after the weekend, Paul looked a little shaken but was otherwise okay. The official diagnosis was that he had suffered a bronchial spasm brought on by too much smoking. Thankfully, Paul never had another incident like that.

Still, as the sessions continued, the adventures continued. One night the four of us—Paul, Linda, Denny, and I—went to a club called The Shrine to hear some music. The place was owned by an extremely popular Nigerian musician named Fela Ransome-Kuti, and he was appearing there himself that night. He had a phenomenal band with him, too—more than a dozen percussionists, horns, and brass; it was a real big band in the true sense of the word. In addition to being a pop star and originator of the "afrobeat" genre, Fela was also a political activist, and his followers bought his records by the millions. He was a huge star in Africa.

We loved the music—Paul was positively weeping with joy—and everyone was having a fantastic time. Though I abstained, some strong pot was being passed around the table, adding to the high spirits. During the break, some of the musicians came over to say hello. We assumed it was going to be the usual kind of camaraderie that goes on at live gigs everywhere—swapping road stories, talking music, telling jokes—but it was anything but. To our surprise, our visitors were angry and hostile.

"What are you doing in our country?" they demanded. "You've come here to steal our music and our rhythms. Why don't you just go back home?"

I could see Paul getting alarmed; this was not the reception he had been expecting. Somehow he managed to talk his way out of it and got the musicians calmed down enough to leave us alone . . . at which point we made a hasty departure.

As soon as we got safely in the car, Paul turned to me and said, "Whew, that was a close call, wasn't it?" It might have been the pot making him a bit paranoid, but he was under the impression that we had been in danger of getting physically attacked, and he was really scared.

It was a nasty episode, but we thought that was the last of it. We were mistaken. A day or two later Fela himself got on Lagos radio and began publicly accusing us of coming to Nigeria for the express purpose of stealing and exploiting African music. He was a rabble-rouser, but I always suspected that his motives were as much financial as they were social conscience: I felt that Fela saw Paul as competition, and so he felt that Paul was taking money out of his pocket.

It was definitely worrying there for a while—these were really heavy-duty people we were dealing with, and they were making some pretty serious threats. Ultimately, Paul's diplomatic skills saved the day: through intermediaries, he invited Fela to come down to the studio to hear some of the tracks for himself. A grim-looking Ransome-Kuti showed up one after-noon, accompanied by some thuggish-looking henchmen, and took a seat in the back of the control room, arms crossed defiantly. I nervously threaded up the tape and played him some of the songs we had been work-ing on. To our great relief he was satisfied that we hadn't pinched their rhythms after all—in point of fact, there's practically no African influence on the album at all.

Just as swiftly as it had begun, the entire matter was dropped and we heard no more about it. That's why I was so convinced that the whole inci-dent was about money: once Fela realized that Paul's music was nothing like his and wouldn't appeal to his audience, the accusations ended. To be on the safe side, Paul made the prudent decision to not hire any local musicians to play on the album; that way, we could hardly be accused of exploiting any-one, or of stealing their ideas. Ironically, one African musician did appear on *Band On The Run* after all. His name was Remi Kabaka, and he came in to do a percussion overdub on the song "Bluebird" once we were back in Lon-don. Incredibly, he had been born in Lagos.

It seemed a lot longer at the time, but we only spent some seven weeks in Nigeria. The day before we left, Paul and Linda threw an end-of-album bar-becue on the beach to celebrate. A toast was drunk to our success, to our sur-vival, and to our last meal together in the dark continent. In a few hours Wings and company would be flying back to London . . . or so we thought.

Lagos had one final little surprise in store for us, which was actually somehow fitting. It came in the form of a problem with our aircraft, just as we were about to begin boarding our flight. Nobody had any idea when it would be fixed, or how long we would be delayed, but we'd already checked out of the villas and hotel and we were lumbered with staggering amounts of baggage, as well as all the tapes, which we were hand-carrying to ensure their safe arrival. In the end, one of the roadies was dispatched to wait at the air-port with our things and told to call us as soon as there was any news. The rest of us headed off to the nearby country club where Paul, Linda, and Denny had been spending their mornings. It was my first time there and I was pleasantly surprised at how modern the accommodations were. We passed the long afternoon swimming and relaxing until we finally received word that the flight had been cleared to depart. The two hours' time differ-ence worked in our favor, but we still didn't touch down at Gatwick until 3 A.M. To my surprise, there were dozens of journalists and fans waiting there for us. My dad was there, too; he'd offered to pick me up and give me a ride back to London, though I never expected he'd still be there in the middle of the night. It was the first and only time he ever met Paul, who was gracious enough to come over and say hello for a few minutes.

I drove the car back to Crouch End while my dad dozed in the seat beside me. My mind was buzzing with all kinds of thoughts; it felt like years since I'd left London. But my work wasn't completed yet. In a week's time we were due back in the studio, this time at AIR. I hoped that our string of disasters and near calamities was at long last behind us.

After the heat of Nigeria, the cold damp of a London autumn was especially hard to take, but I had precious little time to recuperate from the nasty head cold that I developed due to the drastic change of weather. We still had a fair amount of work to do: Paul wanted to add some overdubs, even full orchestra, to a number of the tracks, and there was one new song—"Jet"— still to be recorded in its entirety; then we had to mix the whole album. Paul was anxious to have the record released in time for the Christmas season— traditionally a period of high sales—so the pressure was on.

All of the tapes we had recorded in Lagos were eight-track, so our first task was to copy those tracks that would be receiving overdubs to sixteen-track format; doing so would give us eight additional tracks to record on. That went smoothly enough, as did most of the instrumental and orchestral overdubs—Tony Visconti's orchestral arrangements provided the icing on the cake, and Paul's old Liverpool mate Howie Casey came in at one point and, in just a single take, played a phenomenal sax solo on the song "Bluebird." But the Lagos curse reared its ugly head one last time when we started recording the backing track for "Jet."

Everything seemed to be in order as Paul and Denny began laying down the drum and rhythm guitar parts. After just a few takes, they nailed it and came into the control room for a listen. We all agreed that it sounded great, so we moved on to the process of overdubbing the other instruments. Everyone was excited by how well the song was coming together, and the creative ideas were flying fast and furious—the sixteen tracks of the tape were filling up rapidly. My assistant engineer on the session was a fellow by the name of Pete Swettenham, who had at one time been the guitarist in a band called Grapefruit, one of Apple's earliest signings. He seemed competent enough, and I thought he was doing a good job, but then I started hearing something funny during the playbacks: the top end on the cymbals wasn't there anymore. "What's going on?" I asked Pete. He sidled over to the multitrack machine, leaned down to have a look, and casually said, "Well, there's a pile of oxide on the tape machine."

What?? This was a major problem, and I was furious that Pete hadn't noticed it earlier. Assistants were supposed to keep the heads of the tape machines scrupulously clean, and they were supposed to stay on top of things like this. Oxide shedding was something that occurred with distressing frequency back in the 1970s because tape manufacturers were experimenting with different ways of adhering the magnetically charged iron oxide particles—the "recording" component in recording tape—to the backing. If the glue was faulty, or if a batch of tape was improperly manufactured, the particles would begin to come off, or "shed." The top end, or treble, would start to disappear from the sound and eventually the tape would become completely unplayable and could even damage the machine. Not only was it irreversible, each time you played back or even rewound the tape, it got worse. The only thing you could do was to quickly make a second-generation copy of the audio on a good reel of tape and hope that the sound hadn't deteriorated too badly by that point. It was just our luck to have this one bad reel of tape just as we were recording such a great song.

Paul, Denny, and Linda were out in the studio, happily playing away, oblivious to the disaster in the making that was occurring in the control room. I had to think quickly: do I tell Paul, or don't I? I mulled it over and finally came to the conclusion that there was no point in telling him. The damage was already done, and making Paul aware of it would only upset him and kill the vibe. It was already late at night and I was hoping they would wrap things up soon and go home so I could make a copy before the tape became unplayable. I decided to try to mask the problem, which was becoming most noticeable on the crack of the snare drum and sizzle of the hi-hat. Every time we'd play the tape back, I would add more treble to the monitors so that Paul couldn't hear that the top end was disappearing.

We finally did what I thought was the last overdub of the night. Breathing a sigh of relief, I looked over at Pete and said, "Thank God!"

Then, of course, Denny said, "How about if we just add one more guitar?" and I thought, *Oh no!* We had almost gotten to the point where you could see through the tape—that's how much oxide had been shed. But to my relief, Paul vetoed the idea and everyone packed up for the night. As soon as they left, I copied "Jet" onto a fresh reel of multitrack tape, and I never said a word to Paul about it, but that's why the song has a distinctively solid sound. Fortunately, that was the only technical gremlin we encountered at AIR.

That was just one of those difficult aesthetic, nontechnical decisions you have to make as an engineer. I simply didn't want to do anything to destroy the creative flow. There was nothing we could do about the problem, anyway, so why spoil the mood of the session? My philosophy then was the same as it is now: the music comes first. The technical aspects of recording are there to serve the artistic aspects, not the other way around, and if sacrifices have to be made technically in order to preserve the artistic integrity, so be it.

At AIR, we did a fair bit of overdub work on the song "Let Me Roll It"— one of my favorite tracks on the album. Critics later interpreted it as "McCartney trying to out-Lennon Lennon," but if Paul was deliberately trying to sound like his former bandmate when he recorded the song, he never said a word about it. In fact, there was no talk of Lennon or any of the other Beatles at all during the *Band On The Run* sessions. Paul didn't ask for the "Lennon" tape echo, he just told me to add some special tape echo. It was actually very similar to the effect we had put on his vocal on the *Abbey Road* track "Oh Darling."

The lead guitar part in "Let Me Roll It" is phenomenal, and it's even more amazing considering that it was double-tracked. Paul played that, not Denny, and he did an excellent job of doubling the part with exactly the same phrasing and attitude. The guitar sound is a little reminiscent of John's ultra-distorted guitar on "Revolution," but it just happened that way—we weren't specifically trying to duplicate the sound. More eerily, there's a bad edit after the last chorus that adds an extra beat, just as happened on "Revolution." It was just a mistake that Paul liked; it wasn't designed to poke fun at Lennon's proclivity for odd time signatures.

Band On The Run was never really designed to be a concept album, but Paul obviously liked the idea: that's why he had me edit little snatches of melodies from other songs and snippets of French dialogue into "Picasso's Last Words." He also came up with the suggestion of creating a reprise of the title track to end the album. It wasn't a new recording—we just flew in a section of the original version, and it worked just fine.

The mixing sessions for *Band On The Run* were fun, but hurried. AIR, unfortunately, was completely booked up, so we had to move to another London studio called Kingsway. They had reasonable equipment, but we had a few problems trying to replicate the effects we had available at Abbey Road and AIR, especially the automatic double tracking, so we had to rent in a couple of extra tape machines. It was all sorted out pretty quickly, which was a good thing because we had literally only three days to mix the entire album from start to finish.

Mixes didn't take as long in 1973 as they do now—producers can literally spend weeks at a time mixing a single track in today's digital world—but even then, three days to mix an entire album was ridiculous. The problem wasn't that Kingsway didn't have sufficient time to give us—they did, and even if they didn't, they were so thrilled to have a client of Paul's stature, they would have moved heaven and earth for us if necessary. The problem was a producer/manager by the name of Gerry Bron, who owned a label called Bronze Records.

Sometime earlier, Bron had booked time at AIR for a band of his called Tempest—John Hiseman was their drummer. Gerry specifically wanted me to engineer the sessions, and John Burgess, who was AIR's studio manager, assured him that I would be available. However, the *Band On The Run* overdub sessions had run a bit longer than we expected, and now the Tempest sessions were due to start in just a few day's time. I asked John Burgess if he would ask Gerry to slip his sessions back a few days so that I'd have sufficient time to complete the Wings mixes at Kingsway first. Recording projects almost always run behind schedule, and it is considered common courtesy in the music business to accommodate such requests—the likelihood is that you, in turn, will end up making the same kind of request yourself at some point, so it pays to keep everything on a friendly basis. But to my amazement, Bron refused to put the sessions back, even by a day or two, and he also refused to work with any of the other AIR engineers.

Gerry was actress Eleanor Bron's brother; she had appeared with the Beatles in their second film, *Help!* I have no idea if Paul used that connection to try to get us a little extra mixing time, but if he did, it came to naught. I do know that he asked John Burgess to put pressure on Gerry to accommodate us, and that he was infuriated when John refused to do so. Perhaps there was some kind of history, some kind of problem between Gerry and Paul; if there was, I was unaware of it. It just seemed to me that it was simple one-upmanship, and it was stupid.

Just in case we didn't get all the mixes done in the three days we had allotted, Paul had come up with a contingency plan: he was going to kidnap me. To make it look real, he was literally going to hire a couple of guys to abduct me outside my house and spirit me away to some other studio to finish the mixes. He was serious about it, too—they were going to do it properly so that no one would know where I was. That way, I couldn't be held accountable by Gerry or by AIR for not showing up at the Tempest sessions.

Fortunately, it never came to that. Though we were under considerable pressure, the mixes went smoothly and the atmosphere was pleasant. Paul was confident and in a very up mood at the Kingsway sessions, as were Denny and Linda: we all felt as if we'd been through a storm together and that the silver lining was beginning to appear. The tracks were sounding great, too: the instruments had been recorded with a lot of their effects to start with, so there wasn't a lot of tweaking to do. There was just a great energy to the whole album: the guitars were well played, the drums were upfront, and the bass was solid. All the sounds on *Band On The Run*, in fact, were purposefully built around the interplay between the bass and the drums.

On the third and final day of mixing, I staggered out of the studio at 5 A.M. I hadn't slept for more than twenty-four hours, but I had to be at AIR at 10 A.M. to start the Tempest sessions. I physically carried all the mix and multitrack tapes home with me because we weren't willing to leave them at Kingsway, and I left them on the table in my front hallway while I trudged up the stairs to shower and shave—I knew that if I allowed my head to hit the pillow, I would sleep for days. Fortunately, I somehow remembered to bring the tapes with me to AIR; from there, they would be shipped to both Malcolm Davies at Apple and Harry Moss at EMI for mastering. (In the end, I selected Harry's cut because it had the sound quality that I was after.) I felt like death warmed over all that day, and for some time afterward, but I made the session that Gerry Bron had insisted upon, and I somehow survived the entire experience.

Band On The Run, credited to Paul McCartney and Wings, was released in early December 1973, just in time for the big Christmas market. It was a huge success, spawned several hit singles, got rave reviews, and sold millions of copies. It had phenomenal staying power, too, remaining in the British charts for a staggering two and a half years. Perhaps most important, it regained for Paul the credibility and respect of the record-buying public. It also won a couple of Grammys, including Best Pop Vocal Performance and my third award for Best Engineered Album. If anyone at AIR was still unhappy about my joining the staff, that shut them up. There's nothing a studio loves more than to be able to brag that one of their own has a Grammy sitting on his mantelpiece.

I do think the success of the album took Paul a bit by surprise, though it didn't surprise me. He had been raked over the coals by the critics for his last two solo albums (*Wild Life* and *Red Rose Speedway*) and he was perhaps a bit gun-shy by that point. I know that Paul felt good about what we had done, but I can't say he was overly confident, either. Even if he thought something he'd recorded was going to be a monster hit, he wouldn't say so, he would just wait it out. The whole saga of *Band On The Run* is a triumph of spirit over adversity. It was Paul McCartney's shining moment as a solo artist, and I was honored to be a part of it.

Life After the Beatles:

From Elvis to the *Anthologies*

The studio at AIR was top-notch, and it attracted many of the top musicians in the world, giving me the opportunity to engineer for a wide variety of talented artists, including Jeff Beck, Robin Trower, and Split Enz. I did so many enjoyable records during my years there: half a dozen memorable albums by the fine band America (including *Holiday*, *Hearts*, and *Hideaway*); the Paul McCartney/Michael Jackson duet "Say Say Say"; and the Mahavishnu Orchestra album *Apocalypse*, which teamed fiery jazz-fusion guitarist John McLaughlin with the London Symphony Orchestra. I even had the opportunity to work with the legendary comedian Peter Sellers, recording him singing the title track to his 1975 movie *Undercovers Hero*.

Another project that I was quite proud of was a Gino Vannelli album called *The Gist Of Gemini*, which I both produced and engineered. Gino was a talented French-Canadian singer/songwriter. He and his brother Joe were huge Beatles fans and were constantly in awe of the fact that they were working with the same engineer who'd done *Sgt. Pepper*—and every time they'd bring it up, I would find myself getting embarrassed.

We had some excellent staff at AIR, too. Many of my assistants—people like Pete Henderson, Jon Jacobs, Jon Kelly, Steve Churchyard, and Stuart Breed—went on to establish solid careers as engineers themselves.

Buoyed by the success of the Oxford Circus studios, George Martin soon got the hankering to build another facility, this time on the tranquil Caribbean island of Montserrat. Despite the fact that constructing a state-of-the-art studio in such a remote area was an almost impossible task, we pulled it off. I worked closely with George and my former Abbey Road colleague Dave Harries on the design of the new complex, which opened in 1979, and I was fortunate enough to work there frequently, doing sessions with Cheap

Trick, Art Garfunkel, Jimmy Buffett, Ultravox, the Climax Blues Band, and Little River Band, among others. The studio and its surroundings were gorgeous. There was a huge picture window in the control room overlooking the bay; you could literally sit at the console and watch the sunset at the same time. Sadly, the studio was closed down in 1989 after the island was devastated by Hurricane Hugo.

In early November 1980, Paul reunited with George Martin and me to begin work on what would become his first post-Wings solo album, *Tug Of War*. At one point Stevie Wonder flew down to Montserrat to record the song "Ebony And Ivory" with Paul, a collaborative effort that would yield a huge hit single. Soon after finishing the track, we returned to London and resumed work at the Oxford Circus facility. Life seemed good, safe, secure.

All of that was shattered when my phone rang in the middle of the night on December 8, waking me from a deep sleep. The call was from a close friend in America—the girl who would one day be my wife. Even through the haze of my semiconsciousness I realized that something was wrong.

"Something terrible has happened," she said.

"What??" I asked, alarmed.

She started sobbing. "I can't tell you; you'll find out in the morning."

She couldn't bring herself to tell me that John Lennon had been murdered, slain by a madman.

I couldn't go back to sleep, of course, but in those days there was no television in Britain in the middle of the night, so I turned on the radio. The announcer breathlessly reported endless details of the horrifying news, but his words blurred together, a drone of names, times, places: Dakota. Mark David Chapman. Broken glasses. Grieving widow.

John Lennon dead? The three words made no sense. I couldn't fathom how it could be possible.

By dawn the first detailed reports crackled across the airwaves and the numbing realization was starting to set in, but I also had to face practical matters. I was scheduled to work with Paul and George Martin at AIR in a few hours' time. In fact, Paddy Moloney, leader of the Irish band the Chieftains, was scheduled to fly down from Dublin that very afternoon to overdub pipes on one of the tracks. Yet as the sun rose high in the winter sky, I remained glued to my radio, where descriptions of devastated fans the world over assaulted my senses, a twisted, nightmarish revisiting of the hysteria of Beatlemania. "We are told that the other members of the Beatles have been informed of the news," the announcer intoned somberly. *Well, of course they bloody have*, I thought indignantly: *They were John's family, after all.*

I decided that the only thing I could do was to head into work and see how the day's events would unfold. As I walked through the crowded central London streets, I reflected on the many John Lennons I had known: the supremely self-assured young man who took on George Martin at the Beatles' very first recording session; the brash rebel who constantly pushed the envelope during the making of *Revolver*; the gentle, mellow Lennon who had floated his way through *Pepper*; the acerbic, acid-tongued John who had brought me to the verge of a nervous breakdown during the *White Album*; the disengaged, slightly loopy figure who drifted in and out of the Apple offices.

I couldn't imagine what Yoko was going through, but most of all I wondered how Paul was coping. How could he possibly come to terms with the murder of his close friend? John had been the teenager with whom Paul had commiserated during times of loss, the bandmate with whom he had traveled the world and enjoyed unparalleled success, the composer with whom he had collaborated to create so many great and lasting works. At first I thought that Paul would surely be canceling the session, but then I remembered how he had faced up to Brian Epstein's death so many years before, burying his grief in the work of guiding the group's career.

By the time I arrived at AIR, the building was already surrounded by hordes of screaming reporters and television crews, kept at bay by harried policemen. A quick phone call to George Martin's office confirmed that, as I had suspected, Paul was indeed going ahead with the session. As I busied myself with setting up—really just a futile effort to distract myself—Paddy came in, looking bewildered.

"Unbelievable, just unbelievable," he kept repeating, shaking his head sadly.

After a while a grim George Martin arrived. "What a tragedy" was all he could bring himself to say. Beneath his veneer of British reserve, I could sense that he was shaken to the core.

An hour or so later a number of armed security guards stationed themselves around the studio doors, ordered there directly, we were told, by Paul's brother-in-law John Eastman. A short while later, accompanied by Linda, Paul himself walked in, subdued, pensive, and deep in thought. As we made eye contact I could see the deep sadness welling inside him.

"I'm so sorry, Paul," I mumbled awkwardly.

"I know, Geoff, I know," he replied, his voice barely above a whisper.

For a few moments, the three of us stood there numbly, reminiscing about the impact John Winston Ono Lennon had had on our lives, focusing on the positive, the lighthearted, the absurd. We smiled as we conjured up pleasant memories, but there were tears behind our laughter. Somehow none of us could seem to come up with the right words to say.

There probably *were* no right words to say. After a while our recollections petered out to an uncomfortable silence. The only thing to do, it seemed, was try to submerge our pain in the work at hand. Though we knew in our heart of hearts it was a fruitless exercise, we went through the motions nonetheless. Paddy laid down his parts quickly and efficiently, then, giving Paul an awkward hug, departed for the airport. After he'd gone, Paul picked up his bass and idly ran down a few lines, then wandered over to the piano and improvised for a little while, then picked up a guitar and strummed a few chords. He was more than just in a state of shock. He seemed utterly lost and bewildered.

Finally, an exhausted and drained Paul mumbled a soft "All right, lads, I guess that's enough for today."

Surrounded by Eastman's security men, he walked out the front door and, with quiet dignity, faced the surging phalanx of reporters. That night, he went home and, surrounded by his wife and children, allowed himself to grieve in private. It would be many weeks before we would resume work on *Tug Of War*, an album that critics would eventually hail as Paul McCartney's best work since *Band On The Run*.

John Lennon's death was a personal blow to me that left me devastated for a long time afterward. John may have had an aggressive nature, but he also had a wonderfully dry sense of humor, and a real soft side, too. I read once that when Brian Epstein was in drug rehab toward the end of his short life, John sent flowers and a note saying, "You know I love you." That was the kind of thing nobody else in the Beatles would have dreamed of doing. But that really was like John. When he was in a good mood, he was kind and thoughtful; the problem was the bad moods that overtook him all too often. It was almost as if he was mad at the world a lot of the time, but he was also capable of great caring and compassion. He was a giant talent and a humanitarian, but he was also a contradiction in terms.

The late seventies and early eighties saw the rise of a new kind of music in Britain, which rapidly spread to America and the rest of the world. Punk started out as raw energy and rebellion, and the first punk bands were limited in their musical ability, but the movement soon spawned a second generation of so-called New Wave artists. In particular, there was one artist who caught my eye, and ear. While his lyrics were cutting, they were insightful, too. Most impressive, he knew how to write a catchy melody. In 1981, I finally had an opportunity to work with him when I was asked to produce Elvis Costello's *Imperial Bedroom*.

From the first day I met Elvis, I immediately liked him; he was a true artist in every sense of the word. In many ways, he reminded me of John Lennon. Like John, Elvis had a keen, dry wit that could have an aggressive edge. And, like John, Elvis would often come into a session with a scrap of paper with a half-finished verse scribbled on it, finishing and polishing it off in the studio. Interestingly enough, a few years later Paul would write a few songs with Elvis (including the hits "Veronica" and "My Brave Face"), and describe the experience as "the nearest thing to working with John."

Elvis was almost as impatient as Lennon, too. It was all about capturing the mood and the moment with him, because he was constantly bursting with ideas. Each performance would be radically different in terms of timing, phrasing, almost everything. We couldn't labor over anything, either— if he was in the mood to lay down a vocal, you got it down quickly: there was no "We need ten minutes to get a sound together." We ended up recording more than a dozen backing tracks in the first three days we were in the studio, which would have been fast even by John's standard.

My main production goal was to make Elvis's vocals stand out more. Listening to his previous records, I always used to wish they were more intelligible, because he wrote such great lyrics: I just wanted to hear them clearly. That was a bit of an uphill battle, because Elvis hated having so much voice in the mix at first, though he eventually came around to my way of thinking.

Elvis was willing to let me do a lot of sonic experimentation on *Imperial Bedroom*. As a result, a lot of the sounds on that record are quite adventurous, almost harking back to the *Revolver* days, with things like prepared pianos, backward reverbs, and instruments morphing from one to another. I was trying to do new things vocally, too. In the song "Pidgin English" there are completely different vocal treatments on each voice part, plus each is panned to a different area of the stereo soundfield: hard left, hard right, and center. Throughout the entire project I found myself pulling out all the stops, saying, "Well, it might sound stupid, but let's do it anyway." If I'd given it too much thought, I probably wouldn't have tried even half the things I tried.

Imperial Bedroom was also filled with lush, rich string arrangements, written by Elvis's longtime keyboard player Steve Nieve. Steve was a talented musician, but he had little experience doing orchestral scoring; for one track, he had written an arrangement that called for eighteen violas instead of violins, which would have been the norm. I pointed out that the tricky thing would be finding eighteen top-notch viola players in all of London!

I was very pleased with the way *Imperial Bedroom* turned out. It's got the polish of a record that took a lot of time to record and mix, although it actually came together fairly quickly. It was released in 1982 to glowing reviews, and happily I got the opportunity to work with Elvis once again in 1996 on *All This Useless Beauty*. Elvis Costello has described our work together as a collaboration, with me looking after the sounds and him looking after the music, and that's a fairly accurate description, although it wasn't quite as black and white as that: we each offered input to the other, and the magic came from the blend that resulted.

By the late 1970s I had started to grow a bit disillusioned with the way AIR was being run and I decided to set out on my own as an independent engineer, though I continued to base myself at the company's London and Montserrat facilities. My work schedule remained busy, including continuing sessions with Paul, but there was a new interest in my life, one which was to bring me even greater joy than time spent in the recording studio. Her name was Nicole Graham.

I first met Nicole in 1976. She worked at the Los Angeles office of Chrysalis Records—a company affiliated with AIR—and one of her jobs was to act as George Martin's assistant whenever he was working in L.A. I was in town mixing Supertramp's *Even In The Quietest Moments* album, and I was staying in George's rented house at the time. One day Nicole came over to drop off some papers and I was introduced to her by George. She was tall and slender, with an elegance and demeanor that reminded me of Natalie Wood. It may not have exactly been love at first sight, but I was certainly interested in her, and we soon started seeing each other. Our romance blossomed over a long period of time, which was a good thing because it gave us an opportunity to become best friends first.

Nicole and I were married in Sussex, England, in early 1988. Paul McCartney was my best man, and Linda was our wedding photographer. I was honored to have them there, and we kept things low-key. We were married in the town registry office, and then we went down to the church and had a simple service there. The reception—vegetarian, in Paul and Linda's honor—was held at a local hotel called the Hayes Arms, and they did a fine job. Nicole and I enjoyed the vegetarian cuisine, but many of her mother's family were French and some of them objected; they wanted their meat, and they couldn't understand why we weren't serving any. Paul and Linda were most gracious at the reception; they walked around and chatted comfortably with just about everyone on both sides of the family. We did have to make sure that none of our guests brought cameras, however—the last thing we wanted was pictures published in the tabloids.

After our wedding, we lived in Montserrat for a time, and then eventually settled in L.A. Nicole was outgoing and vivacious and we led a very busy social life. She was a gifted singer and songwriter—in fact, she was working on her debut album years before we got married, recording at the Beach Boys' studio in Santa Monica—and she was also a talented painter and photographer. She had grown up in Los Angeles, and between her job and some of her high school friends, she knew a lot of people in the pop business. I was enormously impressed when she took me on a tour of all the houses the Beatles had stayed in when they visited L.A.

Sadly, Nicole died in 1993 after a long battle with cancer. Paul and Linda were among the first friends to ring me and offer their condolences. A few weeks later I saw Paul at a concert he was doing in Las Vegas; months before, he had asked me to come and record the gig because he was working on a live album. When I arrived in the afternoon for the sound check, he set down his bass, walked over, and gave me a big hug.

"I didn't expect you to come," he whispered in my ear.

"No, I wasn't sure if I was going to come, either," I told him. "I just need something to do, something to keep my mind occupied."

Little did I know that just five years later I'd be the one offering condolences. We were both to lose our wives to cancer at an early age. It was yet another way that our lives curiously intersected, another bond that tied us together.

Over the years, I continued to work with Paul on many of his solo albums, including *London Town*, *Pipes Of Peace*, and *Give My Regards To Broad Street*. *London Town* was an exciting adventure and it was particularly challenging because it was recorded on a boat. Paul had decided to make the album in the warmth of the Caribbean, but there were no adequate recording facilities in that part of the world at the time, so he decided to hire several motor yachts, refurbish one of them, and turn it into a floating recording studio. For weeks we cruised around the Virgin Islands, leisurely recording during the week and soaking up the sun on the weekends. A few months later, I headed up to Paul's farm in Scotland and recorded "Mull Of

Kintyre," which became the biggest-selling single in England to date (ironically, the record that had previously held that distinction was the Beatles' "She Loves You") and eventually sold a staggering six million copies worldwide.

I was working on a project with Paul in early 1994 when he happened to mention casually that Yoko had given him some of John's demo tapes to work on, and that he had been talking with George and Ringo about finishing them off.

"If it all comes together, I'd like you to engineer for us," he told me.

I immediately said yes, but I was flabbergasted. There had been rumors of a reunion for years, with John's son Julian or some other musician substituting for him, but I paid them no mind; given the bad feelings at the end of the Beatles' run, I just assumed it would never happen. But it was indeed about to happen, and Paul wanted me to be part of it. George Martin was not going to be in the producer's chair this time, though. George Harrison's mate Jeff Lynne (a producer and musician who had been a member of the Electric Light Orchestra and who had worked with Harrison in the Traveling Wilburys) was going to fill that role, and the recordings would be completed not at Abbey Road but at Paul's private studio.

By early February the details had been worked out and we all got together to begin work on "Free As A Bird"—one of three sketchy John Lennon songs that Yoko had provided. (A year later, we'd do the same with the song "Real Love"; work on the third track was started but never completed.) Although I hadn't done complete projects with either George Harrison or Ringo since 1970, I had bumped into them from time to time in recording studios or at industry events, so it wasn't exactly a grand reunion, but it was great seeing them anyway. The emotions we all felt when we first heard John Lennon's voice come off that cassette tape were indescribable. We were all on the verge of tears, and we resolved that the only way we were going to get through the sessions was to pretend that John had gone away on holiday and left some tapes for us to finish. Silly as it may sound, we literally fooled ourselves into thinking that he'd be back in a week or two. That was our coping mechanism.

Incredibly enough, within hours we eased right back into our old groove; it felt as if it had been weeks and not years since we'd last worked together. We laughed and joked our way through the sessions, just as we had done in the early days, but there was a sadness, too. A huge piece of the puzzle was missing, and we were reminded of that every time we heard John's distinctively nasal vocal coming through the studio loudspeakers.

In close consultation with Paul and Jeff Lynne, I had to do a good deal of manipulation in order to create a new arrangement and clean up the tape as much as possible. But once the three Beatles got together and began overdubbing their parts, it only took a few days to complete. I was tremendously pleased with the results: from the very first downbeat, you knew it was a Beatles record. Paul's signature bass, Ringo's solid drumming, and George Harrison's soaring leads provided the perfect underpinning to John Lennon's plaintive singing. They always had been the best band he ever played with.

Just a few weeks later, George Martin contacted me as well. "I hear you've been back in the studio with the boys," he told me. "Now it looks like all of the old gang is going to get together once again, because they want us to go through the Abbey Road archives and see what might be of interest."

Some twenty-five years after the dissolution of the group, the three surviving Beatles and Yoko had decided that the public at long last deserved to hear the outtakes, the discarded songs, and the studio chatter, all to be put together in a video and CD package that was going to be called *The Beatles Anthologies*. That was the official company line. Truth be told, it was also a way of thwarting the bootleggers who had for years been making money off of illegal releases of Beatles recordings.

But, to me, it felt just as if we were going to be raiding Tutankhamen's tomb. There were no cobwebs, no musty corridors, no hidden passages, but the feeling was the same. My view was that those songs were treasures that were already frozen in time, like a priceless painting. Would anyone dare to suggest that the background to the *Mona Lisa* be repainted? In essence, I felt that was what we were planning on doing. After all, so many people knew every detail, every nuance of every Beatles recording ever released. Why dissect them again? And why subject incomplete or rejected recordings to public scrutiny?

Yet I felt an obligation to be there. It made sense that the task fell not to outsiders but to George and me, despite my misgivings about the project, and despite the fact that we hadn't worked together for more than a decade. Within a few days we had established a routine that worked well. George Martin sat in one control room with Abbey Road archivist Allan Rouse, painstakingly listening to every single Beatles recording all the way through. When George came upon a segment he thought worth including, it would be sent upstairs to me in another control room, where I would pull the multitrack masters from their original boxes and remix it. (In the case of some of the earliest works—home recordings and acetates done at nonprofessional studios—I had to do some cleanup work as well to make the recording technically presentable.)

I insisted on trying to get as near to the original sound as possible, and that meant we had to acquire a great deal of vintage equipment, including a version of the mixing console that was used in the later Beatles sessions. Amazingly, most of the tapes were in immaculate condition, even though many of them hadn't come out of their boxes for more than thirty years. I encountered very few technical problems, despite the fact that Abbey Road had gone all digital some years before and there was a bit of a snobbish attitude toward working with analog tape. At one point, one of the maintenance engineers sniffed, "We don't carry screwdrivers anymore," when I asked him to line up a tape machine.

As I sat there, surrounded by tape boxes, I often wondered what was going to come out of them, what feelings they would invoke in me. Interestingly, it was the sight and smell of those tapes, even more than the sounds they held, that brought back a flood of memories. Because they had been stored in protective plastic covers inside a temperature- and humidity-controlled vault, the boxes hadn't even yellowed, which was a bit of a shock to me. Each was labeled carefully with the date of the session, the names of the songs recorded, and the track order, and often I recognized my own handwriting and was able to recall the setting in which I wrote those words. All the years that had passed in between didn't seem to exist. It was as if the sessions had happened last week, as if time had been frozen.

George had decided to work his way through the archives in chronological order, so I spent the the first few weeks dealing with ancient acetates, rehearsal tapes, and crude home demos made by the Beatles long before they ever set foot in Abbey Road—recordings made well before I was on the scene. They were interesting to listen to, but since I'd had no personal involvement, they didn't have any special meaning for me. But as I started working with tapes of sessions that I myself had been present at, each triggered its own special set of remembrances and emotions. The handwriting on some of the boxes was that of a teenage assistant engineer named Geoffrey Emerick; in other cases it was the scrawl of my assistants—Phil McDonald, Richard Lush, Ken Scott, John Kurlander. As I listened to each slate announcing the song title and take number, I felt instantly transported to that moment in time, back to a place of innocence and wonder, an era when the sky seemed the limit to idealistic young people the world over . . . and most especially to four lads from Liverpool.

In the early days, the Beatles would travel from one ill-paying provincial gig to the next, huddled together in the back of a small, unheated van. Whenever they would start to become discouraged at the apparent hopelessness of the situation, John Lennon would buck them up by asking the question, "Where are we going, lads?" to which they would respond with a rousing, "To the top, Johnny! To the toppermost of the poppermost!"

We grew up together, and they did indeed achieve their goal. For the rest of my life, I will be proud of the role I played in helping them reach the summit.

· Epilogue ·

I Read the News Today, Oh Boy

There are times when I do indeed feel like the "lucky man who made the grade." When I think about the confluence of circumstance that placed me in that Abbey Road studio on the day that John, Paul, George, and Ringo first turned up in September 1962, and when they last trudged out nearly seven years later, and for all the sessions in between, it's almost spooky. Why was I mesmerized by sound and music at such a young age? Why were those gramophone records waiting to be discovered in my grandmother's basement, and why did I love them so much when I finally found them? And why did that vacancy occur at EMI just as I was casting about, looking for a career in recording?

Some say there are no coincidences. Perhaps I was just destined to be in the right place at the right time, blessed with the right set of skills and abilities, graced with the right blend of self-confidence and perseverance. I've always had the feeling there was some unseen force that guided my life; there were times when I almost felt propelled into becoming the person I am.

One of my nicknames at Abbey Road was "Golden Ears," and though I always thought it was kind of silly, it is true that I can hear things that many other people can't. Music affects me in a unique way, too. Some people can view a painting of a landscape and their imagination allows them to hear birds chirping. For me, it's the opposite: when I hear a piece of music, it literally conjures up visual images. That's why I always thought of mixing as simply painting pictures with sound.

I'm convinced that these kinds of things aren't just genetic. When I first started at Abbey Road, if a producer and arranger were discussing a playback and they were saying that one single bass note was wrong, I'd be sitting in the back of the control room, thinking, "How the hell can they hear that?"

It took me about a year to develop the ability to obliterate everything else I was hearing and listen to just one component. You aren't born with that; it's something you have to train your ears to do.

In 2003, I was privileged to be awarded a prestigious Technical Grammy. The inscription on the plaque reads, "To Geoff Emerick, who, as both producer and engineer, has pushed the boundaries of studio recording techniques to new frontiers of creativity and imagination." Quite a mouthful . . . and quite an honor. But a lot of the credit has to go to the Beatles, and to the other great artists I had the opportunity to record. In particular, the gorgeous, melodic songs composed by John and Paul gave me so much to work with, such a vivid and broad palette of colors. Throughout my entire time with them, all four Beatles were constantly spurring me on to try new ideas; their endless creativity was almost contagious.

I may have built a reputation as an "engineer," but the term always seemed like such a misnomer to me because I wasn't ever especially technical. My title at Abbey Road was "balance engineer," and I viewed my role as just that: I was the person who balanced the music. It was an artistic, creative job; the technical side of things was left to the technicians. That's something that's really changed through the years, to my regret. Many of today's artists are deeply involved with the recording process; they sit behind their computers and agonize over every little detail. But the Beatles trusted George Martin and me to do our job up in the control room, and they did theirs down in the studio. They had no idea how to operate the mixing console or the tape recorders; they didn't want to know, any more than we wanted to learn how to play guitar or write songs. They were the artist, and their focus was solely on the music. That's the way it should be. That's the way great records are made.

Working with the Beatles was unlike working with any other artists. With them, anything and everything was possible; they had zero tolerance for the words "no" or "can't." On the other hand, if something wasn't right, they knew it, right away, and they had no problem changing direction and moving on. There was no prevaricating; no ifs, ands, or buts; no maybes. It was either good or it wasn't.

There are so many more options available to today's engineer than we ever had—unlimited tracks, unlimited ways to manipulate a signal, unlimited time to mix—but I don't see that as necessarily a good thing, because it also makes it possible to constantly defer decisions. Some of today's producers would rather lay down fifteen bad takes and pull bits and pieces from them than work to get the performance right in the first place.

I still love the art of recording just as much as I did when I was a teenager, but the process is simply not as much fun as it was in those days. Then, it took a team of people to get the sounds right and play the parts correctly. But walk into any studio now and all you'll see is someone staring at a computer screen, moving a mouse, cutting, copying, and pasting as if they were doing a spreadsheet; everything is just too clinical. The Beatles were constantly in search of perfection, it's true, but they were looking for the perfect way to convey a feeling, not technical perfection, which seems to be the goal of many of today's records. If someone made a tiny mistake or sang something a little funny in a Beatles session, it would generally be left in if it was felt it added to the character of the record. Sometimes we'd even accentuate the mistakes during mixing, just to underline the fact that the music was being made by fallible human beings. Today, there's plenty of technology, but precious little soul.

That's not to say that I'm not excited about some of today's technological advances. Some of the newer high-resolution digital audio systems sound pretty good to my ears—almost as good as analog tape—and I can appreciate the creative opportunities that surround sound offers; I'm especially looking forward to the time when new music is composed specifically for that medium. I'm still a little dubious about the wisdom of remixing existing stereo recordings in surround sound, even in the hands of a skilled engineer. To me, it's like colorizing a black-and-white film; it can detract from the original artistic vision rather than enhance it. Certainly the original engineer should always be involved wherever possible. Some of the Beatles songs I recorded have been remixed in surround sound without my involvement, and I haven't been overly impressed with the results. In some cases, effects we added in the mix stage were missing altogether, completely changing the character of the song.

Will there ever be another Beatles? I doubt it. It's not down to talent; there have always been gifted young artists, and there always will be. But there aren't breeding grounds like Hamburg anymore, places where bands can develop in anonymity and hone their craft. Every musician is isolated in his or her bedroom now; there's little collaboration, little opportunity for ideas to be nurtured and developed. In addition, today's digital tools—things like Autotuning, which corrects out-of-tune singing and playing—allow even untalented people to make records, too. As a result, the market is glutted with mediocre product, making it harder for the cream to rise to the top.

There are economic reasons as well. Once upon a time, record companies were willing to cultivate artists over a long period of time: being a recording artist was a lifetime career, not a onetime opportunity for a shot at the brass ring. Sadly, those days are gone. If you don't make a large profit for the record company with your debut album, you rarely get a second chance. These corporations simply don't understand that creativity doesn't just happen, and it rarely is a linear process. Sometimes artists need to be given a chance to find themselves over the long haul, and putting too much pressure on them to deliver the goods right away can be completely self-defeating.

There are also precious few producers left that have the musicality of a George Martin. He may have lost control over the Beatles toward the end of their career, but there's no question that his influence was profound in the early days. In my opinion, the most important contribution he made was the way he expanded the band's horizons. When they showed up for their first few sessions, their only instrumentation was two guitars, bass, and drums, with a little John Lennon harmonica thrown in as a gimmick. But George Martin understood the importance of adding other tone colors: even his simple early piano and celeste overdubs gave Beatles records that certain extra something that made them stand apart from the competition. Within a few short years, he was scoring full orchestras for them.

George Martin had a profound influence on me, too, teaching me that the recording studio itself could actually be an instrument. The first time I heard his half-speed piano trick, I was positively inspired; it made me realize that there was new ground to be broken, that the art of recording could be advanced in unorthodox ways. It showed me that records weren't just about capturing a live performance, that there was a whole universe of approaches to take, ways of creating sounds that had never been heard before. As the Beatles became increasingly adventurous, that became my mantra: "Make sure that piano doesn't sound like a piano; make my vocal sound like I'm singing from the moon." George Martin's everlasting legacy will not just be the scoring and arranging he did, but his willingness to accommodate the Beatles as they stretched their artistic wings and learned to fly.

Working with Paul today is very much the same as it ever was. We've both been through a lot in our lives, from the long late-night sessions that went into *Pepper* to the challenges we faced making *Band On The Run*. And, just as I lost my wife at an early age, so too did Paul lose his beloved Linda, five years after Nicole died. I saw a fair bit of Paul during Linda's final illness— we were recording his *Flaming Pie* album at the time—and even though we didn't talk much about it, he knew that I'd gone through the same terrible experience.

In the last months of Linda's life I worked with Paul on her solo album,

Wide Prairie. Sadly, she passed away shortly before we finished it. A few months later, I was listening to the CD test pressings in one of the small editing rooms at Abbey Road. The studio manager had mentioned that Paul was going to be working that day, too, doing another project in Studio One. Paul didn't know I was going to be there, though, and I was a little worried about how he might react if he came in, but during a break he popped his head in to have a listen. Not surprisingly, Paul put on a brave face once again. For a moment or two we listened intently. But then, when he thought no one was looking, he turned to me wordlessly with a tear in his eye. There was no need to say anything. I knew exactly how he felt.

A few years later, George Harrison left us, too. We hadn't seen each other since the *Anthologies* days, but I was deeply saddened to hear the news of his passing. Even though we were never close personally, we always got along well professionally, and I always had great respect for his musicianship and his abilities as a producer. Especially after he got interested in Eastern music, George brought a new dimension to Beatles records and his contribution was inestimable.

I miss him, just as I miss John, Linda, Mal Evans, and all the others who are no longer with us. But life, as George himself said, goes on within you and without you. Today, a little bit older and hopefully a lot wiser, I'm as prone to be tinkering with my photographic equipment at home as I am to be hunched over a console in a recording studio. Watching a gripping new movie is almost as exhilarating to me as hearing a great new record for the first time or mixing an exciting track.

Almost, but not quite. What time are the musicians due in?

· Acknowledgments ·

How does one encapsulate a lifetime inside the pages of a book? There's nothing easy or straightforward about the process, and it cannot be accomplished without the help and support of a lot of good people.

First and foremost, I would like to thank John, Paul, George, Ringo, and all the other incredibly talented musicians I have been privileged to work with throughout the years. The music you brought to the world not only enriched my life immeasurably, but made it a better place to live in. In particular, I'd like to acknowledge Elvis Costello for his gracious eloquence and lyrical artistry.

A very special thank-you goes to Richard Lush, a great assistant and great engineer, who shared good times and bad with me, and to my friends and colleagues Phil McDonald, John Smith, Malcolm Davies, John Kurlander, and Ken Scott, all of whom gave generously of their time to share their recollections of an era long past, but fondly remembered.

I'd also like to express my gratitude to Norman Smith, George Martin, and Stuart Eltham for taking me under their wing and sharing the depths of their knowledge and creativity, as well as to my long-time assistant at AIR, Peter Henderson, and to Richard Langham for showing me the ropes all those years ago.

Rory Kaplan is a mutual friend of both authors and the person who actually introduced us to each other; for that we will forever be indebted. We are also deeply appreciative of the fine work done by our skillful editor, Brendan Cahill; his assistant editor, Patrick Mulligan; our agent, Jennifer Cayea; as well as publicist extraordinaire, Carol Kaye; and Peter Fields, our legal eagle. Thanks also to Mark Lewisohn, Alexander Stuart, and Bob Doerschuk for their invaluable assistance and input, and to Gotham's Bill Shinker, Ray Lundgren, Lisa Johnson, Kathleen Schmidt, and Hector DeJean.

In addition, Howard Massey would like to acknowledge his many friends and loved ones who provided support, tea, and sympathy throughout the long journey of putting this book together, from initial concept to final polishing: Deborah Gremito, Pat Adler, Laura Colona, Maureen Droney, Karen Eisenberg, Steve Epstein, Elizabeth Givner, Remi Majekodunmi, Robin Oshman, Steve Parr, Ken Pilgrim, Darcy Proper, Sharon Rose, Gerri Ryan, Tim Sanders, David Snow, Barney Spivack, Marvin Tolkin, Rich Tozzoli, and Mary Westcott.